Cross
and
Crescent

NEW EDITION

Cross and Crescent

Responding to the challenges of Islam

Colin Chapman

Inter-Varsity Press
Norton Street, Nottingham NG7 3HR, England
Email: ivp@ivpbooks.com
Website: www.ivpbooks.com

First published 1995
Reprinted 1996, 1998, 1999, 2002
This revised edition published 2007
Reprinted 2009, 2011

British Library Cataloguing in Publication Data
A catalogue record for this book is available from the British Library.

UK ISBN: 978–1–84474–192–2

Set in Monotype Garamond 11/13pt
Typeset in Great Britain by CRB Associates, Potterhanworth, Lincolnshire
Printed and bound in Great Britain by Ashford Colour Press Ltd, Gosport,
Hampshire

Inter-Varsity Press publishes Christian books that are true to the Bible and
that communicate the gospel, develop discipleship and strengthen the
church for its mission in the world.

Inter-Varsity Press is closely linked with the Universities and Colleges
Christian Fellowship, a student movement connecting Christian Unions in
universities and colleges throughout Great Britain, and a member
movement of the International Fellowship of Evangelical Students.
Website: www.uccf.org.uk

CONTENTS

ACKNOWLEDGMENTS

I want first of all to acknowledge how much I owe to many groups of students in different contexts and in different countries, with whom I have worked through the material included in this book since I first started teaching in Egypt and Lebanon.

I also want to thank a number of friends who have contributed case studies or read all or parts of the manuscript and made valuable suggestions: John Azumah, Libby Iskander, Christopher Lamb, Musa Gaia, David Greenlee, Muhammad Imran, Philip Lewis, David Marshall, Chawkat Moucarry, Birthe Munck-Fairwood, Bill Musk, Phil and Julie Parshall, John Ray, Ata'ullah Siddiqui, Jay Smith, Sarah Snyder, Richard Sudworth and Sunny Tan.

Most of the work of producing this new edition was done during a semester spent as Senior Mission Scholar at the Oversees Ministries Study Center in New Haven, Connecticut, USA, from September to December 2006. I am immensely grateful to its Director, Dr Jonathan Bonk, and to all the staff and the community there from many different countries who made me so welcome and provided such an ideal context in which to wrestle with both the old and the new issues surrounding Christian-Muslim relations today.

I owe special thanks to Kate Byrom and her colleagues at IVP who have been very patient with my limited computer skills and must have found that a revised edition of a book presents as many challenges as a new manuscript.

✠ ✠ ✠

Unless otherwise stated, quotations from the Qur'an are taken from *The Meaning of the Glorious Koran: An Explanatory Translation*, by Mohammed Marmaduke Pickthall, Mentor, n.d.

PREFACE TO THE SECOND EDITION

The events of 11 September 2001 have profoundly affected the way Islam and Muslims are perceived in the world today. A new edition of this book is therefore bound to look very different from the first edition which was published in 1995. At the very least it needs to address some of the major political issues related to Islam which have come to the surface in recent years. Some of these issues are raised early in the book in the chapter 'Examining our attitudes'. A new chapter on 'Islamic terrorism' has been added, and the chapter on 'Facing the political challenge of Islam' has been considerably revised. In view of the importance of these issues today, some readers may want to turn to these chapters first.

If the political issues are now uppermost in many people's minds, however, it is wise not to allow them to dominate the agenda. In many situations in the world where Christians and Muslims live peacefully side by side as neighbours, these are not the only or the most important issues on their minds, and these political issues can only be understood in the light of the origins and development of Islam. The basic structure of the book, with its five parts, therefore remains the same. Whatever the major issues on the surface and whatever our context, there is value in working through the five stages – focusing first on personal relationships with Muslims (Part One), and then on understanding Islam (Part Two). After exploring discussion and controversy (Part Three) and reflecting on some of the issues that divide us (Part Four), we should be in a better position to explain the Christian faith to Muslims and see ways forward in our relationships with them (Part Five).

Since this new edition is still intended to be a basic introduction to the faith and practice of Islam, it takes little or nothing for granted and attempts to summarize the most important information without going into too much detail. It is also intended to be used as a textbook in courses on Islam in colleges and seminaries of different kinds, and therefore incorporates new material which I have used in teaching, including chapters on 'What is Islam?', 'The qur'anic view of Christians' and 'Explaining Christian beliefs about Jesus'. While covering the basics, however, it also seeks to explore some of the deeper issues involved in Christian engagement with Muslims and Islam.

Islam presents *new* challenges and *new* questions to Christians and to the West today. This new situation is reflected in the new subtitle, *Responding to the Challenges* (plural) *of Islam*. My hope is that a completely revised edition will help Christians to understand Muslims and Islam better in our rapidly changing situations today. It is not an accident that the cross is the main symbol of the Christian faith, and it still has a powerful message both for Christians and for the world of Islam.

July 2007

INTRODUCTION

This book is about relationships between Christians and Muslims, and the relationship between Christianity and Islam.

It is not hard to understand why the cross has been a major symbol – if not the major symbol – of Christianity since the beginning. But what of the crescent? The moon is important for Muslims because they follow a lunar calendar and have their own names for the twelve months of the year. So, for example, the first sighting of the new moon at the beginning of the ninth month of the Islamic calendar signals the start of the fast of Ramadan. Since a new moon is increasing, the crescent symbolizes something that is growing in strength.

The symbol of the crescent, however, has a strange history. The people of Byzantium (Constantinople) used to have a myth that the city had been founded by Keroessa, the daughter of the moon goddess Io-Hera. They therefore used the crescent as a symbol for the city. It continued to symbolize Byzantium when it became the capital of the eastern half of the Holy Roman Empire. For centuries, therefore, it was the major symbol of a Christian empire. In other cultures the crescent has symbolized 'the Great Mother', 'the Queen of Heaven'.

It was then taken over by the Muslims some time after they conquered the city in AD 1453, and for several centuries it was regarded as a Turkish symbol. Since the beginning of the nineteenth century, however, the crescent (usually combined with a star) has come to be regarded as the emblem *par excellence* of the faith and community of Islam all over the world.

Just as Christians often put a cross on the spire or dome of a church, so Muslims put a crescent on top of the minaret or the dome of a mosque. The symbol of the crescent clearly does not play the same role in Islam as the cross does in Christianity. But by putting cross and crescent together in the title, we are simply bringing together the symbols of two major world religions, and asking questions about the relationship between them.

How are the challenges of Islam perceived?

If we are thinking simply in terms of *numbers*, we are very aware that Islam is growing and spreading. Islam has been a missionary religion ever since the time when the Prophet Muhammad brought the tribes of Arabia under the rule of Islam, and Muslims are understandably proud of a great Islamic civilization. They claim that Islam is the fastest-growing religion in the world, with about 1.3 billion adherents, and that it is now poised for the conversion of Europe and North America. Here, then, we have a missionary religion that would like to convert the world; and while the Christian church seems to be contracting in the West, Islam seems to be expanding.

If we are thinking in terms of *culture*, Islam is perceived by many in the West to be an alien culture. So when Westerners think of Muslims, they tend to think of Arabs, Asians, Africans or Turks rather than of white Europeans or Americans. When Muslims expect their women to wear the veil, want their children to go to Muslim schools and insist on *halal* meat, they seem to be foreigners trying to maintain their own kind of society in our country. The smells of their cooking and the way they dress make us feel that we are dealing with a totally different culture which is not interested in integrating into Western society.

When we come to think of *politics*, the whole world has been made aware in recent years of so-called 'Islamic fundamentalism' and 'Islamic terrorism'. Since Muhammad regarded himself as both prophet and statesman, his followers have always believed that 'Islam must rule'. The assumption has been that the territory occupied by Islam (*dar al-Islam*, the House of Islam) would eventually overcome and absorb the territories as yet outside the control of Islam (*dar al-harb*, the House of War). Within a hundred years of Muhammad's death, the Islamic empire had spread as far as Spain in the West and China in the East. If Charles Martel had not stopped their advance at the Battle of Tours in AD 732, Islam might have conquered the whole of Europe. In 1453 the Muslim armies captured Constantinople, and in 1683 they were battering on the gates of Vienna. On several occasions before 9/11 Osama bin Laden was seen on television all over the world calling the West to Islam and warning of a major attack. It is not hard to conclude that 'Islam wants to conquer the world', and it seems that a small minority of Muslims are prepared to use violence to achieve their goals.

The *theological* challenge of Islam to Christianity can be summed up in these words: 'We Muslims have the greatest respect for you Christians as "People of the Book" – alongside the Jews. But we believe that you've got it all wrong about Jesus! Your Trinity of three persons in one God is impossible to understand, let alone explain, and you have elevated the man Jesus to the level of God. Islam is a simple creed without any dogmas, and this belief in one Creator God includes all the truth that had previously been revealed in Judaism and Christianity. It leads to a unified world view which embraces every aspect of life and can draw people of all races together without discrimination.'

The *ideological* challenge of Islam to the Western world goes like this: 'Look where Christianity and the Western intellectual tradition have got you! You may be technically clever and good at making money, but what kind of society have you created – with all its consumerism, sexual immorality and crime? Nazism, fascism and communism are dead, and socialism is struggling. The nationalism that you have exported all over the world has created enormous problems in one country after another. Your questioning of faith has led to agnosticism and atheism, and people do not know what to believe or how to make ethical choices. You have ruled religion out of the public sphere and said that it can be a purely private matter. But we believe that it *cannot* be a private matter and *must* have something to say about how society functions and decides moral standards. Islam offers a genuine and realistic alternative to the West in its decline, a solution to the sicknesses of modern, Western society.'

What is involved in Christian responses to Islam?

Each of the five parts of this book deals with a vital element in a genuinely Christian response to these challenges presented by Islam.

Part One, 'Relating to our Muslim Neighbours', focuses on the way Christians relate to Muslims. We begin at this point because relating to people is more important than acquiring information or mastering new ideas. This means appreciating Islamic culture and reflecting on some of the difficulties that we experience in our relationships with Muslims. It also means being more aware and critical of our attitudes towards Muslims and Islam.

Part Two, 'Understanding Islam', covers basic Islamic beliefs, the practice of Islam, the life of Muhammad and the Qur'an. The study of Islam cannot stop at this point in time, however, and we need to take note of developments in Islam from the beginning up to the present day. In all this we are not simply trying to absorb facts and information. Our aim is to try to understand Islam from within as far as possible. We want to put ourselves in the shoes of Muslims, and learn to sit where they sit.

Part Three, 'Entering into Discussion and Dialogue', deals with some of the main issues that tend to come up in discussions between Muslims and Christians. Some of these are very practical (like 'Why do you eat pork?'), while others are related to political and social issues (like 'Why do so many Christians support the state of Israel?'). Then there are the difficult theological questions (like 'Why do you believe that Jesus is the Son of God?'). Christians clearly need to work out how to respond to questions and objections like these and know how to engage in serious dialogue with Muslims.

Part Four, 'Facing Fundamental Issues', begins by considering some of the difficult theological questions which come to the surface sooner or later when Christians start engaging with Muslims and Islam (for instance, 'Is the God of Islam the same as the God of Christianity?'), and looks at some of the most fundamental differences between the Christian faith and Islam (e.g. in our understanding of revelation and inspiration, our diagnosis of the human condition, forgiveness and salvation, politics and the state). One chapter explores what is involved in thinking biblically about Islam, and this is followed by chapters on two sensitive issues: the cost of conversion and the political challenge of Islam.

Part Five, 'Bearing Witness to Jesus', attempts to get beyond the stage of argument and to concentrate on Christian witness. How can Christians share their faith in Jesus as the most complete revelation of the one true God? We look at an example of a situation in daily life when Muslims and Christians have opportunities to talk about their faith, and how Christians can respond to folk Islam. We then turn to three different examples of how Christians can explain their faith to Muslims: first, through sharing scripture; second, by starting with themes in the Qur'an; and third, by explaining how the disciples of Jesus gradually came to understand who he was. This part ends with a series of case studies illustrating some of the issues facing Christians in different parts of the world in their relationships with Muslims.

In the Conclusion we reflect on what it may mean for Christians to be walking the way of the cross in responding to the challenges of Islam today. If the cross is so difficult, if not impossible, for Muslims to understand, but so central to the faith of Christians, what does it say to Christians who want to go on relating to Muslims and trying to understand them?

PART ONE

RELATING TO OUR
MUSLIM NEIGHBOURS

> If we are to make any progress in dialogue with Muslims we must first of all get inside the world of Islam and make ourselves welcome as guests and friends ... There is also a need for some of us to get inside the Muslim world and meet Muslims on their own territory where they are most at home, and, perhaps, most truly themselves.
>
> *Roger Hooker*[1]

The emphasis in Part One is on personal relationships between Christians and Muslims. Before asking what Muslims believe or how they practise their faith (in Part Two), we think about how we relate to them as people and as neighbours in the different situations in which we find ourselves anywhere in the world. This will involve understanding their culture and examining our own attitudes towards Muslims and Islam.

1. MEETING FACE TO FACE

'Hello! How are you?' This was a speaker's short answer to a student who asked, 'How should I approach a Muslim?' No doubt the questioner had a particular idea in mind of what Muslims are like, and felt some need to learn special techniques for communicating with them.

The short answer sums up the basic point: we approach Muslims as human beings. We meet them as people before we meet them as Muslims. We greet them as individuals with a name before we think of them as representatives of a great world religion. We extend the hand of friendship as neighbours before we self-consciously announce that we are Christians.

Perhaps it is a sad reflection on the state of the Western Christian world that something as obvious as this needs to be said! But unless it is understood and put into practice, all our study of Islam and all the talk about sharing our faith with Muslims is worthless.

Starting where we are

Where we are presently in contact with Muslims, we may need to take stock of our situation and think how we can build on the relationships that we already have. Whom do we know? What is the context in which we meet? How well do we know each other? What kind of relationships do we have – do we know each other as neighbours, colleagues at work, teachers, students or casual acquaintances? How can we go deeper in our relationships?

If we do not already have any natural contact with Muslims in our own situation, we may need to ask ourselves some questions. Are there any situations, for example, where we could get to know any Muslims in a natural way – talking with other parents at school events, chatting with colleagues at work, or being involved in some kind of social work in the community, for example? The great advantage of relationships of this kind is that they can be utterly natural; there need not be anything forced or artificial about them. If we have no such contacts in our different situations, are there ways in which we can take the initiative and go out to meet Muslims – for instance, by visiting a mosque or a Muslim bookshop, by talking to a Muslim shopkeeper or by inviting a Muslim student to our home?

The secret of real dialogue

Assuming, then, that we have some kind of genuine relationships with Muslims, are we hoping for anything more than polite, friendly conversation?

Luke's description of Jesus in the temple at the age of twelve gives us a picture of a kind of dialogue that gets beneath the surface. Jesus' parents find him 'sitting among the teachers, listening to them and asking them questions; and all who heard him were amazed at his understanding and his answers' (Luke 2:46–47 RSV). It is obvious that Jesus relating in this way to the religious leaders of Judaism is not exactly comparable to Christians relating to their Muslim neighbours. But Luke's brief picture shows us what is involved in any meeting of minds when people are exploring each other's faith.

Jesus would have learned his faith in the home and the synagogue. But now he is in the capital city, talking to some of the religious leaders of Judaism. He is sitting among them and listening to what they are teaching. He genuinely wants to know what they think and how they teach the faith of their fathers. When he asks questions, it is not to trip them up and embarrass them, but to draw them out into real dialogue. What impresses the observers about Jesus is that he seems to have understanding (as distinct from intelligence or knowledge) and is able to grasp the important issues. When he offers answers, therefore, it is in response to actual questions which people are asking.

What would it mean to see this as a model for dialogue between Christians and Muslims? 'Sitting among them' might mean visiting Muslims in their homes, or spending time with them socially. For a student in a university or college it might mean having the courage to attend meetings of the Islamic Society and getting to know Muslim students. For Christians who have grown up as members of a minority community in a Muslim country, it might mean working through their fears and trying to relax a little more in the company of Muslims.

'Listening' could mean giving more serious attention to what Muslims themselves are saying – not only what is being said about them – in the media. 'Asking questions' may mean at first asking very basic questions. But as we continue to probe gently, it should become obvious that we are not trying to score points, but are doing all we can to see the world as Muslims see it.

If this kind of deeper exchange is going to be fruitful, we will need that 'understanding' which enables us to discern the most important issues. And if we reach the stage of being able to offer any 'answers', we will then be answering genuine questions in the minds of Muslims and not simply the questions that we think they ought to be asking.

Greetings

The problem for most of us is that we find it hard to break the ice, and for reasons that are perfectly understandable, we are reluctant to cross barriers of language, culture and religion. Muslims all over the world, whatever their mother tongue, are taught the following Arabic greeting: one person says *As-salamu 'alaikum*, or *salam 'alekum* ('Peace be on you'), and the other replies *Wa'alaikumus salam* ('And on you be peace'). Is there any reason why Christians should not learn this greeting, whatever country they are living in, and use it to greet any Muslims they meet?

Some Muslims may not be pleased to hear Christians using a greeting which is generally thought to be a greeting only for fellow Muslims. But others will be pleasantly surprised to be greeted in this way by non-Muslims, and delighted to feel that we have taken the trouble to learn something that is part of their religion and their culture. And it could be even more significant for ourselves if we discover that greetings are more than a mere formality; they convey something about our whole attitude towards another person.

Visiting

'An Englishman's home is his castle', says the proverb. Most Westerners tend to think in the same way, seeing their home as a place of retreat for privacy. They therefore feel they are intruding if they call on someone without an invitation. This is not, however, the mentality of the East and most of the Muslim world. An Egyptian sums up the way most Easterners think about the custom of visiting in this way: 'You honour people more by visiting them in their homes than by inviting them to yours.'

In this respect it is probably true to say that it is we in the West who are out of step with the rest of the world. Throughout the East, in Africa and in Latin America, hospitality is regarded almost as a sacred duty. If someone visits me in my home, I must drop whatever I am doing, however urgent I think it is, because welcoming and entertaining guests has priority over every other obligation. I will offer them something to drink and perhaps even something to eat, and they will have to think twice before refusing what I offer.

What might this mean in practice in relating to Muslims? It may mean that I need to put aside Western ideas of etiquette. So if I meet Muslims and want to get to know them better, it might be natural to say, 'Can I visit you in your home?' rather than 'Would you like to visit me in my home?' Once we begin to feel relaxed and comfortable in the homes of our Muslim friends, it will be natural to think of other occasions when visits would be appropriate. What about visiting, for example, during a Muslim feast? And why not visit after the birth of a child, when someone has returned from a journey or from pilgrimage to Mecca, or during a time of celebration or bereavement?

Another way to meet Muslims is to visit a mosque.

Visiting a mosque

Curiosity is not the only thing that might draw Christians to a mosque. Another reason could be that we want to meet devout, practising Muslims, and to understand them and their faith as much as we can. It is not appropriate to visit a mosque in order to 'evangelize Muslims', although such a visit can sometimes lead to opportunities to share our faith with Muslims. We need to remember that we are visitors, enjoying the hospitality extended to us in someone else's place of worship. If a group of Muslims were to visit our church, we would expect them to come primarily to listen and to learn, rather than to preach to us.

The word 'mosque' is an Anglicized version of the Arabic word *masjid*, a place of prostration, or worship. In addition, the mosque is regarded as a kind of community centre, since many important social functions are held in the mosque or in a hall attached to the mosque. It is also a place for education, and in many cases classes for teaching Islam and the Qur'an are held regularly in the mosque.

What should you do before going?

The leader of a group visiting a mosque should make personal contact before going, with either the imam or some other leader of the community, such as a member of the mosque committee. Women visiting a mosque should wear a scarf to cover their heads. They may in some cases be asked to wear a long skirt or loose trousers, and to have their arms covered. Some mosques may ask women not to visit during menstruation. Men are sometimes expected to cover their heads. You should be prepared to take your shoes off before going to the main prayer room of the mosque.

During your visit, your hosts will probably want to talk about the mosque and explain their faith to you, perhaps at some length. There will usually also be opportunities for you to ask questions. It can be helpful to think in advance of some questions you may want to ask.

You should be prepared to stay for at least an hour, and not be in a hurry to leave. You may be served refreshments, and there may be a further opportunity for you to ask questions. If the leader of your group knows the mosque well, he or she should know how long the visit is likely to take.

If any members of your group have reservations about visiting a mosque, they should not feel obliged to do so. It may be helpful, however, if they can be encouraged to express their feelings openly and discuss them with the rest of the group.

What can you see at the mosque?
You may be welcomed to a mosque by the imam, whose position is roughly similar (but not identical) to that of the minister, pastor or priest in a Christian church. It is worth finding out how the responsibilities of the imam differ from those of a Christian minister or priest. It is possible, however, that you will be welcomed and shown around by a member of the community who may not have studied Islam in any depth.

You may be able to see the place where those who come to the mosque carry out their ablutions – *wudu*, the ritual washing of the hands, arms, face, nose and feet before prayer. Your hosts may be very willing to demonstrate to you how they say their prayers and what the ritual means for them.

In the prayer room or prayer hall itself you will see the *mihrab*, the alcove in the wall that marks the direction of Mecca, the central shrine of Islam, and thus indicates the direction that Muslims face to pray. Muslims generally do not mind if visitors watch them from behind when they are saying their prayers, and they are often willing to demonstrate for visitors the postures that they adopt during their prayers.

The *minbar* is the pulpit with steps, usually made of wood, from which the imam gives a sermon at the Friday prayers. There is often Arabic writing on the walls, which could be:

- the name of God, *Allah*;
- the name Muhammad;
- the *Fatiha* (the first sura of the Qur'an; see chapter 6, 'Muslims at prayer');
- other verses from the Qur'an (e.g. sura 112).

There may be a series of clocks indicating the times for prayer each day and the Friday prayers.

There may or may not be a minaret. In a Muslim country the call to prayer, the *adhan* (usually pronounced *azan*), would be heard from the minaret, often magnified by a loudspeaker. In most mosques in Europe and North America the call to prayer is heard only inside the mosque, and special permission has to be given by the local council for it to be broadcast outside the building.

There may or may not be a separate women's prayer room. If there is no special room, there may be a gallery or a curtained area in the main prayer hall that is used by women.

In many mosques there is a special room for Qur'an classes. Children come here for an hour or more after school each day to learn the Qur'an. It may be worth studying the pictures and posters on the walls.

There may be a hall attached to the mosque used for social functions such as weddings, funerals and important festivals. Some mosques include a morgue.

What should you do after the visit?

It is important for members of the visiting group to meet together, even if only for a short time, to share their impressions of the visit. It may also be appropriate to write to your hosts to thank them for their hospitality. You should think together about the most appropriate way to follow up your visit. You cannot expect to make too much progress on your first visit, and you may well want to arrange further visits to the mosque, or to visit your hosts in their homes. If you invite them to visit your church, do not be surprised or offended if there is some reluctance to do so, and try to work out the reasons for their reluctance.

Where will all this lead?

If we want to work out in advance where all our meeting and visiting are going to lead, the chances are that there is still something wrong in our own attitudes. In the teaching of Jesus, the command to love our neighbours is prior to the command to go out and make disciples of all the nations. It makes little sense to calculate how we are going to share the gospel with our Muslim neighbours if we have not begun to know them, love them and care for them as our neighbours. There needs to be genuine meeting between people.

But how does this emphasis on relationships work out in practice? The following three quotations come from entirely different situations and illustrate different kinds of response to initiatives in friendship. In the first, Roger Hooker describes an important breakthrough in his attempts to get to know his Muslim neighbours while he was working in India:

> When we came to live in Bareilly ... I determined to make contact with the Muslim community, which was obviously a large one. But how to set about it? In Agra I had once paid a visit to the Jama Masjid, but had been asked to leave after about 10 minutes. In Allahabad I had asked a durzi if I could visit his mosque to watch the worship, but this was not allowed. Soon after we got to Bareilly I wrote to the principal of the local Muslim college to ask if I could see round his institution, but I got no reply. One afternoon in February 1969, in sheer desperation, I went for a walk in the old city and climbed the steps of the first mosque I came to. I asked if I could see the maulana. After some time he appeared and asked me what I wanted. I said that I wanted to see round his mosque. He showed me round but of course there was not very much to see, so he invited me to sit down and have a cup of tea. We chatted for about half an hour. He asked me who I was and what I was doing in India. I told him I was a missionary. He said that he, too, had wanted to be a missionary in Africa but his parents wouldn't let him go. We also discovered that we each had a son of the same age and that our respective wives were expecting a second child. As I went down the mosque steps he asked me to come again. For me this was one of the most thrilling moments I had known since arriving in India four years before. At last I had managed to penetrate to the house of Islam, and had met a Muslim as a fellow human being.[1]

The second quotation comes from one of the leaders of a Muslim community who had been welcoming groups of Christian students to his mosque in a British city over a period of years. At the end of a helpful time of questions and discussion, someone said to him, 'Would you and any of your community be interested in visiting a church or coming to our college to hear how we understand our faith?' The answer was polite but clear, and seemed almost to close the door to closer friendships:

There are too few of us looking after our own community, and we don't really have the time to meet with people of other faiths. What's more, it might be confusing for any Muslims who are not sure of their faith. But for those of us who are sure about our faith, there's nothing we can learn from Christians, because it's all there in the Qur'an. We've got it all in Islam.

The third quotation is from a Lebanese Christian working in Iraq before the Gulf War, who describes his experience of mixing socially with friends and colleagues during the month of Ramadan:

The month of Ramadan has just finished. Particularly on this occasion I am having first-class contact with Islam and its practices. The legalism, the Judaism, salvation by works and hypocrisy are just killing. Being invited to so many dinners, I eat so much during this month, but also suffer so much spiritually. I find myself completely helpless being evangelized rather than evangelizing. It is a faith so much rooted in the hearts of people. Anything else contradicting their Book is 'false' because God has actually and verbally spoken.

This person had moved beyond superficial contacts to begin to get beneath the surface. He had also discovered that there is nothing romantic in dialogue at this deeper level; he had begun to experience some of the pain, confusion and vulnerability involved in Christians and Muslims relating face to face.

These three examples underline the priority of personal relationships. If we have started out thinking that we are interested in 'Islam', it should not take long for us to realize that we may need to be thinking about 'Muslims' as much as about 'Islam'.

2. APPRECIATING ISLAMIC CULTURE

It may seem strange to raise the subject of culture so near the beginning of this book. Why put *culture* before *creed*, for example? There are four basic reasons why it may be more helpful to consider *how Muslims live* before studying *what they believe*.

First, we want to relate to Muslims as people – as individuals, families and communities – rather than as representatives of the religion of Islam. Concentrating too much on doctrines and beliefs can easily create barriers and make it harder to accept them as people. Developing cultural sensitivity is an important part of obedience to the commandment 'Love your neighbour as yourself'.

Second, since culture and creed are so interwoven in Islam, an awareness of the culture can often be a helpful way of beginning the study of doctrine and beliefs.

Third, looking at the culture of Muslims makes us more aware of our own cultural bias. Some of the things we find difficult in Islam may have more to do with culture than with religion. If Muslim culture looks strange to us, we can be quite certain that our culture looks strange to Muslims!

Finally, when we come to think about communicating the Christian message to Muslims, we need to be aware of the vitally important distinction between the gospel and culture. What we think of as 'the Christian way of life' may owe more to our culture than it does to the gospel. We must avoid giving the impression that conversion to Christ means rejecting everything in Islamic culture and adapting to a foreign culture (see chapter 30, 'Counting the cost of conversion', and chapter 36, 'Some issues facing Christians today').

How can we begin to appreciate Muslim culture?

One way of learning to appreciate Muslim culture is to allow Muslims to explain their culture in their own words. Here, for example, is an outline of the Muslim way of life as described by Muslims for non-Muslims in a Western context, taken from a leaflet produced by British Muslims entitled *Islam: A Brief Guide*.[1]

Festivals

In Islam festivals are observed to seek the pleasure of Allah, not for pleasure's own sake. They are, however, occasions of joy and happiness. The happiest occasion of a Muslim's life is to see the laws of Allah established in their totality on the earth, ensuring peace and happiness to all Creation. **Idul Fitr** and **Idul Adha** are the two major festivals in Islam:

Idul Fitr falls on the first day after the month of Ramadan, the ninth month of the Islamic calendar. On this day, after a month of fasting, Muslims offer congregational prayer, preferably on open ground. They express their gratitude to Allah for enabling them to observe the fast. Special food is prepared. It is customary to visit friends and relatives, and to make the occasion special for children.

Idul Adha begins on the 10th day of the month of Dhul Hijjah and continues until the 13th. This celebration commemorates the willingness of Abraham when he was asked to sacrifice his own son Ishmael. Abraham showed his readiness and Allah was very pleased. A ram was sacrificed instead of Ishmael on Allah's command. Muslims offer congregational prayer on the day, and they sacrifice animals such as sheep, goats, cows and camels. The meat of the sacrificed animal is shared among relatives, neighbours and the poor.

Other celebrations include the **Hijrah** (migration of the Prophet, the peace and blessings of Allah be upon him), **Lailatul Mi'raj** (Night of the Ascension) and dates of Islamic battles. There is a special night called **Lailatul Qadr** (Night of Power), an odd-numbered night in the last ten days of Ramadan. The Qur'an says it is 'better than a thousand months'. Muslims spend the night offering prayers and reciting the Qur'an.

Islamic festivals are observed according to the Islamic Calendar, which is based on twelve lunar months. The lunar year is about 11 days shorter than the solar year. Festival dates are determined by the appearance of the moon.

Marriage and family life

Marriage is the basis of family life in Islam. It is a solemn, simple contract between a man and woman. Muslim marriages are generally arranged by parents but must be with the consent of the son and daughter, as required by Islamic law (Shari'a). Marriage is performed in a simple ceremony in the presence of relatives, friends and neighbours.

Islam does not allow free mixing of men and women, nor sex before marriage. Extramarital sex is severely punished in an Islamic state, to keep society free from the social problems it causes. No discrimination is made on the basis of sex. Husband and wife are partners in the family and play their respective roles. Divorce, whilst permitted, is the lawful action most displeasing to Allah.

Diet

Muslims are encouraged in the Qur'an to eat what is good and wholesome for them, and are forbidden to eat certain foods. A Muslim is not allowed to eat:

- pigs
- the blood of animals
- animals not slaughtered in the name of Allah
- carnivorous animals

Fish and vegetables are permitted. Islamic law requires animals to be humanely slaughtered by a sharp knife penetrating the inner part of the neck, to allow maximum drainage of blood. The name of Allah must be said at the time of slaughter. All alcoholic drinks are prohibited. These rules root out the harmful effects of food and drink from society.

Dress

Muslims should dress modestly and decently. No particular dress is recommended. The requirements include:

- For men, covering at least from the navel to the knees.
- For women, covering the whole body except the face and hands; according to some scholars, women above the age of puberty should cover the face when going out or meeting strangers.
- Men and women must not dress in a manner that arouses sexual feelings, e.g. transparent, skin-tight or half-naked dress.
- Men are not allowed to wear pure silk or gold.
- Men must not wear women's clothes, and vice versa.
- Symbolic dress from other religions is not allowed.

Simplicity and modesty are encouraged. Dress expressing arrogance is disliked. The style of dress depends on local customs and climate.

Social manners

Islam teaches decency, humility and good manners. Muslims greet one another by saying: **As-salamu 'alaikum** (peace be on you), and the reply is: **Wa'alaikumus salam** (peace be on you too).

Keeping promises, truthfulness, justice, fair play, helping the poor and needy, respect for parents, teachers and elders, love for children and good relations with neighbors are valued virtues in a Muslim. Islam condemns enmity, back-biting, slander, blasphemy, ridicule, use of offensive names, suspicion and arrogance.

Comments on this description of Muslim culture

'Allah' is the ordinary Arabic word for 'God'. It is not associated exclusively with Islam, since it is the word for 'God' used by up to 15 million Arabic-speaking Christians all over the Middle East. When Muslims are speaking English they generally prefer to speak of 'Allah' rather than 'God'. This is partly because it is important for them that the revelation given by God in the Qur'an was in Arabic, and partly because they are afraid of the possible confusion between the one true God and concepts of God or gods in other religions (see chapter 25, 'Theological questions').

Idul Fitr is the feast or festival of *Fitr*. The word *Id* is used for all the main feasts in the Muslim year. The Qur'an does not explicitly say that the son concerned was Ishmael (37:83–113), and for the first three centuries there was a debate among scholars, with some saying it was Isaac and some saying it was Ishmael. At the end of this period it became the accepted belief that it was Ishmael.

The *Hijra* is the migration of the Prophet Muhammad from Mecca to Medina in AD 622. This is regarded as the most significant event in the life of the Prophet (apart from his receiving of the Qur'an). Years in the Islamic calendar are all dated from this central event; for example, AD 2010 is equivalent to the years 1430/1431 AH (*Anno Hegirae*). (See chapter 7, 'The life of Muhammad'.)

Some Muslims believe that the Prophet was taken physically from Mecca to Jerusalem and from there taken up to heaven by night, while others believe that it was simply a mystical or spiritual experience like that described by Paul in 2 Corinthians 12:1–4. In any event, Muslims recognize *Lailatul Mi'raj* (Night of Ascension), referred to in the Qur'an (17:1), as a very significant experience in the life of Muhammad.

The expression generally used to show respect for the Prophet Muhammad is 'The peace and blessings of Allah be upon him' – *sallallahu 'alaihi wassallam*. Muslims show their respect for all the prophets (including Jesus) by using the expression 'Peace be upon him' (abbreviated as pbuh) whenever they mention their names.

	Start of Ramadan	Idul Fitr	Idul Adha
2007	11 September	13 October	20 December
2008	1 September	2 October	8 December
2009	22 August	21 September	28 November
2010	12 August	10 September	17 November
2011	2 August	31 August	7 November
2012	23 July	19 August	26 October
2013	13 July	8 August	15 October

Table 2.1

Since the dates of festivals are based on the lunar year, they occur approximately eleven days earlier each year. So, for example, the approximate dates of the start of Ramadan and of the two main feasts are as shown in Table 2.1.

What is special about Islamic culture?

Some of the aspects of the culture of Islamic communities which are most obvious to people in the West can be listed as follows.

- The family is thought of as the extended family rather than the nuclear family.
- People are more aware of their obligations to their family and their society than of their rights as individuals. Personal interests, views and opinions should be subordinate to those of the group. Religion has more to do with the community than with the individual.
- Great respect is shown to old people and to any who are older than oneself.
- Honour is a very important concept, especially the honour of the family and the whole community.
- Hospitality is an almost sacred obligation. It is so important that one should never, under normal circumstances, turn a visitor away.
- Education tends to rely more on rote learning than it does in the West. Acquiring knowledge is more important than thinking independently or questioning other people's opinions.
- God is concerned about the whole of life – not just about the religious parts of life. There should be no distinction between areas of life that are secular and areas that are sacred.

It needs to be recognized, however, that none of these attitudes and customs is exclusively Islamic. They are regarded as part of the Muslim way of life and are undergirded by Islamic moral teaching (e.g. respect for parents and hospitality), but several of them are part of the culture of Africa and the East – in other words, of most of the world except the West. There are many Christians living in Islamic societies, therefore, whose way of life is very similar to that of their Muslim neighbours in these respects. This means that such cultural differences have little or nothing to do with the religion of Islam.

Some aspects of Islamic culture are very clearly based on the teaching of the Qur'an:

- the prohibition of eating the blood of an animal and certain kinds of animals (2:168; 2:173; 5:3; 6:145; 16:115);
- the prohibition of alcohol (5:90–91);
- the possibility of marrying up to four wives (4:3).

Others are based on the example of the Prophet:

- the Prophet Muhammad instructed his followers to eat with the right hand and to wash their hands before meals;
- the Prophet did not allow men to wear silk or clothes decorated with gold.

Others are based on Islamic tradition:

- Muslims should begin their meals by saying the Arabic words *Bismillahi rrahman irrahim* ('In the name of God, the most Merciful and the most Kind'), and end by saying, *Al hamdu lillahi ladhi at'amana wa sagana wa ja'alana minal muslimin* ('All praise be to God who gave us to eat and drink and made us Muslims');
- dogs are regarded as unclean and are not normally kept as household pets (see chapter 9, 'Tradition').

Some controversial aspects of Islamic culture

The veil (hijab)

In Europe – and especially in France and Britain – in recent years there has been a fierce public debate about the wearing of the veil by Muslim girls in state schools. In most European countries there is no objection to the wearing of veils in state schools. In France, however, a ban by the government on the wearing of veils in schools in 2004 led to vociferous protests from Muslim communities. The subject is discussed in greater detail in chapter 16, 'Women in Islam', and in chapter 36, 'Some issues facing Christians today'. In the meantime we should note that the veil has little or nothing to do with the concept of women submitting to the authority of men. Muslim women who wear the veil in Western countries feel that they are making a statement about their identity as practising Muslims, and are simply obeying the qur'anic command that women should dress modestly. They see the wearing of the veil as no different in principle from Christian women wearing a crucifix as a necklace or Jewish men wearing a *kippa*.

Honour killings

There have been several cases in European countries in recent years in which a Muslim woman has been murdered by her male relatives because she is considered to have dishonoured her family through a sexual relationship or even just a friendship with a man before marriage or outside marriage. Although the punishment for adultery that is laid down in the Qur'an is flogging with a hundred stripes, stoning has been prescribed in Islamic law since the earliest centuries of Islam, and is based on Islamic traditions about the sayings and practice of the Prophet. Most Muslims living in the West today are outspoken in their condemnation of honour killings and want to uphold their country's laws which regard such killings as murder pure and simple and prescribe severe penalties. At the same time it has to be acknowledged that the concept of 'honour' (*izzat* in Urdu, from the Arabic *'izza*, meaning honour, self-respect or reputation) is so deeply ingrained in many Muslim societies (especially in the Middle East, India and Pakistan) that it is sometimes difficult to draw the line between the teaching of Islam on the one hand and the culture of a particular Muslim community on the other. This is an area where extreme sensitivity and patience are required in discussion of these issues with Muslims.

Female circumcision

This is another example of the difficulty of making a distinction between the culture of many Muslim societies and the official teaching of orthodox Islam. Ruqaiyyah Waris Maqsood in a recent introduction to Islam writes, 'Female circumcision (better called female genital mutilation) has nothing to do with Islam but is a barbaric cultural practice that predates Islam.'[2] Dr Nawal al-Saadawi, a prominent doctor and writer in Egypt, has written of her own traumatic experience of undergoing female circumcision as a child of six, and has campaigned vigorously against the practice throughout her life, arguing that it is a barbaric practice which cannot be supported by the teaching of Islam.[3] Most moderate Muslims would agree with her and hope that in the course of time the practice will eventually die out. It is clear, however, that in some of the more conservative Islamic societies the practice is still common, and it continues to provoke severe criticism in Western societies.

What do Muslims think about Western culture?

Another way of appreciating Muslim culture is to try to understand what Muslims feel about *Western* culture. While recognizing the danger of relying on stereotypes, the following are examples of the kind of general comments about Western culture that Muslims (as well as people of other faiths) often make.

- 'Your families in the West are often broken up and fragmented. You think of yourselves as individuals and are concerned about your own happiness and fulfilment. You emphasize the nuclear family, while we think of the extended family.' This is not a peculiarly Islamic view, however, since most cultures, except in the Western world, have the same ideas about the family.
- 'You don't show enough respect for old people. In our religion and our culture, we are taught to show respect for anyone who is older than us. We can't understand, for example, how you shut your old people away in old people's homes.' Here again is an attitude that is strongly supported by Islam but is not exclusively Muslim. Westerners probably need to be deeply challenged by observations and criticisms of this kind!
- 'We don't agree with free mixing between the sexes. We prefer Muslim girls to go to single-sex schools, and we don't allow our teenage daughters to go to night clubs, or at least we strongly discourage them from doing so.' Many Muslims take this view because they want their young people to marry within their own community and because they want to protect them from harmful influences in the society around them. Not all Muslim

families in the West, however, are as strict in their attitudes, and some allow their children considerable freedom.

- 'We don't like the kind of moral standards that we see on TV and in films. We are shocked by all the sex, violence and blasphemous language. If you are outraged by honour killings and female circumcision, we are enraged by the sexual promiscuity that we see in the West.' This reaction is similar to the reaction of many Christians. In some cases Muslims go further than some Christians, and refuse to watch any films or TV, because they believe that the Qur'an's prohibition of idols extends to the representation of the human form both in art and in films.

Some of these reactions have little or nothing to do with Islam, but are common to people of all faiths in the East. One of the problems in understanding Muslim reactions to Western culture is that they tend to focus on the culture of the society as a whole, and find it hard to distinguish between this and the lifestyle of committed Christians.

Some basic dos and don'ts

The following are basic guidelines that may be of help to any who have little or no experience of meeting with Muslims or with people from an Eastern culture. Here again, however, not all of these points are relevant for all Muslims or all Asians. We will need to be guided by people who have more experience than ourselves in relating to the Muslim community in our area.

- A man should not visit a woman in her home when she is alone or be alone with a woman in other situations.
- Men should not be surprised if the women in the family retire to a back room and do not sit with the men of the family and other guests in the front room.
- A man should not look a woman in the eye.
- A man should not shake the hand of a Muslim woman unless she takes the initiative by holding out her hand.
- You should not receive a present or eat with your left hand, since the left hand is associated with functions that are regarded as unclean.

- You should not sit with your legs folded if you are in the presence of an older person.
- If you are sitting on the floor, you should not sit with the soles of your feet facing another person.
- You should show respect for any copy of the Qur'an and the Bible. They should not, for example, be left lying on the floor or under a pile of other books. Muslims show respect for the Qur'an and often keep it wrapped in a special cloth. They are also supposed to go through the ritual of washing before opening the Qur'an. They are therefore surprised and shocked when they see how Christians often treat their holy book.
- It is best not to admire anything in a person's home too much, or to admire someone's child. In the minds of people of some cultures this can be regarded as a kind of coveting and associated with the 'evil eye'.
- If you are entertaining Muslims in your home, you should not offer them pork or alcohol. Strict Muslims will eat only meat that is *halal*, i.e., killed by a Muslim with the proper ritual and using the name of Allah. There need be no embarrassment about asking them if they prefer to have a vegetarian meal. If Muslims offer you meat in their home, there is no reason why you as a Christian should refuse to eat it. Most Christians would say that Paul's teaching about food offered to idols (1 Cor. 8) is not relevant at all to this situation.

Appreciating cultural issues of this kind can go a long way towards helping us to understand Muslims and Islam. But before we go on to look at Muslim beliefs and practices, we may need to ask more questions about ourselves and our attitudes.

3. EXAMINING OUR ATTITUDES

Once we have begun to develop genuine relationships with Muslims and to appreciate their culture, we may need to look more closely at our attitudes towards them and their religion. Some of these attitudes are related to theology and what we believe as Christians, since this is a religion which challenges Christianity at many points. Others, however, are related to culture and politics, since we are dealing here with the gut reactions of Christians in the West to a growing community of Asians and Arabs who have settled in our midst, whose way of life is very different from that of secular Westerners, and whose rhetoric often has profound political implications.

If we are honest with ourselves and can articulate these attitudes, we can try to reflect on them and examine them in the light of the gospel. The following, for example, are comments which are often made by Christians.

'Look at the way they persecute Christians!'

Christians in Pakistan have suffered for many years as a result of the so-called Blasphemy Laws, which have been used unscrupulously by some Muslims to convict Christians in courts of law. Although Christians in Iraq felt reasonably safe under Saddam Hussein, since the war of 2003 they have suffered from kidnapping and murder at the hands of Islamist extremists, and many churches have been attacked. There are many countries in the world where Muslims who want to convert to Christianity (or to any other religion) experience severe harassment from their families, communities or the police, and sometimes lose their lives. The Law of Apostasy, which says that Muslims who renounce their Islamic faith forfeit the right to live, has been enshrined in traditional Islamic law for centuries, even though it is not always practised in every situation today.

It is important that both Christians and Muslims – as well as secular governments – should be willing to acknowledge that in some Islamic contexts there is real persecution of Christians taking place today. We need to be careful, however, that we do not allow the fact of persecution in these situations to create very negative attitudes in our minds towards *all* Muslims. In trying to understand these situations of persecution and working out how Christians outside the situation should respond, these are some factors which we need to keep in mind.

There is a wide range of attitudes among Muslims towards Christians. At one end of the spectrum are Muslims who regard Christians as 'unbelievers' or 'idolaters', using the strong qur'anic word *kuffar* (plural; *kafir* singular) and *mushrikun* (literally 'associators', who put created beings on the same level as God). They therefore see them as little different from the polytheists and idolaters who are so strongly condemned in the Qur'an (see 5:17, 72–73; 9:30). At the other end of the spectrum are Muslims who point to several verses in the Qur'an which are very positive towards Christians (e.g. 2:62; 5:82–83), describing them (along with the Jews) as 'People of the Book' because they possess written scriptures. Since there are also many positions between these two approaches, it is *never* possible to sum up the attitudes of Muslims to Christians in one sentence, as if *all* Muslims *everywhere* have the same attitude towards Christians (see further chapter 27, 'The qur'anic view of Christians'). Christian Troll, a Jesuit Islamic scholar, comments:

> It is precisely this ambivalence that has determined the character of Muslim attitudes to Christianity right up to the present. The ways in which

Christianity and Christians are judged – whether as unbelievers or as
'People of the Book' and monotheists – thus depend to a considerable
extent on the peaceful or tense co-existence of Christians and Muslims,
exactly as in the time of the Prophet.[1]

In every situation where there is discrimination and persecution of
Christians by Muslims, we need to ask questions like these:

- What are the proportions of Muslims and Christians? In some
  situations we may be dealing with the intolerant attitudes of the
  majority community towards a minority community in their
  midst.
- What is the official attitude of the government towards
  Christians? What legal protection is there for Christians? In
  some countries the government does attempt to protect the
  rights of religious minorities, but is sometimes powerless against
  the strong prejudices of very conservative communities.
- Is this persecution the result of a personal quarrel between
  individuals, families or communities which has broadened into
  a wider conflict? This seems to have been the trigger that has
  sparked off attacks against Christians in several countries in
  recent years.
- Is this persecution the result of other factors – especially
  political factors – outside the situation? In the last ten years,
  for example, Christians in a number of Muslim countries have
  suffered because they are inevitably identified in the minds of
  Muslims with 'the Christian West' which is perceived to be
  attacking 'the Muslim East'.
- Is this persecution simply because Christians are practising their
  faith (e.g. by meeting together for worship), or because they are
  breaking a written or unwritten law (e.g. by seeking to spread
  their faith among non-Christians)?

Asking questions like these does not make the persecution any easier
to bear. But it does highlight the wide variety of factors which may lie
behind the persecution, and should make it easier to work out the most
appropriate responses in each situation. Christians outside the situation will inevitably want to help in practical ways without making the

situation even harder for the Christians concerned.[2] (See further
chapter 30, 'Counting the cost of conversion', and chapter 31, 'Facing
the political challenge of Islam'.)

'People in glass houses shouldn't throw stones.' When pointing to
Islamic contexts in which Christians are being persecuted, it is only
fair to recognize that Muslims in the West feel that they experience
discrimination and unfair treatment of different kinds. While this
treatment does not usually amount to the kind of active persecution
of Christians that we are thinking about, Christians in the West must
be willing to acknowledge that attitudes towards Muslims in some
Western countries have hardened in recent years – for a variety of
reasons. Many North African immigrants in France, for example, and
Turkish guestworkers in Germany are economically disadvantaged
and feel alienated from the host community, and this inevitably makes
it hard for them to integrate fully into French and German society.

While recognizing situations of real persecution in other countries,
it is important not to give the impression that *all* Christians living in
Islamic countries are *always* suffering persecution. Christians in the
West are often surprised to find how many Christians there are in
many countries in the Middle East and to learn how open they
can be not only in the practice of their faith but also in sharing it
with others.

When stories of persecution are combined with the big political
issues related to Muslims and Islam, it is only natural that Christians
begin to feel afraid. They then find it harder to trust Muslims or to
develop natural and meaningful relationships with them. If Christians
find that they are responding to Muslims and Islam more out of fear
than out of love, it becomes very much harder for them to obey the
command to 'love your neighbour as yourself' (Matt. 19:19).

'Islam seems to be a religion of violence'

Terrorist attacks carried out by Muslims in recent years – in the name
of Islam – have made many non-Muslims wonder whether the
religion of Islam might be *inherently* violent. There are many verses in
the Qur'an, for example, in which God commands Muhammad
and his followers to fight and even to kill. Here are some verses of
this kind.

And fight for the Cause of Allah those who fight you, but do not be aggressive. Surely Allah does not like the aggressors ... Kill them wherever you find them and drive them out from wherever they drove you out. Sedition is worse than slaughter ... Fight them until there is no sedition and the religion becomes that of Allah. (2:190–193, Fakhry)

Then, when the Sacred Months are over, kill the idolaters wherever you find them, take them [as captives], besiege them, and lie in wait for them at every point of observation. If they repent afterwards, perform the prayer and pay the alms, then release them. (9:5, Fakhry)

The earliest accounts of the life of the Prophet written by Muslims record in some detail the battles which Muhammad fought against the people of Mecca and his violent treatment of the three Jewish tribes in Medina who opposed him.[3] For these reasons it is hardly surprising that one Christian scholar of Islam describes Islam as 'a religion cradled in violence'.[4] Muslims point out that these incidents need to be understood in the context of the ethic of tribal revenge at the time, and remind us that Muhammad was often magnanimous towards his enemies and put no one to death when he and his followers returned to Mecca in triumph. They also quote the Qur'anic verse 'There is no compulsion in religion' (2:256).

If it is ever going to be possible to be scrupulously fair and to get the right balance between those who overemphasize these elements of violence in the origins of Islam and those who downplay them and claim that Islam has always been 'a religion of peace', the following are some of the issues which we may need to address.

Muslims have their own ways of dealing with the texts about warfare in the Qur'an. Islamists in many countries today feel that the world of Islam has been under attack from the West for at least the last two hundred years. They therefore feel that they are in a similar position to the first community of Muslims under Muhammad's leadership, who were under attack from the pagan Meccans, and the verses about *jihad* and warfare can apply equally well to them today. Other Muslims, however, point out that the word 'Islam' is related to the word *salam*, which means 'peace'. They argue that the commands to Muhammad and his followers to fight were related only to that particular context and cannot therefore be applied to

situations today which are totally different. Christians may want
to challenge this defence. But they must at least have the honesty to
recognize that many Muslims have their own ways of dealing with
these difficult texts, and must be willing to listen to this kind of
moderate interpretation.

We need to recognize similar problems that many find in the Bible
– especially in the Old Testament. The book of Joshua describes a
violent conquest of the land, in which most of the original inhabitants
were either absorbed, exterminated or driven out. Christians today
believe that although the name 'Jesus' is a variation of the name
'Joshua' and Jesus is described in the New Testament as a kind of
'new Joshua' (e.g. Heb. 4), it is unthinkable for Christians today to
want to go back to the earlier model of Joshua. It is a sad fact,
however, that wherever Christianity has become the dominant religion
of a nation and the religion of the state, it has been easy for Christians
to slip back into ways of thinking found in the Old Testament. That
model is called 'theocratic' because it was based on the idea that God is
the ultimate authority and that he is exercising his rule through the
king who enforces the law of God and goes out to make war on
the nation's enemies. The only incident in the New Testament in
which any of the disciples committed a violent act was when Peter cut
off the ear of the high priest's servant during the arrest of Jesus (Matt.
26:51–54). But he was rebuked by Jesus, and there is nothing in the
New Testament to suggest that his followers ever engaged in acts of
violence either to defend themselves or to spread their faith. Christians
today, however, are still faced with the difficult question of how to
explain so many stories of violence in the Old Testament, which have
some similarities with the violence reflected in the Qur'an.[5]

Jesus and his followers did not take up arms either against the
Jewish leaders or against the Romans who ruled Palestine as part of
the Roman Empire. He was willing to go to the cross himself and told
his followers that they too must be willing to take up their cross and
suffer as his followers (Mark 8:31–38). He said he was sending them
out 'as sheep among wolves' (Matt. 10:16). For three hundred years
Christians were a tiny minority within the Roman Empire without any
political power. It was only when the Emperor Constantine became a
Christian in 313 and decided to make Christianity the official religion
of the empire that the situation began to change.

In the Christian Empire with its capital in Byzantium there was a close alliance between church and state, and Muhammad must have been aware that this was one of the dominant expressions of Christianity during the time when he was spreading his message in Arabia. Christians today often have very mixed feelings as they reflect on the history of 'Christendom' in Europe – a phenomenon that was not very different from 'the House of Islam' (*dar al-Islam*, the area ruled by Islam). The Crusades were fought in the name of Christianity, and Muslims have never forgotten that when the Crusaders entered Jerusalem they made the streets flow with blood. Many Muslims today see Western political and military involvement in the Middle East during the twentieth and twenty-first centuries as a continuation of the Crusades. Here, then, is another situation in which Christians need to recognize that the criticisms they level against Muslims and Islam can easily be thrown back by Muslims as criticisms of Christians and Christianity. Could this be a situation in which Christians need to remember the words of Jesus, 'Do not judge, or you too will be judged. For in the same way as you judge others, you will be judged, and with the measure you use, it will be measured to you' (Matt. 7:1–2)?

'Islam wants to rule the world!'

Some of the common slogans of Islamists in recent years have been 'Islam must rule!' and 'Islam is the solution!' These convictions about the political ambitions of Islam go back to the origins of Islam. After the Prophet Muhammad established the first Islamic state in Medina, his followers went on to bring the whole of Arabia under the rule of Islam. According to Islamic tradition, before his death Muhammad sent messengers to the rulers of Abyssinia, Egypt, Byzantium and Persia, inviting them to accept Islam and become Muslims. Within a hundred years of the death of the Prophet, Arab Muslim armies had moved across North Africa and into France and Spain, and eastwards across the whole of the Middle East to the borders of India and China. In addition to this early empire there have been other examples of Islamic empires: the Safavids in Persia (1502–1722), the Mughals in India (1526–1858) and the Ottomans in Turkey, the Balkans, the Middle East and North Africa (1512–1918). In other places and at other times, however, Islam has spread peacefully through traders, teachers and holy men.

Throughout its history, therefore, Islam has been not only a missionary religion, but also one that is very interested in power. It has also had its own empires in the past. When the centuries of Western imperialism came to an end in the middle of the twentieth century, Muslim countries gained their independence as separate nation states – but without the unifying focus of the Caliphate, which was abolished by Turkey in 1924. The rise of radical Islam has revived the political ambitions of a number of Muslims, who now want to re-establish the Caliphate, make Muslim countries more genuinely Islamic and recover the political power of the Muslim world. How are we to respond to this new situation?

We need first of all to be more careful about the kind of *language* that we use. To say that 'Islam wants to rule the world' is just as misleading as saying that 'Christianity wants to rule the world'. *Some* Muslims would like Islam to 'rule the world' and everyone in the world to become a Muslim, just as *some* Christians would like Christianity to 'rule the world' and everyone to become Christians. Expressions like these are highly inaccurate and only have the effect of stirring up fear and prejudice.

We need to take stock of the situation we face:

- At the present time Muslims number around 1.3 billion throughout the world, which is around 20.4% of the total population. Christians number around 2.196 billion, making them 31.4%. In some parts of the world (especially in Europe and North America) Islam seems to be growing fast, while in others (e.g. in Africa) Christianity is growing as fast as, or faster than, Islam.
- The birth rate in Muslim communities in the West tends to be higher than that in other communities.
- Many thousands of non-Muslims in the West have converted to Islam.[6]
- Muslims are an overwhelming majority in around forty countries of the world. In some, like Nigeria, the proportion of Muslims and Christians is roughly equal. And 25% of all Muslims, i.e. one out of four of all Muslims, live in countries were they are a minority (as in Europe and North America).

- For every Muslim in the West who has a strong missionary vision there are dozens who are interested only in the survival of the present Muslim communities. They are far more concerned to hold on to their young people and protect them from the influence of a godless society around them than they are to spread the message of Islam. Just as not all Christians have strong desires to spread their faith, in the same way not all Muslims want to spread their faith.

- Western countries could only become Islamic if Muslims became an overwhelming majority of the population, *and* if the majority within their communities actually wanted this to happen. Many Muslims, however, are very nominal in the practice of their faith, and some have come to Western countries to escape from Islamic governments which they have found oppressive.

We need to recognize the complexity of some of the *legal issues* which governments in most Western countries have to address. All citizens of democratic countries in the West – regardless of their religion and their racial origin – have the same freedom both to practise and to propagate their religion. In several countries Muslim communities have become bolder in making requests (if not demands) like these, asking for:

- permission to build mosques and community centres;
- the introduction of *halal* meat for Muslims in schools, hospitals and prisons;
- permission to broadcast the Islamic call to prayer from mosques;
- the appointment of Muslim chaplains in hospitals and prisons;
- the creation of multi-faith prayer rooms in airport terminals;
- the creation of Muslim schools within the state system;
- the introducion of Islamic *shari'a* law for family matters within Muslim communities (e.g. for marriage, divorce and inheritance law).

Some of these requests (like *halal* meat) raise few problems and have been granted by local and national authorities. Others, however (like faith schools), raise complex and sensitive issues which divide Christians and local communities (see chapter 36, 'Some issues facing Christians today'). The boldest request of all (the introduction of Islamic law) raises questions about the ultimate goals of some Muslims and presents a fundamental challenge to the very nature of Western democratic societies (see chapter 19, 'Social and political issues').

We would do well to remember the principle of *reciprocity*. Christians should want to be guided by the Golden Rule in which Jesus says, 'In everything, do to others what you would have them do to you, for this sums up the Law and the Prophets' (Matt. 7:12). This might mean, for example, that Western Christians should ask themselves, 'If we were living as a Christian minority in a Muslim country, how would we like to be treated?' The answer to this question should influence the way we think about Muslim minorities in Western societies. A simple 'tit-for-tat' approach would make us say, 'Since they don't allow Christians to build churches in Saudi Arabia, we shouldn't allow them to build mosques in our country!' But Jesus encourages his followers to take the initiative and follow the Golden Rule – however the other party behaves.

In some situations in recent years Christian leaders – including Dr George Carey, the previous archbishop of Canterbury, and the present pope, Benedict XVI – have been able to appeal to Muslim leaders on the basis of the principle of reciprocity. A delegation of Christian and Muslim leaders from Bradford in England, for example, visited Pakistan some years ago, and while talking about Muslim-Christians in Bradford were able to ask pointed questions about the treatment of Christians in Pakistan. Saudi Arabia regards itself as a special case because of its unique history in the development of Islam, and is generally unwilling to take the principle of reciprocity seriously. But in some of the Gulf States governments and rulers have been generous in allowing expatriate Christian communities to build churches. If Christians are sincere and open in their attempt to follow the Golden Rule, they may be surprised to find that in time *some* Muslims may be willing to work on the same basis. If and when they do so, these Muslims may find that they are opening up issues with fellow Muslims who certainly *do not* want to operate on this basis and have other goals in mind.

In situations like these Christians have special responsibilities and can sometimes play an important role as bridge-builders and peace-makers, simply because they have sympathies *with both sides*. They have learned how to live in societies that are becoming more and more secular, but at the same time, like many Muslims, they would like to see religion having much more influence in public life. Christians therefore usually have to find a middle path between two extremes: on the one hand doing their utmost to resist requests from Muslims, and on the other giving in to every request out of misguided political correctness and a desire not to offend. These therefore are some of the questions that Christians will want to be asking:

- Given our commitment to the human rights of individuals and communities in our midst, is there any reason in law why these privileges should not be extended to Muslim communities?
- What are the likely implications for the rest of the community of granting these requests, and are they acceptable?
- What kind of societies do we want to create? How, for example, do we want religion to be taught in our schools? How do we think children in Muslim schools should learn about faiths other than their own?
- How are secular governments to face the challenge from the more articulate and forceful Muslim leaders who, on the basis of their understanding of Islam, do not want to separate religion from the state and would like the whole of society to conform to Islamic standards?

What we are dealing with, therefore, is two religions, both of which are missionary religions with long histories, facing each other in Western countries where the churches are declining in numbers and influence, and where the dominant secular humanism finds itself at a loss to know how to respond to a radically new kind of challenge. How are secular governments, *which want to keep religion out of the public sphere as much as possible*, to work with these Muslim leaders, *who really do want to bring God into public life and into politics*? It must be obvious by now that these are some of the hardest challenges that Christians are called upon to face in the Western world at the present time (see chapter 36, 'Some issues facing Christians today').

'If Christianity is true, then Islam is false'

If Christianity is true, the argument goes, does it not follow that Islam
is false? If Jesus is the only way to God, does it not mean that Muslims
cannot know God in a personal way? Although we do not have the
space to cover the very delicate and complex question of Christian
attitudes to other faiths in any detail, we must at least notice that there
are many passages in the Bible which express a very negative attitude
towards 'other faiths' (e.g. Deut. 12:1–3, 29–31; 32:17; Ps. 96:5;
1 Cor. 8:4–6).

On the other hand, there are passages which reflect a much more
positive and open approach to people of other faiths (e.g. Gen. 14:18;
Mal. 1:10–11 RSV; Acts 10:30–43; 17:16–31). At the very least, therefore, we need to get beyond the simplistic view that if Christianity
is completely true, Islam and all other faiths must be completely false.
We can hardly say that they contain no understanding of God, his
creation or humanity.

We also need to look again at a crucial verse of scripture, John
14:6, and ask if it really is as exclusive as it sounds. The key to a
proper understanding of these words may be to recognize that
Jesus is speaking here about people coming 'to the Father'. When he
says 'I am the way', he means 'I am the way *to the Father*; no one
comes *to the Father* but by me'. We can therefore fill out the rest of
the verse in this way: 'I am the truth about the Father; no one can
know the truth about the Father except through me. I am the life
of the Father; no one can live in fellowship with the Father except
through me.'

If this is the thrust of what Jesus is saying, he can hardly mean
that a person who does not believe in him knows *nothing* about God
and has *no* relationship with him. But he does seem to be saying that
people cannot know God *as Father*, and enjoy all the blessings of
the father-child relationship, unless they recognize and trust Jesus
as the Son. The testimony of Bilquis Sheikh in *I Dared to Call
Him Father*[7] bears out the fact that Muslims generally believe it is
quite wrong to think of God as 'Father'. Their denial of the sonship of Jesus is therefore linked with their denial of the fatherhood
of God.

Quite apart from the exegesis of this important verse, however, we need to recognize that our attitudes may sometimes be influenced by more than just our desire for correct doctrine. The story of Abraham and his wife Sarah, and their dealings with Abimelech, in Genesis 20:1–18 exposes some of our attitudes towards people of other communities for what they really are. Abraham wants to protect Sarah, but gets her into a difficult situation because he is less than honest in the way he explains who she is. He also suffers from a subtle form of pride which makes him feel that no one apart from himself and his family has any real relationship with God: 'I thought that there would be no one here who fears God.' When God eventually speaks to Abimelech in a dream and Sarah is restored to Abraham, the painful lesson that Abraham has to learn is that some people outside the covenant do have a real reverence for God, and are even able to hear and respond to a direct communication from God.

A similar story in the New Testament is the account of how Peter's racial and religious prejudices are challenged through the events leading up to his meeting with Cornelius (Acts 10). Peter has to allow the Holy Spirit to expose and root out these pernicious prejudices before he, as a Jew, can share the good news with a God-fearing person of a different nationality: 'God has shown me that I should not call any man impure or unclean' (v. 28).

If we as Christians suffer from a feeling of superiority that makes us look down on people of other faiths and other races as if they are inferior, we may need the same kind of upheaval to humble us and enable us to say with Peter: 'I now realize how true it is that God does not show favouritism, but accepts men from every nation who fear him and do what is right' (Acts 10:34–35). Reaching this point does not mean concluding that 'people of other faiths are all right as they are' and 'there's no need any longer to share the good news about Jesus with them'. It is significant that immediately after these words Peter goes on to speak of 'the message God sent to the people of Israel, telling the good news of peace through Jesus Christ, who is Lord of all' (v. 36). But it does mean that in the process of sharing the good news, or perhaps even before we can be in a right frame of mind to do so, we may have to allow the Holy Spirit to do some painful things to deal with attitudes of pride in our conscious and subconscious minds.

'It's impossible to convert Muslims, and we shouldn't try anyway'

Sometimes a 'live and let live' approach shapes Western attitudes towards Muslims: 'We have our religion, they have theirs – so why can't we just accept the situation as it is?' At other times this attitude arises from the conviction that all religions are basically the same, and that it is sheer arrogance for Christians to think that their faith is truer or better than any other. In other cases, however, Christians have reached this conclusion because of the many problems they face in relating to Muslims and the terrible cost often paid by Muslims who recognize Jesus as more than a prophet.

One book in the Bible that speaks to these attitudes is the book of Jonah, which has been described as the high-water mark of mission in the Old Testament. Jonah takes some time to realize that God wants him to convey his message to the people of Nineveh. One reason for his reluctance to answer the call is the feeling that 'if God wants to convert them, he can do it perfectly well without me'. Jonah therefore has to learn that God uses people in his purposes of love for the world. After Jonah obeys the call and preaches a message of judgment and mercy, he is amazed to find how responsive the people of Nineveh are. He expects them to be hardened pagans and can hardly believe that they actually accept his message and express their repentance in a dramatic way.

At the end of the book there is a further challenge to Jonah, the reluctant and unloving missionary, when God says to him, in effect, 'You've been faithful in condemning all that was wrong in Nineveh. But have you secretly enjoyed it all? Do you really care for these people whose faith and way of life are so different from our own? Do you really want them to turn to me in repentance and faith?' (Jon. 4:1–11) Could it therefore be that the book of Jonah has a powerful message not just for individual Jonahs today who try to run away from God's call, but for the whole Christian church running away from the challenges of Islam?

It is also worth pointing out that it is not we who 'convert' people. In the New Testament we have in Paul an example – almost larger than life – of how God can change the direction of a person's life. The Christians of Judea got the message that 'the man who formerly persecuted us is now preaching the faith he once tried to destroy' (Gal. 1:23). Writing towards the end of his life, Paul sees his conversion as proof of how God in his love and patience can turn the hardest hearts: 'For that very reason I was shown mercy so that in me, the worst of sinners, Christ Jesus might display his unlimited patience as an example for those who would believe on him and receive eternal life' (1 Tim. 1:16). If God could change someone as hostile towards Christianity as Saul, is there any reason why he cannot help people of any faith today to change their ideas about Jesus?

'Muslims seem to be very prejudiced and have closed minds'

Yes, maybe in some cases they are – but often it may be a case of the pot calling the kettle black! It is always easier, for Christians as for anybody, to accuse others of being prejudiced rather than to admit that we ourselves have prejudices. We may not be able to change others' prejudices, but we can at least do something about our own.

Once we have made the admission and called our prejudices by their proper name, it can be a relief to find that the New Testament has so much to say on this subject. It is reassuring to know, for example, that the prejudices which many Christians have towards Muslims are very similar to the prejudices the Jews showed towards Samaritans at the time of Jesus. Just as the apostle John had to say, 'Jews have no dealings with Samaritans' (John 4:9 RSV; the NIV says, 'Jews do not associate with Samaritans'), so in many situations today it is sadly true that 'Christians have no dealings with Muslims', or at least as few dealings as possible. When we try to explain these prejudices in the minds of the Jews, we find that there were at least three major reasons.

The first reason was *racial*. The Jews despised the Samaritans for their mixed ancestry, which resulted from intermarriage between Jews in the northern kingdom of Israel and Assyrians who were brought to the area after the fall of Samaria in 721 BC (2 Kgs 17:24–41).

The second reason was *religious*. The Samaritans had a temple on Mount Gerizim that rivalled the Jerusalem temple, and they recognized the Torah (the Pentateuch) but not the Prophets and the Writings.

The third reason for these prejudices was *political*. There had been tensions and rivalries between the two communities over many centuries.

If Christians today think of Muslims in anything like the same way as the disciples thought of the Samaritans, we will have to learn that loving our neighbour involves putting aside our prejudices and doing something very positive to overcome the social, political, cultural and religious barriers which separate us. We may need to see how Jesus dealt with prejudices in the minds of his disciples.

By his example

The disciples were surprised, for example, that Jesus spoke to a woman at Jacob's well, and no doubt doubly surprised that she was a Samaritan (John 4:1–42, especially v. 27). He was not prepared to be bound by all the social and religious prejudices of his fellow Jews.

By his teaching

It can hardly have been an accident that Jesus chose a Samaritan as the main character in the story which we know as 'the parable of the good Samaritan'. His Jewish listeners would have been shocked to find that the priest and the Levite come out so badly in the story, and that the hero is from that despised and heretical community to the north! If we wanted to capture the original impact of the parable, we would need to say that if Jesus were addressing Protestants in Northern Ireland, the good Samaritan would have been a Catholic; if he were speaking to Palestinian Arabs, the person who so unexpectedly showed kindness would have been a Jew; if he were talking to Armenians, it would have been 'the good Turk'. In this way Jesus was, among other things, encouraging his disciples to reject such stereotypes and to believe that sacrificial love often comes from sources which we in our arrogance think most unlikely.

By his sending of the Holy Spirit

Jesus specifically mentions Samaria as one of the places where his disciples are to take the good news: 'You will be my witnesses in Jerusalem, and in all Judea and Samaria' (Acts 1:8). A few chapters later we learn how this worked out in practice. Luke tells us that 'When the apostles in Jerusalem heard that Samaria had accepted the word of God, they sent Peter and John to them' (Acts 8:14). It seems that the leaders of the church may have felt that the coming of the gospel to Samaria was such a significant development that they had to send an official apostolic delegation to the city to welcome the new believers. In view of all the animosities between Jews and Samaritans in the past, some public gesture was called for to show to all the world that in the church there would be no place for any bad feeling between Jewish and Samaritan believers.

There may be elements of truth in all these different sentiments which we have explored. Challenging and revising them, however, will involve learning more about Islam – both the ideal Islam and the actual Islam, being sure of our facts, and recognizing that Muslims often think the same about us. Most of all it will mean exposing our prejudices to the light of the gospel of Jesus and allowing the Holy Spirit to show us 'the mind of Christ'.

PART TWO

UNDERSTANDING ISLAM

Great Spirit, grant that I may never criticize a man until I have walked a mile in his moccasins.
An American Indian prayer

One tries to get inside the mind and heart of Islam, to get the feel of it, to be at home within it.
Roger Hooker[1]

You have got to know and yet never try to teach a Muslim his own religion.
Jens Christensen[2]

The intention is to describe, rather than to pass judgment, on the phenomena of religion ... Our first need is to understand.
Ninian Smart[3]

The task before the modern Muslim is immense. He has to rethink the whole system of Islam without completely breaking with the past.
Muhammad Iqbal[4]

The aim of Part Two is to present Islam as much as possible from the point of view of Muslims, to describe the faith and practice of Islam in a way that Muslims will recognize as accurate and fair. We are trying to put ourselves, as it were, in the shoes of Muslims and understand their world view. We are not at this stage trying to compare Islam with Christianity, except where there is some significant similarity or difference that can help us to appreciate better some aspect of Islamic belief or practice.

4. WHAT IS ISLAM?

'Islam is what Muslims say it is.' If we accept this principle, it must mean that non-Muslims can observe Muslims and study Islam from the outside, but have no right to say what is 'real Islam' or 'true Islam'. Our best starting point, therefore, is to take a summary of the meaning of Islam written by Muslims – like this one from *Islam: A Brief Guide*:

> Islam is a complete way of life. It tells man about the purpose of his creation and existence, his ultimate destiny and his place among other creatures. More importantly, it provides him with Guidance (*Hidayah*) to lead a balanced and purposeful life which will enable him to avoid the Hellfire (*Jahannam*) and be rewarded with a place in Paradise (*Jannah*) in the life after death.
>
> The Arabic word *Islam* means voluntary surrender to the Will of Allah and obedience to His commands. Allah, also an Arabic word, is the unique name of God. Muslims prefer to use Allah rather than God. Allah is the universal Creator of all mankind. The Islamic way of life is based on total obedience to Allah. This is the way to obtain peace both here and in the hereafter; hence, Islam also means peace.
>
> A person who freely and consciously accepts the Islamic way of life, and sincerely practises it, is called a Muslim.

At a later stage we will look at the different branches of Islam and some of the movements within it (see chapter 14, 'Branches and movements within Islam'). At this stage, however, it may be helpful to try to give names to the most significant expressions of Islam that we see in the world today. Islam is not monolithic; it has many different 'faces'. Figure 4.1 attempts to give names to four of these and show how they relate to each other.

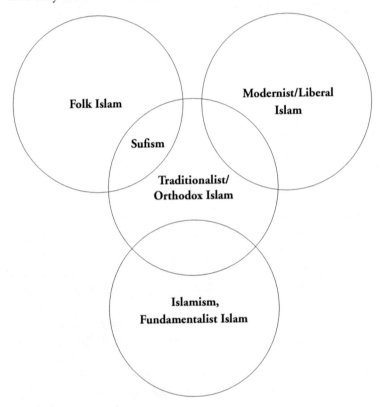

Figure 4.1

The different faces of Islam

Traditionalist, orthodox Islam

These are Muslims who seek to preserve the beliefs and practices of Islam as faithfully as possible with the minimum of concessions to the modern world. They tend to be critical of the other main expressions of Islam – folk Islam, modernist or liberal Islam, and Islamism.

Folk Islam or popular Islam

This is the kind of Islam practised – especially (but not only) in rural areas all over the world – by Muslims who are influenced by the primal religion of their area more than by the teaching of orthodox Islam (see chapter 12, 'Folk Islam or popular Islam').

Modernist/liberal Islam or Islamic modernism

This has developed out of the attempt of Muslims since the end of the nineteenth century to adapt the beliefs and practice of Islam to the modern world (see chapter 14, 'Branches and movements within Islam', and chapter 15, 'Issues facing Muslims today'). The emphasis here is on embracing change and allowing religion to change, and thereby reinterpreting Islam in a way that accommodates Western and modern ideas.

Islamism, Islamic fundamentalism, radical or revivalist Islam

These are Muslims who have sought to return to a pure form of original Islam, but at the same time to respond to the many political challenges to the Muslim world in the last century. They are convinced of the perfection and self-sufficiency of Islam, and believe that Western ideas, science and technology should be embraced only on Islamic terms.

Sufism

This is located in Figure 4.1 somewhere between folk Islam and traditionalist, orthodox Islam because, while some its teachings have been adopted by many orthodox Muslims, others are closer to folk Islam (see chapter 11, 'Sufism', and chapter 12, 'Folk Islam or popular Islam').

It is probably hazardous to attempt to suggest figures for each of these four main groups. But one British Muslim, Ishtiaq Ahmed, suggests the following figures: modernists 15%; Islamists or revivalists 15%; traditionalists (which would include folk Islam in Figure 4.1) 70%.[1]

While we need to start, as we have done, by trying to define Islam in the words of Muslims themselves, sooner or later we may need to start thinking in terms of 'Muslims' as much as 'Islam'. There is clearly a basic core of beliefs and practices which form the heart of Islam and which all Muslims recognize as the norm, the ideal to which they should strive, and which holds them together. But there are so many differences between Muslims in different situations that it is dangerous to assume that *all* Muslims believe and practise their faith in the way that traditionalist, orthodox Islam requires.

In trying to build up an understanding of individual Muslims we meet, these are some of the questions we may need to ask in order to build up a profile of the kind of Muslims they are.

- Which branch of Islam do they belong to, Sunni or Shi'ite, and do they belong to any subgroup within the two main branches (see chapter 14, 'Branches and movements within Islam')? Which school of law does their community follow (see chapter 10, 'Law and theology')?
- Do they associate with any particular movement – like the Muslim Brotherhood or one of the many movements which originated in the Indian subcontinent (see chapter 14, 'Branches and movements within Islam')?
- What country do their families come from originally – Europe and North America, or North Africa, the Middle East, Turkey, Iran, India, Pakistan, Bangladesh, Malaysia, Indonesia, etc.?
- How do they understand their identity as Muslims in relation to their nationality? Do they feel they are Muslims first, and British, French or American second, or the other way round?
- Are they committed or nominal? Do they say their prayers five times a day and attend the mosque on Friday? Do they fast during Ramadan?
- In dealing with the problems of everyday life, do they turn to the practices of folk Islam?
- Apart from the prescribed prayers, how do they pray? Have they been influenced by Sufism? What is their approach to spirituality?
- How do they respond to modernity? Do they embrace everything in the modern world gladly, or reject as much as they can? Do they appear open, tolerant and liberal in their thinking?

- Are they politically motivated? Are they concerned about issues of justice in society and the world, or are they more concerned about their spiritual lives and their relationship with God?
- How do they respond to Christians and Christianity? Are they open, friendly and tolerant, or cautious, suspicious and critical?

In asking these questions we are not making any judgments on individuals, but simply trying to appreciate the variety and diversity of Muslims. Having tried to recognize this diversity, we turn now to consider the core beliefs and practices which hold them together.

5. BASIC MUSLIM BELIEFS AND PRACTICES

In this chapter we consider the basic beliefs of Islam (the Muslim creed) and the 'five pillars' (the basic duties) of Sunni (orthodox) Islam. This is what most, if not all, Muslims would recognize as the normative beliefs and practices that have been handed down through the centuries from the Prophet Muhammad and the first Muslim community.

Basic beliefs

The following verse from the Qur'an gives a summary of the fundamental beliefs revealed by God to the Prophet Muhammad:

> The messenger believeth in that which hath been revealed unto him from His Lord and (so do) the believers. Each one believeth in Allah and His Angels and His scriptures and His messengers ... (2:285)

According to a saying of the Prophet recorded in Islamic tradition (see chapter 9, 'Tradition'), Muhammad summarized the basic articles a Muslim must believe as 'God, and his Angels, and His Books, and His Apostles; the Last Day, and the Decree of both good and evil'.

Islam: A Brief Guide provides a good example of a contemporary statement of what it calls 'the three fundamental Islamic beliefs':

Tawhid – The oneness of Allah
Risalah – Prophethood
Akhirah – Life after death

Tawhid is the most important Islamic belief. Everything in existence originates from the one and only Creator, who is also the Sustainer and the sole Source of Guidance. This belief should govern all aspects of human life. Recognition of this fundamental truth brings a unified view of life which rejects any division into religious and secular.

Allah is sole source of Power and Authority, and is to be worshipped and obeyed. He has no partner; Tawhid is pure monotheism. Allah is not born, and He has no son or daughter. Human beings are His subjects. He is One; He is eternal; He is the First and the Last; and there is none like Him.

Belief in Tawhid brings total change in a Muslim's life. It makes him bow down only to Allah, Who sees all of his actions. He must work to establish the laws of Allah in all areas of his life, in order to gain His pleasure.

Risalah means prophethood and messengership. Allah has not left man without Guidance for the conduct of his life. Since the creation of the first man, Allah has revealed His guidance to mankind through His prophets. Prophets who received books from Allah are called messengers. All the prophets and messengers came with the same message; they urged the people of their time to obey and worship Allah alone and none other. Whenever the teachings of a prophet were distorted by people, Allah sent another prophet to bring them back to the Straight Path (*Siratul Mustaqim*). The chain of *Risalah* began with Adam, included Noah, Abraham, Ishmael, Isaac, Lot, Jacob, Joseph, Moses, David and Jesus, and ended with Muhammad (peace be upon them all). Muhammad (the peace and blessings of Allah be upon him) is the final messenger of Allah to mankind.

The revealed books from Allah are: the Torah (*Tawrah*), the Psalms (*Zabur*), the Gospel (*Injil*) and the Qur'an. The Qur'an, which was revealed to Prophet Muhammad (the peace and blessings of Allah be upon him), is the final book of Guidance.

Akhirah means life after death. Belief in *Akhirah* has a profound impact on the life of a believer. We are all accountable to Allah on the Day of

Judgment, when we will be judged according to how we lived our lives on the Earth. A person who obeys and worships Allah will be rewarded with a place of happiness in Paradise; the person who does not will be sent to Hell, a place of punishment and suffering.

Allah knows our every thought and innermost intention; angels are recording all our actions. If we always keep in mind that we will be judged by our actions, we will try to make sure that we act according to the Will of Allah. Many of today's problems would disappear if we had this awareness and acted accordingly.

Basic practices

The Qur'an has many expressions to describe people who follow the religion of Islam, such as 'those who surrender' (*muslimun*), 'the God-fearing', 'those who believe and do good works', 'the righteous', etc. *Islam: A Brief Guide* summarizes the 'five pillars of Islam' as follows.

> Islam has five basic duties, often called the 'pillars of Islam'. Performed regularly, correctly and sincerely they transform a Muslim's life, bringing it into line with the wishes of the Creator. Faithful practice of these duties should inspire a Muslim to work towards the establishment of justice, equality and righteousness (*Ma'ruf*) in society, and the eradication of injustice, falsehood and evil (*Munkar*).
>
> 1. *Shahadah* is the conscious and voluntary declaration of: *La ilaha illallahu Muhammadur rasulullah.* 'There is no god except Allah, Muhammad is the Messenger of Allah.' This declaration contains the two basic concepts of Tawhid and Risalah. It is the basis of all actions in Islam; the other four basic duties follow this affirmation.
>
> 2. *Salah* (compulsory prayer) is offered five times a day, either in congregation or individually. It is a practical demonstration of faith, and keeps a believer in constant touch with his Creator. The benefits of *Salah* are far-reaching, long-lasting and immeasurable. *Salah* prepares a Muslim to work towards the establishment of true order in society, and the removal of falsehood, evil and indecency. It develops self-discipline, steadfastness and obedience to the Truth, leading to patience, honesty and truthfulness in the affairs of life.

The five daily prayers are

Fajr	between dawn and sunrise
Zuhr	between midday and mid-afternoon
'Asr	between mid-afternoon and sunset
Maghrib	just after sunset
'Isha	between nightfall and dawn

Five times a day, *Salah* provides a wonderful opportunity for a Muslim to improve his life. It is a system of spiritual, moral and physical training which makes him truly obedient to his Creator. Each *Salah* takes just a few minutes to complete.

3. *Zakah* (welfare contribution) is a compulsory payment from a Muslim's annual savings. It literally means purification, and is an annual payment of 2.5% on the value of cash, jewellery and precious metals; a separate rate applies to animals, crops and mineral wealth. *Zakah* is neither a charity nor a tax: charity is optional, whilst taxes can be used for any of society's needs. *Zakah*, however, can only be spent on helping the poor and needy, the disabled, the oppressed, debtors and other welfare purposes, as defined in the Qur'an and Sunnah. *Zakah* is an act of worship. It is one of the fundamental principles of an Islamic economy, which ensures an equitable society where everybody has a right to contribute and share. *Zakah* should be paid with the conscious belief that our wealth and our property belong to Allah, and we merely act as trustees.

4. *Sawm* is the annual obligatory fast during the month of Ramadan, the ninth month in the Islamic calendar. From dawn to sunset every day a Muslim refrains from eating, drinking, smoking and from sex with his marital partner, seeking only the pleasure of Allah. *Sawm* develops a believer's moral and spiritual standards, and keeps him away from selfishness, greed, extravagance and other vices. *Sawm* is an annual training programme which increases a Muslim's determination to fulfil his obligations to the Creator and Sustainer.

5. *Hajj* (pilgrimage to the House of Allah) is an annual event, obligatory at least once in a lifetime for Muslims who have the means to perform it. It is a journey to the House of Allah (*Ka'bah*) in Makkah, Saudi Arabia, in the

month of *Dhul Hijjah*, the twelfth month of the Islamic calendar. *Hajj* symbolizes the unity of mankind; Muslims from every race and nationality assemble in equality and humility to worship their Lord. The pilgrim, in the ritual clothing of Ihram, has the unique feeling of being in the presence of his Creator, to Whom he belongs, and to Whom he must return after death.

Many Christians are surprised to see the simplicity of the basic creed of Islam – very much shorter and less complex than a basic Christian creed! Everything flows from belief in one Creator God and in Muhammad as the last and final Messenger sent by God. The 'five pillars' are obligations – duties required of all Muslims. Many may not practise them faithfully, and in facing the problems of daily life many will follow more closely the practices of folk Islam (see chapter 12). Three of the pillars – prayer, fasting and pilgrimage – are very public activities in which other Muslims are involved. This is not a faith that is practised in secret or by individuals, but very much in public and (ideally) by the whole Muslim community.

6. MUSLIMS AT PRAYER

One way of attempting to understand Islam is to try to enter sympathetically into the mind and heart of Muslims at prayer. Constance Padwick's classic *Muslim Devotions: A Study of Prayer Manuals* explains the value of this approach, which is based on the conviction that

> in Islam, as in any other faith, a stranger desiring not to remain a stranger could best feel the pulsing life of religion through a study of the devotions actually in use ... We should desire to have worship, Muslim or Christian, judged not by what it means to the lukewarm and the untaught, but by what it gives to those who try to enter fully into its life.[1]

The call to prayer

The following is a transliteration, together with a translation below each line, of the call to prayer (*adhan* – often pronounced *azan*) which is chanted in Arabic five times a day, with some variations, from mosques throughout the Islamic world.

Allahu akbar, Allahu akbar, ashhadu an la illaha ill-Allah;
God is most great, God is most great; I bear witness that there is no god
but God;

Ashhadu anna Muhammada rasulu-Allah. Hayya 'ala-ssalah. Hayya 'alal-falah;
I bear witness that Muhammad is the Apostle of God. Come unto prayer.
Come unto good.

Allahu akbar, Allahu akbar, la illaha ill-Allah.
God is most great, God is most great, there is no god but God.

Christians living in the Muslim world who hear the call to prayer
regularly could ask themselves whether there are any ways in which
they too can hear these words as a call to prayer – to pray *with* and *for*
Muslims whenever they hear it.

The ablutions

Before Muslims say the prescribed form of prayers five times a day,
they must prepare themselves to offer prayer by carrying out the ritual
ablutions (*wudu*). These are the different stages through which they
must go.

- Wash both hands up to the wrists three times.
- Rinse the mouth three times.
- Sniff water to the nostrils.
- Wash the tip of the nose three times.
- Wash the face three times.
- Wash the arms three times from wrist to elbow.
- Pass the wet hand over the head and both hands over the back
  of the head to the neck.
- Wash inside and behind the ears with wet fingers.
- Wash both feet thoroughly up to the ankles.

The compulsory prayers (*sala* or *salat*)

The following are the main stages in the basic sequence of the ritual
prayer (called a *raka'a*), which is repeated with variations three or four

times at the different times of prayer, together with an English translation of words that have to be said in Arabic.

1. Stand upright on the prayer mat, facing the Ka'ba (the Black Stone) in Mecca, and say some words expressing your 'intention' (*niyya*) either aloud or silently, for example, 'I intend to say four *raka'as* of the dawn prayers for Allah facing the Ka'ba.'

2. Raise your hands to your ears and say, 'God is most great' (*Allahu akbar*). Place your right hand on your left just below your navel or on your chest and say, 'O Allah, glory and praise are for you, and blessed is your name, and exalted is your Majesty; there is no god but you. I seek shelter in Allah from the rejected Satan. In the name of Allah, the most merciful, the most kind.'

3. Recite the *Fatiha* (the first sura of the Qur'an; see below), and recite other verses of the Qur'an.

4. Bow from the waist saying 'God is most great', and place your hands on your knees saying 'Glory to my Lord, the Great'. Then stand up saying 'Allah hears those who praise him. Our Lord, praise be to you.'

5. Prostrate on the floor with your forehead, your nose, both palms and both knees touching the ground, say 'God is most great. Glory to my Lord, the Highest.' Then stand up again, saying 'God is most great'. Sit upright with your knees bent and your palms on your knees. Prostrate again, say 'God is most great'. Then get up again, saying 'God is most great'.

6. Say other prayers (called *du'a*), either memorized or extemporaneous, such as 'O Allah, I have been unjust to myself and no one grants pardon for sins except you; therefore, forgive me with your forgiveness and have mercy on me. Surely you are the Forgiver, the Merciful.'

7. Turn your face to the right (whether or not there is someone praying beside you), saying 'The peace and mercy of Allah be on you', and then to the left with the same words.

In observing the postures which Muslims adopt for their prayers, Christians should remember the following points.

- Muhammad may well have learned some of these postures from Syrian Christian monks.
- Prostration is found in the Bible (Ezek. 1:28).
- Muslims are trying to express their total submission to God in a physical way.
- Muhammad first taught Muslims to pray towards Jerusalem, like the Jews. It was only when his message was rejected by the Jews that the direction for Muslim prayer was changed to Mecca, in accordance with a qur'anic revelation.

The *Fatiha* – the opening sura of the Qur'an

This is Kenneth Cragg's English translation of the *Fatiha*, a prayer that is included in every form of ritual prayer and always recited in Arabic.[2] It has been described as 'the essence of the Qur'an'[3] and 'the quintessence of Islamic doctrine'.[4] Setting the *Fatiha* alongside the Lord's Prayer enables us to see the similarities and differences in the two prayers.

In the name of the merciful Lord of mercy.
Praise be to God, the Lord of all being,
The merciful Lord of mercy,
Master of the Day of Judgment,
Thee alone we worship
And to Thee alone we come for aid.

Guide us in the straight path,
The path of those whom Thou hast blessed,
Not of those against whom there is displeasure,
Nor of those who go astray.

Our Father in heaven,
Hallowed be your name,
Your kingdom come,
Your will be done,
on earth as it is in heaven.
Give us this day our daily bread;
And forgive us our sins
As we forgive those who sin against us.
And lead us not into temptation;
but deliver us from evil.

For the kingdom, the power and the glory are yours for ever and ever.

Christians may be surprised to find more common elements in the two prayers than they expected, such as worship and praise, and prayer for help and guidance. They may feel uncomfortable with the last two lines of the *Fatiha* – especially when they hear that some qur'anic commentaries point out that the people referred to are Jews and Christians. They will no doubt recognize, however, that some of the psalms contain similar sentiments.

One striking difference between the two prayers is that Muslims do not address God as 'Father'. This is partly because the idea of 'Father' could suggest the idea of the sonship of Jesus, which is strongly rejected; and partly because 'Father' suggests a more intimate relationship with God than is appropriate for Muslims, who believe they are more like 'servants' approaching God as 'Lord' or 'Master'. Another difference is that while the Lord's Prayer includes a prayer for forgiveness, there is no corresponding prayer in the *Fatiha*, although it speaks of God as merciful and compassionate.

Other kinds of prayer

Since the prescribed prayer (*sala*) is one of the 'pillars' of Islam, it is a duty required of all Muslims. It needs to be distinguished from *du'a*, which is entirely voluntary and can be said in any language. The following are some examples of written prayers that are used by Muslims.

O Allah, whatever you want to give me, no one can stop it from coming to me, and whatever you want to prevent from coming to me, nobody can give me. (A prayer used by the Prophet after every prayer)

Lord of all,
And King of all,
And Predestinator of all –
I pray to Thee to grant me:
Wholesome knowledge,
And virtuous deeds,
And real faith!
And grant that we may experience
The repentance of the faithful,

The submission of the submissive,
And the deeds of the virtuous,
And the conviction of those who are convinced,
The fidelity of the God-fearing,
And the High Degree of the successful.[5]

O Almighty Allah,
My Creator, Owner and Sustainer,
Watcher of my deeds,
I implore You, beseech You, beg You,
to accept this humble effort of mine,
help the readers of this book to the Light of Guidance
and grant me pardon on the Day of Judgment
When nothing except Your Mercy and Blessings
Will be of any help.
Amin.
(Prayer at the beginning of Ghulam Sarwar's *Islam: Beliefs and Teachings*)[6]

7. THE LIFE OF MUHAMMAD

We begin by trying to understand what Arabia was like in the sixth and seventh centuries, since the life of Muhammad can only be understood in this context. A summary of the most important events of his life is followed by an outline of the period of the Caliphs, the immediate successors of the Prophet. The final section in this chapter attempts to underline the importance of certain aspects of the life of Muhammad for understanding Islam and Muslims today.

Arabia before the time of Muhammad

Muslims refer to the time before Muhammad as *al-jahiliyya*, the 'Age of Ignorance'. Some of the tribes in Arabia were nomadic Bedouin of the desert; some were semi-nomadic, while others were permanently settled in smaller towns (such as Ta'if) or larger cities (such as Mecca and Yathrib, i.e. Medina). Total loyalty to one's tribe was always expected, and while individual tribes were united by alliances, there was no unity in the area as a whole. Blood feuds between tribes were settled by the tribal ethic of revenge and reprisal.

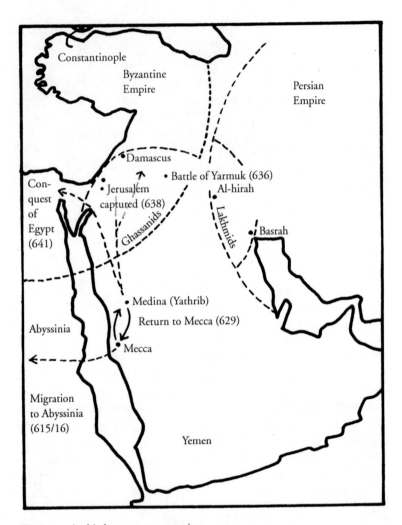

Figure 7.1 Arabia between two empires

The two great world powers in Muhammad's time were the Byzantine Empire and the Persian Empire, and Arabia was affected by the power struggle between these two great powers.

The Byzantine Empire (covering Asia Minor, Syria, Egypt and south-eastern Europe, with its capital in Constantinople) was fiercely Orthodox Christian in doctrine and strongly opposed to doctrines it regarded as heretical, such as Monophysitism and Nestorianism.

It supported the Ghassanid dynasty in Syria as a buffer state against the Arabs. The Persian Empire under the Sassanid dynasty (stretching from Iraq to Afghanistan, with its capital in Iraq) supported the Lakhmid kingdom of Hira in Iraq as a buffer against the Arabs. In AD 614 the Persians captured Jerusalem from Byzantine power; but in 628 the Byzantines defeated the Persians and regained control of Jerusalem. Both empires were exhausted by the struggles, leaving a power vacuum at the time when Islam was beginning to spread.

There was a flourishing caravan trade along routes running north-south and east-west. Mecca had become an important commercial centre, as well as a centre of pilgrimage. There were many social evils: for example, female infants were often buried alive, and women were not well protected.

Although there is some evidence of belief in one supreme God (Allah), whose role was similar to that of the 'High God' in many traditional religions in different parts of the world, religious practices centred round a host of lesser deities like the moon god, the sun goddess and various tribal deities. At Mecca three goddesses in particular were worshipped: Manat, al-Lat and al-Uzza. There were also many idol cults, and incense and animal sacrifices were offered in temples to spirits of caves, trees, wells, stones and so on. Superstitious rituals were practised at many shrines, and there were annual pilgrimages to the major shrines such as the sanctuary of the Ka'ba at Mecca, a cube-like structure which had the Black Stone (probably a meteorite) built into one of its walls. There was a strong belief in fate, and little or no belief in an afterlife. A rich tradition of Arab poetry had developed.

There were some Jewish communities or tribes, especially in the south of Arabia and in and around Medina. Some Arabs had become monotheists of a sort (known as *hanif*), perhaps through Jewish or Christian influences. Several nomadic tribes had previously embraced Christianity. The area of Yemen in the south had been Christian since the early sixth century and a large church had been built at Najran. In Mecca itself the Christians were mostly foreigners, such as black slaves from Abyssinia and labourers and traders from Syria. According to tradition, Muhammad's first wife Khadija had a cousin, Waraqa bin Naufal, who had become a Christian. Muhammad may well have had some contact with Syrian monks in the desert.

The life of Muhammad

Table 7.1 is an outline of the most significant events in the life of the Prophet, based on the earliest Islamic sources.

---

c. 570	Birth of Muhammad into the tribe of Quraysh in Mecca. His father died before he was born, and his mother died six years later. He was brought up by his grandfather and his uncle, Abu Talib.
c. 592	According to tradition, Muhammad began travelling to Syria with trading caravans, and on one of these journeys met Bahira, a Syrian Christian monk.
595	Muhammad married Khadija, aged forty, a wealthy widow, and began working with her in her trading business.
610	Muhammad received his first call to be a prophet while meditating in a cave on Mount Hira near Mecca. The first of the 'revelations'. He shared these first with Khadija and then with others. The first who accepted the message were his cousin, 'Ali, then a merchant friend, Abu Bakr, and Muhammad's servant, Zayd.
615/16	Persecution from Muhammad's own tribe of Quraysh forced fifteen of his followers to emigrate, seeking asylum in the Christian kingdom of Abyssinia. Muhammad and his 'Companions' remained in Mecca, still suffering ostracism.
619	Khadija and Abu Talib, Muhammad's uncle and protector, died. Muhammad's position in the tribe was now less secure. This was the lowest period for Muhammad and was later described as his 'year of grief'.
	The 'Night Journey' (*Isra'*) to Jerusalem and 'Ascent to Heaven' (*Mi'raj*), understood by Muslims as either a miraculous event in which he was physically transported to Jerusalem on a winged horse named Buraq, or a spiritual experience. From Jerusalem he ascended to heaven where he met several of the great prophets, including Abraham, Moses and Jesus.
	After Khadija died, Muhammad took other wives (see chapter 16, 'Women in Islam').
622	The Emigration or Migration (*Hijra*) to Yathrib, later called Medina, in response to a request from a group of Muslim converts ('Helpers', *ansar*) there who hoped that he would resolve the

conflicts between the different communities in Medina. The *hijra* marks the beginning of the Muslim era.

624   Muslims began raiding caravans from Mecca, which led to a series of battles: the Battle of Badr, where Muslims (with 324 men) defeated the Meccans (with 950 men). Following this a Jewish tribe in Medina, the Banu Qaynuqa, were expelled from Medina for plotting against Muhammad.

625   In the Battle of Uhud, Muslims were defeated by the Meccans. Another Jewish tribe in Medina, the Banu Nadir, were expelled.

627   The Battle of the Ditch or Trench, in which the Muslims repelled a Meccan attack on Medina by building a ditch round the city. A third Jewish tribe, the Banu Qurayza, were punished for working with the Meccans: around 600 men were beheaded and the women and children sold into slavery.

628   The Treaty of Hudaibiya between Muhammad and the Meccans, which enabled him to return to Mecca on pilgrimage the following year.

629   Muhammad and the Muslims returned to Mecca on 11 January with 10,000 men. The Meccans submitted without fighting. Muhammad then declared a general amnesty, and all the 360 idols in the Ka'ba were destroyed – except an icon of the Virgin Mary and Jesus. Muhammad then returned to Medina. Missionaries were sent out to other parts of Arabia, and a mass movement began of tribes embracing Islam. Messengers were sent to the rulers of surrounding countries, calling them to Islam.

630   Muhammad mounted a campaign to Tabuk in the north of Arabia to avenge the defeat of his forces by the Byzantines in Palestine, but failed to engage with the Byzantine army.

631   Muhammad made his last pilgrimage to Mecca.

632   Muhammad died and was buried in Medina.

Table 7.1

The successors of Muhammad

The successors of the Prophet are known as 'caliphs', and the first four are known as the 'Rightly Guided' or 'Righteous' Caliphs. This period of thirty years is regarded as a Golden Age of Islam (see Table 7.2).

632–4	The first caliph, Abu Bakr, was chosen because he had been nominated by Muhammad to lead the prayers during his final illness. He prevented many tribes from breaking away from the new Islamic state during the Wars of Apostasy. He defeated the Byzantine army in 634, and under his rule Islam spread to Syria, Iraq and Yemen.
634–44	The second caliph, 'Umar, was nominated by Abu Bakr. He authorized the collection of the suras of the Qur'an. In 635 he attacked Damascus, capturing it in 637; he defeated the Byzantine army at the Battle of Yarmuk in 636, and captured Jerusalem (638) and Alexandria (642). He gained control of Syria, Egypt and Persia, and gave Jews and Christians in Arabia the choice of converting to Islam or leaving Arabia. He was stabbed to death by a Persian Christian slave.
644–56	The third caliph, 'Uthman, established the official text of the Qur'an and had other texts burned. A weak leader, he was accused of granting favours to relatives. His leadership provoked rebellion, and he was assassinated.
656–61	The fourth caliph, 'Ali, was Muhammad's cousin and son-in-law. He fought against the followers of 'A'isha, Muhammad's widow, at the Battle of Camel, then against Mu'awiya, the governor of Syria, who proclaimed himself caliph. After a truce in 660, Mu'awiya ruled over Syria and 'Ali's power declined. He was murdered by a rebel. His conflict with Mu'awiya led to the split between Sunnis and Shi'ites (the 'party of 'Ali').

Table 7.2

These four caliphs were succeeded by the Umayyad dynasty, which ruled in Damascus from 661 to 750. Power then passed to the Abbasids, whose capital was Baghdad, which remained the centre of Islamic power from 750 to 1258.

Christianity at the time of Muhammad and Muhammad's relations with Christians

One significant detail recorded in several Islamic sources is that Khadija's first reaction on hearing of Muhammad's revelations was to send him to her cousin, Waraqa bin Naufal, who was a Christian. This is al-Bukhari's account of what happened.

> Khadija then accompanied him [Muhammad] to [her cousin] Waraqa
> bin Naufal ... Waraqa was the son of her paternal uncle, i.e. her
> father's brother, who during the pre-Islamic period became a
> Christian and used to write the Arabic writing and used to write
> of the Gospels in Arabic as much as Allah wished him to write.
> He was an old man and had lost his eyesight. Khadija said to
> him, 'O my cousin! Listen to the story of your nephew.' Waraqa
> asked, 'O my nephew, what have you seen?' The Prophet described
> whatever he had seen. Waraqa said, 'This is the same Namus
> (i.e. Gabriel the Angel who keeps the secrets) whom Allah had sent to
> Moses. I wish I were young and could live up to the time when your
> people would turn you out ...' [1]

Most of the Christians with whom he came in contact were not Arabs but foreigners from neighbouring countries, many of whom had settled in Arabia because they had been persecuted elsewhere. They kept themselves aloof from the Arabs and continued to worship in their own languages. It is generally agreed by Western scholars that (in spite of what is recorded in al-Bukhari above) Muhammad could not have had access to any books of the Bible in Arabic.

The Christian church was deeply divided over doctrinal disputes. Ever since the great councils of Nicaea (AD 325) and Chalcedon (451), the churches in the East had been arguing about the doctrines of the Trinity and the person of Christ. These disputes are reflected in several qur'anic verses (e.g. 5:14). Several groups rejected the doctrines of Chalcedon:

- The Monophysites emphasized the divinity of Jesus and gave the impression that Jesus was not fully human. The Abyssinian Christians, for example, were Monophysites and were supported by the Byzantines.
- The Nestorians in the East accepted the two natures of Jesus but thought that they were separate. Nestorian Christians were supported by the Persian Empire.

- The Gnostics tended to think that matter was evil and that salvation depended on an experience of mystical enlightenment. They denied the incarnation, and some believed that Jesus was not crucified.

In spite of official statements of church doctrine at the great councils, there was considerable diversity in the beliefs of ordinary Christians, reflected for example in the variety of Christian writings which were circulating throughout the region. Although by today's standards some of these beliefs would be regarded as heretical, they might not have been regarded as such at the time. Tarif Khalidi makes the point, therefore, that 'Islam was born amid many, often mutually hostile, Christian communities and not in the bosom of a universal church'.[2]

For the first three hundred years Christianity was the religion of a persecuted minority in the Roman Empire. It became the official religion of the empire in 315 after the Emperor Constantine had converted to Christianity. From now on Christianity was inevitably associated with political power, and the Byzantine emperors stood firmly for the Orthodox faith, fiercely persecuting the different heretical sects. For many Arabs, therefore, Christianity was synonymous with Byzantine domination and fierce repression of any beliefs that differed from the religion of the state. A Syrian Christian, Abu l-Faraja, explained why Syrian Arab Christians were happy when the Arabs took over from the Byzantines (called here 'Romans'):

> When our people complained to Heraclius [the Roman emperor], he gave no answer. Therefore the God of vengeance delivered us out of the hands of the Romans by means of the Arabs. Then, although our churches were not restored to us since under Arab rule each Christian community retained its actual possessions, still it profited us not a little to be saved from the cruelty of the Romans and their bitter hatred towards us.[3]

The significance of the life of Muhammad for Muslims and Islam today

The following features of the life of Muhammad are particularly important for understanding aspects of Islam as it is understood and practised today.

The Jahiliyya

The period before the revelation of the message of Islam to the Prophet is known as the *Jahiliyya*, 'the Time of Ignorance' (see 48:26). This term has been taken up by many Islamists in recent years who are critical of societies which claim to be Muslim but are not practising real Islam. They describe these Muslim countries today as being in a state of *Jahiliyya*, comparable to the ignorance and decadence that prevailed before the coming of Islam.

The Meccan period

During the thirteen years of his ministry in Mecca, Muhammad was simply a preacher of the message of Islam with a small group of followers. He was frequently persecuted by the people of Mecca, who saw him as a threat to their society and to their commercial trade. It has been pointed out that the position of this first group of Muslims in Mecca is similar to that of Muslims who live as minorities in Western countries. It is also possible to see some similarities between the position of Muslims living in so-called 'Christian' countries in the West and the Muslims who were sent by Muhammad during this period to seek asylum in the Christian kingdom of Abyssinia.

The Hijra *and the Medinan period*

Muhammad must have seen the invitation to move from Mecca to become the ruler of Medina as an opportunity to create an Islamic community which lived by the revelation that he was receiving. The *Hijra* therefore marks a fundamental turning point in the life of the Prophet, a crucial change well summed up in the title of William Montgomery Watt's classic study of the life of Muhammad, *Muhammad: Prophet and Statesman.*[4] The experience of Muhammad in Medina and the history of the rise and development of Islam in the early period produced the strong conviction that 'Islam must rule'. Islamists today believe that most Islamic countries have been influenced too much by the West and would like these countries to become much more like the first Islamic state in Medina, where the whole community came under Islamic law.

Meccan and Medinan suras

Muslims today are very aware of the differences in content and style between the *Meccan suras* and the *Medinan suras*. In the Meccan period, for example, Muhammad is not making any laws, and when he encounters opposition to his message from the Meccans he is commanded by God to be patient. In the Medinan period, however, the revelations include many new laws for the Muslim community, and Muhammad and his followers are commanded to fight against those who oppose them and reject the message of Islam. Muslims who live as minorities in Western countries may feel as powerless as Muhammad and his followers did in Mecca. Some Muslims and non-Muslims have therefore been asking whether the message of the Meccan suras might be more relevant to their situation today than the laws revealed in the Medinan suras. There is a lively debate on this issue today, and some Muslims have gone so far as to suggest that the Meccan suras contain the abiding message of Islam and therefore should take precedence today, while the Medinan suras should be regarded as relevant primarily to the situation of Medina at that time and not necessarily as the model for all Muslims everywhere and at every time.[5]

Mecca, Medina and Jerusalem

Muslims believe that the Ka'ba in Mecca was first built by Adam and later rebuilt and restored by Abraham and Ishmael. After Muhammad and his followers left Mecca, their sights were set on returning there eventually to reclaim the Ka'ba for the worship of the one God. Ever since then, Muslims – wherever they are in the world – have always prayed in the direction of Mecca, and pilgrimage to Mecca has been regarded as a sacred duty, an obligation that is required of all Muslims if they are able to undertake it. Similarly Medina, as the site of the first Islamic state and the first mosque, has always been considered the second most holy site for Muslims. And because Muhammad experienced his Night Journey to Jerusalem (the *Isra'*) and from there ascended to heaven (the *Mi'raj*), Jerusalem has been regarded as the third most holy site for Muslims. Christians do not generally feel anything like the same attachment to Jerusalem and the land of Palestine that Muslims feel towards Mecca and Medina. Apart from the Byzantines and the Crusaders, Christians have generally not felt that it was necessary for Christians to rule Jerusalem.

Territoriality

When some tribes believed their alliance with Muhammad and the Islamic community had ended with his death, the Muslims fought the Wars of Apostasy in order to bring these tribes back under the rule of Islam. Whenever territory has been conquered by Muslims, they think of it as being part of *dar al-Islam* (the House of Islam) and find it unthinkable that it should ever cease to be part of the world of Islam. It has therefore always been painful for Muslims to remember that they once ruled much of Spain from the early 700s, but were expelled during the Reconquista which ended in 1492. Bringing land under the control of Islam and keeping it within Islam has always been a very fundamental goal for Muslims who know anything of their history. Building mosques in Africa, for example, has been seen as a way of claiming land for Allah and for Islam, in the hope that it will one day be settled and perhaps even ruled by Muslims.

Muhammad's relationships with Jews

We have seen that Muhammad had very difficult relationships with the three Jewish tribes in Medina. They generally opposed his message, and sometimes sided with the Meccans against the Muslim community. References to these Jewish communities in the Qur'an are often quite harsh and critical (e.g. 5:82–83; 4:153–161). When Islam spread throughout the Middle East, Jewish and Christian communities were not forced to convert to Islam, but were tolerated as protected communities and allowed to practise their own faith (see chapter 13, 'The spread and development of Islam'). Jewish communities were never numerous or powerful enough to present any challenge to the Muslim rulers, and although there were occasional periods of persecution, relations between Jews and Muslims were generally reasonably good. The situation changed, however, in the 1880s with the birth of the Zionist movement and the influx of many Jews into Palestine. Muslim Palestinians have inevitably made a connection between their own difficult experience with the Zionist immigrants and the experience of the Prophet Muhammad with the Jews of Medina. It is hardly surprising, therefore, that many Muslims today relate the harsh words about Jews in the Qur'an to the Zionist Jews in Israel.[6]

Muhammad as an example
Colin Turner comments:

> There is something 'Muhammadan' about a religion in which believers are
> encouraged to base their lives on the example bequeathed to them in the
> form of Muhammad's *sunna* or practice. Interest in the incidental detail of
> Muhammad's life has always been enormous for this very reason: to know
> what Muhammad did is to know what everyone must do. There are some
> who endeavour to emulate Muhammad in everything they do, down to the
> most trivial thing such as putting on shoes, or taking off clothes.[7]

Although it is always emphasized that Muhammad was an ordinary
man, and although in the Qur'an he and his followers were told by
God to seek forgiveness (e.g. 17:73–75; 80:1–10; 40:55; 47:19; 48:1–2),
he has come to be regarded by Muslims as the best man who has ever
lived, and is therefore regarded as a model of the ideal human being.
When the name of Muhammad is written alongside the name of Allah
in mosques, one is always told that Muhammad is never to be elevated
to the level of the divine. In folk Islam in some countries like India and
Pakistan, however, some Muslims believe that Muhammad existed in
heaven before he was born, and because he will be an intercessor for
Muslims on the Day of Judgment, he has come to be venerated almost
as if he is divine. Here is another example of the significant difference
between folk Islam and ideal Islam (see chapter 12).

Attacks on Muhammad
It is important that Westerners understand why Muslims all over the
world have in recent years been so sensitive to attacks or ridicule
directed at the Prophet. Andrew Rippin explains why Muslims react
with such feeling:

> Those who insinuate evil of Muhammad or who cast aspersions on him are
> considered to be insulting Islam ... 'attacking' Muhammad is, of course,
> attacking the way of life of individual Muslims, for their way of life is
> understood to rest on the example of the founder of their religion. If
> something is felt by Muslims to be a denigration of one aspect of the life
> of Muhammad, then by implication such may be seen as an attack on the
> whole way of life of each and every Muslim ...[8]

All the teachers of Islam would insist that however important the Prophet Muhammad is in Islam, ultimately he is only the human channel through whom the Qur'an was revealed. We now turn, therefore, to see what the Qur'an means to Muslims.

8. THE QUR'AN

If Christians want to appreciate what the Qur'an means to Muslims, they need to understand that *the Qur'an is to Muslims what Jesus is to Christians*. It is a mistake to make a direct comparison between the role of Jesus in Christianity and the role of Muhammad in Islam, or between the place of the Bible in Christianity and the place of the Qur'an in Islam. This point has been made forcefully by Wilfred Cantwell Smith:

> Muslims and Christians have been alienated partly by the fact that both have misunderstood each other's faith by trying to fit it to their own pattern. The most usual error is to suppose (on both sides) that the roles of Jesus Christ in Christianity and of Muhammad in Islam are comparable ... If one is drawing parallels in terms of the structure of the two religions, what corresponds in the Christian scheme to the Qur'an is not the Bible but the person of Christ – it is Christ who is for Christians the revelation of (from) God.[1]

For a statement of how Muslims think of the Qur'an today, we turn once again to *Islam: A Brief Guide*.

The Qur'an is the sacred book of Muslims, and the final Book of Guidance from Allah, sent down to Muhammad (the peace and blessings of Allah be upon him) through the angel Gabriel (*Jibra'il*). Every word of the Qur'an is the Word of Allah. Revealed over a period of 23 years in the Arabic language, it contains 114 chapters (Surahs) – over 6,000 verses. Muslims learn to read it in Arabic and many memorise it completely. Muslims are expected to try their best to understand the Qur'an and practise its teachings.

The Qur'an is unrivalled in its recording and preservation. Astonishingly, it has remained unchanged even to a letter over fourteen centuries. In the Qur'an Allah addresses human beings directly. Its style cannot be compared with any other book. The Qur'an deals with man and his ultimate goal in life. Its teachings cover all aspects of this life and the life after death. It contains principles, doctrines and directions for every sphere of human activity. The theme of the Qur'an broadly consists of three fundamental concepts: *Tawhid, Risalah* and *Akhirah*. The success of human beings on this Earth and in the life hereafter depends on belief in and obedience to the teachings of the Qur'an.

The origins and interpretation of the Qur'an

How was the Qur'an first written down and collected?
According to the Qur'an and later tradition, many revelations came to Muhammad with the command, 'Recite...' (as in 96:1). The Arabic word here (*iqra*) is related to the word *Qur'an*. Some scholars have suggested, however, that the word *Qur'an* is probably not originally an Arabic word, and that it may have been derived from the Syriac word *qeryana*, which was used by Christians in Palestine and Syria for scripture readings in church.[2]

Muhammad recited the revelations to his followers, who memorized them all carefully. Some of the revelations had probably been written down by the middle of Muhammad's time in Mecca (before the *Hijra*). And it is likely that Muhammad used scribes during the time he was in Medina.

Much of the Qur'an had probably therefore been written down in one form or another during the lifetime of Muhammad. He himself no doubt brought together many different passages and arranged them in a special order, which was then kept by his companions. These collections would have included the main part of each sura.

One strong tradition, recorded in al-Bukhari, reports that during the so-called Wars of Apostasy (AD 632–4), 'Umar, who later became the second caliph, was concerned about the fact that many of those who could recite parts of the Qur'an had been killed in the battle of Yamama in 633. Fearing that much of the Qur'an might be lost if more of them were killed, he urged the first caliph, Abu Bakr, to make an official 'Collection'. Abu Bakr was unwilling to do so at first, since he had received no authorization from Muhammad. Later, however, he agreed and commissioned Zayd ibn Thabit, one of Muhammad's scribes, to carry out the task. The tradition goes on to say that he collected the verses 'from pieces of papyrus, flat stones, palm-leaves, shoulder-blades and ribs of animals, pieces of leather and wooden boards, as well as from the hearts of men'. He left his finished work with Abu Bakr, and after his death it was passed to 'Umar. From him it passed to his daughter Hafsa.

These same Islamic sources report that during the caliphate of 'Uthman (644–56), disputes about the reading of the Qur'an arose among the Muslim troops from Syria and Iraq who were engaged in expeditions to Armenia and Azerbaijan. These disputes were so serious that the general had to report the problem to 'Uthman. After consulting some of the senior Companions of the Prophet, 'Uthman commissioned Zayd ibn Thabit to make a further, final 'Collection' of the Qur'an. He and three members of noble families in Mecca worked on the principle that wherever there were differences of reading, they should follow the dialect of Quraysh, the tribe to which Muhammad belonged. In this way the whole of the Qur'an was revised between 650 and 656, and this became the authoritative text of Islam, known as the 'Uthmanic recension.

How reliable is the present text of the Qur'an?
Al-Bukhari gives the following account of what happened with the 'Uthmanic text of the Qur'an:

> 'Uthman said to the three Quraishi men, 'In case you disagree with Zaid bin Thabit on any point in the Qur'an, then write it in the dialect of Quraish as the Qur'an was revealed in their tongue.' They did so, and when they had written many copies, 'Uthman returned the original manuscripts to Hafsa. 'Uthman sent to every Muslim province one copy

of what they had copied, and ordered that all the other Qur'anic
materials, whether written in fragmentary manuscripts or whole copies,
be burned.[3]

Evidence for the existence of readings of the text which are different
from the 'Uthmanic version can be found in many of the early
commentaries, such as those of al-Tabari and al-Zamakhshari.
Although the majority of the variant readings concern vowels and
pronunciation, there are occasional differences in the consonants,
and the order of the suras is sometimes different. Short vowels in
Arabic are indicated by diacritical points above or below the letters.
These were not introduced to the Arabic language until after the
Qur'an had been distributed. Thus the earliest surviving manuscripts
which date from the eighth and ninth centuries have only consonants
without all the diacritical points which were added later on.

One example of the textual differences is in 3:19, which in the
standard text reads 'religion with Allah [i.e. the true religion] is Islam'.[4]
Some of the other readings of this text, however, say 'religion with
Allah is *hanafiyya* [monotheism]'. Another example is in 21:112 where
the standard text says, 'He said [*qala*], "My Lord, judge according
to the truth…"' Scholars have pointed out that the text makes
more sense if the verse reads, 'Say [*qul*]…' as in many other verses in
which God is addressing the Prophet, giving him the words that he is
to declare.[5]

What is the Muslim doctrine of scripture?

Muslims believe that the revelation of the Qur'an was itself a miracle,
since Muhammad was not able to read or write. This belief is summed
up by the Arabic word *i'jaz*, meaning the inimitability, incomparability
or miraculous nature of the Qur'an. It means that according to the
Muslim understanding, 'The Qur'an … has no equal: however hard he
may try, man will never be able to match the holy Book in terms of
eloquence, beauty or wisdom.'[6] This belief is based on such verses in
the Qur'an as these:

> Those who follow the messenger, the Prophet who can neither read
> nor write, whom they will find described in the Torah and the Gospel
> (which are) with them. (7:157)

And thou [O Muhammad] wast not a reader of any scripture before it, nor
didst thou write it with thy right hand, for then might those have doubted,
who follow falsehood. (29:48)

Muslims have generally understood an Arabic word used in the
Qur'an (*ummi*) to mean 'illiterate', and for this reason M. M. Pickthall
translates the phrase 'the Prophet who can neither read nor write'. By
the end of the tenth century Muslim apologists were making a great
deal of this point to argue for the miraculous nature of the Qur'an.
How, they argued, could someone who could neither read nor write
compose out of his own mind such beautiful Arabic? According to the
Qur'an, the Prophet never performed any miracles. When challenged
to perform a miracle to authenticate his claim to be a prophet, he
simply pointed to the incomparable nature of the revelations he had
received directly from God.

A number of Christian scholars, however, have suggested that this
was not the original meaning of the word *ummi*. The same word is
used in 62:2 and is translated by Majid Fakhry as follows: 'It is He
Who has raised up from the common nations a Messenger of their
own...' Kenneth Cragg suggests 'the unlettered prophet', 'the
prophet to the people without a book', meaning those who are as
yet without scriptures.[7] If this was the original meaning of the word
ummi, it would mean that Muhammad was aware that the Jews and
Christians had their own scriptures, and that he saw himself as the
Prophet called by God to give the Arabs their own scriptures in their
own language. Chawkat Moucarry says:

> As an Arab Prophet, Muhammad was from the 'Nations' (or 'the Gentiles')
> who had no Scripture. Unlike the 'People of the Book', the Arab people
> (and more generally the 'Nations') had not been given a written revelation
> from God until the Qur'an was revealed to Muhammad. Thus Muhammad
> is the *ummi* Prophet in the sense that he is 'the Gentile Prophet'.[8]

Can the Qur'an be translated?

Since the Qur'an was revealed in Arabic, the Arabic of the Qur'an is
an essential part of the message, and part of the appeal of the Qur'an
for Muslims lies in the beauty of the Arabic. Since the Qur'an is
thought of as the Word of God revealed in Arabic, and since much of

the quality of the original is lost in translation, translating it is even harder than translating Shakespeare. In the past, translation was generally discouraged, if not actually forbidden. Today, however, some translations have the approval of Muslim scholars, although they are regarded as a kind of paraphrase and have to be given titles such as *The Meaning of the Glorious Qur'an*.

What is the place of the Qur'an in the experience of Muslims?

Since the Qur'an was first communicated orally by Muhammad to his followers, the Qur'an for Muslims is first and foremost a book to be recited, and the word 'Qur'an' is derived from the Arabic word for 'recite' (*qara'*). Although the Qur'an needs to be read and studied, nothing can take away from the importance of the recitation of the Qur'an. 'Muslims see the reciting of the Qur'an', says Jan Slomp, 'as a way of communion with God.'[9] Moreover, learning the text by heart is extremely important, and public recitations of the Qur'an are popular, particularly at the time of certain festivals. In this context also it is possible to understand why Arabic calligraphy is so significant for Muslims. In the words of Reza Aslan, 'Islamic calligraphy is more than just an art form; it is the visual representation of the eternal Qur'an, the symbol of God's living presence on earth.'[10] Starting a Qur'an school has often been a major priority for Muslim missionaries in different parts of the world, whereas for Christian missionaries the priority has been to translate the Bible into the local language.

How do Muslims interpret the Qur'an?

The first important principle is that Muslims have always tried to interpret verses of the Qur'an by studying them in their original context. To do this they have asked questions such as these: What do we know about incidents in the life of the Prophet that help us to interpret the meaning of a particular passage? What do we know from the sayings of the earliest Companions of the Prophet that can help us to interpret the text? Studying the 'Occasions of Revelation' (*asbab al-nuzul*, literally 'reasons for revelation') is therefore an important principle of interpretation.

The first great exegete of the Qur'an was Ibn Abbas, a cousin of Muhammad. The earliest important commentary on the Qur'an which

exists today was written by al-Tabari (died 923) and gathered together
all that was best in the earlier commentaries. Two other well-known
commentators were al-Zamakhshari (died 1143) and al-Baidhawi (died
1286). The following example of a discussion about the context in
which a revelation was given comes from Ibn Ishaq's *Life of the Apostle
of God*. It refers to two different explanations of the context in which
important passages concerning Christians (28:535 and 5:82–83) were
revealed.

> It is said that these Christians came from Najran, but God knows
> whether that was so. It is also said, and again God knows best, that it
> was in reference to them that the verses [were revealed] 'Those to whom
> we brought the book aforetime, and they believe in it. And when it is read
> to them they say We believe in it. Verily it is the truth from our Lord.
> Verily aforetime we were Muslims,' as far as the words, 'We have our
> works and you have your works. Peace be on you; we desire not the
> ignorant.'
>
> I asked Ibn Shihab al-Zuhri about those to whom these verses had
> reference and he told me that he had always heard from the learned that
> they were sent down concerning the Negus [Christian ruler of Abyssinia]
> and his companions and also the verses from the sura of The Table from
> the words, 'That is because there are of them presbyters and monks and
> because they are not proud' up to the words 'so inscribe us with those who
> bear witness.'[11]

The second important principle used in exegesis of the Qur'an is
known as 'Abrogation', which means that a revelation that came from
God at one particular time could be 'abrogated', that is superseded or
replaced by a new revelation given later. This principle is based on
verses such as these:

> Such of our revelations as We abrogate or cause to be forgotten, We bring
> (in place) one better or the like thereof. Knowest thou not that Allah is able
> to do all things? (2:106)

> And when We put a revelation in place of (another) revelation, – and Allah
> knoweth best what He revealeth – they say: Lo! thou art but inventing.
> Most of them know not. (16:101)

Richard Bell explains the doctrine of abrogation as it was developed by Muslim scholars.

> The idea underlying the doctrine is that certain commands to the Muslims in the Qur'an were only of temporary application, and that when circumstances changed they were abrogated or replaced by others. Because the commands were the word of God, however, they continued to be recited as part of the Qur'an.[12]

The doctrine of abrogation has been developed in two further, significant ways. In the first, according to some Muslims, *hadith* sometimes abrogates verses from the Qur'an, so that some rulings in Islamic law are based on *hadith* rather than the Qur'an. Second, the idea has been developed to teach that since the Qur'an came *after* the Jewish and Christian scriptures, it effectively abrogated them. For this reason many Muslims believe that there is no need for them to read the previous scriptures, because everything that is true in them has been repeated in the Qur'an, and all the mistakes in them have been corrected by the Qur'an.

Are Muslims able to study and analyse the Qur'an as Christians study the Bible? Muslims have generally been unwilling to adopt the same critical approach to the Qur'an that Christians have used with the Bible. If the Qur'an is the very Word of God, it is unthinkable that we should try to analyse it in the same way that we would analyse an ordinary book. It is with this in mind that Andrew Rippin writes of 'the general lack of critical reflection upon the Muslim historical sources in general'.[13] An Egyptian named Abu Zaid argued that 'the Qur'an is a literary text, and needs to be analysed through a literary approach', but was condemned as an apostate in 1995.

Translations of the Qur'an

The following are some of the best-known and most accessible translations of the Qur'an in English.

Marmaduke Pickthall, *The Meaning of the Glorious Koran*,
    Mentor, n.d.

A. Yusuf Ali, *The Holy Qur'an: Text Translation and Commentary*,
   The Islamic Foundation, 1975
A. J. Arberry, *The Koran Interpreted*, Cambridge University Press,
   1964
N. J. Dawood, *The Koran*, Penguin, 2000
Kenneth Cragg, *Readings in the Qur'an: Selected and Translated*,
   Collins, 1988
Majid Fakhry, *An Interpretation of the Qur'an*, Garnet, 2002
M. A. S. Abdel Haleem, *The Qur'an: A New Translation*, Oxford
   University Press, 2005

Reading the Qur'an

Although the Qur'an is slightly shorter than the New Testament,
it is probably just as hard for Christians to read the Qur'an from
beginning to end as it is for Muslims to read the Bible from Genesis
to Revelation! The following, therefore, are some suggestions of
ways to start reading the Qur'an. Verse numbers are as in the
standard Cairo edition which is followed in most English translations. Some translations of the Qur'an, however (like that by Yusuf
Ali), use a different system for numbering the verses. In this case one
needs to look a few verses *before* or *after* the numbers as they are given
here to find the correct verse.

The shortest and earliest suras
1 – The *Fatiha* (see chapter 6, 'Muslims at prayer').
96 – Said to be the first sura revealed to Muhammad.
73, 74 – Both claimed variously to be the second sura, revealed after
some months.
82, 84, 93 – Short suras at the end of the Qur'an.

Some well-known passages
2:255 – A well-known verse about the sovereignty of God.
2:256 – 'There is no compulsion in religion.'
24:35–36; 5:54; 50:16 – Passages which have been a source of
inspiration to mystics.
59:22–24 – Verses about 'the most beautiful names' of God.
17:1 – Muhammad's 'Night Journey'.

Typical passages
About the creation – 3:189–191; 13:2–4; 31:10–11; 32:4–9; 45:3–5.
About heaven and hell – 2:24–25; 38:49–60; 44:47–57.
About prophets – 2:124–136; 6:84–88.

Laws
About marriage – 4:3.
About theft – 5:38.
About usury – 2:275–279.
About obedience to parents – 29:8.
About wine – 2:219.
About pork – 2:173.
A summary of the moral law – 2:83, 177.

Using the index
Look up subjects such as Abraham, marriage, divorce, Jews, Christians, Satan and adultery.

Complete suras
2 – The Cow. Generally said to be the first sura revealed at Medina, this is one of the longer suras, but contains many important qur'anic themes.
4 – Women. Also a longer Medinan sura covering a wide variety of subjects, including marriage, orphans, inheritance, fighting, treatment of hypocrites and idolaters, the sins of the Jews, and the denial of the crucifixion of Jesus.
12 – Joseph. This account can be compared and contrasted with the story of Joseph in Genesis 37 – 50.

Important verses in the Qur'an

About the Qur'an itself
The Qur'an revealed in the Arabic language – 12:2; 46:12.
Muhammad 'the seal of the prophets' – 33:40.
The Qur'an reveals clearly what Jews and Christians have hidden in their scriptures – 5:15.
Some revelations to the Prophet can be 'abrogated', or superseded, by later revelations – 2:106; 16:101; 22:52.

About the Bible
The Qur'an recognizes these earlier biblical revelations:

- the *Tawrat* (revealed to Moses) – 2:87; 3:3;
- the *Zabur* (revealed to David) – 4:163;
- the *Injil* (revealed to Jesus) – 5:46–48.

The Qur'an confirms the message of previous scriptures – 2:91; 3:1–4; 3:84; 4:47.
God has protected the scriptures – 5:48; 18:27.
Muhammad is to consult the scriptures already revealed if he is in doubt about what is being revealed to him – 10:94–95.
Jews and Christians are accused of tampering with their scriptures:

- they are ignorant of their scriptures – 2:78;
- they conceal them – 2:146, 159, 174; 5:15;
- they change them – 2:75;
- they sell false scriptures for gain – 2:79;
- they believe parts and disbelieve other parts – 2:85.

About Christians
Passages which are sympathetic – 5:82–83; 2:62, 136–137; 5:68–69, 82; 22:40.
Appeals to Christians to accept Muhammad's message because it confirms the *Injil* – 3:64–71; 29:46.
Passages which are more critical – 5:14–15; 51:72–73; 9:29–31; 57:27; 4:171 (see chapter 27, 'The qur'anic view of Christians').

Passages about Jesus
The annunciation and the birth of Jesus – 3:35–47; 19:16–35.
The ministry of Jesus – 3:49–54; 5:110–117; 57:27; 61:6.
The death of Jesus – 4:155–159; 3:55; 19:33; 5:117.
Jesus and God – 3:59; 4:171–172; 5:72–75, 116–117; 9:30–31.

9. TRADITION (*HADITH* AND *SUNNA*)

The word *hadith* means literally a communication, narrative or record, and came to be used for a record of the actions and sayings of the Prophet and his Companions. The word *sunna* means literally a way, or a path, and thus came to mean 'the way of the Prophet' or 'the Prophet's example', that is, the way the Prophet did or said something, and therefore the way that Muslims should follow.

Thus the *hadith* enshrines the *sunna*, and the two words have come to mean the same thing, and refer to the whole body of traditions about the Prophet collected after his death. The importance of tradition as it was developed by his followers is summed up by Kenneth Cragg: 'By *hadith/sunna* Muhammad shaped and ordered his community, we might say, from the grave.'[1] 'The *hadith* literature', in the words of Alfred Guillaume, 'is the basis of that developed system of law, theology and custom which is Islam.'[2]

Collections of *hadith*

Table 9.1 shows the authors of the six most important and authoritative collections of *hadith*:

al-Bukhari	died 870
Muslim	died 875
Abu-Dawood	died 889
ibn Majah	died 887
Tirmidhi	died 892
An-Nasa'i	died 915

Table 9.1

The first of these collections, the *Sahih* of al-Bukhari, has been described as 'arguably for the vast majority of Muslims the most important "religious text" after the Qur'an'.[3]

Further questions about tradition

How were hadith *and* sunna *recorded?*
Every *hadith* has two parts. The first features the names of those who handed it on ('A told me, saying that B said C had informed him, saying D mentioned that he heard E relate, "I heard F ask the Apostle of God such and such" '). This chain of authority is known as the *isnad*, which means literally 'supports'. The second part is the substance or content of the report of what the Prophet said or did (*matn*). In Muslim understanding only the *sunna* of the Prophet and the original Muslim community could supply a rule of conduct for believers. It needs to be noted also that there are two kinds of *hadith*. A small number of them, known as *hadith qudsi*, 'divine saying', are the words of God put into the mind of the Prophet but not recorded in the Qur'an; the vast majority, however, are *hadith nabawi*, 'a prophetic saying', in which the Prophet speaks in his own words but giving an authoritative opinion.

How reliable is hadith?
In the two hundred years after the death of Muhammad during which the genuine traditions about the Prophet were circulating widely, other traditions were circulated by people who wanted to gain authority for a particular view (often related to political issues) by attributing it to the Prophet himself. The Muslim community was therefore faced with the problem of how to distinguish between genuine traditions which

could be traced back to the Prophet or his Companions, and contradictory, doubtful or even spurious traditions invented later.

The problem was solved by the collectors of *hadith*, who classified them in the following categories.

- 'Sound' (*sahih*): traditions where there are no weak links in the chain of authorities, and the content is not inconsistent with accepted Muslim belief.
- 'Fair' (*hasan*): where the links in the chain of reporters are incomplete, or there is incomplete agreement about the reliability of the authorities.
- 'Weak' (*da'if*): where some of the transmitters of the tradition are not regarded as reliable, or there are doubts about the content of the report.

In this way discussion about the reliability of *hadith* developed into a science, known as *'ilm ul-hadith*.

How is hadith used?

A wide range of Muslim practices and beliefs are based not on the Qur'an, but on *hadith*. Chawkat Moucarry lists some of these as follows:

- circumcision;
- the five canonical prayers;
- Muhammad's intercession on the Day of Judgment;
- Muhammad's night journey and ascension to heaven;
- Muhammad's miracles;
- God's ninety-nine most beautiful names;
- the death penalty for apostasy;
- the death penalty for sexual immorality;
- Jesus' return to earth at the end of time.[4]

Gai Eaton explains why *hadith* is so important in the everyday life of Muslims:

> If the Muslim is to tap that same source and become 'one who understands', he has no choice but to model himself on this 'perfect exemplar', imitating Muhammad so far as he is able, both in his character

and in his mode of action. Since the Prophet is 'closer to the believers than their [own] selves' (Q.33.6), it can be said that he is the believer's alter ego or – to take this a step further – more truly 'oneself' than the collection of fragments and contrary impulses which we commonly identify as the 'self'.

This is why the *hadith* literature is of such immense importance in the everyday life of the Muslim; and the record is so extensive that it is always possible, even among learned people, for someone to astonish and delight his friends by quoting to them a 'Prophet story', or a saying of which they had not previously heard. The intimate knowledge we have of Muhammad's life (much of which we owe to 'A'isha) is, from a practical point of view, just as important as his religious teaching and the example he set in affairs of greater consequence. The believer feels close to him in life and hopes to be closer still after death, loving him not only as master and as guide but also as brother-man. It is in the light of this relationship that we may understand parts of the record which often appear trivial to the occidental, such as 'A'isha's meticulous account of the manner in which they washed from a single bowl after making love, and her added comment, 'He would get ahead of me and I used to say, "Give me a chance, give me a chance!"' ...

Al-Ghazzali (d. AD 1111), who is one of the most widely accepted authorities, wrote of the true Muslim as one who 'imitates the Messenger of Allah in his goings out and his comings in, his movements and his times of rest, the manner of his eating, his deportment, his sleep and his speech'. So a man should sit while putting on his trousers and stand while putting on his turban, start with the right foot when putting on his shoes and, when cutting his nails, begin with the forefinger of the right hand; and al-Ghazzali mentions the case of a pious man who never dared eat a melon, much as he wished to do so, because he could not discover the precise manner in which God's Messenger ate melons. Did he cut them to segments? Did he perhaps scoop the flesh out with a spoon? We shall never know. But this outward observance is, of course, meaningless unless it both reflects and engenders a profound inward conformity to the perfect exemplar, given us by God as 'a mercy to mankind', a conformity of the believer's soul to the soul of Muhammad.[5]

Examples of *hadith*

The following examples illustrate the wide variety of subjects covered by *hadith* – such as details about the life of the Prophet, moral teaching, and regulations about clothes, eating, marriage, the pursuit of knowledge, apostasy and gaining Paradise.

'A'ishah said: The first revelation that was granted to the Messenger of Allah (peace and blessings of Allah be on him) was the true dream in a state of sleep, so that he never dreamed a dream but the truth of it shone forth like the dawn of the morning. Then solitude became dear to him and he used to seclude himself in the cave of Hira, and therein he devoted himself to divine worship for several nights before he came back to his family and took provisions for his retirement; then he would return to Khadijah and take more provisions for a similar period, until the Truth came to him while he was in the cave of Hira; so the angel (Gabriel) came to him and said, Read...

If a man goes an inch towards God, God will come a yard towards him. If he goes a yard towards God, God will come a furlong towards him.

Intentions count for more than actions.

The man who marries perfects half his religion.

Never did God allow anything more hateful to him than divorce. With God, the most detestable of all things allowed is divorce.

He who believes in Allah and the Last Day should honour his guest.

By Allah, I [Muhammad] ask Allah's forgiveness and turn to Him in repentance more than seventy times a day.

Modesty is part of faith.

Gold and silk are lawful to the women of my Umma and forbidden to the men.

The angels do not enter the house in which there is a dog or pictures.

Say Allah's name (*Bismillah*) and eat with your right hand and eat from near you.

If anyone has got an atom of pride in his heart, he will not enter Paradise.

The seeking of knowledge is a must for every Muslim man and woman.

No one of you (really) believes (in Allah and His religion) till he wants for his brother what he wants for himself.

I have been commanded to wage war on the people till they testify that there is no deity save Allah, and that Muhammad is the Apostle of Allah, (till they) say the prayers and give the legal alms.

The blood of a man who is a Muslim is not lawful [it may not be lawfully shed], save if he belongs to one of three (classes): a married man who is an adulterer; one who owes his soul for another soul [a murderer]; one who abandons his religion, thus becoming one who splits the community.

In response to a question put to Muhammad: 'Is it your opinion that if I pray the prescribed [prayers], fast during Ramadan, allow myself what is allowable and treat as disallowed what is forbidden, but do nothing more than that, I shall enter Paradise?' the Prophet answered 'Yes'.

No child is born but that Satan touches it when it is born whereupon it starts crying loudly because of being touched by Satan, except Mary and her son.

Whoever knows himself, knows his Lord.

God is as one thinks of him.

You should worship Allah as if you are seeing Him, for He sees you even if you do not see Him.

Communal prayer is twenty-seven times better than the prayer of a man alone in his house.

Truly what the Messenger of Allah has forbidden is like what Allah has forbidden.

Behold, I have left among you two things: you will never go astray as long as you hold fast to them – the Book of Allah and my *sunna*.

God created Adam in his own image.

Make sure you treat the Copts [in Egypt] well for they are your kith and kin.

(In response to the question of how to purify oneself) He should always remember that Allah is with him wherever he is.

Leading a good life is to worship God as if you see him.

God is beautiful and he loves beauty.

The best *jihad* is to speak a word of justice to an oppressive ruler.

Always speak the truth, even if it is bitter.

When one of you yawns, he should close his mouth with his hand, else Satan would enter.

God will send this community a person who will renew its faith at the beginning of every hundred years.

If any one of you sees an abhorrent action, let him correct it with his hand; if he cannot, let him do it in words; if he cannot, let him do it in his heart – which is the weakest degree of faith.

Hadith qudsi: 'My mercy prevails over my wrath.'

If my servant likes to meet me, I like to meet him, and if he dislikes to meet me, I dislike to meet him.

My servant draws not near to Me with anything more loved by Me than the religious duties I have enjoined upon him, and My servant continues to draw near to Me with supererogatory works so that I shall love him. When I love him I am his hearing with which he hears, his

seeing with which he sees, his hand with which he strikes and his foot
with which he walks. Were he to ask [something] of Me, I would surely
give it to him, and were he to ask Me for refuge, I would surely grant
him it.

To underline the importance of *hadith* for Muslims, it may help
Christians to recognize that for Muslims *hadith* is vital for understanding the Qur'an and knowing how to live as a Muslim. The Qur'an is
the very Word of God – even the Words of God – and Muhammad
was the human vehicle through whom that divine revelation has been
given. The Christian idea of incarnation is totally ruled out. But at the
risk of misunderstanding, it could be said that the Word of God
in the Qur'an is embodied – even 'incarnated' – in the life of the
Prophet. *Hadith* is so important for Muslims, therefore, because it is
here that Muslims have direct access to the sayings and deeds of the
Apostle of God. For Muslims, in the words of Andrew Rippin, *hadith*
is 'the living Qur'an quite literally'.[6]

10. LAW (*SHARI'A*) AND THEOLOGY (*KALAM*)

Law

Christians will no doubt find it hard to understand why we need to give attention to law, since the concept of law seems foreign to Christians who are taught that salvation is by faith, not by works. While Christians recognize that each church has its own order and discipline, the only law they are conscious of is the law of their country or international law.

The importance of law in Islam is summed up succinctly by Joseph Schacht:

> Islamic law is the epitome of Islamic thought, the most typical
> manifestation of the Islamic way of life, the core and kernel of Islam itself.[1]

The relationship between law and theology is explained by Kenneth Cragg and Andrew Rippin in this way:

> Islam understands law as religion, religion as law ... Law, rather than
> theology, has the prior emphasis in Islam. Broadly, it is obedience to the
> will of God, rather than fellowship in the knowledge of God's nature,

which is paramount. Revelation is for direction of life, rather than
disclosure of mystery ... Islam is essentially submission, rather than
'communion'.[2]

Theology ... is not only subordinate in importance to law as a discipline
but also incorporated within the whole legal framework. Since all law
comes from God, law is, in fact, theology as such, for both topics deal with
the contemplation of human action in relationship to the divine; because
of the practical aspects of Islamic life, law requires study in a way that
theology does not.[3]

The process of formulating Islamic law took between 200 and 250
years. Thus by about 850 Islam 'reached the fully developed form in
which it was to persist down to modern times ... The major items of
belief and practice had been settled and an agreed body of authoritative sources had emerged.'[4]

The basis of law

The four sources (*usul*), principles or pillars of law in Sunni Islam are
as follows.

1. The Qur'an, which contains in principle the whole of the *shari'a*
   law.
2. The *sunna* (*hadith*), which clarifies or elaborates the teaching
   of the Qur'an, explaining the example of the Prophet as a
   model.
3. The consensus of the community (*ijma'*). The word means
   'convergence', as in 'convergence of opinion'. This principle is
   based on a saying of Muhammad: 'My community will never
   agree on an error.' The consensus of the community is reached
   in practice by the process of 'enterprise' (*ijtihad*, literally 'effort',
   'struggle'), which is the activity of the scholars (*ulama*) who
   formulate legal precepts dealing with new situations, using all
   the sources of the law with a kind of logical reasoning or
   rational argument.
   'The inner function of *ijma'*,' says H. A. R. Gibb, 'as the
   instrument by which the Community regulates its spiritual life,

is to secure and to preserve the integral spiritual unity of all Muslims as a spiritually governed society.'[5] From about AD 900 it was felt that all essential questions had been finally settled if a consensus had gradually emerged. All that remained to be done after this was the explanation, application and interpretation of the law that had been laid down.

4. The principle of analogy (*qiyas*). When there is no clear ruling that emerges from the Qur'an or the *sunna*, scholars try to find some comparable ruling that will suggest an appropriate parallel, relying on personal judgment (*ra'y*) and the application of discretion in legal judgments based on the 'good of the community' (*istihsan*).

The science of law is called jurisprudence (*fiqh*). The four main schools of law in the Sunni tradition differ according to the emphasis they place on each of the four sources. Each tends to be strong in certain countries or regions and are 'schools' rather than 'sects'.

The *Hanafi* school was founded by Abu Hanifa (died 767) in Iraq. Here the main emphasis is on the Qur'an, and the *sunna* is regarded as secondary, while some role is allowed for reason.

The *Maliki* school was founded by Malik ibn Anas (died 795) in Medina. This is the oldest of the schools and is very conservative. It regards the Qur'an and the *sunna* as the main sources of authority, but allows some place for consensus.

The *Shafi'i* school was founded by al-Shafi'i (died 820), who lived in Baghdad and Egypt. This position represented a compromise between the Maliki and Hanafi schools, and rejected the role of private judgment. It was al-Shafi'i who established the important principle that the *sunna*, the tradition, should be based only on the traditions of the Prophet.

The *Hanbali* school was founded by Ahmad ibn Hanbal (died 855) in Baghdad. This was the most conservative of all the schools, accepting only the Qur'an and the *sunna*, and rejecting both consensus and analogy. This is the school that is followed in Saudi Arabia today.

Alongside *shari'a* there developed a kind of unwritten Islamic custom known as *'urf*. In addition to the *shari'a* courts, therefore, there existed in many countries *'urfi* courts to decide on questions related to customs.

The completion of this process of formulating Islamic law is described by Michael Nazir-Ali in this way:

> By the beginning of the third century after the Hijra, Muslim jurisprudence had been codified by the jurists of the four schools of law. The *ulema* now reached a consensus, which has only recently been challenged, that the four schools were 'final' and that the work of the jurists henceforward would be only the interpretation and application of the codified law.[6]

Examples of Islamic law

Islamic legal scholars developed a classification which divides all human actions into one or other of the following five categories:

- obligatory (*fard, wajib*); i.e. mandatory, so that omission can be punished;
- recommended (*mandub*); i.e. actions that are rewarded, while omission is not punished;
- permissible (*mubah*); i.e. actions that are neutral and permitted and therefore legally indifferent;
- disapproved (*makruh*); i.e. actions that are deplored or abhorred, but not punished;
- forbidden (*haram*); i.e. prohibited and also punishable by law.

The following is a typical ruling on the subject of 'Growing the Beard':

> Letting one's beard grow and become thick is a feature of dignity. It should not be cut so short that it appears like a shaved beard, nor should it be left so long that it becomes untidy. It is also a sign of manhood. Ibn 'Umar related that the Messenger of Allah said, 'Differ from the polytheists: let your beards (grow) and shave your moustache' (Bukhari and Muslim). Bukhari's version adds: 'Whenever Ibn 'Umar made the *hajj* or *umrah*, he would hold his beard in his fist, and whatever exceeded his fist, he would cut off.'[7]

Abdur Rahman I. Doi summarizes the position of Islamic law concerning the marriage of a Muslim man to a Jewish or Christian woman as follows:

Islam considers the Jews and the Christian as 'People of the Book' (*Ahl al-Kitab*) because they believe in the Torah and the Evangil, the Books revealed to the prophets Musa and 'Isa respectively. Marriage with a woman of the People of the Book (*kitabiyyah*) is permitted in Islam: 'This day are all things good and pure made lawful unto you. The food of the People of the Book is lawful unto you and yours lawful unto them. Lawful unto you in marriage are not only chaste women who are believers, but chaste women among the People of the Book revealed before your time, when you give them due dowers, and desire chastity and not lewdness nor secret intrigues' (5:6).

There is a consensus of opinion among the Sunni schools that marriage with Jewish and Christian women is permitted. It was also the practice of the Companions of the Prophet (*Sahabah*) like 'Uthman ... and others.

However, in spite of this, Abdullah ibn 'Umar was of the opinion that a Muslim should not marry a Jewess or a Christian woman. He used to say, 'Allah has forbidden us to marry the polytheists, and I do not understand it as being other than manifest polytheism when a woman says that her Lord is 'Isa, when he is but a servant from the servants of Allah.'

Although we also respectfully submit that no doubt some pious *Sahabah* and some of the Followers (*Tabi'un*) did marry the *kitabiyyah* women, yet Muslims of today must think long and deeply before contracting such marriages ... [8]

Doi explains the traditional ruling on apostasy (*al-Ridda*):

Al-Riddah means rejection of the religion of Islam in favour of any other religion either through an action or through words of mouth. The act of apostasy thus puts an end to one's adherence to Islam ... The following Qur'anic verse explains the gravity of sin and the crime of apostasy: 'How shall Allah guide those who reject faith after they accepted it and bore witness that the Apostle was true and the clear signs had come unto them. But Allah guides not the people unjust of such the reward is that on them rests the curse of Allah, of His Angels and of all mankind in that will they dwell; nor will their penalty be lightened, nor respite be their lot, except for those that repent (even) after that and make amends; for verily Allah is oft-forgiving, Most Merciful.'

The punishment for apostasy is prescribed in the following Hadith of the Prophet: 'It is reported by Abbas ... that the Messenger of Allah said:

"Whoever changes his religion (from Islam to anything else), brings end to
his life." '

The punishment by death in the case of apostasy has been unanimously
agreed upon by all the four schools of Islamic jurisprudence... [9]

Theology

We have already noted the basic creed of Islam (see chapter 5, 'Basic
Muslim beliefs and practices'). The following brief survey outlines
some of the major theological issues that Islam has had to face during
the past 1,400 years.

The question of succession

Who were the rightful successors of the Prophet? How should the
leaders of the community be chosen? This was the fundamental issue
that led to the split between Sunnis and Shi'ites. Should the successor
of the Prophet be chosen by the community, as the Sunnis argued? Or
should he be from the Prophet's family, as 'Ali (Muhammad's cousin
and son-in-law) and the Shi'ites argued? 'Ali eventually became the
fourth caliph; but when his first son Hasan renounced his claim to
succeed his father, and his second son Husayn was killed in the Battle
of Kerbala in 680, the family had no hope of competing with the
claims of the Umayyad caliphs who were now ruling in Damascus.
Throughout the centuries the Shi'ites have had their own approach to
the question of the leadership of the community, which has been
particularly important since the Islamic Revolution in Iran in 1979 (see
further chapter 14, 'Branches and movements within Islam').

The definition of 'Muslim'

What makes a person a Muslim? When the centre of power in the
Muslim world moved from Medina to the city of Damascus, and
the Islamic Empire spread in every direction, the leaders of the
Muslim community were exposed to all the temptations of power
and wealth. Inevitably some protested against the worldliness and
compromise that they felt were invading Islam, and they challenged
the community to define more carefully what makes a person a
Muslim. One group called Kharijites ('Seceders') were puritanical in
their approach, and called for a strict definition of what it means to be

a good Muslim. They argued that a Muslim who committed serious sin and refused to repent became automatically an unbeliever, an apostate. Another group called Murji'ites ('Postponers') took a more lenient view of moral standards, saying that only God could decide who was a good Muslim, and that he would give his verdict on the Day of Judgment. They argued that an outward profession of faith combined with inward assent was sufficient to make a person a Muslim. While the Murji'ites disappeared, the Kharijites continued as a distinct group. A third position, which became the accepted position, was that while a basic faith in Islam is enough to make a person a Muslim, there are different degrees of faith and believers should strive to develop in the practice of their faith.

The challenge of rationalism

What is the place of reason in faith? As the Muslim community came in contact with Greek culture and civilization in such places as Damascus, they found they had to face all kinds of intellectual questions that might never have occurred to the first Muslims in Arabia. Islam had to come to terms with Greek philosophy, just as Christianity had been trying to do for centuries. These, therefore, were some of the questions that were discussed:

- Is it reasonable to believe in God's predestination of everything, including both good and evil? Are there not many verses in the Qur'an which speak of human beings as responsible and free to choose for themselves?
- Can one prove the existence of God by reason alone?
- How are we to understand the language of the Qur'an? Are anthropomorphic expressions (e.g. about the 'face' or the 'hands' of God) to be understood literally or figuratively?
- If the Qur'an is the very Word(s) of God, how is it related to God? Was it created in time, or was it uncreated and eternal? Did it come to being as it was being recited by Muhammad, or had it existed from eternity in heaven?

The Mu'tazilites took a position that might be described as 'rational-ist' or 'modernist', with a strong emphasis on reason and on the justice of God. They questioned the more extreme expressions of predestination and argued for the freedom of the will, insisting that individuals have power over their own choices and actions. They believed that if the Qur'an is thought to be eternal, it becomes something divine alongside God. They also taught that anthropomorphic language must not be understood literally. The influence of this movement was curtailed in the eleventh century – partly for political reasons. But modernist, liberal Muslims have revived many of these issues, attempting to make the Islamic faith more rational and acceptable to people in the modern world.

Al-Ash'ari (873–935), after having been a Mu'tazilite theologian for some years, abandoned their philosophical method and returned to a more orthodox, traditional position. He rejected their teaching on free will, for example, and taught that the Qur'an was uncreated. He came down strongly on the side of predestination, while allowing a place for human freedom and responsibility. He emphasized the transcendence of God, and in discussion of the problems of religious language he frequently appealed to the formula *bi la kayf* (meaning literally 'without how', i.e. 'without asking "how?" '). So in emphasizing the qualitative difference between God and humanity, he believed that God's justice is different from any human concept of justice. His teaching determined the direction in which traditional Islamic theology was to move for several centuries, and he is regarded as one of the greatest theologians in Islam.

At a later stage further challenges came from those who, influenced by Greek philosophy, believed that the universe is eternal, that there is no resurrection of the body, and that philosophy is more important than prophecy, but they are connected because they are related to the same human faculty of imagination. The person who demonstrated that these ideas were heretical and who re-established orthodox theology was al-Ghazali (died 1111), who came to be recognized as another of the greatest theologians in Islam.

The definition of orthodoxy

What is unacceptable belief? Because Sunni Islam has never had leaders comparable to bishops and popes and has never convened councils to make credal statements like the Apostles' Creed and the Nicene Creed, it has never attempted to define its theology in the same way that Christians have done. What has happened is that a kind of consensus has developed over the centuries, based on the teaching of the most influential scholars. In the twentieth century, however, the Muslim community in Pakistan was forced to draw some lines because of the prominence of the Ahmadiyya movement. Founded by Mirza Ghulam Ahmad Khan (1836–1908), it began as a reform movement, attempting to revitalize Islam from within. It had a strong missionary emphasis, organizing missionary work in many parts of the world. Its founder claimed to be a kind of *Mahdi* ('Messiah'). Because these claims seemed to question the finality of the Prophet Muhammad, the movement was declared non-Muslim by the government of Pakistan in 1973.

The question of development and reinterpretation

To what extent can Islamic law and theology develop and change through time? How dynamic and progressive can they be? It has generally been thought that the process of formulating Islamic law ended around the ninth century and that only those who have been schooled in all the traditional disciplines of Islamic study can be called scholars (*'ulama*). In recent years, however, many Muslims have started questioning the idea that law cannot develop and evolve further since 'the gate of *ijtihad*' closed many centuries ago. They have also begun to ask whether lay people, who are not Islamic scholars in the technical sense, might have a contribution to make in these discussions.

The status of shari'a law

What should be the basis of law in Muslim countries? When most of the Muslim world came under European colonial rule in the eighteenth century, civil courts took over the powers of the Islamic *shari'a* courts, which then came to be responsible mainly for family law. Law codes were based on different kinds of Western law (British or French, for example). Many Muslims have argued that Islamic law should not need to be supplemented, let alone superseded, by legal systems coming from non-Islamic sources. This is one of the goals of Islamists who want Muslim states to base their constitution and law on the *shari'a*. Other Muslims, however, have resisted this attempt to go back to the *shari'a* and want to see law codes based on a combination of *shari'a* and Western law. Kemal Ataturk took the step of abolishing *shari'a* law altogether in Turkey in the 1920s.

Some examples of Islamic theology

Al-Ghazali's theological treatise on *The Ninety-Nine Beautiful Names of God*, written at the end of the eleventh century, explains the meaning of all the names, such as 'Compassionate' and 'Merciful', that are given to God in the Qur'an and in Muslim tradition. One of the introductory chapters discusses whether or not it is possible to know God:

> Since there is no likeness of Him, He or 'His nature' is not known by other than Him. So al-Junayd – may God's mercy be on him – was right when he remarked: 'Only God knows God' ... So, by God, no one other than God knows God, in this world or the next.
>
> This is the way in which one should understand the one who says 'I know God' and the one who says 'I do not know God.' If you were to show a piece of intelligible writing to a reasonable person and say to him: 'Do you know its writer?' and he said 'No,' he would be speaking truly. But if he said, 'Yes: its writer is a man living and powerful, hearing and seeing, sound of hand and knowledgeable in the practice of writing, and if I know all this from the sample how can I not know him?' – he too would be speaking truly. Yet the saying of the one who said, 'I do not know him' is more correct and true, for in reality he does not know him. Rather he only knows that intelligible writing requires a living writer, knowing, powerful, hearing, and seeing; yet he does not know the writer himself. Similarly, every creature knows only that this ordered and precisely disposed world requires an arranging, living, knowing, and powerful maker.
>
> Therefore, it is impossible for anyone other than God truly to know God most high.[10]

A creed written by al-Ash'ari (died 935) summarizes what orthodox Muslims believe about some of the key issues:

> They hold that on earth there is neither good nor evil except what God wills, and that things come to be by the will of God ... a person has no acting power to do anything before he (actually) does it, and ... the evil actions of human beings are created by God and the (good) works of human beings are created by God, and ... human beings are not able to create anything ...
>
> They hold that the Qur'an is the speech of God and uncreated ...

They assert the intercession of the Messenger of God, and that it is on behalf of great sinners of his community...

They think it proper to pray for the welfare of the imams of the Muslims, not to rebel against them with the sword, and not to fight in civil strife...

They count true the appearance of the Dajjal (Antichrist) and the killing of him by 'Isa ibn Maryam (Jesus, son of Mary).[11]

A twentieth-century credal statement following the tradition of al-Ash'ari, in answer to the question 'What does it mean to believe that God Most High is dissimilar to ... creatures?', gives the following answer:

It means to believe that nothing is like God Most High, neither in his essence, nor in his attributes, nor in his acts ... It means to believe that the essence of God ... does not resemble creatures in any way. Whatsoever you might conceive in your mind, God is not like that, 'Like Him there is naught' (Surah 42:11) ... nothing that is attributed to God can resemble that which is attributed to creatures...[12]

11. SUFISM

'The function of Sufism', says H. A. R. Gibb, 'was to restore to the religious life of Muslims the element of personal communion with God which orthodox theology was squeezing out.'[1] It has also been described as 'the interiorization and intensification of Islamic faith and practice'. Since Sufis themselves think of Sufism as 'the living spirit of the Islamic tradition ... Islam's life-giving core ... co-extensive with Islam',[2] it is probably misleading to speak of Sufism as 'Islamic mysticism', and it may be more helpful to think of it in terms of 'Islamic spirituality'. It deserves a chapter on its own for the following reasons.

- It has been a major source of spiritual fervour almost since the beginning of Islam, introducing an intense personal devotion to the daily life of believers, and producing famous saints who have inspired love and devotion.
- Many Sufi ideas were integrated to the mainstream of Islamic thought through the life and teaching of al-Ghazali (died 1111).
- It has influenced every level of Muslim society and contributed significantly to the social fabric and to the spread of Islam. In

the words of Colin Turner, 'Sufism was central to Islam and an integral component of the spiritual make-up of many, of not all, Muslim communities and societies, operating in its various forms and guises throughout all levels of society.'[3]

- It has experienced a revival in the last century and is therefore very much alive in contemporary Islam, often influencing political and social action.
- It still proves to be one of the most attractive features of Islam to non-Muslims, especially for a number of converts in Western countries.
- In the first centuries it was deeply influenced by Christian spirituality, and at a later period it has influenced Christian mystics such as John of the Cross and Teresa of Avila.

The word *sufi* probably comes from the word *suf,* meaning 'undyed wool'. A *sufi* was someone who wore *suf,* rough and uncomfortable clothes made of wool. By the ninth century the word *tasawwuf* was being used to mean 'being a *sufi*'.

The origins of Sufism

H. A. R. Gibb sums up the emergence of Sufism by saying, 'The main impulse arose out of primitive Islamic asceticism, governed by the eschatology of the Koran and the fear of Hell, and passing into a positive search for God, then into the quest of the mystical experience of oneness with God.'[4] Michael Nazir-Ali summarizes six reasons for the emergence of Sufism as outlined by Muhammad Iqbal, the poet-philosopher of Pakistan:

> ... the *political unrest* during the eighth and ninth centuries AD, which drove people of devotion to seek a contemplative life away from such conflict; the *barrenness* of much rationalistic theology which led people to appeal to a super-intellectual source of knowledge; the dead hand of *legalism* in the major traditions and their bitter opposition to creative thinking; *inter-faith dialogue* which had been encouraged, and, indeed, practised by some of the Caliphs; and *moral laxity*, which had been brought about by unparalleled prosperity; the *presence of Christianity* as a working ideal of life ...[5]

It is not hard to see how this kind of movement developed during the Umayyad period as a protest against the worldliness that had come into Islam. Some were calling for a simpler and more austere way of life, closer to that of the Prophet. Similarly, whenever religion and worship seemed in danger of becoming a formality without any deep personal conviction, there were those who longed for a faith that had reality for the individual. This 'hunger of the heart' led many Sufis to seek to recover the intensity of the spiritual experiences of the Prophet. If Muhammad had had his 'journey to heaven' (the *Mi'raj*), could the believer not enjoy something of the same kind of experience? They appealed to verses in the Qur'an such as the following:

> We verily created a man and We know what his soul whispereth to him, and We are nearer to him than his jugular vein. (50:16)

> And when My servants ask you about Me, say: 'I am near; I answer the prayer of the supplicant when he calls...' (2:186, Fathry)

> O ye who believe! Whoso of you becometh a renegade from his religion, (know that in his stead) Allah will bring a people whom He loveth and who love Him, humble toward believers, stern toward disbelievers, striving in the way of Allah, and fearing not the blame of any blamer. (5:54)

> Allah is the Light of the heavens and the earth ... Light upon light, Allah guideth unto His light whom He will. And Allah speaketh to mankind in allegories, for Allah is Knower of all things. (24:35)

> To Allah belong the East and the West. So whichever way you turn, there is Allah's Face. Indeed, Allah is Omnipresent and Omniscient. (2:115, Fathry)

Muhammad and his followers had been in contact from the beginning with Christian monks and hermits. They must have learned something from their ascetic lifestyle and their regular patterns of devotion. Later mystics were influenced by Christian ideas of different kinds, such as the speculation about the *logos*, the eternal Word of God, and they applied similar ideas to Muhammad. The emphases on asceticism, seeing the self as illusory, and the quest for inner enlightenment and union with God all have a very Eastern flavour. If they did not actually come from the East, they would certainly have been strengthened through the considerable interaction with Indian thought that took place at various stages in Islamic history.

Basic practices and emphases in Sufism

'Recollecting' or 'remembering' the name of God in prayer (dhikr)

This has been one of the most fundamental features of Sufi practice since the beginning, carried out either by the individual in private or by a group when they meet together for spiritual exercises. It is based on qur'anic verses such as 'Remember me then and I will remember you...' (2:152), and 'O believers, remember Allah often; and glorify Him morning and evening' (33:41–42).

An individual or a group repeat methodically certain names of God, words from the Qur'an or the *Shahadah*. *Dhikr* is sometimes accompanied by music (the flute, for example) or dancing, and occasionally by the use of drugs. For many Muslims the idea of remembering the name of God is very close to the Christian idea of 'practising the presence of God'.

The following directions regarding the practice of *dhikr* come from an Algerian Sufi, Shaykh al-'Alawi (1869–1934).

Any reasonably sensitive man will be conscious of the influence on him of the name he mentions. If we admit this we are bound to believe that the Name of God also produces an influence on the soul, as other names do, each one leaving the particular imprint that belongs with it and corresponds to it. I think you are aware that a name is ennobled with the nobility of him who is named, inasmuch as it carries his imprint in the hidden fold of its secret essence and meaning. Al-Ghazzali writes in his commentary on the Name Allah: 'That which the slave gets from this Name is Ta'alluh, or deification,' by which is meant that his 'heart and his purpose are drowned in God, so that he sees naught but Him.'

He also wrote: My son, rid thy heart of all attachment save unto God. Go apart by thyself and say with all thy powers of concentration: Allah, Allah, Allah. When thy thoughts are muddied with other than God, thou hast need of negation: La ilaha ('There is no god but...'). But once thou hast withdrawn from all things in contemplation of Him Who is Lord of all, thou takest rest in the bidding: Say: Allah ... Open the door of your

heart with the key of saying – La ilaha illa Allah 'There is no god but God,'
and the door of thy spirit by saying: 'Allah'.[6]

Belonging to a group

Meeting together with other Sufis in a group has always been
important, and these groups – brotherhoods, communities or associa-
tions, as they are sometimes called – have something in common
both with Christian orders such as the Franciscans, and with the cell
groups, house groups and base communities with which Christians
are familiar. 'Sufi ecstasy', says Kenneth Cragg, ' ... was essentially
corporate in its nature.' This is how he describes the corporate action
of the group in their 'remembering' of the name of God:

> *Dhikr*, for Sufis, meant a corporate action, a circle of rhythmic utterance,
> often accompanied by swaying (or whirling) of the body, controlled
> breathing, and accelerating tempo, until an ecstatic trance was reached.
> To say rhythmically and endlessly: *Allahu, Allahu, Allahu* or *Allahu akbar,
> Allahu akbar* ('God greater! God greater!') or the formula: *La ilaha illa Allah*
> ('There is no god but God ...') with its limpid 'ls' and its 'a' vowels, served
> to induce that hypnotic state in which ecstasy was near at hand.[7]

Sufi guides

All the Sufi orders were founded by holy men who trained others to
follow the particular discipline of the brotherhood. People in the
group would have their own spiritual director, guide or master, a
murshid, sheikh or *pir* to guide them in their spiritual journey. Many
of these saints were thought to have miraculous powers, and to be
able to communicate *baraka* (blessing or power). 'It was ultimately
the quality of their spiritual disciplines', says Kenneth Cragg, 'and the
genius of their founders and saints which held them together.'[8] The
brotherhoods also often brought together people of the same craft in
special guilds.

Walking the mystic 'way' (tariqa)

Sufi teachers all had their own understanding of the mystic path and
taught their own spiritual discipline to a group of disciples, who would
then teach others. The word *tariqa* therefore came to be used for an
order or a brotherhood. In Sufi teaching there are certain key stages

through which the believer who is seeking union with God must go: (1) repentance and renunciation, combined with the fear of God; (2) contentment and tranquillity, with patience and self-control; leading to (3) the final stage, which is variously described as the vision of God, union with God, spiritual illumination or knowledge, absorption into God or the love of God. While Islamic theology emphasized the transcendence, the otherness and the justice of God, Sufism emphasized his nearness, compassion and love. The ultimate goal is to reach the stage where there is an unveiling of God, so that the believer enjoys a vision of God's presence both in the world and in the soul.

The questioning of selfhood and the quest for union with God

Sufis have taught that although we all assume we are self-contained individuals, distinct from other people and from God, we need to think again about our sense of individuality. Can we not strive until, instead of thinking of the relationship between ourselves and God in terms of 'I' and 'He', we reach the stage where we can speak of a single 'we', and are no longer aware of our own individual self? In this way we may reach the state of *fana'*, annihilation, dying to self and being totally absorbed in God, the passing away of the self, as either a momentary or a continuing experience. Colin Turner says, 'The idea of the "purification of the soul" which lies at the heart of Islamic spirituality entails the gradual surrender of all human claims to sovereignty, and to realize that it is God and not man who is the real Centre of the human universe.'[9]

This idea that union with God is possible and leads to identity with the Godhead was expressed in an extreme form by al-Hallaj, who was crucified for blasphemy in 992. When he said, 'I am the real, The Truth [*ana-lhaqq*],' he was understood to be claiming to be God. What he probably meant, however, was that when the truth of God enters the soul of the individual there is an intermingling of the divine spirit and the human spirit. This is therefore a kind of incarnation of the divine spirit in individuals, who achieve deification.

Missionary zeal

Not only did the Sufi brotherhoods help to keep believers together, they were also among the most effective agents in spreading the message of Islam. In many parts of the world it was wandering Sufis who took the message alongside, or independent of, the soldiers and traders. By the twelfth century a large number of Sufi orders had been established, with their own communities and with branches in other places. These orders spread widely, creating further subdivisions all over the Muslim world. These Sufis were generally open to the culture of their new converts, and were prepared to incorporate many of their practices (which could often be described as folk religion or 'superstitions') into their Islamic practice. This was particularly true in Africa, the Indian subcontinent and the Far East.

Jesus as a model

Jesus came to be regarded by many Sufis as a model of holy living. Thus for al-Hallaj Jesus was more of a model than Muhammad. And Ibn Arabi, remembering that the Qur'an speaks of Muhammad as 'the seal of the prophets', described Jesus as 'the seal of the saints'.

Sufism and orthodox Islam

During the early centuries, orthodox Muslims made criticisms such as these of Sufi teaching and practice.

- It encourages individualism, egotism and emotionalism.
- If the inner meaning of prayer and pilgrimage is more important than carrying them out, Muslims will come to believe that observance of the five pillars is not important.
- In its emphasis on the quest for union with God, it seems to blur the distinction between the Creator and the creature and can easily end in pantheism.
- It can easily develop into a syncretistic type of folk Islam because it allows, if not encourages, esoteric speculation, popular superstition and magic, and the desire for supernatural demonstrations of power.
- It is divisive of Islam because of the creation of so many different *tariqas*.
- There is sometimes excessive reliance on the teaching of a sheikh, and total obedience to him.
- Some Sufis use music and dance, and some use drugs.

The theologian al-Ghazali (died 1111) played a significant role in resolving the conflict between Sufism and traditional Islam. He had been trained in all the traditional disciplines of qur'anic study, law and theology, and had made a thorough study of Greek philosophy. He surprised his contemporaries when he gave up his post as a theological professor in Baghdad in order to become a Sufi. His greatest concern was to reach certainty in faith, and he came to believe that this could be gained through neither philosophical thought nor theological inquiry, but only through immediate personal experience of God. Although he later returned to teaching, he never ceased to follow the Sufi way.

His contribution was particularly significant because he brought the best of the Sufi tradition within the mainstream of orthodox Islam. 'Al-Ghazali tried', says Ninian Smart, 'to do justice to the actual experience of the Sufis and the requirements of orthodoxy and the religion of worship ... [He] succeeded in welding together orthodox piety and the inner quest of the contemplative. Through this synthesis Sufism gained an honorable and recognized place in orthodoxy.'[10]

One of the greatest Sufi writers was Ibn Arabi from Spain (died 1240), who wrote many books about Sufism, explaining Sufi theory in great detail. Because of his emphasis on the idea of union with God and the unity of all existence (*wihdat al-wujud*), he has been accused of blurring the distinction between God and his creatures. Thus Sufism became less and less orthodox, and at times verged on pantheism. Wahhabism in the eighteenth century was a strong protest from orthodox Muslims against ideas and practices of this kind that had come into Islam from Sufism and from folk Islam.

Examples of Sufi writing

Here are examples of sayings, prayers and poetry written by Sufis:

My hope is for union with you, for that is the goal of my desire ... I have ceased to exist and have passed out of myself. I have become one with God and altogether His. (Rabi'a al-Adawiya, died 801)[11]

O my God, if I worship Thee from fear of Hell, burn me in Hell, and if I worship Thee from hope of Paradise, exclude me thence; but if I worship

Thee for Thine own sake then withhold not from me Thine eternal beauty. (Rabi'a)[12]

O God, my concern and my desire in this world is that I should remember Thee above all the things of this world, and in the next, that out of all who are in that world, I should meet with Thee alone. This is what I would say, 'Thy will be done.' (Rabi'a)[13]

In general ... how is the mystic way described? The purifying which is the first condition of it is the purification of the heart completely from what is other than God Most High; the key to it, which corresponds to the opening act of adoration and prayer, is the sinking of the heart completely in the recollection of God; and the end of it is complete annihilation in God. (Al-Ghazali)[14]

God speaks to everyone ... He speaks to the ears of the heart, but it is not every heart which hears Him. His voice is louder than the thunder, and His light is clearer than the sun, if only one could see and hear. In order to do that, one must remove this solid wall, this barrier – the Self. (Jalal ud-Din Rumi)[15]

There are many roads to the Ka'bah ... but lovers know that the true Holy Mosque is Union with God. (Jalal ud-Din Rumi)[16]

Kenneth Cragg suggests that the following description of a modern Algerian saint, Abu-l 'Abbas al-'Alawi (1869–1934), conveys 'the genius of Sufism at its finest':

In his brown jallabah and white turban, with his silver-gray beard and his long hands which seemed when he moved them to be weighted with the flow of his barakah (blessing), he had something of the pure archaic ambience of Sayyidna Ibrahim (Abraham), the friend of God. He spoke in a subdued, gentle voice ... His eyes, which were like two sepulchral lamps, seemed to pierce through all objects, seeing in their outer shell merely one and the same nothingness, beyond which they saw always one and the same reality – the Infinite. Their look was very direct, almost hard in its enigmatic unwaveringness, and yet full of charity. Often their long ovals would grow suddenly round as if in amazement, or as if enthralled by some marvelous spectacle. The cadence of the singing, the dances and ritual incantations seemed to go on vibrating in him perpetually. His head would sometimes rock rhythmically to and fro while his soul was plunged in the unfathomable mysteries of the Divine Name hidden in the dhikr, or remembrance.

He gave out an impression of unreality, so remote was he, so inaccessible, so difficult to take in, on account of his altogether abstract simplicity ... He was surrounded, at one and the same time, with all the veneration due to saints ... Yet, as another observes, he belonged to that class of men often to be met with in North Africa, who can pass without transition from deep thought to action, from the mysteries of the next world to the life of this, from the vast sweep of ideas to the smallest details of native politics.[17]

12. FOLK ISLAM OR POPULAR ISLAM

It has already been shown how the hunger of the heart expressed itself in the ideas and practices of Sufism. But where does one draw the line between the purer expressions of Sufism (which may or may not have been acceptable to the orthodox) and the popular superstitious and magical practices that have been, and still are, so widespread in the world of Islam?

Some want to draw a sharp distinction between two aspects of Sufism: on the one hand its strong personal disciplines and its highly developed teaching about the mystic way, and on the other its superstitious practices. Other observers find it hard to draw any distinction between Sufism and all the manifestations of popular Islam that they see.

Without resolving this debate, this chapter deals with the difference that seems to exist between the 'purer' kinds of Islam described in the textbooks (as outlined in the previous pages) and the Islam that is actually practised by many Muslims all over the world. The one is usually called 'ideal', 'orthodox', 'qur'anic' or 'normative' Islam. Over against this, there are a number of practices which seem at first sight to be inconsistent with this pure form of Islam, and which are therefore often grouped together under the heading 'folk Islam' or 'popular Islam'.

Examples of folk or popular Islam

All the following practices, many of which can be described as magical, can be observed in a wide variety of Muslim contexts.

- Wearing an amulet (*ta'wiz*) as a lucky charm to ward off evil spirits.
- Warding off 'the evil eye' through displaying a representation of the eye on a house or car.
- Writing a verse from the Qur'an on a piece of paper, putting the paper in water and then drinking the water.
- Using the names of God in a magical way.
- Drinking water from a particular spring because it is regarded as having magical powers.
- Visiting shrines built over the graves of especially holy people, and making pilgrimage to them to obtain blessing (*baraka*) or to seek relief from any kind of trouble or evil. Sometimes people visit shrines as a substitute for going on pilgrimage to Mecca. Many of these saints are regarded not only as examples of holy living, but also as intercessors between individuals and God.
- Veneration of the Prophet Muhammad. Although the Qur'an teaches that Muhammad was an ordinary man who needed to seek forgiveness from God, popular piety has often tended to exalt the status of the Prophet and to attribute to him qualities that seem to be semi-divine or even divine.
- Many of the phenomena which Christians associate with charismatic gifts, such as healings, visions and miracles of different kinds, can be found in Islam.
- Many other ideas and practices familiar to Western societies today, such as astrology and occult practices, can be found in Muslim societies as well (see chapter 36, 'Some issues facing Christians today').

It needs to be emphasized that whereas in some situations these practices are widespread and public, in others they are not so common and certainly not evident to the casual observer. Some Muslims regard many practices of this kind as dangerous compromises with paganism – the kind of paganism against which the Prophet Muhammad was constantly fighting – and believe they are inconsistent with the teaching and the spirit of the Qur'an. They have accused Muslims who practise them of being superstitious infidels. Others see no fundamental difference or conflict between the so-called 'high' and 'low' expressions of Islam.

The world view of folk Islam

For the vast majority of Muslims, Satan (*al-Shaytan*, or *Iblis*) is a very real being. And many believe in the existence of spirits of different kinds which are variously called *ghul*, *'ifrit*, or *shayatin* (plural). Many would believe in 'the evil eye', convinced that a person, through envy (*hasad*) or any kind of ill-will, can actually cause real physical harm to other people or their possessions. Few Muslims, therefore, would have any problems with this description of the unseen world in a recent textbook about Islam by Ruqaiyyah Waris Maqsood:

> The universe consists of that which is seen and understood by our five senses, and that which is unseen (known as *al-Ghayb*). What we see and understand is only the tip of the iceberg in the vastness of God's creation. The two most important non-physical entities are angels and jinn.
>
> Angels are the agents and servants of God, the means by which He governs the universe and the channels by which humans become aware of Him. They do not have free-will, but carry out God's wishes. They are sometimes seen by people in times of crisis; many sensitive people feel aware of their presence when they pray and meditate. They may take any shape or form.
>
> Each human is assigned two special angels as guardians and 'recorders'; they activate a person's conscience, and note down every good and evil deed in each person's 'book', the record which they will see and understand, and on which they will be judged on the Day. All good deeds are recorded for ever, but if a person repents, the record of the evil deed is wiped out...
>
> Jinn are also non-physical beings, and they can be either good or evil, having free-will like humans. They are thought to inhabit unclean places,

and can often frighten and confuse human beings by involving themselves
in their lives and homes. Occasionally they attempt to possess human
bodies and have to be exorcised. They are not always malevolent, however,
and Surah 72 mentions jinn that were converted to Islam.[1]

Paul Hiebert, a Christian anthropologist whose main experience was
in India, explains how folk religion of different kinds all over the
world meets the needs of ordinary people who face the problems and
questions of daily life.

Folk religion answers several immediate questions. The first of these has to
do with the present meaning of life and death. Life cycle rites, such as birth
and initiation rites, marriages and funerals, makes sense out of life by
ordering it into stages and marking the traditions . . .

The second question has to do with the well-being of a person or
groups, and the threat of misfortune. Life is precarious at best. It is
constantly beset with illnesses, plagues, barrenness, accidents, drownings,
fires, droughts, earthquakes and disasters of all sorts. To prevent these,
people use amulets, talismen, magic, astrology, demon traps, spirit
repellants, rituals and many other practices. And when these strike, they
turn to diviners, shamans, medicine men, magicians, spirit healers,
witchdoctors and many others.

The third question has to do with success and failure. How does one
find a suitable spouse for a child, succeed in business, win in gambling or
pass school examinations? How does a tribe insure its prosperity and
guarantee victory in battle? Divination, omens, astrology, magic, ancestors,
tribal gods and surrounding spirits can bring success. Similarly, curses,
medicines, black magic, sorcery and witchcraft can secure the failure of
rivals and enemies.

The fourth question has to do with the need to plan one's life and the
fear and frustration of the unknown, whether past, present or future. Who
stole the money? Who would make the best king? Which plane will crash?
To answer these questions one needs guidance by means of divination,
dreams, oracles, omens or prophecies.

The fifth question has to do with a person's relationships with other
humans, ancestors, local spirits, gods, demons, animals and plants. Here
we find such phenomena as 'love magic', fertility rites, medicines to test
the faithfulness of a spouse, sorcery, witchcraft, curses and the like . . .

This is his explanation of the difference between high religion and folk religion:

> One of the crucial differences between high and folk religions has to do with their purposes. High religion seeks truth. It provides people with their ultimate map and story of reality. Consequently it turns to revelation, insight and reason. While it deals with power, it does so in a framework of truth.
>
> Folk religion, on the other hand, focuses on power and problem solving in everyday life. It is, therefore, basically pragmatic. Any method will do so long as it works. Moreover, several methods may be used simultaneously. A father with a sick son will ask the mullah to pray to God for him, tie an amulet to his arm to drive off evil spirits and give him modern medicine to kill the germs, all at the same time.
>
> Given this difference between high and folk religion, it should not surprise us that leaders in high religion are often displeased with common folk who turn to religion simply for an immediate, pragmatic solution to present-day problems.
>
> Power is central to our understanding of folk Islam.[2]

A text illustrating aspects of folk Islam

Folk Islam naturally cannot be studied through texts in the same way as other aspects of Islam. The following document, however, called 'Ode of the Shawl' or 'The Prophet's Mantle' (*Qasidatu-l-burda*), is an excellent example of one aspect of folk Islam, the veneration of the Prophet. The author, al-Bushiri, was an Egyptian who lived in the thirteenth century. He wrote the poem in praise of the Prophet while paralysed following a stroke. After writing the poem, he claimed that the Prophet came to him in a dream, wrapped him in his mantle and healed him completely.

The poem has had a strong hold on the popular imagination of Muslims, and is still recited all over the Arabic-speaking and the Muslim world on social and religious occasions. It is also used as an amulet for protection against disease and as a cure. The following is a selection of the verses which speak about the Prophet Muhammad, many of which express ideas which orthodox Muslims would never associate with the Prophet.

Muhammad, Lord of both worlds and both races
   and both peoples, Arab and non-Arab,
Our Prophet, who commands and forbids,
   there is none more just than he in saying 'No' or 'Yes'.
He is the Friend whose intercession is to be hoped for
   Assaulting every kind of fearful threat . . .
He excelled the prophets in bodily form and character,
   nor did they approach him in deed or in honour [nobility] . . .
For it is he whose inner meaning and outward form are perfect;
   wherefore the Creator of souls chose him as a friend.
He is free from peer in his excellent qualities,
   so that the essence of goodness is in him undivided.
Leave aside what Christians claim for their Prophet,
   and judge what you will in praise of him; and be reasonable . . .
For the excellence of the Apostle of God has no limit which
   may be expressed by word of mouth.[3]

Many of the sayings of the Prophet Muhammad recorded in *hadith* offer guidance as to how to deal with the different kinds of forces which seek to do us harm.

Lower your utensils and tie your waterskins and close your doors and keep your children close to you at night, as the jinns spread out at such time and snatch things away.

These privies are frequented by jinns and devils. So when anyone amongst you goes there, he should say, 'I seek refuge in Allah from male and female devils.'

When a person enters his house and mentions the name of Allah at the time of entering it and while eating food, Satan says (addressing himself): You have no place to spend the night and no evening meal; but when he enters without mentioning the name of Allah, Satan says: You have found a place to spend the night and an evening meal.

13. THE SPREAD AND DEVELOPMENT OF ISLAM

This chapter presents a brief overview of the spread and development of Islam by focusing on six major themes. Under the first five headings we note some important events and then seek to understand their significance for the history of Islam.

The first Islamic conquests

632	The death of Muhammad.
632–61	The 'Rightly Guided' Caliphs (Abu Bakr, 'Umar, 'Uthman, 'Ali).
632–4	The Wars of Apostasy; Arabia is brought back under Islam.
635	Damascus is attacked; and surrenders 637.
636	Battle of Yarmuk.
638	Jerusalem surrenders.
642	Alexandria and Egypt surrender.
636–46	Iraq and Persia surrender.
647	First raid into Tunisia; Kairouan founded 670.
656–61	Civil war within Muslim community; Kharijites challenge leadership of 'Ali and secede; Sunni-Shi'ite split.

661–750	The Umayyad dynasty in Damascus.
661	Mu'awiya, governor of Damascus, defeats caliph 'Ali; centre of power moves from Medina to Damascus.
691	Dome of the Rock built in Jerusalem by caliph 'Abd al-Malik.
711	Muslim armies reach the Indus River (Sindh in Pakistan). General Tariq crosses from Gibraltar into Spain.
732	Charles Martel defeats the Muslims at Poitiers/Tours in France; Muslim advance is halted.
750	Umayyad dynasty in Damascus is overthrown by a revolt; centre of power moves from Damascus to Baghdad under the Abbasid dynasty (750–1258).
756	A descendant of the Umayyad dynasty establishes a rival caliphate in Cordoba, Spain.

Table 13.1

When Muhammad died, a number of tribes in Arabia stopped paying tribute to the Muslim rulers, arguing that the agreement they had made ended with his death. This rebellion was regarded as apostasy from Islam, and in the 'Wars of Apostasy' force was used to bring them back under Islamic rule. One of the most outstanding military leaders in this early period was Khalid bin Walid, who 'contributed more than any other man, apart from Muhammad, towards the creation of Islam as a world power'.[1] He was criticized for his harsh treatment of prisoners, and was later dismissed by the caliph 'Umar. This is how William Montgomery Watt describes the process by which Arabia came under Islamic rule:

> Since apart from alliances, every tribe was against every other tribe, a tribe had to be either for Muhammad or against him after his conquest of Mecca. Neutrality was impossible when his power could be felt in most parts of Arabia. The decision to be for Muhammad or against him was basically a political decision. The religious aspect came in because Muhammad insisted that those who wanted to become his allies must accept him as a prophet, and this involved becoming Muslims.[2]

During the lifetime of Muhammad, Byzantium and Persia were the two great world powers, and although they had both been weakened in the wars they fought against each other, they still presented a considerable threat to the expansion of the Muslim Arabs and Islam. According to Islamic tradition, Muhammad sent messengers before his death to the rulers of Byzantium, Persia, Abyssinia and Egypt, inviting them to accept Islam. One version of the text of the letter he sent to Emperor Heraclius reads as follows:

> In the name of God, the Merciful, the Compassionate. From Muhammad
> ibn Abdullah to Heraclius, Emperor of Byzantium. Peace be upon the
> rightly-guided. I call you to the religion of Islam. If you convert you will
> be saved and God will double your reward. If you do not convert,
> responsibility for the salvation of your subjects rests with you.[3]

Part of the significance of this invitation is that in traditional Islamic thinking, a refusal from any group to embrace Islam provides a justification for attacking them. If they have rejected the invitation to accept Islam, the Muslims have justification for making war on them. In 634 the patriarch Sophronius in Jerusalem said in a sermon that the Arabs who were plundering around Jerusalem 'boast that they will conquer the whole world'.[4]

Some Christian communities welcomed the arrival of the Muslims. Syrian Christians, for example, saw Muslim Arab rule as an alternative to the harsh rule of Byzantium, and in Egypt the Muslims helped the Copts to depose a puppet patriarch and recall their own patriarch. The Copts joined forces with the Muslims to drive out the Byzantines, and paid less tax to the Muslims than they had done to Byzantium.

All non-Muslims living under Islamic rule paid a land tax (*kharaj*). Jews and Christians were treated as *dhimmis*, members of protected communities, and paid in addition a special poll tax called the *jizya*. They were not allowed to do military service or pay the alms tax that was paid by Muslims. The *dhimma* system remained in force until it was modified in the nineteenth century by the *millet* system introduced by the Ottoman Empire and then set aside with the creation of nation states (see chapter 31, 'Facing the political challenge of Islam').

It is an unhelpful and misleading half-truth to say that 'Islam was spread by the sword'. Muslims cannot deny that Arabia came under the rule of Islam *partly* through peaceful preaching and *partly* through conquest. It was Muslim Arab armies which spread out across

Palestine and Syria, Iraq, Persia and North Africa, and there was some fierce fighting when General Khalid brought the Punjab in North-west India under Islamic rule. Muslims would claim that even when Islamic rule spread through conquest, there were few forced conversions. John Taylor, a Christian scholar of Islam, attempts to be scrupulously fair in this description of what was involved in the spread of Islam in the early period:

> When Islam spread rapidly over much of the civilized world it spread first as a military and political success story; yet it was sometimes centuries before the inhabitants of the conquered lands voluntarily became Muslims. On the other hand, the motives in the minds of the caliphs behind the military expansion was that ultimately there should be those conversions to Islam; in the minds of the soldiers, as in every other generation, there was the desire for the spoils of war; but the Muslim conquests were remarkable for their discipline and lack of wanton destruction.[5]

If *jihad* was one of the main motives underlying the expansion of Islam, many Muslims today feel that it is very misleading to translate it as 'holy war'. Andrew Rippin gives the following explanation of how the scholars of Islam came eventually to understand the concept of *jihad*:

> The necessity of the armed struggle against the unbelievers was clearly indicated in the Qur'an, as in Qur'an 22:39: 'Permission is given to those [believers] who are fighting [the disbelievers] because they have been wronged. Surely God is able to give them victory!' Whether this was a defensive or offensive struggle mattered little because the resistance of people to Islam was often taken to be the equivalent to an attack on Islam. The final goal of *jihad* must then be a world which has been brought under the control of Islam and is, by definition, peaceful.
>
> Underlying the idea of *jihad* is a unified Muslim community, the *umma*, which has the collective duty to expand Islam ... An expansionist war would not be undertaken without first issuing a call for the unbelievers to join Islam; should there be resistance to that call, then the war was justified. This notion of a unified community underlying the idea of *jihad* is crucial because it emphasizes the political (as opposed to religious) significance of the doctrine, certainly as it evolved.[6]

The spread of Islam in Africa and Asia

900 onwards	Muslim traders begin crossing the Sahara into West Africa. They settle along the coast of East Africa. By 1400 Zanzibar is Islamicized.
c. 1000–1250	Military conquest of North India under Mahmud, a Turkish ruler of Ghazna (Afghanistan); the first Muslim sultan in India is installed.
1054	The Almoravid dynasty in Mauretania conquers the area of Ghana in West Africa north of the river Niger.
c. 1000–1100	After centuries of penetration by Muslim traders into West Africa south of the Sahara, several sultans are converted to Islam.
1206	Another Turkish dynasty brings North and North-east India under Islam; the sultanate of Delhi is set up.
1220	Mughal invasion of Persia under Genghiz Khan.
1258	Baghdad is destroyed.
1200–1300	Islam reaches Indonesia; Java is converted to Islam.
c. 1700–1800	There is a string of Muslim states south of the Sahara between the Atlantic and the Red Sea.
1800–80	Jihad Wars in West Africa bringing Muslim tribes to more faithful adherence to Islam. Muslims begin to penetrate inland in East Africa.

Table 13.2

Muslim armies conquered North-west India by force. The Turkish general, Mahmud, regarded his war in the Punjab as a war against infidels and idolaters; Hindu idols were smashed and some Hindu priests executed. But the tolerance that had earlier been offered to Jews and Christians was later extended towards Zoroastrians, Hindus and Buddhists on the subcontinent.

Islam penetrated into West Africa first through traders who crossed the Sahara. After several centuries of trading relationships, some kings and sultans converted to Islam. 'In this context,' says Jacques Jomier, 'Islam was above all an Islam of finance, of men of letters, of warriors, of traders. The role played at a very early stage by the pilgrimage of rulers to Mecca and the existence of schools in which Arabic was taught should be noted. In fact, Arabic script was adopted and cultural links were established with Muslim centres in North Africa, Mecca and Cairo.'[7]

If we try to list some of the main factors which contributed to the appeal of Islam as it spread in Africa and Asia, these would seem to be some of the most important: liberation from foreign rule; the tolerant spirit of Islam; its closeness to the Christian faith; its willingness to accommodate local religion and culture; its simplicity and rationality; and the moral superiority of its culture and civilization.[8]

In later stages of the spread of Islam in West Africa, some of the Muslim brotherhoods or orders, like the Qadiriyya, played an important role. A series of Jihad Wars, for example under Uthman Dan Fodio, was also significant for bringing large areas under the control of Muslim rulers and enforcing a stricter observance of Islam. According to Jacques Jomier, 'It took a long time for the mass of the people to be affected. It seems that it was the brotherhoods on the one hand and the holy wars waged by the Fulani kingdoms in the eighteenth and nineteenth centuries on the other which allowed the penetration into the bush and the countryside.'[9]

In the course of its spread in Africa, Islam has often been accepted on the surface, without radically changing the world view and practices of African traditional religion. In most of Africa this has created a strong folk Islam which looks very different from traditional orthodox Islam. In the words of Jacques Jomier, 'Since Islam asks only for a simple profession of faith from the new convert, he and even his descendants often continue to think and act in ways which are very dubious.'[10] When Islam gained power, however, traditional customs and structures were banned and destroyed.

In many places in Asia, Islam was spread largely by traders, teachers and holy men, but also by local wars. According to Fazlur Rahman, 'Those people who spread Islam were mainly Sufis who attracted non-Muslim masses towards Islam by their spiritual activity and their broad humanitarian services to all sorts of people whether Muslim or non-Muslim.'[11] Muslims were considered superior because they were literate, were engaged in healing, and were more wealthy.

The slave trade, which began in the early period of the spread of Islam and was directed from the Middle East and Arabia, played a

significant role in the extension of Islamic influence and power in both
East Africa and West Africa. It took large numbers of Africans into
the Middle East who eventually converted to Islam. Similarly, within
Africa itself the slave trade and enslavement escalated during the Jihad
period, resulting in large-scale enslavement by Muslim compatriots of
Africans who practised traditional religions. The social disruptions
engendered by the slave raiding coupled with the fact that slaves always
adopted the religion and way of life of their masters contributed to the
conversion of a significant proportion of Africans to Islam.[12]

At the beginning of the Abbasid dynasty in Baghdad in 750 the
Islamic world was still united, and its empire was still highly successful
and powerful. Two caliphs in particular, Harun al-Rashid (786–809)
and al-Ma'mun (813–33), are particularly remembered for the splend-
our of their courts and for scientific and cultural achievements during
their reigns. This Golden Age lasted until the end of the tenth century.
During this period, however, the political unity of the empire was
declining, as one province after another gained its independence. From
now on the caliph only enjoyed an honorary position of leadership
over the Muslim world.

Relationships between Islam and Europe

711	The Moors cross from Gibraltar into Spain.
732	Charles Martel defeats the Muslim armies at Poitiers/Tours.
1060	Beginning of campaign to drive the Moors out of Spain (the Reconquista).
1096–1291	The Crusades.
1095	Pope Urban II calls for a Crusade at Clermont in France.
1096	The Crusaders capture Jerusalem.
1169	Saladin (Salah al-Din) recaptures Jerusalem.
1291	The fall of Acre and the end of Crusader rule.
1396	The Turks enter Eastern Europe.
1453	The fall of Constantinople to the Ottoman Turks.
1565	Turkish attack on Malta repulsed.
1683	Turkish attack on Vienna repulsed.

Table 13.3

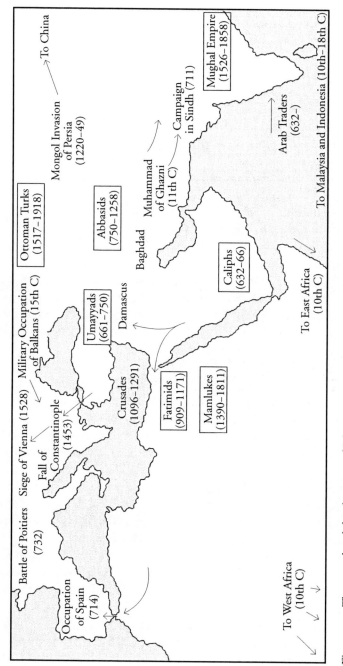

Figure 13.1 The spread and development of Islam

Even today Muslims look back with pride to the nearly 800 years of Islamic rule in Spain. This was a time of peaceful coexistence between Muslims, Christians and Jews, with all three communities contributing to the flowering of culture, science and medicine. Buildings which still stand today combined Islamic and Spanish styles of architecture. There were well-known Islamic scholars like Ibn Hazm and Ibn Arabi, and mystic Jewish philosophers like Maimonides. The title of Salman Rushdie's novel *The Moor's Last Sigh* is the name of the place from which Boabdil, the last Moorish king of Granada, took his final look at the city after surrendering it to the Spanish in 1492.

In spite of the peaceful coexistence of Muslims and Christians in Spain, the attitudes of Europeans towards Islam during the Middle Ages can be summed up with the words 'ignorance', 'fear', 'suspicion' and 'hostility'. The first translation of the Qur'an into Latin was in 1143. But most Europeans knew little about Islam, and what they did know included some very malicious distortions of the faith and practice of Islam. They feared and despised Islam at the same time, and no doubt also felt a certain envy towards a civilization that was in many respects superior to their own.[13]

Although the Crusades were not perceived at the time by Muslims as religious wars and did not have a serious long-term effect on Muslim rule in Palestine and Syria, they have had a lasting impact for two main reasons. First, they embittered relations between Christians and Muslims for centuries. From now on the attitudes towards Christians living under Islamic rule and towards Christians in Europe became harder. Second, the Crusades severely weakened Eastern Christianity, leaving Byzantium more exposed to attack from the Turks, who were growing in power and pressing westwards from the twelfth century. The fall of Byzantium to the Turks in 1453 can therefore be seen as an indirect result of the Crusades.

The Crusaders were finally expelled in 1492, but in the minds of many Muslims today the Crusades have never ended. When Columbus sailed westwards for the New World in 1492, he was looking for new sources of wealth which could be used in the struggle against the Muslim world. And when General Gouraud entered Damascus at the head of the French forces in 1917 and stood at the grave of Saladin, he said, 'Saladin, we have returned. My

presence here constitutes a victory of the Cross over the Crescent.'[14]
Many Muslims have seen the recent wars in the Middle East as a
continuation of the Crusades, with the Christian West trying to rule
over the Muslim East.

Islamic empires and dynasties

Under this heading we note the times and places where Muslims were
'a dominant force on the world stage, united in a single international
community and unaffected by differences of language, culture and
outlook'.[15]

750–1258	The Abbasid dynasty in Baghdad.
969–1171	The Fatimid dynasty (Shi'ite) rules in Egypt.
969	Cairo is founded as their capital and becomes the centre of the Islamic world.
1254–1517	The Mamluk Dynasty in Egypt.
1453	The Ottoman Turks capture Byzantium (Constantinople). Beginning of the Muslim advance into the Balkans.
1492	The fall of Granada; Muslims are finally driven out of Spain.
1503–1722	The Safavid Empire in Persia. Shi'ite Islam becomes the state religion of Persia.
1512–1917	The Ottoman Empire, based in Turkey, rules Asia Minor, Syria, Palestine, Iraq, Arabia, Egypt, parts of North Africa and the Balkans.
1529, 1683	Ottoman Turks attack Vienna, but are driven back.
1526–1858	The Mughal Empire in North India.

Table 13.4

When Muslims are critical of centuries of Western imperialism which
they believe was in one way or another associated with Christianity, it
is only fair to point out that Islam too has had its empires. Is there
not, for example, some similarity between Muslim rule in Andalusia
(Spain) and the British Raj in India? There is little to be gained by
comparing the record of Western 'Christian' imperialism with that
of 'Islamic' imperialism. *Both* faiths have created empires; *both*

communities inevitably look back to the past with mixed feelings – certainly with a sense of pride for all that was achieved, but also at times with shame for the violence which was sometimes associated with their expansion. So, for example, if Christians in the West need to try to understand what it felt like for Muslims on the Indian subcontinent or in Indonesia to be under Western 'Christian' rule for two centuries, Muslims need to ask themselves what it was like for Christians in the Middle East to be living under Islamic rule for fourteen centuries.

European imperialism

1757	Start of British expansion in India.
1792	William Carey begins his work in India.
1798–1801	Napoleon's occupation of Egypt; first period of European rule in a Muslim country.
1800–12	Henry Martyn's work in India and Persia.
1854	Pfander's public debate at Agra in India.
1881	Britain takes control of Egypt after the Urabi revolution.
1857	The Indian Mutiny/War of Independence.
1910	The Edinburgh Missionary Conference.
1917	General Allenby enters Jerusalem.
1918	Defeat of Ottoman Turks and end of Ottoman Empire.
1922	Caliphate abolished by Ataturk in Turkey.
1948	State of Israel established.

Table 13.5

This period marks what Colin Turner calls 'the slow but inexorable decline of the Muslim world, culturally, economically and politically'. He continues:

> For as the three great empires of the medieval Muslim world – the Ottomans in Asia Minor, the Safavids in Iran, and the Moghuls in the Indian sub-continent – entered the eighteenth century, they did so against a backdrop of gradual decay, disillusion and discontent, moving from 'golden age' to old age with depressing inevitability.[16]

The whole of the Muslim world (except Arabia, Turkey, Iran and Afghanistan) was under Western imperial rule at one time or another, in some cases for two hundred years. The significance of this can only be understood against the background of centuries of the great Islamic empires and the basic conviction that 'Islam must rule'. Kenneth Cragg explains why Muslims have found it difficult to accept the idea of Muslims being ruled by non-Muslims:

> Islam was largely under non-Muslim government in wide areas of its dispersion. Western imperial control did not, by and large, affect the practice of religion. It did not close mosques, forbid Ramadan, pilgrimage, or prescribe belief. By all these 'religious' tests (as westerners might see them), Islam was altogether free. But, politically, in many cases, Muslims did not rule themselves. Recall the basic conviction, arising from its origins, that Islam must rule. Recall the long caliphal history when Islam did rule. From the Hijrah on, Islam had bound religion and rule to one. Not, then, to have Muslim rule, however free the rituals, is not to be Islam in a full sense. It is a state of exile, the puzzle and pain of which caused much debate in the nineteenth century. In India, for example ... Islam was bewildered and dismayed.[17]

Muslims tend to associate Western imperialism with Christian mission, since in many cases missionaries followed the traders and the soldiers, taking advantage of their relationship with the imperial powers to spread the Christian message. The perception of Muslims is that these two movements came basically from the same source – the desire of the Christian West to dominate the world. Historians would say that the relationship between mission and imperialism was much more complex, and that similar analyses can be suggested concerning the relationship between Islamic mission and Islamic expansion.

The political and economic decline of the Muslim world forced many Muslims to do some serious soul-searching. If Islam is supposed to be victorious, they asked, and if imperial rule and prosperity are signs of God's vindication of Islam, why has he allowed the Muslim world to decline so far? In response to all that Westerners brought to the Muslim world, some Muslims tried to work out the reasons for the success and prosperity of the West and were determined to learn all

they could from the West. The *Tanzimat* reforms in the Ottoman
Empire, for example, which began in 1839, introduced highly
significant changes, making all religious communities equal before
the law. They were 'the most far-reaching yet attempted in the Muslim
world, and easily the most revolutionary'.[18] Others may have appreci-
ated the material benefits that they were receiving, but resisted some
of the ideas that were associated with Western thinking – such as its
questioning of faith and its separation of religion and state. This
is how the basic dilemma of Muslims is summed up by Andrew
Rippin:

> The rise of Europe as a colonialist power ... shattered a deeply held
> Muslim idea – even, it might be said, one of the basic presuppositions
> of Islamic existence. A crisis of identity faced those who did not get
> carried away on the Western bandwagon and who wished to investigate
> the roots of the problem. The modern situation was perceived to be
> one of a fundamental challenge to Islam, therefore; the failure to
> be able to respond would be the failure of Islam as a religion. What,
> then, is the status of Islam when it is not in political ascendancy in
> the world?[19]

The creation of the state of Israel in 1948 is seen by most Arabs and
Muslims as the last – and perhaps the most bitter – example of
Western imperialism. From their point of view, Jews (mostly from
Europe) were coming as colonizers to settle alongside the small
Jewish communities which had existed in Palestine for centuries, but
in the process were dispossessing thousands of Palestinians. All this
was happening in the heartlands of Islam and under the protection
of Western powers (especially Britain and the USA). But whereas
Western imperialism elsewhere in the world gave way to the creation
of independent states – many of them Islamic – the Zionist state of
Israel has remained as a thorn in the flesh to the Arab and Muslim
worlds. It is often perceived as an unwanted transplant or even as a
cancerous growth at the heart of the Islamic world. Westerners may
want to challenge this perception; but if we want to understand the
anger that has been building up within the Muslim world in recent
decades, it is important that we try to understand what the creation of
Israel has meant for Muslims.[20]

Movements of revival and reform

Against the background of despair and defeat created by the decline of great Islamic empires and Western rule over most of the Muslim world, we turn now to consider ten people who led movements for the reform and renewal of Islam between the eighteenth and twentieth centuries. All of them were in one way or another responding to the profound impact of Western imperial rule. All had to work out their diagnosis of the decline of the Muslim world and their recommendations as to how to recover the pure Islam of the Prophet's time. How much could they respond *positively* to all that the West was offering, and how much did they need to respond *negatively*? In the first half of the nineteenth century Muslims tended to be more positive towards the West. But gradually their responses became more negative as they saw what European imperialism was doing to their part of the world and understood the less than altruistic motives of the colonizers.

Shah Wali Allah (1702–62) of Delhi worked for the renewal of Islam in India through a return to the pure Islam of the Prophet's time and the ideals of Sufism. For him this meant getting rid of Hindu elements that had crept into Islam, and encouraging the hope that Muslim government would once again be restored. In Wali Allah's view of Islam, 'a broad, humanistic sociological basis is overlain by a doctrine of social and economic justice in Islamic terms and crowned by a Sufi world view' (Fazlur Rahman). According to S. M. Ikram, a Pakistani historian, 'More than anyone else he is responsible for the religious regeneration of Indian Islam.'

Muhammad ibn 'Abd al-Wahhab (1703–91) was an Arab sheikh who was trained in the school of Hanbali jurisprudence and the teaching of Ibn Taymiyya (died 1328). After years of travel in Iraq and Persia, he returned to Arabia at the age of forty and began a movement for the purification of Islam. The main targets of his attack were (1) aspects of popular Islam, such as the veneration of saints, visiting the tombs of saints, belief in the intercession of the Prophet and saints, and other forms of what he regarded as superstition; (2) the lowering of moral standards among Muslims; and (3) additions to basic Islamic beliefs and practices from the Sufis, philosophers and theologians. He appealed to the Qur'an and the *sunna* as the only sources of authority and rejected all other later Muslim authorities, and saw the Islamic state founded by the Prophet in Medina as the model that represented the Golden Age of Islam. This movement became the official brand of Islam for Saudi Arabia when it was created in 1932, and from there has spread all over the Islamic world. Osama bin Laden and many of the Islamic radicals today have their roots within this tradition.

Sayyid Ahmad Khan (1817–98) of Delhi was much more positive than many other Muslims towards modern scientific knowledge, and argued that it was fully compatible with Islam. He also tried to convince fellow Muslims that Islam and Christianity have much in common. He founded the famous Aligargh College. 'It is to him', says Trevor Ling, 'that a great deal of credit must be given for the awakening of the Muslims of India to a new understanding of the possible place of Islamic religion in the modern world.'[21]

Jamal al-Din al-Afghani (1839–97) was probably born in Iran, but spent most of his life in different Muslim countries, especially Afghanistan, India and Egypt, and later in Istanbul. He was more concerned with the social and political issues facing Muslims, and argued that if Muslims were to benefit from Western technology, they must at the same time recover the spiritual tradition and culture of Islam. In his concern to unite the Muslim world against Western imperialism, he became the leader of a pan-Islamic movement which called for the creation of an Islamic world state.

Muhammad 'Abduh (1849–1905), a disciple of al-Afghani, was an Egyptian theologian who taught at the Al-Azhar University in Cairo, and was critical of the rigidity and conservatism of many orthodox theologians whose minds seemed closed to everything in the modern world. He stood for a liberal and open kind of Islam, arguing that faith and reason were compatible, and that there need be no contradiction between faith and modern knowledge. He wanted to see greater flexibility in the formulation of Islamic law, believing that traditional laws should in certain cases be replaced by laws more appropriate to the social context. He was not, however, prepared to apply modern critical methods to the study of the Qur'an. As a result of his teaching, a new kind of secular modernism grew up in the Middle East, some of whose adherents called for the separation of religion and state. At the same time there was opposition from fundamentalist groups who wanted to return to the Qur'an and *sunna*.

Muhammad Iqbal (1873–1938) was for many years the leader of the Muslim League, a movement founded in 1906 to focus on the political aspirations of Muslims in India. From 1930 he began to argue for a separate Muslim state in India, and because of his widespread influence he is generally regarded as 'the spiritual founder of the state of Pakistan'. He believed that the interpretation of Islamic law needed to be opened up in a radically new way. He is also well known for his writings as a poet and philosopher.

Mawlana Abul A'la Mawdudi (1903–79) was a journalist and a self-taught Islamic scholar who founded the organization *Jama'at-i-Islami* (Community of Islam) in 1941. Although at first he opposed the idea of establishing a separate Muslim state, when the state of Pakistan came into existence in 1947 he settled in it, making his aim 'the thorough Islamization of the government of Pakistan and its purging from all Western moral, spiritual and political values and practices'. His writings have been widely distributed in many languages, and through the movement he created he continues to have a profound influence on Muslims all over the world who want to see the establishment of genuinely Islamic societies.

Hasan al-Banna (1906–49) was brought up in a small village in the Nile Delta in Egypt and learned much of his Islam from his father, who was a graduate of the Al-Azhar University in Cairo. While working as a teacher in Ismailiyya on the Suez Canal, he became acutely aware of the depressed state of the Muslim world – politically, culturally and economically. He and some friends bound themselves together by an oath in 1928 and founded a movement for moral and spiritual regeneration called the Muslim Brotherhood (*al-Ikhwan al-Muslimun*). During the 1930s and 1940s the movement grew rapidly and became more political, being officially banned at times by the government for demanding that the *shari'a* should be established as the law of the country. After a member of the Brotherhood assassinated the prime minister who had banned the movement, Banna himself was assassinated by the secret police. The Brotherhood, although officially suppressed in some Arab countries, is still very active under other names. Banna and Mawdudi were the first Muslim thinkers to call for the creation of 'the Islamic state' and the full implementation of *shari'a* either by peaceful means or through revolution and violence.

Sayyid Qutb (1906–66) worked for some years as a school teacher in Egypt and then as a government official in the Ministry of Education. While he admired many things in the West, as a result of two years spent in the USA between 1948 and 1950, he became a strong critic of what he saw as degenerate Western societies. He worked with the Muslim Brotherhood, and was critical of the secularist approach of Nasser's revolution in Egypt. During the nine years that he spent in prison (when he was sometimes tortured), he wrote one of his most important works, *Signposts on the Way*, which was published in 1964 after his release from prison. He applied the concept of *al-jahiliyya*, the Age of Ignorance, to Islamic countries today, and believed that violence and terrorism were justified in the *jihad* to overthrow existing governments which were not sufficiently Islamic. His writings have inspired some of the more extreme Islamist groups like *Islamic Jihad*, *Takfir wal-Hijra*, *Hizb-ut Tahrir* and *al-Qa'ida*.

Ayatollah Khomeini (1900–89) was born into a family in which both his father and grandfather had been religious scholars. At the age of nineteen he began his studies in the religious sciences under Shi'ite scholars, mostly at the holy city of Qom to the south of Tehran. He soon attracted the attention of his teachers and colleagues because of the way he combined a deep spirituality and mysticism with a passionate concern for social and political issues. He found himself in opposition to the Iranian monarchy, which he saw as a totalitarian dictatorship determined to eliminate Islam as a cultural, social and political force. After his first public statement against the government in 1943, he became a popular leader who expressed the aspirations of his people. He was arrested in 1963 after protesting a series of measures that he believed would bring the country further under foreign influence. He was later released, and during periods of exile in Turkey, Iraq and France (1964–79) his influence spread through the tapes of his lectures and sermons which were distributed through the network of mosques within Iran. He received a rapturous welcome when he returned to Tehran in 1979 after the Shah had left the country. In a legal ruling (*fatwa*) some months after the publication of the book *The Satanic Verses* in 1988, he pronounced the death sentence on its author, Salman Rushdie. He introduced the doctrine of *vilayat-i faqih*, the vice-gerency of the theologian/jurist, which means in practice that the nation needs to be led by men of religion rather than politicians, and he remained the leader of the Islamic Revolution in Iran until his death in 1989.

Having surveyed the spread and development of Islam over fourteen centuries, we now turn to look at the main branches of Islam and some of the many movements that are active today.

Muslims believe that there is much more unity among Muslims than there is among Christians. One of the reasons for this unity is the simplicity of the 'five pillars' and the core beliefs of Islam. Another reason may have been the authority and comparative unanimity of orthodox jurists and theologians over the centuries. At the same time, however, there are many significant differences between the various branches of Islam and the different movements within it at the present time. Writing about Muslims and Islam in Europe today, Philip Lewis says that 'Islam is far less homogenous than outsiders commonly suppose'.[1]

The break between Sunnis and Shi'ites

The break between the two main branches of Islam – Sunnis and Shi'ites – goes back to AD 661, the year that 'Ali, the fourth caliph, died.

The word 'Sunni' comes from the Arabic *sunna*, meaning the way or practice of the Prophet. Sunnis accepted all the four Rightly Guided Caliphs who led the community in Medina, and later accepted the claim of Mu'awiya, the governor of Syria, to take over the caliphate and become the leader of the Muslim community after the death of 'Ali. The Abbasid caliphs who ruled in Baghdad from 750 to 1258 were all Sunnis. The caliphate then passed to the Fatimids in Cairo, who were Shi'ites, and it was revived again by the Ottomans in 1725, but was abolished by Ataturk in 1924. Approximately 90% of the Muslims in the world today are Sunnis.

The word 'Shi'ite', or 'Shi'i', comes from the Arabic word *shi'a*, meaning 'party', and refers to 'the party of 'Ali'. The fundamental reason for this major split within the Muslim community was the belief of these Muslims that the leader of the Muslim community

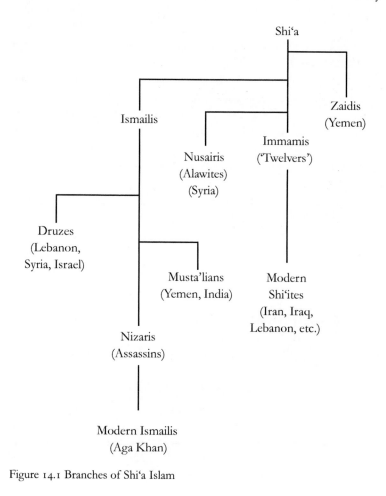

Figure 14.1 Branches of Shi'a Islam

ought to be someone from within the family of the Prophet. Of the four caliphs, therefore, they accepted only 'Ali, the fourth caliph, who was the husband of Fatima, the Prophet's daughter, and therefore the Prophet's son-in-law.

When Ali was assassinated in 661, his followers wanted Ali's two sons to take over the leadership. But Hasan declined to be caliph and Husayn was killed in the Battle of Kerbala in 680. The martyr-dom of Husayn is extremely significant for Shi'ites and is re-enacted annually during the feast of Muharram. The tomb of Husayn in Kerbala has become an important shrine for Shi'ites.

The Shi'ite community was led by a succession of twelve imams, although they had no political power within the larger Sunni com-munity. The twelfth imam disappeared or went into hiding (known as 'Occultation') in 874. It is believed that from his position of Occultation he has guided the Shi'ite community until now and will one day reappear to ensure the vindication of the Shi'ite community. The largest group of Shi'ites in the world are called 'Twelvers' because of their belief in the twelve imams. Some groups of Shi'ites are known as 'Seveners' because they acknowledge only the first seven imams. Over the centuries they have subdivided into several smaller groups as follows.

Shi'ism became the state religion of Persia in 1501. It has become particularly significant as a result of the Islamic Revolution in Iran in 1979 and the spread of Iran's influence within Iraq and Lebanon.

Distinctive beliefs of Shi'ites

The imams who have led their community have been regarded as infallible teachers. While Sunnis have looked to the community to discern the consensus that was developing among them, Shi'ites have looked to their imams to give them definitive interpretations of Islamic belief and practice.

There is a strong belief that the twelfth imam will one day emerge from his Occultation and return to the world as 'the *Mahdi*' (a word that means literally 'the guide'). This has created a strong eschato-logical hope among Shi'ites which has many similarities to Christian belief in the second coming of Christ. This belief is especially strong in Iran today, and Shi'ites there believe that the Islamic Revolution that was led by Ayatollah Khomeini and continues under his successors is preparing the way for the imminent return of the Mahdi.

Shi'ites have their own commentaries on the Qur'an and their own distinctive ways of interpreting it, which are generally less literal and more free and open. They also have their own collections of *hadith*.

Because of the importance of the martyrdom of Husayn, they have a strong appreciation for the place of patient endurance of suffering. They do not believe, however, that Husayn's suffering has any redemptive value. For most of their history they have been a power-less minority in the Muslim world. This makes their new-found power in Iran, Iraq and Lebanon all the more significant.

Shi'ites have held to a belief known as *taqiyya*, which is often translated as 'dissimulation'. This is the belief that it is legitimate for Muslims not to tell the truth about their Shi'ite faith if it will help them to save their lives. This idea developed in the context in which the Shi'ite minority experienced discrimination, if not persecution, from the Sunni majority and its political and religious leaders during the Abbasid period.

The Islamic Republic of Iran, created in 1979 under the leadership of Ayatollah Khomeini, is highly significant because it marks the first time for many centuries that Shi'ites have gained political power. The decline of Iraq has made Iran a major player in the politics of the Middle East, and its alliances with the Shi'ite majority in Iraq and the Shi'ite community in Lebanon present a significant challenge to Sunni Muslims elsewhere in the Middle East.

Modern movements within Islam today

The following movements reflect the ethnic origins of different Muslim communities in Britain, but also give some idea of the diversity of the movements which exist in many Western countries.[2]

The Deobandis

A movement named after Deoband, a town north of Delhi, at which an Islamic seminary was founded in 1867 to strengthen the Islamic identity of Indian Muslims in a context where they had to survive without the support of political power since the British now ruled. It sought to reconstruct personal and communal life according to

Islamic norms freely embraced. To this end it sought to publicize widely Islamic legal decisions (*fatwa*), encourage social distance from non-Muslims and their influences, and embody a reformed Sufism critical of some aspects of folk Islam as practised at Muslim shrines.

Tablighi Jama'at (The Faith Movement)

A revivalist movement within the Deobandi tradition, with a strong emphasis on individual moral and spiritual renewal rather than on political goals. It was founded by Maulana Ilias (died 1944). The European headquarters are at Dewsbury, West Yorkshire, where large conferences are held. It embodies an isolationist ethos with regard to non-Muslim wider society.

Barelwis

A movement named after the home town of its founder, Ahmad Raza Khan, of Bareilly in North India (died 1921). It affirms traditional Sufism and the legitimacy of certain aspects of folk Islam, such as practices surrounding shaikhs (elders, or holy men) and shrines. This movement has rooted Islam in the hearts and minds of ordinary non-Arabic-speaking people through its development of devotional songs in vernacular languages (*qawwalis*).

Jama'at-i-Islami (The Islamic Party)

A politico-religious party embodying the notion of Islam as a comprehensive ideology and critical of pietistic Islam. Founded in 1941 in Pakistan by Abul A'la Mawdudi (died 1979). It has developed a strong political agenda in the British context. Groups in Britain within this tradition are UK Islamic Mission, The Islamic Foundation (Leicester), Young Muslims UK and The Islamic Society of Britain.

Ahl-i-Hadith (The People of Tradition)

A movement with an emphasis on individual personal faith rather than social or political awareness. The Islamic Propagation Centre (IPC) operates from their Birmingham office and distributes literature and videos (e.g. the debates of Ahmad Deedat, a South African anti-Christian polemicist). This movement is closest to the influential Saudi-supported Salafi movement and enjoys their financial support.

The Salafi movement

The term refers to the 'virtuous ancestors' – the first three generations of Muslims after the Prophet's death. The term is the preferred self-description of the Saudi 'Wahhabi movement', named after its founder, Muhammad ibn 'Abd al-Wahhab (died 1791). It is a puritanical, literalist tradition which has no time for any innovation (*bid'a*) – anything not rooted in the original textual sources of Islam. This means it is opposed to Sufism and Shi'a Islam alike. It has been influential in Britain through its extensive funding of Islamic centres, mosques and hundreds of religious scholars trained in Saudi Arabia at Saudi expense.

Muslim Council of Britain (MCB)

Founded in 1997 to promote co-operation, consensus and unity in Muslim affairs in the UK. Its structures include national, regional and local components, although support is strongest in London and weaker elsewhere in the UK. It is seen by many in the Barelwi tradition as a Sufi Wahhabi/Islamist tradition. This is why the latter organized an alternative national organization in 2005, the *British Muslim Forum*, which embodies their more accommodatory, Sufi ethos.

Hizb ut-Tahrir (The Party of Liberation)

Founded in 1952 in Palestine as a breakaway movement from the Muslim Brotherhood, it has developed a radical ideology working for the revival of the Islamic state using the word *Khalifa* ('The Caliphate'). It is active especially on campuses of British universities under a variety of names. It is a political movement with a high profile and significant as the first non-Asian group to win support among British Muslims. Its anti-democratic stance and frequently anti-Western diatribes – including anti-Semitism – have meant that since 7/7 the government has threatened to ban it. It has generated even more radical splinter movements, such as Al Muhajirun, whose leader Omar Bakri has now been banned from Britain.

The Taliban

Among the Pakistani Muslim community in the UK there is a smaller grouping with roots in the Frontier Province who share the same religious tradition (Deobandi) and ethnicity as the Taliban. Within this group, some will sympathize with the Taliban. This does not, however, equate to support for al-Qaʻida and Osama bin Laden.

Ahmadiyya

A movement founded by Mirza Ghulam Ahmad Khan (died 1908). In 1973 it was declared by the government of Pakistan to be heretical because of its claims that its founder was a prophet after Muhammad. It is therefore regarded by most Muslims as a sect outside the fold of Islam.

15. ISSUES FACING MUSLIMS TODAY

This chapter seeks to explain nine basic issues currently facing Islam and Muslims in the world. As in all the chapters in Part Two, the intention is not to criticize or to supply 'Christian answers'. The aim is still to understand, to sit where Muslims sit, and to seek to enter, as far as possible, into the dilemmas that they face in today's world. Similar questions could easily be listed which face Christians today.

1. Islam and the nation state: What does it mean for a state to be Islamic?

There are at present approximately forty-nine Muslim majority states, which together account for around 75% of the total number of Muslims in the world. They do not, however, all have the same kind of constitution, and do not all give the same place to Islamic law. While it is true that Muslims generally do not like to separate religion and state, *in practice* there are many different models of the role of Islamic law in relation to the state. Islamic countries today can therefore be divided into the following categories.

a. Islamic states where Islamic law is used almost exclusively,
   e.g. Saudi Arabia, Pakistan, the Gulf States. Iran comes into
   this category, but is slightly different because it is based on
   Shi'ite ideas introduced by Ayatollah Khomeini about *vilayat-i
   faqih*, the rule of the legal scholar.
b. Islamic states which use mainly *shari'a* law, e.g. Malaysia,
   Sudan.
c. States which use some *shari'a* and Western models, e.g. Egypt,
   Tunisia, Jordan, Morocco, Yemen and Indonesia.
d. States with a secular legal system, e.g. Turkey and the Central
   Asian Republics.

One of the demands of Islamists is that Muslim countries should
reject Western models entirely and return to Islamic law as the only
source of law in the country. Traditionalist, orthodox Muslims
would not go as far as this, but would want their governments to be
more consistent in upholding Islamic standards. Many moderate
Muslims, however, are willing to accept the present variety of
models in Muslim-majority states, and to be more pragmatic in the
way the laws of their country are framed. Appreciating the spirit of
Islamic law and seeking the common good in rapidly changing
situations are more important for them than strict adherence to
traditional Islamic law.

2. Pluralism and Muslim minorities: Can Muslims accept pluralism, and how should Muslims justify their existence as minorities in non-Islamic countries?

There are some verses in the Qur'an which seem to encourage a
positive acceptance of other faiths (e.g. 2:62; 5:48; 49:13). But as long
as Muslims continue to divide the world into *dar al-Islam* (the House of
Islam) and *dar al-harb* (the House of War) and want to engage in *jihad*
in order to bring the whole world under the rule of Islam, it is difficult
for them to accept the existence of so many different religions
alongside Islam in a pluralist world.

One of the most significant developments in the last fifty years,
therefore, has been the growth of Muslim communities in non-Islamic
countries. They now number about 25% of all Muslims, which means

that about one in four of all Muslims now lives in a very *un*-Islamic kind of situation. The basic dilemma faced by Muslims living in this kind of secular state was summed up in the following way by the late Zaki Badawi, an Egyptian Muslim who had lived for thirty-three years in Britain and became a highly respected Muslim leader and spokesperson in the country.

> As we know, the history of Islam as a faith is also the history of a state and a community of believers living by Divine law. The Muslims, jurists and theologians, have always expounded Islam as both a Government and a faith. This reflects the historical fact that Muslims, from the start, lived under their own law. Muslim theologians naturally produced a theology with this in view – it is a theology of the majority. Being a minority was not seriously considered or even contemplated. The theologians were divided in their attitude to the question of minority status. Some declared that it should not take place; that is to say that a Muslim is forbidden to live for any lengthy period under non-Muslim rule. Others suggested that a Muslim living under non-Muslim rule is under no obligation to follow the law of Islam in matters of public law. Neither of these two extremes is satisfactory. Throughout the history of Islam some pockets of Muslims lived under the sway of non-Muslim rulers, often without an alternative. They nonetheless felt sufficiently committed to their faith to attempt to regulate their lives in accordance with its rules and regulations in so far as their circumstances permitted. In other words, the practice of the community rather than the theories of the theologians provided a solution. Nevertheless Muslim theology offers, up to the present, no systematic formulation of the status of being a minority. The question is being examined. It is hoped that the matter will be brought to focus and that Muslim theologians from all over the Muslim world will delve into this thorny subject to allay the conscience of the many Muslims living in the West and also to chart a course for Islamic survival, even revival, in a secular society.[1]

These are new questions for Muslims and are both theological and political at the same time. Some have seen the first *Hijra*, the migration of some of Muhammad's followers who sought asylum in Christian Abyssinia, as an important precedent with suggestive similarities to the position of Muslims in non-Muslim Western societies. But it is not always easy for traditionalist Muslims to accept the kind of pluralism that exists in many countries of the world.

3. Unity: How should the unity of the Muslim world be expressed?

After centuries of Islamic empires followed by centuries of Western imperialism, by the 1960s Muslim countries throughout the world had regained their independence through the creation of nation states. The major preoccupation for many years was nation-building and the creation of supportive alliances. But some Muslims were asking how these different Muslim states could work together and how they should express their unity.

For many centuries the caliphate, located in the capital of the Ottoman Empire in Istanbul, represented an important focus of unity for the Sunni Muslim world. When it was abolished by Kemal Ataturk in 1924, Muslims were faced with the question of how the unity of the *umma*, the 'people' of Islam, should be expressed. Should it be through a single federation that links together all the Muslim countries in the world? Or should Islam accept the existence of independent nation states as inevitable and as the only realistic way of surviving in the modern world?

Islamic radicals in recent years have been extremely critical of nationalism, seeing it as an alien concept which was imposed on the Muslim world by the West. Some of them want to revive the caliphate as a way of creating a new focus for the unity of the Muslim world, and use the Arabic word *Khalifa* to express these hopes. The word has therefore become an important slogan for Islamists, a rallying cry expressing their hopes for a new kind of unity in the Muslim world which would come about through the restoration of Islamic states based on *shari'a*.

Various organizations have been created to develop closer links between Muslim countries – such as the Organization of the Islamic Conference (OIC) – and the heads of Muslim states meet from time to time. Those who go on pilgrimage to Mecca have a powerful sense of the unity of the Muslim world. But it is hard to find anything in Islam today that is comparable to the ecumenical movement and the

World Council of Churches. The bitter conflict between Sunnis and Shi'ites in Iraq and elsewhere in the Middle East is presenting a new challenge to the Muslim world. And the dilemma of how to express the unity of Muslim peoples in political terms in the world as it is today still remains.

4. Economics: Is there a uniquely Islamic approach to questions of wealth and poverty?

Many Muslims in recent years have been extremely critical of both capitalism and socialism, and have often said that Islam offers a middle ground between the two extremes. Although communism is no longer a valid option, certain aspects (such as the one-party state) have some attraction for Muslims in certain countries. The philosophy of the Ba'ath Socialist Party until now in Syria and in Iraq under Saddam Hussein until 2003, for example, has been described as 'the largest dose of Marxism that the Muslim mind can take'.

One particular area in which Muslims have tried to be consistent in following Islamic teaching is that of banking. The Qur'an explicitly forbids the taking of usury (*riba*) in verses such as these:

> Allah hath blighted usury and made almsgiving fruitful. Allah loveth not the impious and guilty ... O ye who believe! Observe your duty to Allah, and give up what remaineth (due to you) from usury, if ye are (in truth) believers. And if ye do not, then be warned of war (against you) from Allah and His messenger. And if ye repent, then ye have your principal (without interest). Wrong not, and ye shall not be wronged. (2:276–279; cf. 3:130; 4:161; 30:39)

If the Qur'an forbids the charging or receiving of interest, how is a modern bank to function? How are farmers and traders to raise the capital needed to start a business? Some see the development of Islamic banks in many countries as a bold attempt to obey qur'anic commands in the modern world and demonstrate an effective alternative to capitalism. The basic concept in Islamic banking is that if the lenders can share the *profits*, they must also take an equal share of the *risks* involved in any enterprise. As Paul Grieve explains, 'The fund as the investor, and the entrepreneur as the initiator and manager of the enterprise, share the risk, and the depositors behind the fund, who provide the capital, are paid a portion of the profit rather than a fixed rate of interest.'[2]

Others suspect that no economy can survive in the modern world without capital generating interest, and hold that Islamic banks in practice charge interest of a kind but simply call it by another name. Some of these questions are particularly acute when we recognize the irony in the uneven distribution of resources in the Muslim world. The wealthiest countries (such as Saudi Arabia) have the fewest people, while the poorest countries (such as Bangladesh) have the largest populations and the fewest natural resources.

Alongside these questions raised by Islamic law and tradition, there are the pressing questions posed by the big issues facing the human race: poverty, corruption, inequalities in world trade, global warming, HIV/Aids and terrorism. The Muslim understanding of human beings as God's 'caliphs' with a responsibility to care for creation on behalf of God should provide a firm theological basis for addressing concerns of this kind. It is perhaps significant that it is in the context of economic issues that Kenneth Cragg writes, 'Never before since the rise of their faith have Muslims had to reckon on so many fronts with so vigorous a challenge to both creed and will.'[3]

5. Questions about truth and scripture: How does Islam respond to questions about the truth of its scriptures?

Some of the most fundamental questions raised by Western philosophy in the last three hundred years have been in the area of the theory of knowledge (epistemology). The basic questions have been: 'How can we know anything?' and 'How can we know that anything is true?' These in turn have led to further questions about the truth of the Bible and the whole Christian revelation. The difficulty that Muslims have in responding to questions of this kind was summed up by Wilfred Cantwell Smith in these prophetic words written in 1967:

> Muslims do not read the Qur'an and conclude that it is divine; rather, they believe that it is divine, and then they read it. The Muslim world, also, is moving to what may possibly become a profound crisis, too;

in that it also is just beginning to ask this question, instead of being
content only with answering it. Young people in Lahore and Cairo,
labor leaders in Jakarta and Istanbul, are beginning to ask their religious
thinkers, and beginning to ask themselves, 'Is the Qur'an the word
of God?'
Answering this question has been the business of the Muslim world for
over thirteen centuries. Asking it is a different matter altogether, haunting
and ominous.[4]

Muslims generally have been very reluctant to ask critical questions
about the origins of the Qur'an. If it is the very Word of God, existing
in eternity alongside God, how can one possibly think of asking about
sources: where did the Prophet get this idea or that story from? By
definition, the Prophet could not have contributed anything to the
Qur'an because he received it from God and then recited it to others.
Some scholars like Fazlur Rahman have wanted to allow for a greater
element of creativity on the part of Muhammad in the process of
revelation, but have encountered strong opposition from traditional
scholars and have generally only been able to develop these ideas in
Western academic contexts.[5]

Salman Rushdie's *The Satanic Verses* (1988) raised questions about
truth in a particularly provocative way. Muslim criticism of the book
focused largely on the mocking way in which the Prophet was
portrayed by a writer who was born and bred a Muslim. Another
major challenge of the book, however, was that it questioned the very
idea of divine revelation. How, it asks, are we to know whether the
revelations that came to Muhammad were from God or from Satan?
How can we know whether there is a God anyway? The Rushdie affair
demonstrated that there is something 'haunting and ominous' about
asking this kind of question in the Muslim world. It confirmed that the
situation has not changed very significantly since 1945 when H. A. R.
Gibb made this comment about the difficulty Muslims have had in
accepting new ways of thinking about the study of history:

There is no stronger proof of the superficiality of the Western impact upon
the Muslim peoples than the fact that the immense revolution in historical
thought in the West in the nineteenth century has not yet penetrated into
the Muslim world.[6]

6. Israel: Can Islam tolerate the Zionist state?

'A dagger in the heart' is how an Indian Muslim, Rafiq Zakaria, sums up the feelings of Muslims all over the world and of Arabs in particular over the existence of Israel.[7] 'It has involved thousands of ordinary Muslims', says Kenneth Cragg, 'in the sharpest of personal distresses.'[8]

Why is it that the existence of a small state near the heart of the Arab and Muslim world causes Muslims such pain and leads some Middle Eastern leaders to describe their opposition to Israel in terms of *jihad*? Ronald Nettler explains how the establishment of Israel, coming so soon after Western colonial intrusion in the Middle East, was seen as 'the ultimate affront' to the Arab world.

> The Arabs reacted to Jewish aspirations and activities here with a sense of bewilderment, outrage, shock and embitterment, because they regarded Zionism from the beginning first as another manifestation of Western domination and secondly, but even more importantly, as an attempt by Jews to do something that was not legitimate: to seek political independence and that in the midst of what the Arabs regard as their own territory. This was for Islam and the Arabs the ultimate affront. How could the despised Jews, who had for centuries under Muslim rule been dhimmis and thus living in their proper place, have had the nerve and the ability to do something like this? This was to the Arab mind even more of a shock than the earlier Christian influence in the area.
>
> For the Arabs had hardly begun to come to terms with the initial shock of the Christian displacement of Islam when they were dealt another blow, by another minority which had no legitimate right to seek independence for itself – a minority which, unlike the Christians, had not during Islamic times expressed itself in a politically independent way. The Christians, after all, had possessed their empires for centuries – a distasteful fact which Islam had been forced to swallow, sometimes after a bitter struggle – while the Jews had all the time kept their proper status as dhimmis, a people without power under both Christianity and Islam.[9]

It needs to be said that not all Muslims feel the same way about Israel, and there is always a danger of creating stereotypes. But alongside all the questions about human rights and international law involved in the Arab-Israeli conflict, one cannot escape the fact that there is an Islamic dimension to the conflict which has become increasingly prominent with the rise of movements like Hamas and Hizbollah, and which deeply affects the way Muslims all over the world feel about the state of Israel. It may be that the failure till now to reach any resolution of the conflict on the basis of international law has contributed to the intensification of the Islamic elements in the conflict.

Muslims have their own reasons for their claims to the ancient city of Jerusalem and to Palestine – reasons which are based as firmly as Jewish claims on scripture, history and continuous occupation. The basic dilemma for Muslims, therefore, is whether they can accept the existence of the Jewish state – at least within its 1967 borders – or whether their rejection of the Jewish state is so deep-rooted that they must continue to struggle to dismantle it and create in its place a state which is Islamic or one in which all its citizens, whatever their race and religion, are equal.[10]

7. Human rights: Can Muslims accept concepts of human rights as widely understood today?

Most Muslim states, but not all, have signed the different international agreements on human rights, such as the UN Declaration of Human Rights of 1948. But several of these countries, especially in the Middle East, have been challenged both by outside observers and by their own nationals over their record on human rights. In many cases the policies of governments have more to do with social and economic factors than with Islam. It must also be recognized that Western countries (the USA in particular) which have spoken most loudly about the need to respect human rights have themselves been criticized for what are seen to be abuses of human rights. Some Muslims feel that Western ideas of human rights are being imposed on the rest of the world and are tied up with all the newer forms of imperialism.

Traditionalist, orthodox Muslims generally have several problems with the language of human rights as it is usually understood.

- This language speaks only of human rights and says nothing about human responsibility to God.

- There is no acknowledgment of God as the ultimate source of all law, and it is always assumed that laws are to be made by human beings without reference to the divine law.
- There is a real tension between the concept of non-discrimination on the grounds of gender, religion or belief, since in traditional Islamic law there are three fundamental inequalities: between Muslims and non-Muslims; between men and women; and between slaves and free men and women.
- The UN Declaration of Human Rights gives every individual the right to freedom 'to change' – and not just to practise – 'his belief or religion'.

Various Muslim organizations have drawn up statements of human rights, such as the Universal Declaration of Human Rights, produced by the Islamic conference of Europe in 1981, and the Declaration of Human Rights in Islam, drawn up by the Organization of the Islamic Conference (OIC) in 1990. While these statements go some way towards expressing modern understandings of human rights – but in Islamic terms – there are sometimes significant differences between the Arabic and English versions of these documents, and the tension between traditional Islamic ideas and more recent ideas remains evident. This is an issue of great complexity, in which Muslims and non-Muslims must be willing to respond to each other with great sensitivity.[11]

8. Democracy: Is Islam compatible with democracy?

The root of the problem here is that modern Western ideas of democracy insist on the sovereignty of the people and their inalienable right both to choose their governments and to create their own laws. Islam, on the other hand, finds it impossible to rule God out of the equation and insists that every society in which Muslims live should recognize the sovereignty of God. Thus Paul Grieve points out that 'the core difficulty with "democratic Islam" is that the will of the people can never be supreme, but must always be subject to the will of God, from whom flows all power'.[12]

The Islamist solution is spelled out simply by Abul A'la Mawdudi: 'There is no remedy for this present injustice except to swap man-made laws and accept, unconditionally and without reservation, the law of

God.'[13] Most modernist Muslims and many traditionalist Muslims, however, would insist that since the Prophet Muhammad clearly believed in and practised the principle of consultation (*shura*), there can be no fundamentally Islamic objection to a nation electing its own leaders through democratic processes. Thus, in the words of Mumtaz Ahmad,

> Most modern Muslim thinkers have maintained that since the Qur'an commands Muslims to conduct their affairs through *shura* or mutual consultation, the rule of autocratic kings is not allowed and that a constitutional and representative form of government either with or without a king, is the only type of government permissible.[14]

9. The struggle between fundamentalists and modernists: Which side will win?

There is 'a titanic struggle', in the words of Peter Riddell and Peter Cotterell, 'taking place between moderates and radicals for the hearts and minds of the Muslim masses in the middle...'[15] Gilles Kepel makes the same point in the title of his most recent book, *The War for Muslim Minds: Islam and the West*. Ziauddin Sardar comments that 'the fight against terrorism is also an internal Muslim struggle within Islam. Indeed it is a struggle for the very soul of Islam.'[16] And John Esposito speaks of 'the struggle for the soul of Islam going on today', ending his book *Unholy War: Terror in the Name of Islam* with these words:

> While some forms of terrorism, like some forms of cancer, respond to radical surgery, this deadly disease can only be effectively countered first by under-standing how it originates, grows stronger, and spreads and then by taking action. The cancer of global terrorism will continue to afflict the international body until we address its political and economic causes, causes that will other-wise continue to provide a breeding ground for hatred and radicalism, the rise of extremist movements, and recruits for the bin Ladens of this world.[17]

Reza Aslan speaks of the conflict in terms of 'another Muslim civil war':

> The tragic events of September 11, 2001, may have fueled the clash-of-monotheisms mentality among those Muslims, Christians, and Jews who

seem so often to mistake religion for faith and scripture for God. But it also initiated a vibrant discourse among Muslims about the meaning and message of Islam in the twenty-first century. What has occurred since that fateful day amounts to nothing short of another Muslim civil war – a *fitnah* – which, like the context to define Islam after the Prophet's death, is tearing the Muslim community into opposing factions.[18]

All these writers – two of them Muslims – are very aware of the seriousness of this conflict. It is far too soon, however, for anyone to predict whether, how or when this conflict will be resolved.

16.WOMEN IN ISLAM

Muslims often argue that Islam has liberated women, giving them a dignity that no other religion has given them. Non-Muslims, on the other hand, have often been critical of the treatment of women in Islam. If one side has used this issue to commend Islam and the other to attack it, might it not seem wiser to leave such a sensitive and controversial issue completely alone? There are three reasons why it may be appropriate at least to open up the subject.

1. The family plays such an important role in Islam that it is impossible to understand Muslim culture without understanding something of the place of women in Islam.

2. A study of the role of women in Islam leads us straight to several subjects which are crucial for our understanding of the nature of Islam, such as the place of the Qur'an, the traditions about the Prophet, and Islamic law (*shari'a*). If we can understand how Muslims think about this crucial subject, we should be able to appreciate more of their total world view.

3. Tackling this subject should make us aware of some of the pitfalls in any comparison of Christianity and Islam. There are

three in particular which we need to avoid: comparing what
we think is the worst in Islam with the best in Christianity;
criticizing Islam for the faults and weaknesses in individual
Muslims without recognizing that Christians have often been
guilty of exactly the same things; and judging Muslims in the
past by contemporary moral standards, which for many of us
are simply those of the Western world in the twenty-first
century.

Once again our task is to try to understand rather than to be judg-
mental, and to enter with as much sympathy or empathy as possible
into a culture which is very different from our own.

The teaching of the Qur'an about women and marriage

The following are the main points in the teaching of the Qur'an, with
references to some of the relevant verses.

- Men and women were created 'from a single soul', morally equal
  before God (4:1; 3:195; 9:71–72; 33:35).
- God has created all living beings in pairs, male and female, and
  marriage is ordained by God (51:49; 30:20–21; 42:11); men and
  women need each other in marriage (2:187; 16:72).
- God will reward both men and women in Paradise (3:195; 16:97;
  43:70).
- Men are commanded to treat women kindly (4:19).
- Passages which appear to teach that women are inferior to men
  because 'men are a degree above them' are generally interpreted
  to mean that husbands are responsible for leadership of the
  family and for maintaining their wives; wives are to be obedient
  and chaste, and can be beaten if they are disobedient (4:34;
  2:228; 3:35–36).
- Women should dress modestly and draw their cloak or veil
  around them when they go outside; but there is no suggestion
  that they should be completely veiled (33:59; 24:30–31).
- Men may marry up to four wives, provided they treat them all
  fairly and equally (4:3–4; 4:129). This permission was given after
  the Battle of Uhud, when seventy Muslim men were killed, and

is therefore seen as a way of caring for widows and unmarried women in any community where there are not enough men. Some interpreters today believe that since it is virtually impossible for a husband to deal absolutely fairly with more than one wife, the passage should be interpreted to mean that polygamy is discouraged, if not actually proscribed.

- The same verse that allows up to four wives also teaches that a Muslim may have any number of slave-concubines in addition to the four legal wives (4:3).
- Muslim men may marry Jewish or Christian wives (5:5), but may not marry women from any other religion (2:221).
- Intercourse is not allowed during menstruation (2:222); women are to be regarded as 'tilth for you (to cultivate)' or 'a field of tillage' (2:223).
- Adultery is to be punished severely (4:15–18; 17:32; 24:20).
- Divorce is permitted (2:225–242; 60:1–2; 65:1–2), but only after an attempt has been made at reconciliation (4:35). It would seem that no provision is made in these verses for a wife to divorce her husband.
- A person's estate is to be divided among his or her relatives after death (2:180). A husband is to receive a half of his wife's estate, while a wife should receive a quarter of her husband's estate (4:7–12).
- Descriptions of Paradise include 'dark-eyed virgins' or 'wide-eyed houris' (e.g. 44:54; 52:20; 55:56; 56:22–24).
- Special respect is due to the wives of the Prophet Muhammad.

The teaching and example of Muhammad

These are some of the relevant sayings of the Prophet concerning women which have been recorded in Muslim tradition, and which are therefore given considerable authority by Muslims.

Paradise lies at the feet of your mothers.

(In answer to the question 'Who deserves the best care from me?') Your mother, your mother, your mother; then your father, and then your nearest relatives.

The best among you is the one who is the best towards his wife.

O people, your wives have certain rights over you and you have certain rights over them. Treat them well and be kind to them, for they are your partners and committed helpers.

A people with a female ruler will never be successful.

The following basic facts about the wives of Muhammad are based on authoritative traditions and are accepted by all Muslims.

- Khadija was forty years old at the time of her marriage to Muhammad, and had been widowed twice. She was his only wife for twenty-five years and bore all Muhammad's children except one. She died at the age of sixty-five.
- At the age of fifty, Muhammad married Sawda, whose husband had emigrated to Abyssinia to escape persecution and then died there.
- In the same year there was a proposal of marriage to 'A'isha, who was around seven or eight years old, the daughter of his companion Abu Bakr. The marriage was not consummated until after the *Hijra* in 622 when she was around nine years old, and she became his favourite wife. For six years, until he reached the age of fifty-six, Muhammad had only these two wives, Sawda and 'A'isha.
- Between the ages of fifty-six and sixty Muhammad contracted marriages with nine women, including Hafsa and Juwairiya, both widows whose husbands had been killed in battle; Zaynab bint Jahsh, a cousin of Muhammad who had been the wife of his adopted son Zaid and became Muhammad's wife after he received a special revelation permitting him to marry her (recorded in the Qur'an, 33:37); Safiyya, a Jewish princess; and Mariya, a Coptic (Egyptian) Christian slave girl, who was given to him by the Christian archbishop of Alexandria, and who bore Muhammad's only son, Ibrahim. He died at eighteen months.

Gai Eaton explains how Muslims understand polygamy today and the traditions concerning Muhammad's married life.

In accordance with the Qur'anic injunction, he treated his wives equally in all material matters and in matters of justice. He divided his nights fairly between them and he drew lots to determine who should accompany him on his campaigns; but, as he himself said, a man's affections are outside his control and his particular fondness for 'A'isha was common knowledge. Jealousy was inevitable, and he tended to make light of it. Once he came to a room where his wives and other members of the family were assembled bearing in his hand an onyx necklace, which had just been presented to him. Holding it up, he said: 'I shall give this to her whom I love best of all!' He allowed a pause while they whispered together, sure that he would give it to the daughter of Abu Bakr. When he had left them long enough in suspense, he called his little granddaughter to him and clasped it round her neck. 'If the revelation comes to me when I am under the coverlet of a woman,' he said once, 'it is only when I am with 'A'isha.' She herself, as was mentioned previously, was not without a streak of jealousy. He asked her once, half-teasing, if she would not like to die before him so that he could bury her and pray at her funeral. 'I should like that well enough,' she said, 'if I did not think that on returning from my funeral you would console yourself with another woman.'

The tense and delicate balance between the glory of Muhammad's prophethood, his closeness to God and his visionary gifts, the Herculean tasks he undertook and accomplished in the world, and the warmth and liveliness of his household is at the heart of the Muslim view of life; if this is understood, Islam is understood.[1]

Islamic law concerning women

Since the Qur'an does not contain a complete system of law, the Muslim community had to develop its laws gradually after the death of Muhammad, using the Qur'an and the traditions about the Prophet as their starting point. It was in the period from about 850 to 950 that the *shari'a* came to be codified and developed into a complete and all-embracing system of law. During this time the four main schools of law emerged, each of them placing different emphasis on the four main Islamic sources of authority (see chapter 10, 'Law and theology').

These were some of the basic provisions concerning women and marriage contained in the *shari'a*.

- A man may marry up to four wives.
- The husband has to pay a dowry to his wife at the time of the wedding. The first part of the dowry consists of jewellery or cash, which is spent on the bride's trousseau or household furnishings. The second part is payable in cash or in kind in case of divorce.
- The testimony of two women is equivalent to the testimony of one man.
- Temporary marriage (*mut'a*) was marriage for a limited period (varying from a few days to many years), which involved the payment of a dowry, however small. Probably a pre-Islamic custom in Arabia, the practice was given legal sanction in the Qur'an (4:24) and the traditions of the Prophet. It became a common practice in Shi'ite Islam, mainly in Persia, but the practice is not allowed by Sunnis.
- Women can own property. Wives have a right to their own earnings, and they can give away their property and earnings as they wish. A woman has a right to a proportion of the inheritance of her dead father, husband or childless brother, but only half of the share of other male relatives, since men have greater financial responsibilities.
- A Muslim man should marry a Muslim woman. A Muslim man may in some cases marry a Jewish or Christian woman. But a Muslim woman is not allowed to marry a non-Muslim man.
- Divorce (*talaq*) is allowed on the grounds of incompatibility, cruelty, injustice, prolonged absence, adultery, insanity and incurable or contagious diseases. Although in the past Muslim women have not generally been allowed to divorce their husbands, it is now allowed in many Muslim countries. There are strict rules to ascertain the paternity of a child in cases where a divorced wife is pregnant.
- Abortion is strictly forbidden, although in Tunisia today it is legally possible, and in many other countries it is practised clandestinely.

The role of women in the history of Islam

Many women have played a significant role in the history of Islam. 'A'isha, for example, was the source of a large number of traditions about the life of the Prophet. During the Battle of the Camel she took up arms against 'Ali. One of the Prophet's granddaughters, Sayyida Zainab (died 684), has been venerated as a saint for many centuries, and her tomb in Cairo is still an important shrine today.

Rabi'a of Basra (died 802) was one of the earliest and best known of the Sufi saints. She is especially remembered for her prayer, 'O my Lord, if I worship Thee from hope of Paradise, exclude me thence, but if I worship Thee for Thine own sake then withhold not from me Thine eternal Beauty.' Many women after her played an important part in the Sufi movement, and women have been as deeply influenced by the movement as men. Princess Radiya, for instance, ruled in Delhi for four years from 1236 until she was supplanted by one of her brothers.

In the twentieth century women played prominent roles in many Muslim countries. Halide Edib Adivar, for example, was active in public life in Turkey as a teacher, journalist and author from the early 1900s until her death in 1964. Begum Ra'ana, the wife of the first prime minister of Pakistan, was ambassador to the United Nations and in 1979 gained a human rights award from the UN. Benazir Bhutto in 1988 became the first woman to be prime minister of a Muslim country (Pakistan) and was elected again in 1993. Several Muslim women from France and North Africa have competed for their countries in the Olympic Games.

Law reform in the twentieth century

Turkey was the first Muslim country to bring in a family law in 1917. In Egypt a series of laws was passed between 1920 and 1929, and in 1943 a new law of inheritance was passed. Similar laws were passed in Jordan in 1951, and in Syria in 1953. In 1979 amendments to the 1929 personal status law were passed, giving women better rights in divorce and for alimony and child custody. Tunisia made polygamy illegal in 1956, and in 1959 made all sex discrimination illegal. Amir Taheri describes some of the obstacles to the reform of laws relating to the status of women in countries of the Middle East.

> The 1980s could be described as a period of retreat for those who
> supported the cause of legal equality and more individual liberties for

women. Under pressure from Islamic fundamentalists most Middle Eastern governments have either postponed or cancelled earlier policies in favour of more rights for women.[2]

The feminist movement in Islam

Reforms initiated by such rulers as Muhammad 'Ali and Isma'il Pasha in the nineteenth century were intended to enable Egyptians to attain the same cultural level as Europeans, and therefore encouraged some women to changes aspects of their traditional Islamic way of life. Reformers such as Jamal al-Din al Afghani, Muhammad 'Abduh and Qasim Amin pressed, for example, for better education for girls and women, and spoke against the practice of polygamy.

In 1919 the leadership of the movement passed to Huda Sha'rawi (1879–1947), the chairperson of the Women's Executive of a major political party in Egypt. In that year she led a demonstration of veiled women to support Egyptian nationalism. In 1923, after leading an Egyptian delegation to the meeting of an International Alliance for Women in Rome, she threw her veil into the sea as she disembarked on her return to Egypt. Through the growing influence of the movement, a new marriage and divorce law was passed in 1928.

The feminist case has been argued strongly in recent years by a growing number of Muslim women who have tried to understand the culture of both the Muslim and the Western worlds. Fatna Sabah, for example, a North African sociologist, is critical of the record of traditional Islam over its attitudes to women. This is how she explains 'the ideal of female beauty in Islam'.

> The ideal of female beauty in Islam is obedience, silence and immobility, that is inertia and passivity. These are far from being trivial characteristics, nor are they limited to women. In fact, these three attributes of female beauty are the three qualities of the believer vis-à-vis his God. The believer must dedicate his life to obeying and worshipping God and abiding by his will.
>
> In the sacred universe, the believer is fashioned in the image of woman, deprived of speech and will and committed to obedience to another [God]. The female condition and the male condition are not different in the end to which they are directed, but in the pole around which they orbit. The lives of beings of the female sex revolve around the will of believers of the male sex.

Using Sabah's analysis, Fatima Mernissi, a sociologist working at the Research Institute of the University of Rabat in Morocco, tries to explain why some recent feminist thinking represents such a threat to traditional ways of thinking in Islam.

> What happens when a woman disobeys her husband, who is the representative and embodiment of sacred authority, and of the Islamic hierarchy? A danger bell rings in the mind, for when one element of the whole structure of polarities is threatened, the entire system is threatened. A woman who rebels against her husband, for instance, is also rebelling against the umma, against reason, order and, indeed, God. The rebellion of woman is linked to individualism, not community (umma); passion, not reason; disorder, not order; lawlessness (fitna), not law.

When she explains the dilemma facing many Muslim women in the modern world, Christian readers will recognize the uncanny parallel with the tensions among Christians over traditional responses to feminism.

> In the struggle for survival in the Muslim world today, the Muslim community finds itself squeezed between individualistic, innovative western capitalism on the one hand, and individualistic, rebellious political oppositions within, among which the most symbolically loaded is that of rebellious women. The common denominator between capitalism and new models of femininity is individualism and self-affirmation. Initiative is power. Women are claiming power – corroding and ultimately destroying the foundation of Muslim hierarchy; whence the violence of the reaction and the rigidity of the response. Femininity as a symbol of surrender has to be resisted violently if women intend to change its meaning to energy, initiative and creative criticism.[3]

Islamization and the demand to return to the *shari'a*

In several countries groups of Muslims are calling for their govern-ments to adopt a new legal code which is based on the *shari'a* rather than on Western law codes. Abdur Rahman I. Doi writes as a traditionalist, orthodox Muslim, expressing the feeling that Muslims have absorbed too much from the West in their attitudes towards women and need to recover a more traditionally Islamic approach.

> During the days of European colonialism and the scramble to take over the Muslim world, the influence of feminism spread to Muslim countries. The first victims of the glittering Western way of life were the Muslim rulers of various Muslim countries. In the days of the political decline of Islam, they were made to believe that the Muslim world was lagging behind because of the 'maltreatment and slavery of women' ...
>
> I would like to appeal to Muslim scholars the world over to re-examine the role they played in this most difficult period of Islamic history when the Christian West had almost dominated the Muslim world. I have a feeling that perhaps they went too far in proposing reforms in the Shari'ah. Perhaps with the best of intentions, they proposed so-called 'reforms' in the matter of the Shari'ah and galloped on the unbridled horse of reason and imagination, giving fatawa [juristic opinions] which did great damage which they did not live long enough to see.
>
> Many of my Egyptian friends will not be happy to read that not only did Egypt shelve, and to a great extent discard, the Islamic system of values as taught by the Qur'an and the Sunnah by adopting Western culture and the Western way of life, but it also exported it to other Arab and Muslim countries.[4]

The wearing of the veil

There has been so much controversy about the wearing of the veil in European countries in recent years, that it is worth quoting in full the text of the qur'anic verse which speaks about women wearing the veil.

> And tell believing women to cast down their eyes and guard their private parts and not show their finery, except the outward part of it. And let them drape their bosoms with their veils and not show their finery except to their husbands, their fathers, their husbands' fathers, their sons, the sons of their husbands, their brothers, the sons of their brothers, the sons of their sisters, their women, their maid-servants, the men-followers who have no sexual desire, or infants who have no knowledge of women's sexual parts yet. Let them, also, not stamp their feet, so that what they have concealed

of their finery might be known. Repent to Allah, all of you, O believers, that perchance you may prosper. (24:31, Fakhry)

Commenting on this verse, Paul Grieve says:

> There is simply no Qur'anic justification ... for the veiling and segregation of women practised by many Muslims for centuries and still continued in some contemporary societies. In fact, there is evidence in the original Muslim sources that in Medina during Muhammad's lifetime women mixed freely and unveiled with men.[5]

Westerners are often surprised to find out that Muslim women who wear the veil can be highly educated, working women. Hinde Taarji, a Moroccan journalist, wrote a book in 1991 entitled *Les Voilees de l'Islam*, in which she recorded the results of interviews with women throughout the Arab world who had decided to wear the veil (*hijab*). These are some of the reasons given for wearing the veil.

- It can liberate women by helping them to escape from masculine aggression in public and encouraging men to respect them. The veil will not necessarily destroy the emancipation of Muslim women.
- It is a sign of total commitment to Islam, and provides the security and stability of a familiar code in a changing society.
- It has little or nothing to do with a desire to remain secluded in the home, since many who wear the veil want to go out to work.
- It indicates to men that Muslim women can have their own interpretation of Islam, in spite of the fact that men have traditionally been the guardians of orthodox Islamic teaching. These veiled women are 'entering the centre of Islam' – with the approval of men.

Some observations and conclusions

There is always going to be a huge gulf between the ideal that is taught by religious teachers and how people within that community actually carry it out. In recent years dozens of books have been published, some written by Muslims and others by non-Muslims, which describe in considerable detail the position of women in certain countries like Afghanistan, Iran and Saudi Arabia.[6] Some of these accounts have been challenged by Muslims, who argue that they are sensational journalistic reports. Cases of honour killings have been reported in the media.

It is often difficult to draw a dividing line between what is local and cultural and what is Islamic. It is often argued, for example, that the *burqa*, the black veil covering the head and the whole body, is a pre-Islamic custom incorporated into Islam.

The status of women has changed considerably as a result of Western influence. The claim of Islamists that the Muslim world has been influenced too much by Western culture proves the point that many of the changes in the status of women in the Muslim world in the last two hundred years have come about through European penetration. While this continues to fuel the anger and resentment of the Islamists, there must be many Muslim women who are profoundly grateful for reforms which, they would say, have greatly improved their position.

Considerable numbers of Western women have converted to Islam in recent years. Sometimes it happens through marriage, but in many cases they convert because they are disgusted at the promiscuity in Western societies and are attracted by the higher moral standards of Islam.

In many cases we are dealing with the failings of human nature rather than the failings of Islam. In her autobiography, Benazir Bhutto, former prime minister of Pakistan, attributes inequalities in the treatment of boys and girls in her society not to Islam, but to the way men have interpreted religion.

> There was no question in my family that my sister and I would be given the same opportunities in life as my brothers. Nor was there in Islam. We learned at an early age that it was men's interpretation of our religion that restricted women's opportunities, not our religion itself. Islam in fact had been quite progressive towards women from its inception.[7]

Although we may believe that the Christian faith provides a better basis for the dignity of women than any other faith, we need to admit that the Christian church has not always had a very good record in its attitudes to women. We may be able to explain this to ourselves by saying that at certain periods Christians cannot have been fully aware of the distinctive Christian teaching, or that they were more influenced by their culture than by the gospel. Our problem often is, however, that Muslims do not generally find it easy to distinguish between Christian teaching and Christian practice.

A survey of this kind should at least enable us to gain some insight into the role of women in Islam and develop some sympathy for the aspirations of women in different Muslim communities. We should also have recognized the need for greater humility and deeper repentance over Christian failures to live up to the standards set before us in the Christian tradition.

'Islamic terrorism' is a very recent phenomenon; but it did not develop in a vacuum. It can only be understood in the context of the development of Islamism or 'Islamic fundamentalism' in the twentieth century. We look first, therefore, at groups and individuals that helped to create the soil in which the movement developed, before going on to ask why some Islamists have engaged in violence and how other Muslims and non-Muslims have responded to this terrorism carried out 'in the name of Islam'.[1]

Antecedents in Islamic history

In the first century of Islam the *Kharijites*, literally 'Outsiders', were a very conservative, strict and puritanical movement, seeking to recall Muslims to the basic teaching of the Qur'an and the example of the Prophet and his immediate successors. They went as far as to wage war against fellow Muslims whom they regarded as infidels, and assassinated 'Ali, the son-in-law of the Prophet.

The *Assassins* (from the Arabic *hashishiyya*, suggesting the idea of 'hashish takers') were extremist, secret communities of Shi'ites, based in Persia and Syria from the eleventh to the thirteenth centuries. They were sent one by one by their leader, the Grand Master, to kill individuals with a dagger – usually political, military or religious leaders of the Abbasid dynasty in Baghdad. They carried out their targeted assassinations knowing that they would be killed by their captors, and were not allowed to commit suicide.

Ibn Taymiyya (1263–1328) was a scholar and political activist who had to move from Iraq to Damascus because of the Mongol invasion. Starting from a literalist interpretation of the Qur'an and the *sunna*, but asking for the doors of *ijtihad* to be opened to allow reinterpretation of the sources, he called for the renewal and reform of Islamic societies. He also pointed to the first state in Medina as the model of the Islamic state. Although the Mongols were Muslims, ibn Taymiyya issued a legal ruling (*fatwa*) describing them as unbelievers (*kuffar*) and apostates who needed to be resisted by force. He has been described as 'the spiritual father of (Sunni) revolutionary Islam'.[2]

In the eighteenth century there were a number of revivalist movements in the Sudan, Libya, Nigeria, India, South-east Asia and Arabia, where Muhammad ibn 'Abd al-Wahhab (1703–91) founded the movement known as *Wahhabism*. This fundamentalist, puritanical form of Islam was later used by Abdulaziz ibn Saud in a kind of holy war to gain control of the Hejaz in 1927 and then to establish the kingdom of Saudi Arabia in 1932. In 1933 an agreement was signed with Standard Oil Company of California allowing them to extract oil. Wahhabism therefore became, in the words of Bernard Lewis, 'the official, state-enforced doctrine of one of the most influential governments in all Islam – the custodian of the two holiest places of Islam...' Commenting on the way the historical accidents of Saudi politics and the discovery of oil have been so significant, he adds, 'The custodianship of the holy places and the revenues of oil have given worldwide impact to what would otherwise have been an extremist fringe in a marginal country.'[3]

Key ideologues in the twentieth century

Hasan al-Banna (1906–49) was a school teacher who became actively involved in the campaign to get the British out of Egypt, and founded the Muslim Brotherhood in Egypt in 1928. Attributing the weakness of the Muslim world to its departure from true Islam and to the corrupting influence of the West, he called for *jihad* to implement reforms in society. He was therefore using a concept which, as we shall see, was well established in Islamic tradition, but was applying it in a new way to his own political context.

Mawlana Abul A'la Mawdudi (1903–79) was a journalist in the Indian subcontinent who shared the same outlook as al-Banna. He described Islam as 'a comprehensive system that tends to annihilate all tyrannical and evil systems in the world and enforce its own programme ... a revolutionary concept and ideology which seeks to change and revolutionize the world social order and reshape it according to its own concept and ideals'. He founded the Jama'at-i-Islami in 1941 and supported the creation of Pakistan as an Islamic state. His writings were widely distributed all over the Muslim world and had a profound influence on Muslims in many different contexts.

Sayyid Qutb (1906–66) was involved in education for many years, and joined the Muslim Brotherhood in the 1950s. Because of his opposition to the government of Nasser, he spent nine years in prison. His most important work, *Signposts on the Way* (1964), transformed the teaching of al-Banna and Mawdudi into 'a rejectionist, revolutionary call to arms'. The fact that he was executed by the Egyptian government increased his popularity and influence, and turned him into 'a martyr for the Islamic revival'.[4]

Dr Abdullah Azzam, originally from Jordan, was a strong advocate of militant, global *jihad*, and is significant because he was one of Osama bin Laden's university teachers in Saudi Arabia. He wrote:

> Jihad and the rifle alone: no negotiations, no conferences, and no dialogues ... jihad will remain an individual obligation until all other lands that were Muslim are returned to us so that Islam will reign again: before us lie Palestine, Bokhara, Lebanon, Chad, Eritrea, Somalia, the Philippines, Burma, Southern Yemen, Tashkent and Andalusia [southern Spain].[5]

Significant dates

It is hard to exaggerate the significance of the Six Day War in June 1967 in the development of Islamism. The humiliating defeat of the Arab armies which attacked Israel is seen by Muslims and Arabs as the lowest point ever reached by the Muslim world. Egypt's brief victory in October 1973 restored some sense of pride, and was followed by the Arab oil embargo. But the shame of the defeat in 1967 still remains.

The Islamic Revolution in Iran in 1979 ousted the pro-West Shah and brought into existence the Islamic Republic, led by Ayatollah Khomeini. America became the main target of Muslim anger and contempt, being labelled as 'The Great Satan'.

In 1979 the Soviets invaded Afghanistan, and this was an event which had a profound effect on Osama bin Laden.

In 1989 the Soviet forces were forced to withdraw from Afghanistan, driven out by Afghan fighters who were supported by Osama bin Laden's al-Qa'ida and Muslim fighters from the Arab world, and supplied with weapons from the USA. Defeating the army of the second most powerful nation in the world gave an enormous boost to the confidence of these Muslim fighters, encouraging them to turn their attention to the most powerful nation of all, the USA. 'The Soviet-Afghan war', says John Esposito, 'marked a new turning point as jihad went global to a degree never seen in the past.'[6]

When Iraq invaded Kuwait in 1990, American forces were stationed in Saudi Arabia. This was another deeply traumatic experience for Osama bin Laden, and set him on a collision course with the Saudi government.

In 1996 Osama bin Laden fled from the Sudan to join the Taliban in Afghanistan, who by 1998 had taken over most of the country. In August 1998 bin Laden issued his first *fatwa* calling for US forces to be driven out of Saudi Arabia. In the same month there was the bombing of the embassies in Nairobi and Dar es Salam. A later *fatwa* called on all Muslims to kill US citizens and their allies.

On 11 September 2001 around 3,000 people were killed in the attacks in New York and Washington. In March 2004 around 200 were killed in the bombings on the trains in Madrid. The attacks in London on 7 July 2005 killed 52 people.

The invasion of Iraq in March 2003 by the USA and its allies (with Britain as the most significant) removed Saddam Hussein and his Ba'ath party from power. The continuing occupation has exposed the divisions between the three main communities – Shi'ites, Sunnis and Kurds – and has led to a situation in which a national insurgency has been fed by Islamists of many kinds from outside the country.

What is most significant from this brief survey is that bin Laden
and those associated with him represent what Esposito calls 'the
radical fringe of a broad based Islamic jihad that began in the late 20th
century', and that al-Qa'ida represents 'a watershed for contemporary
Islamic radicalism'. What is new is the way in which from the 1990s
America and the West have become 'a primary target in an unholy war
of terrorism'.

Major grievances of Islamists

The basic grievances of all Islamists – whether or not they resort to
violence – can be listed as follows.

1. The weakness and humiliation of the Muslim world, which is
   seen as largely the result of Western imperialism in the
   nineteenth and twentieth centuries. Justifying the attacks of
   9/11, bin Laden said, 'Our nation [the Muslim nation, the *umma*]
   has been tasting humiliation and contempt for more than 80
   years.' He was referring here to the role of Western powers in
   destroying the Ottoman Empire and reshaping the whole of the
   Middle East.

2. New forms of Western imperialism – political, military,
   economic and religious – which have taken the place of the old
   imperialism, but which are seen as more subtle and dangerous.
   Colin Turner sums up the feelings of many Muslims in this way:
   'While independent Muslim states emerged one after the other
   with welcome rapidity, the underlying and increasingly
   unpalatable truth was lost on no-one: in the vast majority of
   cases, the individuals, groups and parties that had shaken off
   the shackles of European domination and led their lands to
   freedom were, more often than not, members of the Western-
   educated – and, more than likely, Western-oriented – elite.
   Although their rise to power did indeed signal the formal end
   of European control over the Muslim Middle East, the fact was
   that it was relatively easy for Europe – and, increasingly, the
   USA – to continue to dominate the region by proxy. Economic
   aid and the proliferation of industrial, agricultural and
   educational projects were but a few of the mechanisms

employed by Western powers to retain a degree of control over their former colonies – and, indeed, over countries never before colonized in the literal sense of the word such as Iran. Gradually it became clear to many Muslims in the Middle East that they had not thrown off the yoke of Western colonialism at all.'[7]

3. The failure of the ideologies imported from the West – especially capitalism, communism/socialism and nationalism. These are perceived as 'bankrupt ideologies foisted on them from outside'.[8] While some aspects of modernity are enthusiastically embraced, others are vigorously rejected. It is argued that since these foreign ideologies have failed so conspicuously, the only solution is for Muslims to return to their own Islamic roots.

4. The establishment of the Zionist state of Israel in the heartlands of Islam, carried out with the support of the West, especially by Britain and later by the USA. One-sided American support for Israel since 1967, and especially since the 1980s, enables Israel to hold on to the occupied territories. There is continuing, deep anger over the dispossession of the Palestinians in 1948–9 and the continuing illegal occupation of the West Bank.

5. The presence of foreign troops in Saudi Arabia since the early 1990s and the Gulf War. Sacred territory, containing the two most holy Islamic sites, is felt to have been invaded by infidels. Although American forces have now been withdrawn from Saudi Arabia, their presence in the Gulf and in Iraq since 2003 is seen as deeply offensive because Baghdad was 'the seat of the caliphate for half a millennium and the scene of some of the most glorious chapters of Islamic history'.[9]

6. Corrupt and autocratic governments in Islamic countries which are not truly Islamic and are colluding with the West. For many Islamists the main target for their anger is their own governments. 'From their point of view,' says Bernard Lewis, 'the ultimate struggle is not against the Western intruder but against the Westernizing traitor at home. Their most dangerous enemies, as they see it, are the false and renegade Muslims who rule the countries of the Islamic world and who have imported and imposed infidel ways on Muslim peoples.'[10]

7. Double standards. We are constantly reminded, for example, that the West will go to war to force Saddam Hussein to comply with a UN Security Council Resolution calling on him to withdraw from Kuwait, but will do nothing to force Israel to comply with similar UN Resolutions in 1967 requiring it to withdraw from occupied territory.

The words of Mohammad Sidique Khan, believed to be the leader of the 7 July bombings in London, in a video broadcast on Al-Jazeera television in September 2005 articulated many of these grievances, which for him were focused on Iraq.

> We are at war and I am a soldier ... The lands and interests of the states that took part in the aggression on Palestine, Iraq and Afghanistan are considered targets for us, so anybody who seeks peace should stay away from these states ... Blair has brought catastrophe to his people in the middle of the capital and will bring more, God willing, because he is still fooling his people and insisting and stubbornly treating them like ignorant fools when he keeps repeating that what happened in London has nothing to do with the crimes he has committed in Palestine, Afghanistan and Iraq.[11]

Islamism is therefore the angry response of Muslims who are painfully aware of the decline of Islam and the resurgence of the West. We could say that for Muslims, it should not be like this – that the world of Islam (*dar al-Islam*) becomes subject to the non-Muslim world (*dar al-harb*). This might be called 'the great reversal': in their minds, '*We Muslims* should be ruling over *them*, non-Muslims, not *them* ruling over *us*!' The proud giant has been stung, wounded and humiliated, and Islamism is one major response of the awakening giant.

'Islamic terrorism'

Those who turn to terrorism are a minority among the Islamists, but their violence has to be seen in the context of the whole Islamist movement. While most of the world – including many Muslims – vehemently condemn terrorism of any and every kind, especially when carried out in the name of God and religion, it is important for us to clarify what is meant by the term 'Islamic terrorism'.

Even the United Nations in September 2005 was unable to reach a consensus on the definition of the word 'terrorism'. This was largely because many found it impossible to accept that the killing of innocent civilians in the context of defensive resistance to illegal oppression or conquest should always be classed as 'terrorism'.

We need to be cautious about linking the words 'Islamic' and 'terrorism'. Since many of those Muslims who have engaged in terrorism claim openly that they are acting in the name of Islam, there is some justification for describing these actions as 'Islamic'. But we shall soon see that the majority of Muslim leaders in the West seem to condemn these actions as totally un-Islamic. We ought therefore to be careful about attaching the word 'Islamic' in such a blanket way to every terrorist action carried out by Muslims.

We need to recognize that in many (if not most) situations, terrorism is the angry and violent response of individuals or communities to violence that has been done to them. What has been done to them in the first place, however, is not often called 'terrorism', largely because it is carried out not by individuals but by governments and their armies. Observers are often quick to condemn the terrorism, but slow to say anything critical about the actions to which the terrorists are responding. Terrorism itself, it seems, is not the root of the problem; it is usually a reaction to a perceived injustice, and therefore needs to be seen as a symptom of other underlying problems.

Responses of Muslims to terrorism carried out by Muslims

If we focus on the aftermath of both 9/11 and 7/7, we see that these events have put many Muslims on the spot, forcing them to declare what they think about the attacks. From the reactions of people on the street and the public statements of scholars and leaders, it seems that there have been three different kinds of responses.

'These were genuinely Islamic actions carried out against the enemies of Islam in accordance with Islamic teaching'
One of the hijackers had written before his death, 'Remember the battle of the Prophet... against the infidels, as he went on building the Islamic state.' The Al-Muhajirun movement in the UK on 12 September 2001 addressed fellow Muslims in the UK in these words: 'Muslims, stand

together and unite our Ummah to fight against the enemies of Allah . . .
and his Messenger Muhammad in this time of need.'[12]

'These actions cannot possibly be justified in terms of Islamic teaching'
Dr Zaki Badawi of the Muslim College in London made this statement on 13 September 2001: 'Those who plan and carry out such acts
are condemned by Islam, and the massacre of thousands, whoever
perpetrated it, is a crime against God as well as humanity.'[13] Similarly,
Ziauddin Sardar wrote on 23 September 2001

> To Muslims everywhere I issue this *fatwa* (legal ruling): any Muslim
> involved in the planning, financing, training, recruiting, support or
> harbouring of those who commit acts of indiscriminate violence against
> persons or the apparatus or infrastructure of states is guilty of terror and
> no part of the Ummah. It is the duty of every Muslim to spare no effort in
> hunting down, apprehending and bringing such criminals to justice.[14]

This, therefore, is the position of those who believe that these
extremists 'hijack Islamic discourse and belief to justify their acts of
terrorism' and who dissociate themselves totally from their actions.[15]

*'We sympathize with their motives, but can neither support nor condemn their
actions'*
Many Muslims on the streets in different countries have been caught
in a dilemma because they could understand the thinking of the
hijackers and shared some of their anger. They have had some sympathy with them, but could not bring themselves either to condemn or
to approve of their actions. It is particularly difficult for Muslims to
condemn an action or a judgment by fellow Muslims who are acting
out of Islamic motives, and many believe that they have no right to
declare that someone who claims to be a Muslim is not a real Muslim.
This reaction therefore represents 'an uneasy balance between denial
and approval'.[16]

Crucial theological questions for Muslims

The basic question here is this: how can a religion whose historical
origins were undeniably associated with a considerable amount of

violence present itself today as 'a religion of peace'? When Muslims today reflect on their scriptural sources and their history, therefore, there are at least three questions that they have to address.

What are the different meanings of jihad?

The Arabic word *jihad* simply means 'struggle', and is used in the Qur'an to speak of struggle 'in the path of God'. A typical appeal to the Medinan Muslims says, 'O believers, fear Allah and seek the means to win His favour. Fight [*jahidu*] in His way so that you may prosper' (5:35). At certain stages of Islamic history, *jihad* has been seen as the struggle for moral and doctrinal rigour within Islam itself. Over the centuries, however, it has become, in the words of John Esposito, 'a defining concept or belief in Islam, a key element in what it means to be a believer and follower of God's will ... a universal religious obligation for all true Muslims to join the jihad to promote a global Islamic revolution'. For many Muslims it has come to be regarded as the sixth pillar of Islam, alongside the other five (confession of the faith, prayer, fasting, almsgiving and pilgrimage), and therefore an obligation that is laid on all Muslims.

This is Esposito's summary of how *jihad* was understood for centuries in Islamic law.

> Islamic law stipulates that it is a Muslim's duty to wage war not only against those who attack Muslim territory, but also against polytheists, apostates, and People of the Book (at first restricted to Jews and Christians but later extended to Zoroastrians and other faiths) who refuse Muslim rule. Muslims gave these people two choices: conversion or submission to Muslim rule with the right to retain their religion and pay a poll tax (a common practice applied to outsiders, within and outside of Arabia). If they refused both of these options, they were subject to war. Muslim jurists saw jihad as a requirement in a world divided between what they called dar al-islam (land of Islam) and the dar al-harb (land of war). The Muslim community was required to engage in the struggle to expand the dar al-islam throughout the world so that all of humankind would have the opportunity to live within a just political and social order. One school of law, the Shafii, posited a third category, the land of treaty (dar al-sulh), a territory that had concluded a truce with a Muslim government.[17]

In recent years many of the more liberal Muslims in the West have frequently focused on the more spiritual meanings of *jihad*, quoting for example one particular saying of the Prophet spoken when returning from a raid: 'We are returning today from the lesser *jihad* to the greater *jihad*.' The point that is made by these Muslims is that the greater *jihad* is the spiritual struggle against evil within, and the lesser *jihad* is the physical, military struggle. It is very understandable that many Muslims today quote this *hadith* and want to make this distinction. But Bernard Lewis is entirely justified in pointing out that 'For most of the fourteen centuries of recorded Muslim history, *jihad* was most commonly interpreted to mean armed struggle for the defence or advancement of Muslim power.'[18] Mawdudi defines *jihad* as 'exerting oneself to the utmost to disseminate the word of God and to make it supreme, and to remove all the impediments to Islam – through tongue or pen or sword…'[19]

Is jihad *only defensive, or can it sometimes be offensive?*
Some qur'anic verses, while giving permission to fight, strongly condemn aggressive warfare.

> And fight [*qatilu*] for the Cause of Allah those who fight you, but do not be aggressive. Surely Allah does not like the aggressors. Kill them wherever you find them and drive them out from wherever they drove you out. Sedition is worse than slaughter [*qatl*] … Fight them until there is no sedition and the religion becomes that of Allah… (2:190–193, Fakhry)

There are other verses in the Qur'an, however, which include very strong and clear calls to Muslims to fight. One of the best known is the so-called 'sword verse'.

> Then, when the Sacred Months are over, kill the idolaters wherever you find them, take them [as captives], besiege them, and lie in wait for them at every point of observation. If they repent afterwards, perform the prayer and pay the alms, then release them… (9:5, Fakhry)

Many Muslims are aware of the differences of tone between verses encouraging an aggressive approach and those that are much more moderate. Most scholars argue that every verse of this kind needs to be understood in the context in which it was revealed to the Prophet, and cannot therefore be made the basis for a general rule. Others, however, have argued that the later, stronger verses about fighting abrogate the earlier verses which condemn aggression.

Islamic law which was formulated in the three centuries after the death of Muhammad insisted that *jihad* could only be defensive. It included many stipulations about the circumstances in which *jihad* could be declared, and laid down many rules about the conduct of war. Muslim scholars therefore had a real problem in giving a justification for their wars of conquest in the Middle East and North Africa. Perhaps, however, it would be more accurate to say that one of the purposes of conquest was to extend Islam, but by creating a total Islamic environment rather than by forcing individuals to become Muslims.[20]

For many Islamists today *jihad* can be both offensive and defensive at the same time, since attacking enemies wherever they are may be the most effective form of defence. Thus bin Laden justifies his attacks on America in terms of self-defence: 'America and its allies are massacring us in Palestine, Chechnya, Kashmir and Iraq. The Muslims have the right to attack America in reprisal ... We ourselves are the target of killings, destruction, and atrocities. We are only defending ourselves. This is defensive *jihad*.'[21]

We seem, therefore, to be left with a real tension between the two significantly different approaches adopted by Muslims, which are summed up by Esposito in this way:

> Muslims who insist that the defence of Islam is the only justification for jihad, and that all of the wars in the early days of Islam were defensive, have been criticized by others who believe that the restriction of jihad to defensive wars alone is a product of European colonialism and an unwarranted accommodation to the West.[22]

Can suicide in jihad *be regarded as martyrdom?*
The belief that Muslims who die while engaged in *jihad* go immediately to Paradise is based on verses like these:

> And do not think those who have been killed in the Way of Allah as dead; they are rather living with their Lord, well provided for. (3:169, Fakhry)

> Those who have emigrated and were driven from their homes, were
> persecuted for My sake, fought and were killed, I will forgive their sins and
> will admit them into Gardens, beneath which rivers flow, as a reward from
> Allah. (3:195, Fakhry; see also 3:157; 4:69, 100; 22:58; 47:5)

Martyrs are greatly honoured in the community; their bodies are not
washed and they are buried in the clothes they were wearing at the
time they were killed. Suicide, however, has always until recently been
regarded by Muslims as a mortal sin, totally forbidden. One of the
sayings of the Prophet is that 'Whoever kills himself with a blade will
be tormented by that blade in the fires of hell.'[23]

Martyrdom has played an especially important part in the thinking
of Shi'ites because of the martyrdom of Husayn, the grandson of
Muhammad, in 680. In the Iran-Iraq War, hundreds of thousands of
Iranian boy soldiers walked into certain death to prepare the way for
regular soldiers. What seems to have happened in recent years is that
because of the many situations in which Muslims have been engaged
in the defence of Muslim territory, suicide has become acceptable
both to some Shi'ites and to some Sunnis in the context of *jihad*. It
has come to be regarded by some Muslims as a legitimate way of
fighting against the enemies of Islam. As one martyr said before
his death, 'The quickest and safest way to Paradise is to die fighting
for it.'

The dilemma facing Muslims, therefore, as they reflect on their
struggles in the light of their scriptures, is well summed up by Peter
Riddell and Peter Cotterell:

> Is Islam a religion of peace, as Muslim moderates (and Tony Blair and
> George W. Bush) say, or is it a religion prone to violence and holy war,
> as statements by radical groups suggest? ... [T]he answer lies not in an
> either/or response, but rather in a 'both ... and' response. The Islamic
> sacred texts offer the potential for being interpreted in both ways. It
> depends on how individual Muslims wish to read them ...[24]

We might say that both the Islamists and the moderates are singing
from the same sheet of music, but they are singing different tunes.

Because at this stage we are still trying to understand Muslims and
Islam, we are not attempting to offer an immediate response to the

phenomenon of 'Islamic terrorism'. Before Christians respond, they need to make sure that they really have understood what it has felt like for Muslims to be at the receiving end of all that the West has done to the Muslim world over centuries – and what it continues to do. Christians can of course point out that there is absolutely nothing in the New Testament which could justify the use of force to further the cause of the Christian faith. But they will have to reckon with the fact that Christians at many times in the past have not only resorted to violence, but have appealed to the Bible (and especially the Old Testament) as a basis for their actions. If Muslims have to face up to the gap between the ideal and the actual, so do Christians.

In attempting to understand Islam, we began Part Two with the question 'What is Islam?' and continued with chapters on the fundamentals of Islamic belief, practice and history. Having tried to sit where Muslims sit and see the world as they see it, we now turn to consider some of the issues that have arisen and still arise when Christians and Muslims come together and become aware of all that they share and all that divides them.

PART THREE

ENTERING INTO DISCUSSION
AND DIALOGUE

The areas of conscious difference with Christians seem to act like a magnet
which draws their mind in any conversation.
Roger Hooker[1]

It is hardly too much to say that the intellectual challenge to Christianity
from Islam at the present time is greater than any challenge Christians have
had to meet for fifteen centuries, not excluding that from natural sciences.
W. Montgomery Watt[2]

O that I could converse and reason, and plead, with power from on high.
How powerless are the best-directed arguments, till the Holy Spirit renders
them effectual.
Henry Martyn[3]

Having tried in Part Two to present Islam as Muslims understand and
practise it, we have now to consider the main controversial issues that
tend to arise in conversation between Muslims and Christians. In
some cases these are issues over which Muslims and Christians have
been talking and arguing for centuries. We are trying to understand
why many of these issues are important for Muslims, and to work out
positive and fruitful ways of responding to the challenges presented
by Muslims.

18. QUESTIONS AND OBJECTIONS CONCERNING CHRISTIAN PRACTICE

Each question or comment is followed by a short answer. It should be emphasized that what are set out here are nothing more than suggestions for answers which can be given immediately. They are not intended to be exhaustive and are no substitute for hard thought and study.

'Why do you eat pork, which is unclean?'

The Jews were taught in the *Tawrat* (Torah) that pork was unclean. People today think that this was partly because of hygiene; but it was also a sign that they were God's special people. Jesus, however, taught that cleanness and uncleanness in God's eyes are more a matter of what goes on secretly in our hearts than a matter of what we eat or do not eat. This is the teaching that he gave when he had a dispute with the Jewish teachers about keeping traditions concerning cleanliness:

> Nothing outside a man can make him 'unclean' by going into him. Rather, it is what comes out of a man that makes him 'unclean' ... Don't you see that nothing that enters a man from the outside can make him 'unclean'?

For it doesn't go into his heart but into his stomach, and then out of his body ... What comes out of a man is what makes him 'unclean'. For from within, out of men's hearts, come evil thoughts, sexual immorality, theft, murder, adultery, greed, malice, deceit, lewdness, envy, slander, arrogance and folly. All these evils come from inside and make a man 'unclean'. (Mark 7:15–23)

'Why do you drink alcohol?

In the *Tawrat* there is no command to refrain from drinking alcohol, although there were individuals who took a special vow not to drink alcohol and called themselves 'Nazirites' (Num. 6:2). In the *Injil* (Gospel) we are taught that Jesus *did* drink wine, but that John the Baptist (*Yahya* in the Qur'an), his cousin who prepared the way for him, did *not* drink. This means that since there is no law on the subject, we are free to follow the spirit of the teaching of Jesus, which is that we should practise self-control and be careful stewards of what God has given to us. Christians believe that it is wrong to be drunk. Some choose voluntarily not to drink alcohol, but others feel free to drink in moderation.

'Do you drink wine in church?'

We do have a special service instituted by Jesus which we call 'Holy Communion', 'the Lord's Supper', 'the Eucharist' or 'the Mass'. It is a time when we remember the death and resurrection of Jesus. Many Christians have a taste of wine (some substitute juice for the wine) and a small piece of bread or wafer at this service, following the pattern of Jesus' last meal before he died.

'Christianity makes impossible and unrealistic moral demands, such as "turning the other cheek". Islam doesn't demand more than is reasonable, or expect an unnatural degree of self-denial.'

Christianity does set very high moral standards, but this is because God is holy and says many times in the Bible, 'Be holy, for I am holy' (Lev. 11:44). When we read the teaching of Jesus, we try to understand the spirit of what he said rather than treat his words as a series of laws which have to be obeyed to the letter. 'Turning the other cheek', for example, means at the very least that when we are insulted, we do not reply with an insult.

Although we recognize that the standards set by Jesus are very high, we believe in God's forgiveness. When, therefore, we know we have fallen short of God's standards and ask forgiveness, we can be sure that God has forgiven us. We also believe that the Holy Spirit of God lives within us when we trust Jesus. He works in our conscience, prompts us about how we should behave in particular situations, and gives us power beyond our own natural power to follow the way of Christ.

'Islam has no priesthood, no special caste of people who are set aside to perform priestly functions which no one else can perform.'

In many churches there are certain services (such as Holy Communion or the Lord's Supper, baptism and marriage) which can be led only by a priest or an ordained minister, although in some churches there are no ordained ministers. Different churches give different answers to explain the reasons for this, but all agree that these ceremonies are not a special kind of magic. They believe that, for the sake of good order in the church, the services should be led by a person who is authorized by the whole church to lead them. While there are significant differences between the main branches of the church (Orthodox, Catholic and Protestant), there is no suggestion that the priest is a kind of mediator without whom we cannot come into the presence of God.

19. SOCIAL AND POLITICAL ISSUES

What follows are questions that Muslims often put to Christians and people in the West regarding social and political issues. Again, each one is followed by a brief possible response.

'Children don't obey their parents in the West as they do in Muslim countries.'

Islam emphasizes obedience to parents very strongly. Christians agree with this teaching because one of the Ten Commandments says, 'Honour your father and your mother' (Exod. 20:12). So both Christianity and Islam have the same teaching at this point. This is an example of how the Christian way of life is not being followed in the West. The methods of discipline that are used in some societies rely on the pressure of the extended family and the community. But these pressures tend to be weaker in Western societies, with the result that young people of all religious communities do not see the same need to obey and respect their parents.

As Christians living in a society that is not Christian, we try to teach our children the right way to live and behave, but when they reach a certain age we do not feel we can force them to live in a certain way. We want to leave them free to choose the right way for themselves, because we believe that they will be stronger in the end if they follow this way without being forced to. Many issues of this kind have more to do with *culture* than with *religion*.

'Look at how degenerate the West has become! If this is what Christianity has done for the West, it isn't a very good advertisement for Christianity.'

For many centuries during the Middle Ages, it was assumed that almost everyone in Western countries was a Christian, just as in Muslim countries today everyone is regarded as a Muslim unless he or she belongs to another religion. The situation in the West today, however, is very different: only a minority would call themselves committed or convinced Christians, while the majority would say that they are Christians only in name (because they believe in God, but not in Jesus), or that they have no religious beliefs at all.

Christians would argue that violence and permissiveness in the West today are the results not of following Christian teaching, but of refusing to follow Christian teaching. If Muslims say that the West is in a bad state because of Christianity, it is all too easy for Christians to reply that the Muslim world is in a bad state because of Islam. Can we not get beyond this kind of accusation and try to understand that *both* Christians *and* Muslims face the same difficult problems and challenges in the modern world?

'Why do Christians tend to support the state of Israel without question?'

Many Christians do give strong support to Israel, partly because of their sympathy with the Jewish people, and partly because some Christians teach that the establishment of the state of Israel is the fulfilment of promises and prophecies given by God in the Bible. Most Christians, however, disagree strongly with this way of interpreting the Bible. While they accept the existence of Israel within the 1967 borders, they are critical of some of the policies of Israel and point out some of the problems involved in the idea of a 'Jewish state' in this particular part of the world. Official statements from church leaders have encouraged Christians to have a more balanced view of the conflict. They are very aware of the injustices suffered by Palestinian Arabs and want to work for a just solution that allows Jews and Arabs to live side by side in peace.[1]

'Why do you not allow us to practise Islamic law within our own Islamic communities in the West?'

There is nothing to prevent Muslims arranging inheritance on the basis of Islamic law and dividing a person's estate according to the proportions laid down in Islamic law. But Islamic law concerning marriage would not be acceptable because it allows up to four wives. It is a fundamental assumption in Western states that every person comes under the same law, and there cannot be a different law on these important issues for every religious community.

'Why do Christians object to the introduction of Islamic law in countries with large Muslim communities?'

Muslims themselves in these communities are not all agreed, and some of them oppose the introduction of Islamic law. Where Islamic law has been introduced, it has created many problems for non-Muslims. Although it is supposed to be applied only to Muslims, non-Muslims are bound to be affected, for example, by regulations concerning dress. It has often been used to discriminate against minorities (see chapter 36, 'Some issues facing Christians today').

QUESTIONS AND OBJECTIONS
CONCERNING CHRISTIAN BELIEFS

The following are some of the main objections that Muslims tend to put to Christians about their beliefs. All we are attempting to do here is to suggest the kind of short answers that we can give, which (we hope) will lead to further discussion. Chapter 22 goes into some of these issues in greater depth.

'Do you believe in the Trinity? Do you believe in three gods?'

We do not believe in three gods! We believe in one God as strongly as any Muslim. When we speak of God the Father, God the Son and God the Holy Spirit, we are not thinking of three separate and distinct gods. Christianity is a monotheistic religion, as much as Islam. The word 'Trinity' is not found in the Bible, but the idea is taught in the Bible.

'Why do you say that Jesus is the "Son of God"?'

Jesus called himself 'the Son' and spoke of God as 'the Father' and 'my Father'. We do not believe that Jesus was the son of God in any literal or physical sense; this idea is as repugnant to us as it is to Muslims. We believe that 'God is love' in his very nature, and that there has always been a relationship of love between God the Father, God the Son and God the Holy Spirit, even before the creation of the universe. Jesus of Nazareth is more than a prophet, since he was fully human and fully divine. When we say that Jesus is the Son of God, what we mean in the simplest possible language is that he was like God in a way that no other human being has ever been. When we look at Jesus, therefore, and see what he was like, we have some idea of what God is like. We could say that in a profound sense, *God is like Jesus.*

'Why do you believe that Jesus was crucified?'

The New Testament explains that it was not out of weakness that God allowed Jesus to be crucified. It was his way of showing up the evil in human nature in its true colours. But it was also his way of showing how much he loves us and wants to forgive us for all our sins. Christians see the death of Jesus as a sacrifice for sins, as the one final and complete sacrifice which does away with the need for any other sacrifice offered to gain forgiveness of sins. God allowed Jesus to experience death because all human beings have to die. But by raising him from the dead, God not only vindicated Jesus and revealed his true identity, but destroyed the power of death once and for all for those who trust in him.

'Your Scriptures have been corrupted.'

We know you have been taught that our Scriptures have been corrupted. But according to the Holy Qur'an, the message which God revealed to the Prophet Muhammad confirmed the previous Scriptures: the *Tawrat* revealed to Moses, the *Zabur* revealed to David, and the *Injil* to Jesus. If these Scriptures, which were in the hands of the Jews and the Christians at the time of the Prophet Muhammad, were *already* corrupt, how could the Qur'an be a confirmation of these corrupt Scriptures? Can you tell me who corrupted the Scriptures, and when it was done? Since the Holy Qur'an teaches that God watches over and protects his Word revealed in the Qur'an (15:9), can we not trust him to watch over other scriptures as well? Would you like to read the life of Jesus as it is recorded in the *Injil*? How can you say that our Scriptures are corrupted if you have not read them?

'Your Scriptures are full of mistakes and contradictions.'

Christians are aware of the so-called contradictions that you find in the Bible, because Christian scholars have been aware of them for a long time. But they have their own way of explaining these differences, and some of them can be explained very easily. Others raise harder questions of interpretation. Are you prepared to listen to the way we explain these difficulties?

Some Christians say that they find contradictions in the Qur'an. How would you feel if we were to criticize the Qur'an? But we do not want to do so, because we are not interested in criticizing the Qur'an. If Muslims do not like Christians criticizing the Qur'an, why do Muslims criticize the Bible?

The basic reason why you have problems with the apparent contradictions in the Bible is that you are comparing the Bible with the Qur'an. You believe that the Qur'an is the very words revealed directly to Muhammad, and you assume that the Bible was revealed in exactly the same way. Christians do believe that the Bible is the Word of God, and that God through his Holy Spirit inspired the different books of the Bible. But the Word of God in the Bible has come through a large number of different authors. The Bible is therefore for us *both* the Word of God *and* the words of human beings. The fundamental problem between us at this point is that we have different views of revelation. Muslims believe that the supreme revelation God has given was in the form of *a book*, the Qur'an. Christians, however, believe that the supreme revelation was given in *a person*, Jesus (see further chapter 28, 'Crucial differences').

'We recognize Jesus as a prophet. Why don't you recognize Muhammad as a prophet?'

If we recognized Muhammad as a prophet in the way that you do, we would be Muslims. We are glad to accept the teaching of the Qur'an about the one true God which we also find in our Scriptures. But we cannot believe the whole Qur'an, because its teaching is different at many points from the teaching of our Scriptures.

We believe that Jesus was the last of the prophets, God's final word to the world. We see Jesus as the most complete revelation of God in the form of a human being. We cannot believe that there could be any more complete revelation of God after Jesus. Would you light a candle when the sun is shining?

'Why do you not recognize that the Bible foretells the coming of Muhammad?'

Two verses are often used to support this argument. The first is the words from Deuteronomy about a new prophet who was to come: 'The LORD your God will raise up for you a prophet like me from among your own brothers' (Deut. 18:15). This could hardly refer to Muhammad, since Moses says that this prophet is to be raised up 'from among your own brothers', that is, from among the children of Israel.

The second verse is the words of Jesus about the coming of the Paraclete, 'I will ask the Father, and he will give you another Counsellor to be with you for ever – the Spirit of truth' (John 14:16–17; cf. John 14:26; 15:26; 16:7). Christians have always interpreted these words as a prediction about the coming of the Holy Spirit. Jesus never spoke about another prophet who was to come after him.

'All religions are basically the same. Why worry about the differences?'

This attitude comes as a surprise to Christians who have been accustomed to questions which are highly critical of Christian beliefs. It is often much harder to answer, simply because it seems to be so generous and tolerant towards Christians. This apparently charitable and tolerant view of other faiths springs in some cases from a genuine desire to avoid the painful controversies of the past. In other cases, however, it arises out of complacency and indifference, and may suggest that the person is not interested in the search for truth and wants to avoid discussion of differences between faiths.

This is not how the Qur'an speaks about other faiths! Although it is generous towards Jews and Christians because they are 'People of the Book', it is very critical of them in certain respects. Muhammad therefore openly invited them to reject some of their distinctive beliefs and to accept the religion of Islam. The Qur'an is much less generous, however, towards 'idolaters', and during the first few centuries of the spread of Islam, those who were not Jews or Christians were offered the choice of accepting Islam, slavery or death.

Do you actually know what we believe about Jesus? A detailed comparison between the Muslim's understanding of Muhammad and the Christian's understanding of Jesus should indicate that there are very significant differences between the two faiths. There are dangers in making such comparisons, since the role of Muhammad in Islam is quite different from the role of Jesus in Christianity. But if you know and understand what Christians believe about Jesus (even if you do not believe it), you can hardly say that the differences between the two religions are insignificant.

21. GUIDELINES IN DISCUSSION WITH MUSLIMS

This chapter outlines ten basic 'dos and don'ts' in discussion with Muslims.

1. Be prepared to speak about anything!

Do not feel that you need always to be speaking about 'religious' subjects. You should be happy to speak about any subjects that are of interest to them or to you, which arise naturally out of the situation.

2. Do not start an argument if you can possibly help it.

Whenever you see the warning signals in yourself, remember Paul's words addressed to Timothy, the young and enthusiastic Christian worker: 'Don't have anything to do with foolish and stupid arguments, because you know they produce quarrels. And the Lord's servant must not quarrel; instead, he must be kind to everyone, able to teach, not resentful' (2 Tim. 2:23–24).

If you do find yourself in an argument, do not be too concerned about 'winning' it! Even if you win an argument, you may lose the person. Building a genuine relationship of trust and friendship is more important than defeating someone in an argument.

3. Resist the temptation to criticize Islam.

The words of Jesus about standing in judgment on other people are surely relevant to our dealings with Muslims: 'Do not judge, or you too will be judged. For in the same way as you judge others, you will be judged, and with the measure you use, it will be measured to you' (Matt. 7:1–2). In other words, if you criticize Islam, its civilization, its belief and its whole way of life, you may be inviting Muslims to do the same to you and your faith.

The words that follow are also relevant: 'Why do you look at the speck of sawdust in your brother's eye and pay no attention to the plank in your own eye? ... You hypocrite, first take the plank out of your own eye, and then you will see clearly to remove the speck from your brother's eye' (Matt. 7:3–5).

4. Do all you can to remove misunderstandings (e.g. about Christians worshipping three gods, about Jesus being 'Son of God' in a physical sense, about the West being Christian, etc.).

Even if you do not feel you have achieved very much by doing so, you may at least be clearing the ground, making it easier for someone to see Jesus and understand the Christian way more clearly. Robert Bruce, a missionary in Persia in the nineteenth century, used to say, 'I cannot say I am reaping a harvest; I am not even planting seed. Perhaps all I am doing is removing the stones.'

5. Try to distinguish between what is important and what is less important.

Do not spend all your time debating secondary issues (like eating pork and drinking wine), if you then have no opportunity to deal with more important underlying issues such as the role of law, the human condition, forgiveness, etc.

6. Be prepared to admit the mistakes and crimes of Christians in the past and present.

Paul's words in Romans 2:24 about the Jews of his time can easily be paraphrased and made to apply to the Christian church throughout its history: 'Christ's name is blasphemed in the Muslim world because of you.' Therefore we need to be willing to say with the psalmist, 'We have sinned, even as our fathers did; we have done wrong and acted wickedly' (Ps. 106:6). This means, for example, admitting our shame about the Crusades.

7. Do not be too impatient with discussion about political and social issues.

It is often tempting to avoid questions of this kind, either because they are very complex and we do not know enough about them, or because we think they are very secondary and take us away from 'the real thing'. But Jesus talked about hungering and thirsting after right-eousness/justice. And since these questions usually express very genuine concerns that are often related to justice, we should be willing to discuss them when they are important for others. Something of the spirit of Christ can be conveyed even in dealing with difficult questions like these.

8. Do not underestimate the power of personal testimony.

If you believe that you know God in a personal way, do not be afraid to say so, and to say why you believe that this kind of personal relationship is possible. If you believe that your sins have been forgiven and that you have no fear of the Day of Judgment, explain the basis of your confidence in God's forgiveness.

9. Be content to explain one small aspect of the gospel at a time.

Do not feel you have failed if you have not been able to explain 'the whole gospel' at one time. There is no single technique for explaining the gospel to a Muslim. We must resist the temptation to think that one simple technique is bound to produce results and save us from much heartache and agony.

Encourage your friend at the appropriate time to read one of the Gospels. Luke is perhaps the best one to start with (see chapter 33, 'Using the Bible'). Matthew is also valuable, and the Sermon on the Mount is especially powerful for Muslims, although some find it difficult because it is so Jewish. Mark introduces a stumbling block in the very first sentence by speaking of Jesus as 'the Son of God'. John may be helpful as a second Gospel to read, or with Muslims who have been influenced by Sufism.

10. Be yourself, be honest and vulnerable, and open to learn.

Do not try to be something other than what you are! Others can probably see through you and know how genuine you are. They will easily be able to recognize whether or not you like them and respect them.

Honesty and openness about yourself (how you live and what you believe) may encourage your friends to be honest and open about themselves. Being vulnerable will always communicate a great deal about who you are, what you believe and what is most important for you.

Be open to learn. You should never feel that you know all the answers and have nothing to learn. You should always be open to be challenged by what you hear from Muslims and what you see in their lives.

This chapter goes deeper into some of the objections touched on in chapter 20. In each case we need first of all to listen carefully to what lies behind the objection. Only then can we reflect on how to respond.

'The Bible has been corrupted.'

The Qur'an speaks of three Scriptures that were revealed before the Qur'an:

- the *Tawrat* (Torah), revealed to Moses (3:93);
- the *Zabur* (Psalms), revealed to David (4:163; 17:55; 21:105);
- the *Injil* (Gospel), revealed to Jesus (5:46).

Jews and Christians are called 'People of the Book' or 'People of the Scriptures' (2:105; 3:64), and Muslims are told that they must believe the previous Scriptures as well as the Qur'an:

> O ye who believe! Believe in Allah and His messenger and the Scripture which He hath revealed unto His messenger, and the Scripture which He revealed aforetime. Whoso disbelieveth in Allah and His angels and His

scriptures and His messengers and the Last Day, he verily hath wandered far astray. (4:136; cf. 5:66, 68)

Muslims are to believe the previous Scriptures because the Qur'an confirms the truth of them:

> As for that which We inspire in thee of the Scripture, it is the Truth confirming that which was (revealed) before it. (35:31; cf. 2:97)

> And if thou (Muhammad) art in doubt concerning that which We reveal unto thee, then question those who read the Scripture (that was) before thee. Verily the Truth from thy Lord hath come to thee. So be not thou of the waverers. (10:95)

There are, however, four verses in the Qur'an which speak about the 'corruption' or 'falsification' (*tahrif*) of these previous Scriptures. The word that is used, *harrafa*, is usually translated 'change':

> Have ye any hope that they will be true to you when a party of them used to listen to the Word of Allah, then used to *change* it, after they had understood it, knowingly. (2:75)

> Some of those who are Jews *change* the words from their context [or 'pervert words from their meanings', Bell] ... distorting with their tongues and slandering religion. (4:46)

> They *change* words from their context and forget a part of that whereof they were admonished. (5:13)

> ... the Jews: listeners for the sake of falsehood, listeners on behalf of other folk who come not unto thee, *changing* words from their context... (5:41)

The charge of corruption often goes beyond the accusation of the falsification of the *text* to claim that there are serious errors in the *content* of the Bible. These are three of the most common examples that are given.

- The Pentateuch cannot have been written by Moses, because Deuteronomy 34:5–8 speaks about his death.

- The four Gospels are full of contradictions.
- Jews and Christians have removed prophecies about the coming of Muhammad.

How should we attempt to answer this charge that the Scriptures have been corrupted?

1. None of these verses suggests that the text *of the Bible has been corrupted.*
One of the accusations seems to be that certain Jews deliberately mispronounced words spoken by Muhammad, probably playing on the resemblance between certain Arabic and Hebrew words (see 3:78). They are also accused of taking words in their Scriptures out of context and changing the meaning of words.

In other verses the Jews are accused of 'hiding' or 'concealing' their Scriptures.

A party of them knowingly conceal the truth. (2:146; cf. 2:159, 174; 3:72)

O people of the Scripture! Now hath Our messenger come unto you, expounding unto you much of that which ye used to hide in the Scripture... (5:15; cf. 6:92)

This probably means that in discussion with Muslims, the Jews refused to quote verses that would support the teaching of Islam. This could have included predictions about prophets to come in the future, which might be interpreted as referring to the coming of Muhammad.

There are only two verses in which accusations of this kind are made explicitly against Christians. In one of these the Christians are accused of hiding or concealing parts of what God had revealed in their Scriptures (2:140). In the other they are blamed for forgetting part of God's revelation in Scripture (5:14).

2. The accusation about the corruption of the text of the Bible was developed by later Muslim apologists.
Muslim writers from the time of Muhammad to the eleventh century consistently understood the qur'anic verses about 'corruption' to mean that Jews and Christians had *misinterpreted* their Scriptures.

'Umar, for example, the second caliph, believed that Christian monks and teachers had distorted the teaching of the Bible by giving false interpretations, or simply by covering up clear teaching, for instance about the coming of Muhammad. Similarly, al-Tabari (839–923), one of the earliest authoritative commentators on the Qur'an, records a saying of Muhammad in which he admits that the Torah is God's truth, but accuses the Jews of suppressing its teaching and altering its contents. A work attributed to al-Ghazali (died 1111), called *An Excellent Refutation of the Divinity of Jesus According to the Gospels*, quotes many passages from the Bible, and especially the New Testament, without ever questioning the trustworthiness of the text.

The accusation that Jews and Christians had tampered with the text of their Scriptures first appeared in the writings of Muslim apologists from the eleventh century, and it was probably developed to explain the many discrepancies between the Bible and the Qur'an. Al-Juwayni (died 1085), for example, wrote a treatise in which he argued that the Scriptures must have been corrupted because the Qur'an says that the coming of Muhammad was foretold in the previous Scriptures, which the Christians denied. He based his argument also on the differences between the four Gospels. Ibn Hazm (994–1064), a more polemical writer from Spain, lists contradictions within the Bible and discrepancies between the Qur'an and the Bible to prove that the text has been corrupted.

Not all Muslim apologists, however, have adopted this argument about the corruption of the text. Muhammad 'Abduh (1849–1905), for example, an Egyptian reformer who worked for the renewal of Islam, wrote in his commentary on the Qur'an that although he believed the Jews had altered their Scriptures, he accepted the text of the Gospels as authentic.

3. In answering Muslims who say that our Scriptures have been corrupted, we can politely but firmly ask in reply, 'When do you believe they were corrupted and by whom?'

If they say they were corrupted *before* the time of Muhammad, we can ask them to explain why the Qur'an says that the message revealed to Muhammad was a confirmation of previous Scriptures.

> He hath revealed unto thee [Muhammad] the Scripture with truth,
> confirming that which was (revealed) before it, even as He revealed the

Torah and the Gospel. (3:3, literally 'confirming what is between their
hands'; cf. 2:136; 4:136; 10:95; 41:43)

It is clear that the Scriptures referred to here must be *those which the Jews
and Christians had in their hands at the time.*

Believe in what We have revealed confirming that which ye possess. (4:47,
literally 'what is with you'; cf. 2:91)

And unto thee have We revealed the Scripture with the truth, confirming
whatever Scripture was before it, and a watcher over it. (5:48; cf. 6:116;
10:65; 18:28)

How then could Muhammad say, on the one hand, that the revelations
contained in the Qur'an simply confirm the Scriptures of the Jews and
Christians and, on the other hand, that the Scriptures which the Jews
and Christians have in their hands have been corrupted?

If they say that the Scriptures were corrupted *after* the time of
Muhammad, we can point out that the manuscripts on which our
present Bible is based were written centuries before the time of
Muhammad. For example, the Dead Sea Scrolls, which include
manuscripts of every book of the Old Testament except one, were
written before AD 68. One of the oldest Greek manuscripts of the
whole of the New Testament, the Codex Alexandrinus, dates from
the fifth century and can be seen by anyone in the British Museum in
London. Manuscripts of some parts of the New Testament can be
dated to the early second century.

4. Muslims speak of God as the protector of his Word.
There are verses in the Qur'an which speak about God 'watching
over' Scripture.

Lo! We, even We, reveal the Remainder, and lo! We verily are its Guardian.
(15:9)

This suggests that it is unthinkable that God could allow any of his
Scriptures to be corrupted. There are also several verses which teach
that nothing can alter the words of God (6:34; 10:64; 18:27).

5. Many Muslims claim that the Gospel of Barnabas is the original Injil *revealed to Jesus.*

It is not difficult, however, to show from internal evidence that the Gospel of Barnabas cannot be an authentic writing from the first century.

- It contains historical anachronisms: for example, the feudal custom of a vassal owing his lord a portion of his cup; a notary recording a case in court; wine casks made of wood rather than wineskins; medieval court procedures; certain images come from the fourteenth-century poet Dante, including the idea of 'circles of hell'; it uses the Latin Vulgate translation which was written in the fourth century; there is a reference to the Year of Jubilee being celebrated every hundred years, but in the Old Testament it was celebrated every fifty years, and was not until 1343 that Pope Boniface issued a papal declaration that it should be celebrated every hundred years.
- It contains elementary errors in geography: for example, it locates Nazareth on the shores of the Lake of Galilee, and speaks of Jesus sailing to Nazareth.
- There are historical errors: it says that Jesus was born while Pilate was governor of Judea (but he did not become governor until AD 26/7).
- It contradicts the Qur'an at several points: for example, it claims that Jesus said, 'I am not the Messiah, but after me shall come the Messiah,' whereas in the Qur'an Jesus is frequently called the Messiah (*al-masih*); and it supports the doctrine of free will, which the Qur'an rejects.

From other internal evidence it is generally thought that the Gospel of Barnabas was written in Italy in the sixteenth century. The author was probably a Spaniard of Jewish background who had recently converted to Islam. The Italian manuscript was discovered in Amsterdam in 1709. There is no evidence of its existence before that time, and no references to it before the sixteenth century. Some Muslim scholars today have no hesitation in saying that they believe this to be a forgery, and regret that it is still used by many Muslims.

6. Underlying the charge of corruption is the Muslim understanding of revelation and inspiration of Scripture, which is different from the Christian understanding.

As long as Muslims approach the Bible with the idea that it must have been revealed directly to the minds of prophets in precisely the same way that they believe the Qur'an was revealed to Muhammad, they are bound to have problems with the Bible. It simply does not read as if it were dictated by God (see further chapter 28, 'Crucial differences').

7. At some stage it may be necessary to discuss questions concerning biblical criticism.

Muslims today who like to engage in controversy of this kind often take a keen interest in these subjects and are well aware of what some scholars – especially those who are more radical and critical in their approach – have written about the Bible. Christians can sometimes be at a disadvantage in discussions of this kind if they have not had an opportunity to study these issues for themselves. They need to be able to point out to Muslims that there are many Christian scholars who do not have such a negative approach towards the text and who still hold very orthodox Christian beliefs.

8. Even if we convince Muslims with these arguments, we have not solved the problem for them!

As far as Muslims are concerned, since the New Testament speaks of Jesus as 'God' or 'the Son of God', *it must by definition be corrupted* – regardless of what the Qur'an or Muslim apologists say. Our arguments, therefore, have limited value unless we can persuade our Muslim friends to read one of the Gospels with a slightly more open mind. We will then need to be prepared to tackle fundamental issues that arise from reading the text – such as the divinity of Christ, the Trinity and the crucifixion.

'Jesus was not the Son of God.'

The Muslim denial of the divinity of Christ is based on such passages as the following:

And they say: Allah hath taken unto Himself a Son. Be He glorified! Nay, but whatsoever is in the heaven and the earth is His. All are subservient unto Him. (2:116)

It befitteth not (the Majesty of) Allah that He should take unto Himself a son. Glory be to Him! When He decreeth a thing, He saith unto it only: Be! and it is. (19:35; cf. 19:19–92)

And the Jews say: Ezra is the son of Allah, and the Christians say: The Messiah is the son of Allah. That is their saying with their mouths. They imitate the saying of those who disbelieved of old. Allah (Himself) fighteth against them. How perverse are they! They have taken as lords beside Allah their rabbis and their monks and the Messiah son of Mary, when they were bidden to worship only One God. There is no god save Him. Be he glorified from all that they ascribe as partner (unto Him)! (9:30–31)

Say: He is Allah, the One!
Allah, the eternally Besought of all!
He begetteth not nor was begotten.
And there is none comparable unto Him. (112:10)

The following points may help in working out our response.

1. The original background to these denials of the divine sonship of Jesus seems to have been Muhammad's denunciation of the gods and goddesses in Mecca who were thought to have sons and daughters.
Although Muhammad probably had contact with some Christians during his early ministry in Mecca, his main conflict was with the pagan idolaters who worshipped, for example, Allat, al-'Uzzah and Manat, the daughters of Allah.

At a later stage Muhammad directed his protests at Christian beliefs about Jesus, which must have seemed to him to belong to the same category as these pagan ideas. But his original protest was against the debased polytheism he encountered at Mecca. This is clear from such passages as the following:

Yet they ascribe as partners unto Him the jinn, although He did create them, and impute falsely, without knowledge, sons and daughters unto Him.

Glorified be He and high exalted above (all) that they ascribe (unto Him). (6:101)

We will want to say to Muslims that Christians reject the idea of Jesus being the Son of God in any physical sense as strongly as they do. The idea of Jesus being born of a union between God and the Virgin Mary is utterly abhorrent to us as Christians. If this is what the first Muslims understood by this term, it is as blasphemous to us as it is to Muslims.

2. There are good reasons for believing that the 'Trinity' rejected by Muhammad was not the Trinity of the Father, Son and Holy Spirit, as we understand it. The following verse is attempting to correct the misunderstanding that Jesus and Mary had been made into gods by Christians.

And when Allah saith: O Jesus, son of Mary! Didst thou say unto mankind: Take me and my mother for two gods beside Allah? he saith: Be glorified! It was not mine to utter that to which I had no right. (5:116)

It is not hard to understand how the portrayal of Mary in Christian icons at the time could have given any observer the idea that Mary was to be honoured and worshipped in the same way as Jesus.

3. There is no need to make too much of the title 'Son of God' in discussion with Muslims, and there is good biblical precedent for avoiding names and titles that cause offence and create misunderstandings.
Although the word 'Messiah' (Christ) came from the Old Testament, the idea had been distorted by the Jews in their speculation about the coming messianic age. Since Jesus never referred to himself as the Messiah, it must have been because he refused to conform to the popular conception of the Messiah as a political or military figure. He preferred to speak of himself as 'the Son of Man' (a title almost certainly taken from Dan. 7:13ff.) and alluded to himself as the Suffering Servant (from Isa. 53, etc.; cf. Mark 10:45). Thus when Peter confessed that Jesus was the Christ, Jesus went on to say, 'The Son of Man must suffer' (Mark 8:29, 31). Similarly, when the high priest said, 'Tell us if you are the Christ,' Jesus answered, 'Yes, it is as you say ... But I say to all of you: In the future you will see the Son of Man ...'

(Matt. 26:63–64). It was as if Jesus was saying, 'I am not the Messiah in the sense that you understand the word. And because the term is so open to misunderstandings, I prefer to speak of myself as the Son of Man.' When Pilate asked a similar question, 'Are you the king of the Jews?' Jesus answered, 'Yes, it is as you say' (Matt. 27:11). In John's version, Jesus went on to describe his ministry in terms of declaring the truth (John 18:33–37) (see further chapter 35, 'Explaining Christian beliefs about Jesus').

If Jesus avoided the term Messiah so deliberately, we today have every justification for avoiding the title 'Son of God' as much as we can in speaking with Muslims. There is no dishonesty or compromise in trying to find other ways of speaking about Jesus.

4. Our belief in Jesus as the Son of God is based on the words and actions of Jesus himself, and not only on the teaching of John, Paul and the other apostles. When Muslims say it was Paul and the early Christians who corrupted the simple *Injil* which Jesus proclaimed, we need to show that Paul's teaching was entirely consistent with the teaching of Jesus and his disciples. According to the Gospels, Jesus said and did things which amounted to a claim that he was equal with God.

- He said he would one day judge all people (Matt. 25:31–46; John 5:22–23).
- He said he could give people eternal life (John 5:19–21; 11:25–26).
- He forgave sins (Mark 2:5–7).
- He called God 'Father' or 'my Father' and, when speaking to his disciples, spoke of 'your Father'. He never spoke of 'our Father', except when giving his disciples words to use in prayer. He thus made a clear distinction between his own relationship with God and his disciples' relationship with God (Matt. 12:50; 6:6; John 20:17).

There are at least two important ideas implied in this Father-Son relationship: he was claiming that he knew God in a unique way (Matt. 11:25–27) and that he was completely obedient to the will of God (John 8:27–29, 55). When the Jews heard him speaking of God as his Father, they understood that he was claiming to be equal with God, and this claim was one of the main reasons for the opposition which led to his death. There are about 150 verses in the Gospels in which Jesus speaks of God as 'Father'. They are an integral part of the teaching of Jesus and cannot be cut out without changing the whole message.

5. The sonship of Jesus is not a purely theological issue; it has profound implications for our understanding of who we are and the kind of relationship God wants to have with those who trust in him.

If the Qur'an teaches us to think of ourselves as slaves or servants of God, the New Testament offers us the possibility of becoming sons and daughters of God who know, love and obey God as Father. Jesus spoke of God as 'my Father' and shocked his contemporaries by addressing God as '*Abba*' (almost the familiar 'Father' or 'Dad'). The wonder of the gospel is that Jesus also gave his disciples the right to address God as 'our Father' (Matt. 6:9). Paul shows the same familiarity in speaking of God as '*Abba*' (Rom. 8:15). When we trust in Jesus, he gives us the right to become sons and daughters of God (John 1:12–13).

6. The Qur'an uses 'son of' language metaphorically.

The Qur'an itself offers possible starting points for discussing Jesus' claim of divine sonship.

- The Qur'an recognizes that the expression 'son of' can be used in a metaphorical sense. For example, the expression 'son of the way' (*ibni-ssabil*, 2:215) is translated 'wayfarer'.
- One verse suggests a different idea of what it might mean for God to have a son: 'If Allah had willed to choose a son (*walad*, child), he could have chosen what he would of that which He hath created. Be He glorified! He is Allah, the One, the Absolute' (39:4).

These words do not rule out the possibility of God having a son, although the idea of sonship assumes that the son is a creature and not of the same nature as God himself. In the following verse, however, there is no such assumption about the kind of sonship implied: 'Say: "If (God) Most Gracious had a son, I would be the first to worship"' (43:81, A. Yusuf Ali's translation). The implication of this verse seems hard for some Muslims to accept, which must explain why M. M. Pickthall gives a completely different translation: 'Say (O Muhammad): "The Beneficent One hath no son. I am first among the worshippers."'

Although the Qur'an frequently says that God makes no difference between the prophets, there are many ways in which Jesus, son of Mary, is unique: he was born of a virgin; he worked miracles; he was given titles which no other apostle or prophet was given – 'exalted (above others) in degree', 'supported with the Holy Spirit' (2:253), 'a messenger of Allah, and His word which he conveyed unto Mary, and a spirit from Him' (4:171), 'illustrious in the world and the Hereafter, and one of those brought near (unto Allah)' (3:45).

It can sometimes be helpful to ask Muslims to give their explanation of the uniqueness of Jesus, and then to offer our explanation from the *Injil.*

Many Christians have found that one of the most useful bridges in the Qur'an is the following verse which speaks about Jesus.

> O People of the Scripture! Do not exaggerate in your religion nor utter aught concerning Allah save the truth. The Messiah, Jesus son of Mary, was only a messenger of Allah, and His Word which He conveyed unto Mary, and a spirit from Him. So believe in Allah and His messengers, and say not 'Three' – Cease! (it is) better for you! – Allah is only One God. Far is it removed from His transcendent majesty that he should have a son. His is all that is in the heavens and all that is in the earth. And Allah is sufficient as Defender. (4:171)

This verse accuses Christians of claiming too much for Jesus, although it seems to suggest that Christians believe in three gods rather than in one. In spite of this, however, if we are prepared to listen to Muslims' understanding of the titles 'Word' and 'Spirit', they may be open to listen to what we mean when we speak of Jesus as 'the Word'. Our words are a part of us – they express our mind and our will. Similarly, if we cannot separate our words from ourselves, how can we separate Jesus the Word from God?

Muslims believe that Jesus is a Word from God in the sense that he was created by divine fiat, by the word of God. Christians believe that he is the Word of God in the sense that he is the one who expresses the mind and will of God most fully to the human race. Through Jesus, God has spoken and acted in a unique way (see further chapter 34, 'Starting from the Qur'an', and chapter 35, 'Explaining Christian beliefs about Jesus').

In using the Qur'an in this way, we are not trying to prove from the Qur'an that Jesus is divine. Rather, we are using the Qur'an as a bridge, and trying to understand and explain the differences between this understanding and the Christian understanding of the same titles given to Jesus in the Qur'an and the Bible.

'Jesus was not crucified.'

The most important verses in the Qur'an about the crucifixion come in a passage which lists many of the sins of the Jews: they worshipped the calf (4:153); they broke the covenant made at Sinai; they disbelieved the revelations of God; they killed his prophets (4:155); they spoke against the Virgin Mary 'a tremendous calumny' (4:156). The passage continues:

> And because of their saying: We slew the Messiah Jesus son of Mary,
> Allah's messenger – They slew him not nor crucified, but it appeared so
> unto them; and lo! those who disagree concerning it are in doubt thereof;
> they have no knowledge thereof save pursuit of a conjecture; they slew him
> not for certain. But Allah took him up unto Himself. Allah was ever
> Mighty, Wise. There is not one of the People of the Scripture but will
> believe in him before his death, and on the Day of Resurrection he will be a
> witness against them ... (4:157–159)

The traditional interpretation of this passage is that God raised Jesus up to heaven in a miraculous way before he was actually crucified, and that someone else who looked like him was crucified in his place. This interpretation has been linked with a saying of Muhammad about the return of Jesus to earth at the end of the world.

Many Muslims today, therefore, believe that when Jesus returns, he will establish Islam as the one true religion. Jews and Christians will believe in him in the same way that Muslims believe in him now. He will die and be buried. Finally, on the Last Day, he will be raised along with all people, exposing the false beliefs about him held by Jews and Christians.

There are at least three possible ways of understanding and responding to this traditional interpretation of the text.

1. The Qur'an does not actually deny the crucifixion; all it denies is that it was the Jews *who carried out the crucifixion.*

It is pointed out that a verse in another sura refers in similar terms to the victory of the Muslims over the forces of Mecca at the Battle of Badr: 'Ye (Muslims) slew them not, but Allah slew them. And thou (Muhammad) threwest not when thou didst throw, but Allah threw, that He might test the believers by a fair test from Him' (8:17).

David Brown offers the following suggestion as to how the reference to the crucifixion in 4:156–158 can be explained in the light of 8:17.

> These verses are intended to be a rebuke to the Jews, and particularly to Muhammad's contemporaries in Medina, for various acts of unbelief, and they only refer in passing to the story of the crucifixion. Within this context of an attack on the Jews for their opposition towards Muhammad as well as for other acts of unbelief, the reference to the crucifixion does no more than dispute the claim made by the Jews that they had disposed of the Christian Messiah and repudiated his claims to be an apostle of God by crucifying him. In particular, the phrases 'they did not kill him, nor did they crucify him', do not necessarily mean that there was no crucifixion, but that, even if there was, it was God who was responsible for all that happened during the last hours of the Messiah's life and that the Jews had done whatever they did only by permission of God's will . . .
>
> These verses, therefore, do not explicitly deny the Christian story of the crucifixion, for they refer primarily to Jewish claims against the Christians.[1]

This interpretation can perhaps be supported by three other passages in the Qur'an which appear to speak about the death of Jesus and imply that he died like every other human being. The significant words are given in italics.

- In the account of the birth of Jesus, the infant Jesus speaks to the people from the cradle: 'Peace on me the day I was born,

and *the day I die*, and the day I shall be raised alive!' (19:33)
Similar words are used in the same sura about John the Baptist
(19:15), where they presumably refer to his death and to the
general resurrection of all people.

- In another passage God says to Jesus: 'O Jesus! Lo! I am
  gathering thee and causing thee to ascend unto Me, and am
  cleansing thee of those who disbelieve and am setting those
  who follow thee above those who disbelieve until the Day of
  Resurrection' (3:55).
- In the third passage, Jesus is speaking to God: 'I spake unto
  them only that which Thou commandest me (saying): Worship
  Allah, my Lord and your Lord. I was a witness of them while I
  dwelt among them, and *when Thou tookest me* Thou was the
  Watcher over them' (5:117).

The italicized words in the last two passages are forms of the same
Arabic word *tawaffa*. The first passage could also be translated, 'Truly I
am he who calls you to death,' or, 'It is I who am causing you to die.'
David Brown comments:

> Both these verses refer to the return of Jesus to God at the end of his life,
> and the most straightforward interpretation of them is to suppose that they
> refer to a natural death of Jesus at the end of his earthly life. *Tawaffa* is
> often used in the Qur'an in the sense of bringing a soul to God at death,
> both when the subject of the verb is God (3:193; 10:46), and when the
> subject is the angels (16:28, 32). The word *tawaffa*, however, was originally
> used of a person receiving the full payment of his due or his rights, and
> when used of God in the Qur'an refers to men being called to pay their
> account in his presence, either at death, or in sleep when the soul comes
> to God but is returned to the body for a further term of life on earth.
>
> Thus the use of the word *tawaffa* in these two passages, with reference
> to the Messiah, is ambiguous and its exact meaning must be determined by
> consideration of other verses in the Qur'an: it could mean that Jesus died a
> natural death, but it can also mean that he was taken to heaven without
> undergoing the experience of physical death.[2]

If these verses, therefore, are interpreted as meaning that Jesus died a
natural death on the cross, and if the crucial passage in 4:156–159 is

taken to mean only that the Romans (not the Jews) crucified Jesus, it can be argued that the Qur'an does not deny Jesus' death on the cross. For several centuries there was considerable debate among Muslim commentators about the crucifixion, and many different answers were given by orthodox Muslims. Some Muslims today, who are more liberal in their approach but still consider themselves to be within the orthodox Muslim tradition, reject all theories about a substitute being crucified in the place of Jesus. Kamel Hussein, for example, writes in the introduction to his book *City of Wrong*:

> The idea of a substitute for Christ is a very crude way of explaining the Qur'anic text. They had to explain a lot to the masses. No cultured Muslim believes this nowadays. The text is taken to mean that the Jews thought they killed Christ, but God raised him in a way we can leave unexplained among the several mysteries which we have taken for granted on faith alone.[3]

The main difficulty with this first approach to the apparent denial of the crucifixion in the Qur'an is however careful and convincing our exegesis of the Qur'an may be, it goes against the traditional teaching which most Muslims accept today. It means therefore that we are putting ourselves in the position of trying to correct traditional Muslim teaching. Although some more open-minded and liberal Muslims are willing to accept this interpretation, the vast majority of Muslims accept as dogma that Jesus was not crucified.

2. The crucial text of 4:156–159 leaves open the possibility that Jesus died on the cross and emphasizes what God did to vindicate Jesus in the eyes of the Jews by raising him to heaven.
This is the approach developed by Chawkat Moucarry:

> The Jews wanted to subject Jesus to such a shameful death (cf. Matt. 27:20–23). But did they succeed? They certainly thought they did, but they were under an illusion, for God saved his servant, cleared his name of guilt and justified him by raising him from the dead and lifting him up to be with himself. This amazing act of divine intervention threw the Jews into confusion. Once they realized that the tomb was empty, they no longer knew if they had really killed Jesus. 'Assuredly, they did not kill him'

because God had subsequently brought him back to life, vindicated his name and honoured him by raising him to himself. If we accept this interpretation, the verb *rafaʻa*, 'to lift up' (4:158), would refer to God raising Jesus from the dead as well as raising him to heaven...

The Qur'anic answer implicitly shares the Jews' assumption that it is not possible for Jesus to be *both* God's Apostle *and* to have been crucified. The Jews say: Jesus was not sent by God, since we killed him. The Qur'an replies: Jesus was not killed by the Jews, because he was one of God's greatest messengers. Had he been crucified, God himself would have been defeated. By spoiling the murderous plans of the Jews and rescuing Jesus from their hands God vindicated his own name. He demonstrated, as sura 4:158 states, that he is indeed extremely powerful and wise.

We are faced here with two positions diametrically opposed to each other: the Jews' explanation that 'Jesus *was not* sent by God, which is why he was crucified'; and the Islamic explanation: 'Jesus *was* sent by God, which is why he *was not* crucified.'[4]

3. We start with the traditional assumption of most Muslims that God could not have allowed the crucifixion to happen, and attempt to explain how it is conceivable that God could have allowed it.

This approach can proceed in the following stages.

We can start with the traditional Muslim interpretation that these verses deny that Jesus was crucified, and accept the possibility that the Qur'an may not be entirely consistent with itself. While some verses may suggest a natural death, others suggest a miraculous deliverance.

We take care to distinguish between what the Qur'an seems to deny and what it does not deny. Kenneth Cragg, for example, has drawn attention to the fact that the Qur'an does not deny that the Jews wanted to kill Jesus or that Jesus was willing to be killed. All it seems to deny is that God could allow it to happen.[5]

We should note that before the time of Muhammad there were Christian sects which taught that Jesus was not crucified. Muhammad may therefore have heard the idea from sources of this kind. Geoffrey Parrinder describes some of these heretical ideas as follows.

There early arose in some Christian circles a reluctance to believe that Jesus, as a divine being and Son of God, could really die. Ignatius, writing about AD 115, said that some believed that Jesus 'suffered in semblance'.

The apocryphal Gospel of Peter in the second century said that on the cross Jesus was silent, since he 'felt no pain', and at the end 'the Lord cried out, saying, "My power, my power, you have left me." And when he spoke he was taken up...' The apocryphal Acts of John, about the middle of the second century, said that Jesus appeared to John in a cave during the crucifixion and said, 'John, unto the multitude below in Jerusalem I am being crucified and pierced with lances and reeds, and gall and vinegar is given me to drink. But unto thee I speak.' And later it is said, 'Nothing, therefore, of the things which they will say of me have I suffered ... I was pierced, yet I was not smitten; hanged, and I was not hanged; that blood flowed from me, and it flowed not.'[6]

Some of these ideas were found in the teaching of the Docetists (from the Greek word meaning 'to appear'), who taught that the suffering of Jesus was apparent, not real.

If this was the background to the denial of the crucifixion in the Qur'an, it might explain the difficult phrase *shubbiha lahum* ('it appeared so to them', 4:157). Muhammad could have first heard the idea from heretical Christian circles, and accepted it – not because he believed the teaching of the Docetists, but because the idea of Jesus not being crucified fitted his understanding of the uniqueness of Jesus and of God's obligation to vindicate his apostles. Since Jesus was unique in that he was born of a virgin, worked miracles, and was the 'Word' of God and 'a Spirit from Him', it makes perfect sense to believe that God should rescue him from death through a clearly supernatural intervention.

The Qur'an recognizes that the Jews killed some of the prophets 'wrongfully' (4:155; cf. 5:70; 2:87). Generally, however, the Qur'an teaches that God gives victory to his prophets and is bound to vindicate his servants, and there is no record of any *apostles* being killed. 'Verily Allah helpeth one who helpeth him' (22:40). 'It is incumbent on Us to save believers' (10:104). Thus there are accounts of how God delivers Noah (21:76–77), Abraham and Lot (21:71), and Moses (28:18–28).

There is a compelling logic in this kind of thinking. A government has an obligation to protect its ambassador in a foreign country, because the honour of the whole country is vested in its ambassador and it cannot stand idly by if he is insulted and humiliated in public. In the same way, thinks the Muslim, God cannot and will not stand idly by if his apostles and prophets are treated shamefully. He has an obligation to step in to vindicate them, for in vindicating their honour he is vindicating his own honour (see further chapter 34, 'Starting from the Qur'an').

It can be shown that some of the classical qur'anic commentators (e.g. al-Tabari, al-Razi, al-Qurtabi and al-Baidawi) seem to have accepted the possibility that Jesus may have been crucified, and that a debate on this issue went on for two or three centuries before a consensus developed which effectively made the denial of the crucifixion a dogma accepted by all Muslims. Mahmoud Ayoub, a contemporary Shi'ite scholar, is prepared to accept that Jesus could have been crucified, although he is still unable to accept the Christian interpretation of the significance of the crucifixion. Ayoub's approach is not widely accepted among Muslims, and the vast majority today are still unable to accept the crucifixion as a historical event.[7]

The greatest challenge for us is to find ways of helping Muslims to see the deeper logic which demands that the Messiah *must* suffer before entering his glory. We believe that God *did* vindicate Jesus, but not in the way that the disciples expected. God *did* vindicate and honour him, but not by rescuing him *before* death. He allowed him to go through death on our behalf, and only *after* that raised him from death.

Muslims believe that since forgiveness depends only on God's mercy and on human repentance and belief, there is no need for any sacrifice or atonement. Christians believe that forgiveness somehow involves suffering. God cannot simply forgive, as it were, by decree or a word, since forgiveness that is as easy as this must inevitably undermine the divine law. But by allowing Jesus to die on the cross, God demonstrated his judgment and condemnation of all that is evil, and at the same time showed his sacrificial and forgiving love to all who turn to him.

It may be helpful to remind ourselves that the first disciples had the greatest difficulty in understanding how God could have allowed Jesus to be crucified. Peter's reaction to Jesus' announcement of his cruel death (Mark 8:31–38) is very close to the reaction of Muslims to the idea of an apostle of God being killed. After his resurrection Jesus had to explain the necessity of his sufferings and death to his disciples:

'Was it not necessary that the Christ should suffer these things and enter into his glory?' (Luke 24:26 RSV)

If Muslims can begin to see why it is conceivable that God could allow Jesus his apostle to be crucified, they may be more willing to accept the fact that he *was* crucified (see further chapter 34, 'Starting from the Qur'an', and chapter 35, 'Explaining Christian beliefs about Jesus').

23. LEARNING FROM THE CONTROVERSIES OF THE PAST

If Christians and Muslims have been locked in discussion and argument for 1,400 years, are we any nearer to understanding one another? And are there any lessons we can learn for today from the way these controversies have developed over so many years?

This chapter gives examples of people – some Christians, some Muslims – who have engaged in discussion and dialogue in different situations and with widely differing styles. It is important to notice in each case the context in which the Christians and Muslims were meeting. Which was the majority community, and which the minority? Which side was in the position of power? It will also be helpful for us in several cases to try to evaluate the different approaches, noting their strengths and weaknesses.

Muhammad and the Christians of Najran (c. 632 CE)

It comes as a surprise to many to find that Christian communities existed in parts of Arabia a century or more before the rise of Islam. One such community was based in Najran, south-west of the peninsula (in modern Yemen), from the fourth century, and had its own cathedral and bishop. Ibn Ishaq's *Life of the Apostle of God*, one of the first Muslim biographies of Muhammad, written around 750, describes a meeting between Muhammad and a delegation of sixty Christians who came from Najran. This is a summary of the arguments put forward by each side at the meeting.

Christian arguments. Jesus is God because he worked miracles. For instance, he raised the dead, healed the sick and declared the unseen; he also made clay birds and breathed into them so that they flew away. He had no human father; he was born of a virgin; and he spoke while he was still a baby in the cradle to defend the honour of his mother Mary. Jesus is 'the third out of three', because God says, 'We created, we commanded,' etc. (using the plural). If God were one in the strictly mathematical sense, he would have said, 'I have commanded.'

Muslim arguments. Christians have not 'submitted to God' in the fullest sense because they say God has a son, worship the cross and eat pork. God is eternal, so if Jesus was God, how could he die? How could he leave his place in heaven? Christians associate a created being (Jesus) with God, putting him on the same level as God. God's transcendence and unity must be protected, and they are called in question by the idea of Jesus being God. Miracles do not prove the deity of Christ. And although Jesus did work miracles, he did so 'by the permission of God' and his power was limited; for example, he did not have the power to change day to night. If he really was God, he could have done anything. Jesus was born of a virgin, but he was created by divine fiat without a human father, like Adam. Christian interpretations of the Bible are arbitrary. The Qur'an, by contrast, is one speech from God, and has one meaning that is plain to all. Christians should recognize their error and accept Islam.

This account was no doubt coloured by the way Christian and Muslim apologetics developed after the time of Muhammad. The document is valuable, however, as an early Muslim account of Christian-Muslim dialogue. Some of the Christian arguments clearly reflect Muslim beliefs that probably came originally from heretical Christian sources. Several of the arguments used by the Christians have been used by Christians for centuries, but still appear very unconvincing to Muslims.

John of Damascus (675–753)

John of Damascus was born forty-three years after the death of Muhammad. His father was an important government official in Damascus at a time when the population was still largely Christian, but living under Muslim rule. His grandfather played an important role in the surrender of Damascus to Muslim troops in 635.

John knew both Arabic and Greek, and worked for about thirty years in the ministry of finance. At the age of fifty he left his position, perhaps because top jobs in the civil service were being given only to Muslims. He retired to live in the monastery of St Sabas near Jerusalem, devoting himself to study and writing several major theological works. He is important for our survey since he was the first Christian theologian to think seriously about Islam and to try to help Christians see how it differed from Christianity. One part of his large work *The Fount of Wisdom* dealt with heresies, and he included Islam in this section, describing it as 'the heresy of the Ishmaelites'. He therefore thought of Islam not as a religion in its own right, but as a kind of Christian heresy.

John has been described as 'one of the most serious originators of Muslim-Christian dialogue'. Generally he avoided polemics and put forward serious and open-ended theological arguments. He had close dealings with Muslims from childhood, and had accurate knowledge of the Qur'an and Muslim beliefs and practices. His writings had a considerable influence on later generations of Christians. Some of his arguments (for example, seeking to prove the divinity of Christ from the titles 'Word' and 'spirit' given to Jesus in the Qur'an, and suggesting that Muhammad could not have been a prophet because his coming was not foretold in the Bible and he did not work miracles) became widely accepted in Christian apologetics. Unfortunately, those who followed him seldom had first-hand experience of Islam and Muslims, and often used what John had written simply for political or polemical purposes and to stir up the feelings of Christians against Muslims.[1]

Al-Tabari (died 855)

Al-Tabari was a well-educated Nestorian Christian physician from

Baghdad who converted to Islam at the age of seventy. In the introduction to his book *Refutation of Christianity*, he stated openly that his aim was to destroy the faith of Christians. The main thrust of al-Tabari's attack was that Christian beliefs about Jesus are absurd and self-contradictory, since Jesus is said by Christians to be both God and man. He asked Christians questions like these: Do you believe in one God, or is Jesus a second God? Can God experience suffering and death? Is Christ God or man? Is he the Creator or is he simply a creature?

As a Nestorian Christian for most of his life, al-Tabari may well have held a view of Christ which was very close to that of Muslims, namely, that he was an ordinary man, a prophet, who was used by God. The weakness of this approach, however, was that it failed to recognize that most Christians have generally understood Jesus to have two natures, divine and human. He also refused to recognize the possibility of paradox in religious language.[2]

The correspondence of al-Hashimi and al-Kindi (*c.* 820)

The correspondence of al-Hashimi and al-Kindi has been described as 'one of the most important writings in the history of Muslim-Christian dialogue'. The author of this correspondence must have been a Christian, probably a civil servant living in Baghdad during the caliphate of al-Ma'mum (813–33). By writing in the form of a fictional correspondence between a Muslim and a Christian, he was able to state his own views more openly than he could ever have done if he had written in his own name.

The first letter, of thirty-seven pages, is from the Muslim to the Christian and gives a full and reasonably fair presentation of the beliefs and practices of Islam, accusing Christians of being in error and unbelief, and inviting Christian readers to become Muslims and save themselves from unbelief.

In his reply, of 230 pages, al-Kindi writes about the Christian understanding of the Trinity. He goes on to discuss Muslim claims about the prophet Muhammad, boldly expressing objections and questions which Christians at the time no doubt wanted to put to Muslims but did not dare to – for fear of death. For example:

- How could a man who raided caravans and was of doubtful morals be a prophet?
- Muhammad's claims to be a prophet are not supported by prophecies in the Bible or by miracles.
- Since there is nothing exceptional about the language of the Qur'an, how can Muslims say that the Qur'an is a miracle?
- The pillars of Islam are useless and cannot purify the heart.
- Although the Qur'an says, 'There is no compulsion in religion,' Islam has been spread by the sword.
- Islam is a lax and easy religion compared to the 'narrow way' of Jesus.

In the final section al-Kindi shows from the Gospel of Matthew how the coming of Jesus was predicted by the prophets, giving an outline of Jesus' teaching, life, death and resurrection, and the coming of the Spirit. This work had a profound effect on Christian-Muslim relations for centuries. Muslims felt they had to answer the challenges put forth by al-Kindi, while Christians gained many of their ideas about Islam from these letters and tried to develop al-Kindi's approach to refute Islam.[3]

Ibn Hazm (994–1064)

Ibn Hazm represents 'probably the most violent and systematic attempt to discredit Christianity in the whole history of Christian-Muslim confrontation'. He has been recognized as the 'undisputed Master in the field of anti-Christian polemics'. He came from a Muslim family of Spanish origin and was brought up in the court of the Umayyad caliph in Cordoba. After periods as a prisoner during several coups, then as prime minister, and again as a prisoner, he left political life to give himself to religious studies.

Starting from a very strict and literal approach to all Scriptures, which he regarded as the very words dictated by God, he concluded that the text of the Bible had been corrupted. He attacked Christian belief in the Trinity as an invention of Christians and an absurdity: how can three 'things' be one? He also dismissed the doctrine of the incarnation since it implies a change of nature: if God became man, then he is no longer God. Listing all the discrepancies he could find in the Gospels, Ibn Hazm concluded that the Christian Scriptures were not revealed by God, but fabricated by their human authors. Jean-Marie Gaudeul sums up his approach.

> Ibn Hazm does not try to enter into dialogue with Christians or with his other (Muslim) adversaries. He simply tries to crush and destroy his opponents. His method which reduces the meaning of words to simple elementary notions makes it easy for him to win an argument: words are just weapons for him. But this same method prevents him from reaching any real understanding of the thought of others. Consequently, his arguments may be devastating in a public discussion, but they do not touch the real position of his adversaries.
>
> In a way, his approach is totally logical within his own system of thought, but powerless to take into account another set of principles. At the root of all his argument lies the idea he has of what a Revealed Text should look like, and how this Revelation takes place.[4]

Raymond Lull (1234–1315)

The well-known apologist Raymond Lull was born in Majorca and worked for several years in the service of the king, first as a tutor and later as an adviser. At the age of thirty-one he had a profound conversion experience through a vision of Christ on the cross. Soon after this he began to work out a plan for the evangelization of Muslims, and he joined the Franciscan order as a layman. He spent the next twenty-two years preparing himself through the study of theology, Islam and Arabic, and founding a training centre where other Franciscans could prepare themselves for missionary work among Muslims.

At the age of fifty-two he began lecturing at universities in France and Italy, and wrote more than 200 books of Christian apologetics for Muslims. Finally he decided to engage in direct evangelism himself, and at the age of sixty made trips to Tunis, Cyprus and Algeria. In each case he became involved in public controversy, and was arrested and expelled.

His last evangelistic journey (when he was eighty) took him to Sicily and Tunis. He seems to have begun to work in a less confrontational way and was allowed to engage in debate with Muslim leaders. Before long, however, he changed his style, perhaps out of a desire to die as a martyr. He then moved to Bugia (modern Bejaia) in Algeria, and began preaching openly in the market. He was stoned by the crowd, who were angry at his criticism of Muhammad. He died either at sea or in his native Majorca.

Lull was in many ways ahead of his time. He recognized, for example, that the Crusades had been a terrible betrayal of the spirit of Christ. He therefore called the whole church, including the pope, to believe that the Muslim world could not be won for Christ by force. He saw the need for Christians to study Islam carefully and to give missionaries a thorough training. He also worked hard to develop an effective apologetic that would convince Muslims 'by irrefutable logic'. Many Christians today are still challenged by the example of this man who worked so hard to change traditional Christian responses to Islam and who gave his life for Muslims to come to faith in Christ.

At the same time, however, we need to be aware of the limitations of his approach. His apologetic method probably depended too heavily on rational arguments to demonstrate that Christian doctrines are the most reasonable. He may not have been a very good listener, and his reliance on argument combined with his natural impatience tended to make him provocative in his approach to Muslims.[5]

Henry Martyn (1781–1812)

After his time as a student at Cambridge, Henry Martyn went to India in 1805 as a chaplain of the East India Company at the age of twenty-four. He was an extremely able linguist, and within seven years he had completed a translation of the New Testament into Urdu and a thorough revision of the Persian New Testament, and had started a revision of the Arabic New Testament. The only Muslim who became a Christian as a result of Martyn's ministry was Sheikh Salih (later known as Abdul Masih, meaning 'servant of Christ'), a gifted evangelist who was the first Christian from a Muslim background to be ordained in India.

Because of his poor health, Martyn set out to return to England by land, hoping to meet up with his beloved Lydia, a girl from his home area of Cornwall whom he had known since childhood. During the months he spent in Persia in 1813 on his journey home, he spent a considerable time debating with Muslim teachers in Isfahan. After this he set out again on his journey, but died in Turkey.

Part of Martyn's significance is that while he believed in the need for apologetics, he had real doubts about the value of certain kinds of argument. He was far more at home in personal conversations with small groups of interested Muslims and stressed the need for lasting friendships. It was in this kind of context that he found he could share the religious experience of the forgiveness and peace attained through Christ. He summed up his convictions in words like these: 'I have now lost all hope of ever convincing Mahomedans by argument ... I know not what to do but to pray for them.'[6]

Karl Gottlieb Pfander (1803–65)

Karl Gottlieb Pfander was a German missionary who began work in Istanbul at the age of twenty-two. He moved to India in 1837, where he spoke in public debates and wrote apologetic literature in what came to be known as 'The Muhammadan Controversy'. At the age of fifty-five, he moved back to Istanbul to continue his evangelism, until a change of government policy forced missionaries to give up their work.

Pfander wrote his famous *Balance of Truth* in German and Armenian in 1829, when he was only twenty-six. It was later translated into Persian, Urdu, Turkish, Arabic and English, and has been widely used since then as a basic textbook of Christian apologetics with Muslims. In the introduction, Pfander begins with the question: how can we know whether Christianity or Islam is true, whether the Bible or the Qur'an is the Word of God? He goes on to suggest that any true revelation from God must meet six criteria.

1. It must satisfy the human yearning for eternal happiness.
2. It must accord with the moral law.
3. It must reveal God as just.
4. It must confirm the unity of God.
5. It must make clear the way of salvation.
6. It must reveal God so that people may know him.

Part One is a defence of the text of the Bible, answering the Muslim charge of corruption. Part Two outlines the basic teaching of the Bible, showing how biblical doctrine and morals meet the six criteria. Part Three, 'A Candid Inquiry into Islam's Claim to Be the Final Revelation', answers Muslim arguments about predictions of the coming of Muhammad in the Bible, the miraculous nature of the Qur'an, Muhammad's miracles and his behaviour. Pfander concludes that Islamic doctrine and beliefs do not meet the criteria for establishing genuine divine revelation. The book ends with a strong appeal to Muslims to recognize the claims of Christ and put their trust in him.

In 1854 Pfander took part in a two-day public debate in Agra with a Shi'ite Muslim scholar, Maulana Rahmatullah al-Kairanawi. While both sides claimed victory in the debate, many felt that al-Kairanawi presented a stronger case and could be said to have won the debate. In 1867 he replied to Pfander's *Balance of Truth* in a book called *Manifestation of the Truth*. Both books have been reprinted many times and are still used by Muslims and Christians today. Al-Kairanawi lists contradictions and errors in the Old and New Testaments, arguing that they cannot be inspired. He goes on to give evidence not only for false interpretation of the text by Jews and Christians (*tahrif ma'nawi*), but for falsification or corruption of the text itself (*tahrif lafzi*). The next stage is to argue that many biblical texts are immoral and that certain commands in the Bible have been abrogated or superseded by the Qur'an. There then follows a refutation of the Trinity, and proofs that the Qur'an is the Word of God and that Muhammad is the Prophet of God.

There were several strengths in Pfander's approach in *The Balance of Truth*.

- He knew a great deal about Islam and could quote from the Qur'an, the *hadith* and many other Muslim sources in different languages.
- His style was courteous and polite.
- He could recognize common ground between Christian and Muslim beliefs.

With hindsight, however, we can also recognize certain weaknesses and limitations in his approach.

- His attacks on Muslim beliefs sometimes degenerated into polemics.
- He appealed too much to the reason and the intellect, and not enough to the heart.
- The debate could hardly be an open-ended discussion, because he himself had decided from the beginning the criteria by which genuine revelation is to be determined.
- He was largely unaware of the more critical approaches to history and textual sources which were being developed in Europe. This was the most serious weakness in his response at the Agra debate, since he was unable to respond to al-Kairanawi's challenge which was based on the most recent European scholarship.[7]

Temple Gairdner (1873–1928)

Temple Gairdner was an Anglican missionary who worked in Cairo for thirty-one years. He was a gifted linguist and understood Islam well enough to be able to debate publicly in Arabic with sheikhs from the Al-Azhar University. In his work with Muslims he believed that 'what was most needed for the redemption of Islam was the living exemplification of Christian brotherhood'. In addition to his work with Muslims, therefore, he spent a great deal of his time in pastoral work in the churches. His approach to Islam and Muslims has been summed up in the words, 'Other teachers taught us how to refute Islam; he taught us how to love Muslims.'

Constance Padwick, in her biography *Temple Gairdner of Cairo*, sums up what was most distinctive about Gairdner's apologetic approach.

Gairdner ... found that the literature by which the Christian Church had set forth her living truth to Muslims was a curiously arid, machine-made literature. It was as though the compilers, holy men though they were, had been caught into the argumentative machinery of the schoolmen, and had expended all their vital strength in meeting Moslem arguments with juster arguments. The objector himself might be left on the field prostrate but cursing. The books were starved of personality and of appeal to aught save logic and justice. Moreover, he saw, and it was one of his most fruitful perceptions, that the converts made by this literature were often born in its image – with the spirit of disputation rather than of worship and of love, and apt to hammer rather than to woo and win.

Gairdner believed (for was he not nightly battered with anti-Christian arguments?) that there must needs be an apologetic literature, unafraid of controversial points. Silence, he felt, was tantamount to denial of the truth he knew and lived. But the literature must be humanized and written for fellow men, not only for the defeat of arguers. Moreover, to Gairdner, stories, history, drama, music, poetry, pictures, all that could bear the impress of the Spirit of Christ, was a reasonable part of the Christian apologetic to the whole man.[8]

Ahmad Deedat (1918–2005)

Ahmad Deedat was a South African Muslim apologist who engaged for over thirty years in public debates with Christians. Videotapes of debates before large audiences have been distributed all over the world. Booklets and tracts written by Deedat, with titles such as *What the Bible Says About Muhammad*, 50,000 *Errors in the Bible, Resurrection or Resuscitation?* and *Crucifixion or Cruci-Fiction?*, have given Muslims a wide range of arguments to use in discussion with Christians.

Deedat's approach had much in common with that of Ibn Hazm. His style tended to be aggressive and polemical, and he frequently mocked Christian beliefs to make them appear ridiculous. While many Muslims all over the world continue to use Deedat's material and copy his style, others dissociate themselves from his approach because it represents such a deliberate and open attack on Christian beliefs and does not lead to mutual understanding.

Jay Smith (born 1953)

Smith is an American Christian apologist who has worked for twenty-three years with Muslims. His early years in India were followed by ministry in Africa, and he has lived and worked in London since 1992. Engaging with groups of Christian students on various campuses around the UK, he also leads the Hyde Park Christian Fellowship, which is based in a church in central London, and is a regular speaker at Speakers' Corner in Hyde Park. He has taken part in over forty public debates with Muslims in many parts of the world, and much of his apologetics and polemics are now available in five- to ten-minute videos on Youtube on the internet (see Pfanderfilms at http://www.youtube.com/profile?user=Pfanderfilms).

The strength of Smith's approach can be summed up as follows.

- His continuing engagement with Muslims over many years has forced him and his colleagues to study Islam seriously. One area of special interest has been the history of early Islam, and a textual critique of the early manuscripts of the Qur'an, one of which was discovered in 1975 at the Great Mosque at Sana'a in the Yemen.
- He is not afraid to challenge Muslims about their beliefs and their interpretation of the Qur'an, asking the difficult questions which Christians often want to put to Muslims, but seldom have the background knowledge and confidence to articulate.
- He has spent many years meeting and speaking with Muslims, and especially with radical Muslims on the streets of London and on university campuses all over the world.
- He has developed a wide range of teaching material which he has used to teach Christians how to engage with Muslims, together with other resources which have been written for Muslim readers.

The main criticism of Smith's style is that he blurs the distinction between apologetics and polemics, and does not seem to recognize the limitations of the polemical approaches that have been adopted by both sides over many centuries (see also chapter 36, 'Some issues facing Christians today').

This survey has pointed out strengths and weaknesses of different approaches to arguments between Muslims and Christians over the centuries. It has highlighted in particular the weaknesses and limitations of the more *polemical* approaches adopted by both Christians and Muslims. The following chapter explores how Christians can engage in a more *dialogical* way with Muslims today.

24. EXPLORING DIALOGUE

Is it ever possible to get away from the big theological questions which Christians and Muslims have been arguing about for fourteen centuries? Is it possible to talk freely and frankly with each other about other subjects which are indirectly linked with religious faith, but which avoid starting with the traditional areas of controversy?

In the kind of dialogue explored in this chapter, we are attempting to break out of the fixed positions that Christians and Muslims have frequently adopted in order to see if there can be a deeper meeting of minds. The following pages contain a proposed agenda for discussion, outlining possible questions to be discussed – perhaps between a Christian and a Muslim, or a group of Christians and Muslims, meeting together over a period of time. If the format seems formal and artificial, this outline may at least suggest new models for dialogue that can be explored in an appropriate way in different contexts.

Who are we?

The questions in this section are designed to help us to get to know one another as people and to begin to share what our faith means to us. We want to discover each other's humanity before we learn about each other's creed. Thus a meeting of a group could begin with each person giving a kind of testimony, saying who they are and speaking about their faith.

1. Who are we?

- We are human beings.
- We belong to a family.
- We belong to a community of faith.
- We live in a particular society.

2. What are our basic human needs and how are these met within our own faith?

- Health and well-being: what do we do when things go wrong?
- Values: how do we know the difference between right and wrong?
- Forgiveness: how do we gain forgiveness from God?
- Love: we need to be loved by others and to have people to love.
- Truth: we want to know as far as we can the truth about ourselves and the world.
- A model for humanity: we need an example of the kind of people we ought to be; we need guidance, as we admit in the *Fatiha* and the Lord's Prayer (see chapter 6, 'Muslims at prayer').
- Life beyond death: we want to know what lies beyond the end of our physical life.

What about the past?

Questions under this heading are designed to enable us to think together about how relationships between Muslims and Christians today are affected by what has happened in the past. This is therefore an opportunity for us to try to clear the air, to begin to be open and honest about how we feel about our history and about each other's religion.

In many situations it may be helpful *not* to discuss these questions in any detail, or not to discuss them at all if we do not have enough background knowledge, or if the discussion simply turns to argument. If the questions do not help us to understand each other's point of view better, they should probably be avoided altogether. The following events or developments are all significant because of the way they affect how Christians and Muslims understand their history, and how they see each other in different contexts today.

- The conversion of Constantine, who made Christianity an official religion of the Roman Empire
- The early spread of Islam and the Islamic Empire
- The Crusades and the clash between Christian Europe and Islam
- The spread of Islam in the East
- European colonialism
- The Christian missionary movement
- The establishment of the state of Israel (1948)
- Secularization in the West
- Controversies over Salman Rushdie's *The Satanic Verses* (1988), the Danish cartoons (2006), the Pope's lecture (2006), etc.
- The Gulf War of 1991
- The events of 11 September 2001, and other terrorist attacks such as those in Nairobi, Dar-es-Salaam, Bali, Madrid and London
- The invasion and occupation of Iraq, 2003

How do each of these events or developments affect how Christians think about Islam and how Muslims think about Christianity? Is it true that both Christianity and Islam are missionary religions? Is it possible to separate religion and politics in Christianity and Islam? Is there any value in comparing the record of the two religions?

Is it possible to 'let bygones be bygones' and for each generation of Christians and Muslims to start all over again as if nothing had happened in the past? If not, is there anything we can do to help us to understand each other better?

How has it come about that in some countries Christians are a minority living among a Muslim majority, and in others Muslims are a minority living among a Christian majority? What does it feel like to belong to the minority community? Whichever situation we ourselves are in, can we put ourselves into the shoes of the other community and appreciate how they feel?

What are we up against?

Instead of constantly thinking in terms of 'us' and 'them' and imagining that we are facing each other across a great divide, can we recognize that because Christians and Muslims believe in one Creator God, we have a great deal in common in a world where most people ignore God and where there is so much suffering? Does it help us to recognize that over many of the following issues we face common dangers?

- Hunger
- War and peace
- The environment and global warming
- Human rights
- Materialism
- Secularization
- Racism
- Other social problems (poverty, injustice, drugs, etc.)

How does our faith influence our thinking about these issues? Are there ways in which we can and should be joining hands to fight against evils in our society and the world? For instance, how did Muslims and Christians work together in South Africa to fight apartheid?

Can we find new ways of bearing witness to our faith?[1]

When Muslims throughout the centuries have challenged Christians over their beliefs, they have generally focused on four main subjects: the Trinity, the divinity of Christ, the crucifixion and the authenticity of the Bible. Much of the controversy has sadly been carried out in a polemical spirit, with each side attacking the beliefs of the other, sometimes without really understanding them.

One way of breaking out of the deadlock created by centuries of controversy of this kind is to put on one side (at least initially) the traditional stumbling blocks and start with basic convictions that are

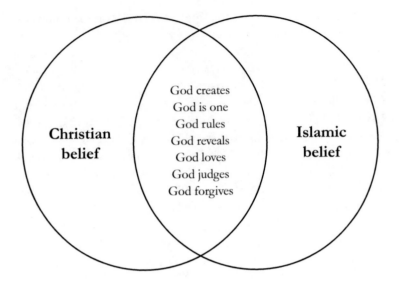

Figure 24.1

common to both faiths, and from there move on to explore differences. The metaphor then changes from attacking each other from the trenches to seeing how far we can walk along the same road before we come to the points at which our paths diverge.

Figure 24.1 contains seven propositions in the area of overlap between the two circles. Christians and Muslims can both assent to these statements without any hesitations.

But what happens when we try to define in greater detail how we understand these statements? As Kenneth Cragg has often said, 'The question is not *whether* but *how*.' The issue between us is not *whether* God forgives, but *how* he forgives; not *whether* he reveals, but *what* he reveals and *how*.

In what follows we begin by attempting to explain as simply as possible how Christians generally understand each of these statements. We then go on to ask questions, pointing to some of the basic issues between Christian and Islamic belief as we understand them.

God creates
Here is an area where Muslims and Christians have a great deal in common – far more than we have when talking with Hindus or

Buddhists. We both insist that God is distinct from the universe which he has created and which is totally dependent on him for its continuing life. We both hold strongly to the idea of stewardship. For Christians the idea can be derived from the creation story in the book of Genesis, in which God gives Adam and Eve responsibility to care for the earth. For Muslims the idea is based on the qur'anic verses which speak of Adam as the *khalifa* (deputy or vice-gerent) of God.

This shared belief should provide a strong basis for discussion about our care for the environment. If we recognize the enormous responsibility that has been given to the human race by our Creator, we ought to have a common starting point for addressing issues concerning water, food, energy resources, the population explosion, HIV and global warming – issues which make many people very fearful about the future of our race and our planet. Frightening developments in technology make our responsibility seem even greater, and perhaps Christians and Muslims may want to join hands in attempting to call our secular friends back to this sense that we have to give an account of what we are doing to our world, not only to one another, but also to our Creator.

There is one area in the doctrine of creation, however, where Christians and Muslims have not always been in agreement. Christians believe that human beings are created 'in the image of God'. One reason why this idea is so important for Christians is that it provides the basis for understanding our relationship with God. If human beings are in the image and likeness of God, there must at least be *some* ways in which human beings are *like* God. Although God is eternal, perfect and infinite in knowledge and power, while human beings are mortal, imperfect and finite, the basic likeness between God and humans makes it possible for us to have a relationship with him. We are not worshipping an unknown God, an entity with which we have nothing in common. Although our relationship with him has been spoiled by sin, it can be restored to be a genuinely personal relationship. When we use words like 'personal', 'good', 'just', 'loving' and 'forgiving' to speak about God, they must have some meaning which is not altogether different from their meaning when applied to human beings.

Another reason why this idea is so important for Christians is that it underlies our understanding of the incarnation. If there is an infinite qualitative difference between God and humankind, it is certainly difficult, if not impossible, for Christians to think that Jesus could be *both* human *and* divine at the same time. Just as water and oil do not mix, so humanity and divinity could never mix. But if the image of God in humankind creates a basic likeness, then it does not seem unreasonable for us to believe that God might choose to reveal himself through incarnation. And if God chooses to do this, we as his creatures, however good our motives, are not in a position to tell him what he can do and what he cannot do.

If we can rejoice in the wide area of agreement in our doctrine of creation, are Muslims able to affirm *anything* in this idea of the image of God in humankind? The expression is certainly found in *hadith*, if not in the Qur'an. Many Muslims, however, would say that something of this kind is implied in the idea of Adam being created from the breath of God: 'He moulded him and breathed into him of His spirit' (32:9).

Is it too simple to suggest that while Muslims tend to want to emphasize the transcendence (*tanzih*) of God and the *difference* between him and human beings, Christians want to emphasize the *likeness*? Have Muslim theologians developed some of these ideas partly in order to sharpen the distinctions between Islam and Christianity? If so, is there any way in which we can narrow down the areas of disagreement?

God is one

The first Christians were not pagans who had believed in many different gods, but orthodox Jews who continued to believe passionately in the oneness of God. They had been brought up from childhood to recite daily, 'The Lord our God, the Lord is one' (Deut. 6:4). In many of our services of worship today we recite a creed which begins, 'We believe in One Lord, Maker of heaven and earth...' We have no difficulty whatsoever with the first part of the *Shahadah*, 'There is no god but God...'

Do Muslims recognize Christians as genuine monotheists who simply have a different understanding of the oneness of God? The Qur'an seems to recognize shared belief of this kind in a verse such as this: 'We believe in that what hath been revealed unto us and revealed unto you; our God and your God is One, and unto Him we surrender'

(29:46). Is this a recognition of common ground? Or does Christian belief in the divinity of Jesus amount to a kind of *kufr* (unbelief) and *shirk* (association)? When the Qur'an says, 'Unbelievers are those who declare: "Allah is the Messiah, the son of Mary…"' (*laqad kafara alladhina qalu …*, 5:17, Fakhry), does this apply to *all* Christians who believe that Jesus is both human and divine and speak of him as 'the Son of God'? Or does it apply only to certain kinds of beliefs about Jesus which were held by particular individuals and groups at the time of the Prophet? If we can accept each other as monotheists, can we go on to share with each other our different understandings of the kind of oneness we are talking about?

God reveals

Christians and Muslims share the conviction that God has not left the human race in total ignorance. But *what* has God revealed, and *how*? Christians recognize the revelation of the law that was given through Moses, but seek to interpret it in the light of the teaching and example of Jesus. They also want to go beyond the revelation of law as an expression of God's will for humankind, and insist that God has revealed something about his character, that in a real sense he has revealed something about *himself*.

This belief is summed up by the evangelist John when he writes, 'No one has ever seen God, but God the One and Only, who is at the Father's side, has made him known' (John 1:18). Jesus speaks of his disciples' relationship with God in terms of knowing God: 'This is eternal life, that they may know you, the only true God, and Jesus Christ, whom you have sent' (John 17:3). The apostle Paul links the work of God both in creation and in revelation when he writes, 'For God, who said, "Let light shine out of darkness," made his light shine in our hearts to give us the light of the knowledge of the glory of God in the face of Christ' (2 Cor. 4:6). Biblical writers therefore are not afraid to speak about 'knowing God'; they are not content with the idea of knowing *about* God, and seem to believe that there is *something* in common between our knowledge of other people and our knowledge of God. Knowing a person means more than knowing *about* that person, because it suggests a genuine personal relationship.

Would all Muslims agree with Isma'il al-Faruqi that 'He [God] does not reveal Himself to anyone in any way. God reveals only His will'? Is he right in saying that 'Christians talk about the revelation of God Himself – by God of God – but that is the great difference between Christianity and Islam'?[2] Qur'anic expressions such as 'desiring the face of their Lord' (*ibtigha' wajhi rabbihim*, e.g. 13:22) and 'people He (God) loves and who love Him' (*qawmin yuhibbuhum wa yuhibbunahu*, 5:54) are clearly anthropomorphic language which needs to be interpreted. But unless they are to be emptied of all content, they seem to suggest the possibility of a personal relationship with God. In considering the Ninety-nine Names of God we are often puzzled about the distinction made by theologians between the *attributes* of God and the *nature* of God, God as he is in himself. And we wonder whether the whole Sufi movement represents a kind of protest against what might appear as the rigidity of the theologians. Does the hunger of the heart not cry out for a relationship with God which has something in common with our relationships with people?

God loves

In the Qur'an we read that *God loves* those who do right, who turn to him, the pure, the God-fearing, the patient, the trusting, the equitable and those who do battle for his cause. But he *does not love* certain other types of people, including aggressors, the corrupt, the evil unbelievers, the ungrateful, the proud and boastful, the unbelievers, the treacherous and the transgressors. In the New Testament John sums up the meaning of the incarnation by saying, 'God so loved the world that he gave his one and only Son ...' (John 3:16). Paul similarly understands it in terms of the love of God: 'God demonstrates his own love for us in this: While we were still sinners, Christ died for us' (Rom. 5:8). For John the supreme demonstration of love is seen in God's action to deal with human sinfulness: 'This is love: not that we loved God, but that he loved us and sent his Son as an atoning sacrifice for our sins' (1 John 4:10).

While the Qur'an and the Bible use the same word, does it have the same meaning in both scriptures? When the Qur'an says that God loves certain kinds of people and does not love others, it seems to be saying that God is pleased with, and approves of, certain kinds of people, but disapproves of others. For Christians the love of God is expressed supremely in self-giving and self-sacrifice. God loved so much that he gave ... His love for rebellious humankind led him to do something to restore the broken relationship and to win back their love. If Muslims speak more about the mercy and compassion than about the love of God, do 'mercy' and 'love' amount to the same thing, or is there a significant difference between the Christian understanding of love and the Muslim understanding of God's mercy and compassion?

God judges

Both Christians and Muslims believe in a process of divine judgment which is going on throughout history and which will come to a climax in the Day of Judgment. The apostle Paul writes, 'The wrath of God is being revealed from heaven against all the godlessness and wickedness of men who suppress the truth by their wickedness' (Rom. 1:18). In addition to all that it says about the Day of Judgment, the Qur'an contains many reminders of God's judgment on individuals and communities in the past, pointing to evidence in the form of ruined towns that were still there for all to see in the time of the Prophet. Christians and Muslims therefore agree over God's opposition to all that is evil and the inevitable judgment that must fall on those who disobey their Creator.

There are, however, significant differences in the diagnosis of the human condition as it is understood by Christians and Muslims. Christians speak of the sin of Adam and Eve as 'the fall', believing that their rebellion against God had consequences which have affected the whole human race. While there are different interpretations of the meaning of 'original sin', there is general agreement that human sinfulness is more than weakness or mistakes, and amounts to something like a disease which affects every part of our nature. God's response to the human condition therefore has to be more radical than the revelation of law, and is summed up in the word 'redemption'. This response is described by Paul in these words:

> God has done what the law, weakened by the flesh, could not do: sending his own Son in the likeness of sinful flesh and for sin, he condemned sin in the flesh, in order that the just requirement of the law might be fulfilled in us, who walk not according to the flesh but according to the Spirit.
> (Rom. 8:3–4 RSV)

What is the Islamic diagnosis of the human condition? Is it simply that human beings are weak, ignorant and forgetful? If this is the Islamic diagnosis, it is understandable that God's remedy for this condition is understood in terms of a law that shows humans how to live, the example of the Prophet as the best human being who has ever lived, and the Islamic community to keep us on the Straight Path. From the Christian perspective, however, this diagnosis seems too optimistic and does not reach the heart of the problem. The qur'anic word *zulm* suggests to us a recognition of a rebelliousness, a stubbornness in human nature, which goes far beyond mere weakness, ignorance and a series of mistakes. Is it possible, therefore, that the Bible and the Qur'an could be closer to each other at this point than we have often thought? Could it be that Christian and Muslim theologians have articulated doctrines in a way that overstates the differences between the two faiths? Or are we forced to say that the different divine remedies for the human condition in the two faiths are profoundly affected by the significantly different understandings of what is wrong with human nature?

God forgives

It is interesting that the qur'anic prayer 'forgive us our sins' (*ighfir lana dhunubana*) (3:16) is exactly the same as the line in the Lord's Prayer as it is recited by most Arabic-speaking Christians today. We seek forgiveness, believing that God is merciful and wanting to forgive. And Jews, Christians and Muslims generally agree that repentance for the wrong we have done and a determination not to repeat it are vital conditions of forgiveness.

But how does God forgive? On what basis does he offer forgiveness? The Christian understanding is that forgiveness is no easy matter for God, because forgiveness is costly. We would probably all agree that in human relationships, the greater the sin, the more it costs us to forgive another person. If someone hurts me in a minor way, it may be easy to forgive and to forget what has been done. But if someone wrongs me in a very serious way, and if that person then comes to ask my forgiveness, it will not be easy for me simply to say, 'It doesn't matter.' If I refuse to punish the person who has wronged me and am willing to forgive, I myself have to bear the consequences of the wrong that has been done to me. There is a real sense in which, instead of punishing that person, I am 'bearing the sin' that has been done to me.

At this point we inevitably come back to the question of the adequacy of human analogies to speak about God. Christians would say that if we are able to use words in any way to speak about the relationship between God and humankind, there must be something in common between forgiveness between human beings and divine forgiveness of human sin. Because of the way the Bible speaks of God's response to the sinfulness of humankind, Christians cannot believe that God is not affected in any way by our sinfulness. And when he forgives, he cannot simply say, 'Never mind! It's all forgotten.'

When Christians, therefore, think of Jesus dying on the cross, what they see is a picture both of how sin has to be judged and of how much God suffers in the process of forgiving. Sin is not an object, a 'thing' that can be disposed of. Because it leads to a breakdown in relationships, it cannot simply be brushed aside or forgotten. It has to be shown up in all its seriousness, judged and condemned. But judgment and punishment can never be the last word. When God forgives, therefore, it does not mean that the broken law is forgotten or that our sin is not serious, but rather that the sin is judged and forgiven at the same time. Christians see the death of Jesus on the cross as a window to the heart of God. Our sin has affected him and touched him deeply; and when he forgives, he is, as it were, bearing the consequences of our sin in himself. Just as it *costs something* for humans to forgive each other, in the same way it *costs something* for God to forgive. *Love that suffers* is therefore central in the Christian understanding of divine forgiveness.

How do Muslims understand divine forgiveness? Will they recognize *any* similarities between forgiveness between human beings and God's forgiveness of human beings? How do they resolve the tension between law and grace, between the holiness of God which condemns sin and the love of God which wants to forgive? And is it possible for us to have any assurance of divine forgiveness during our lifetime?

God rules

Both the Bible and the Qur'an speak of almighty God ruling as king in complete control of his world. 'The Lord is king!' says the psalmist (e.g. Pss. 97:1; 93:1; 99:1). Similarly the Qur'an says repeatedly, 'His is the kingdom [*mulk*] of the heavens and the earth and all that lies between them' (e.g. 3:189; 2:107; 5:17, 18). But how does he exercise his kingly rule? How, in particular, does he react when people reject his lordship over their lives? And how will his divine authority be vindicated and recognized in the end?

Christians see God's response to human need in the life of Jesus, whose message was that the kingdom of God was about to be established through him. Because the kingdom of God has not come in all its fullness, Christians in the Lord's Prayer say, 'Your kingdom come.' Those who enter the kingdom of God now, therefore, are those who live under the authority of Jesus as members of the new community he called into being. Muslims, on the other hand, tend to associate the kingdom of God with *dar al-Islam* (the Household of Islam), so that entering the kingdom of God means living according to the law revealed through the Prophet. God's rule must be expressed in a way that touches the whole community and the whole of life. In the words of Mumtaz Ahmad, 'The desire to create a just social order in Islam is not merely a narrow political goal; it is integrally linked with its soteriology because the central aim of Islam is to create the kingdom of God on earth.'[3]

If Christians must understand the Islamic insistence that the rule of God needs to be very public, embodied in a community and not just in the lives of individuals, can Muslims understand the Christian conviction that God's rule cannot always be enforced, but has to be accepted and entered into willingly? If Muslims must begin to understand why, in Christian thinking, the kingdom of God had to come through a suffering Saviour, can Christians understand the Islamic insistence on God establishing his rule through law and the cohesion of the whole community?

Spelling out an agenda for dialogue in this way may appear daunting and discouraging, making us feel that it is all too hard and that we have hardly started any serious dialogue. But maps can be helpful if they enable us to work out where we are, where we have come from and where we might want to go.

FACING FUNDAMENTAL ISSUES

The problem in mission to Islam is theological.
Arne Rudvin[1]

There are several ways of establishing contact or communication between
man and God. The best would have been incarnation, but Islam has rejected
it. It would be too degrading for a transcendent God to become man, to eat,
drink, be tortured by His own creatures, and even be put to death. However
close a man may approach God in his journeying towards Him, even in his
highest ascension, man remains man and very much remote from God.
Muhammad Hamidullah[2]

Islam is a one-way door; you can enter through it but you cannot leave.
Abul A'la Mawdudi[3]

The desire to create a just social order in Islam is not merely a narrow
political goal; it is integrally linked to its soteriology, because the central aim
of Islam is to create the kingdom of God on earth.
Mumtaz Ahmad[4]

Part Four considers some of the harder issues that come to the surface
in a meeting between Christianity and Islam. How, for example, do
we deal with some of the thorny theological questions which the
existence of Islam raises for Christians (chapter 25)? This is followed
by chapters on the Islamic view of Jesus and the qur'anic view of
Christians (chapters 26 and 27). We then try to analyse the crucial
areas of difference in the theological beliefs of the two faiths (chapter
28). Are there any biblical models that may help Christians in their
thinking about Islam (chapter 29)? And finally we look at two of the
most sensitive issues: the implications of conversion to the Christian
faith (chapter 30), and Christian responses to the political challenge
presented by Islam (chapter 31).

25. THEOLOGICAL QUESTIONS

Meeting with Muslims and engaging with the religion of Islam is bound to force Christians to ask fundamental questions about what we believe and what we think about the religion of Islam. This chapter discusses three such questions.

Is the God of Islam the same as the God of Christianity?

There are a number of ways of approaching this question.

1. Analysing the question itself
The question of whether Christians and Muslims worship the same God is a kind of trick question, because it seems to force us to answer with a simple 'Yes' or 'No'. What we need to do is to break the question down into several smaller questions.

- Is the Christian's idea of God the same as the Muslim's idea of God? Most Christians would answer 'No'.
- Is there anything in common between the Christian's idea of God and the Muslim's idea of God? Most would not hesitate to answer 'Yes'.

- Is there enough in common between the Christian's idea of God and the Muslim's idea of God for us to be able to use the same word for 'God'? This is probably the crucial question. Some Christians, like Arne Rudvin, a former bishop of Karachi, believe that there is not enough in common, while others, like Kenneth Cragg, believe that there is. In the words of Michael Nazir-Ali, 'For Cragg the similarity outweighs the disparity, whereas for Rudvin the disparity clearly outweighs the similarity.'[1]

2. The meaning of 'Allah'

The word *Allah* in Arabic is made up of the definite article 'the' (*al-*) and the word 'god' (*ilah*). Originally, therefore, it probably meant something like 'the God', that is 'the High God', the highest deity at the head of the pantheon of gods and goddesses in Arabia at the time of Muhammad.

Muslims who use the Arabic *Allah* for God seem to want to underline the difference between the God of Islam and the God of Christianity. They are concerned about the possible confusion between God (with a capital G) and god (with a small g), and between Islamic ideas and Christian ideas of God. For these reasons Islamic governments in Malaysia and elsewhere have not allowed Christians to use *Allah* in recent translations of the Bible. Against this view, however, it can be argued that such practice is not true to the Qur'an and the practice of the Prophet. In one important verse the Prophet is commanded to say to Jews and Christians, 'O People of the Scripture! Come to an agreement between us and you: that we shall worship none but Allah, and that we shall ascribe no partner unto Him' (3:64). Nothing in the Qur'an suggests that Muhammad ever believed that Jews and Christians, 'the People of the Book', were worshipping a different God.

Christians today who insist on using *Allah* for the God of Islam may be wanting to assert that the God of Islam is totally different from the God of Christianity. Fifteen million Arabic-speaking Christians in the Middle East, however, speak of God as *Allah*, and would never think of using a different word.

3. An analogy

Suppose, for the sake of argument, that there is a country somewhere in the world where the sun is never clearly visible. People are aware of the sun because they can see the shape of the sun behind the clouds and know that the sun is the source of heat. But they never see the sun in a cloudless sky. Contrast this with people who live in the Mediterranean. They see the sun very clearly and feel its heat. Is it the same sun for both people in both places? It must, of course, be the same sun, although each group of people has a very different mental image and experience of it.

If the analogy is acceptable (even though somewhat artificial), it would suggest that Muslims and Christians are talking about the same being, even though their ideas of that being and their experience of him may differ considerably. We must not, however, press the analogy too far, since no human being can 'see God' or have complete knowledge of him. As Paul said, 'Now we see but a poor reflection as in a mirror; then we shall see face to face' (1 Cor. 13:12). There are many places on the ground between the Mediterranean and the country where the sun never shines!

If we cannot accept the analogy, we have to think in terms of two completely different astronomical bodies, such as the sun and the moon, one being the energy centre of a planetary system and the other a planetary satellite, and assume that Christians and Muslims are talking about two totally different beings. This assumption is likely to make communication between Christians and Muslims extremely difficult, if not impossible.

4. The example of Paul

When Paul was speaking to a Greek audience at the Areopagus in Acts 17, he did not hesitate to use the word *theos* both for the 'unknown God' and for the God who raised Jesus from the dead – in spite of the fact that the Greek word in its different forms could mean either 'a god' or 'gods', male and/or female. He believed that there was enough in common between the concept of God in the mind of these pagan Greeks and his concept of God for him to use the same word (Acts 17:23–24, 30–31).

5. The testimony of converts and enquirers

Many converts from Muslim backgrounds assume that there is some real continuity in the knowledge and experience of God before and after their conversion to Christianity. They speak as if they had some real knowledge of God as Muslims, and as if Jesus has brought their idea of God into focus in a new way. The experience of Bilquis Sheikh in *I Dared to Call Him Father*[2] points to continuity rather than discontinuity. When converts take a negative view and want to repudiate everything in Islam, it may well be either because the only way they can feel secure in their new faith is to cut themselves off from everything in their past, or because the Christians who taught them have taken a negative view of Islam.

There can, therefore, be no linguistic reason for Christians to choose such a contrived way of speaking about God in Islam and finding a different name for God. And it is hard to find any theological reason for trying to distinguish between the words *Allah* and 'God' in Christianity. The crucial question will always be the *content* that we give to whichever word we use. What is he like, this being about whom we are speaking?

Is there any revelation in Islam? Should Christians think of Muhammad as a prophet? Is the Qur'an in any sense the Word of God?

Once again we need to be cautious about the question of revelation in Islam, because it is framed in such a way as to invite a simple 'Yes' or 'No' for an answer. We therefore need to break the question down into a number of smaller questions, which ought to alert us once again to the danger of simplistic answers.

1. Are we speaking about general revelation or special revelation?
Most Christians would reject the view that Muhammad received new revelations from God which had not been revealed before through the prophets, Jesus or the apostles. No doubt most would also be suspicious of the view that Muhammad's teaching was genuine revelation of God in a form that was especially relevant and appropriate for the Arabs. Many would want to say that if he did receive any special revelation, it came to him not directly from God, but through what he learned from the Jews and Christians.

If, however, we are simply speaking about general revelation, we could say that any revelation Muhammad received was no different from the general revelation that is available to all people. Or we might want to argue that if Muhammad was a sincere seeker after God, any revelation he received was no different in principle from that given (for instance) to Cornelius before his conversion (Acts 10), or to other people who are seeking after God (Acts 17:27).

Using Charles Kraft's memorable phrase, we may want to think of Muhammad as being 'chronologically AD but informationally BC'.[3] In this case, his experiences could have had something in common with those of people in the Old Testament such as Gideon, or possibly even Elijah, even though Muhammad played no part in the salvation history which was worked out through the descendants of Abraham.

2. How did the religion of Islam compare with the religion of Arabia?
It could be argued that Islam was a distinct improvement on the pre-Islamic polytheism and idolatry of Arabia. If the pre-Islamic religion of Arabia had much in common with Canaanite religion, Islam must have had much in common with the monotheism of the Old Testament. Even so, we may want to argue that it is irrelevant to ask how close Islam was to the religion of the Old Testament or how far it was from it. The final product seems to be a denial of fundamental Christian beliefs, and this is all that matters.

3. How are we to understand the development in the experience of Muhammad?
Many Christians are prepared to acknowledge that earlier in his life Muhammad was a sincere seeker after God. He had come to believe in the one Creator God, but did not have the opportunity to read the Bible or find out the truth about Jesus. Because of choices that he made at certain stages in his ministry, however, he wandered away from the truth that he knew, and was further from the truth at the end of his life than he was at the beginning. Other Christians answer this question, however, by saying that what matters is 'the finished product', namely his life and teaching as a whole, and that studying the development of his experience is therefore irrelevant.

4. How are we to understand the Qur'an's rejection of Christianity?
Here again there are at least two possible answers. We can say that what Muhammad rejected was at best a misunderstanding of the gospel, and at worst a travesty of the gospel. We simply do not know how Muhammad would have responded if he had had an opportunity

to hear the true gospel. Because the Christianity he rejected was so imperfect, we cannot immediately put Muslims in the same category as Arians or Jehovah's Witnesses. The other answer would be that since the Qur'an denies the deity of Christ and his death and resurrection, Islam must be seen as a heresy just like any other heresy, ancient or modern. It is irrelevant to ask, 'What would have happened if he had known the true gospel?'

5. How are we to understand the psychological processes of the 'revelations' which came to Muhammad?
Some would say that the descriptions of Muhammad's practices and experiences in the Qur'an and the *hadith* suggest that they had strong similarities with those of ascetics, monks and mystics. But since there is not enough clear evidence to reach definitive answers, we need to look at the content of the revelations rather than speculate over the psychological processes involved. On the other hand, some Christians would not hesitate to say that Muhammad must have had dealings with the occult, and that any 'revelations' he received must have come from evil spirits.

Working through questions like these should force us to recognize all that there is in Islam which is thoroughly consistent with Christian beliefs. We shall probably still want to make a distinction between 'truths' (plural) and 'the truth' (singular), and will remain genuinely puzzled about the mixture of truth and error which Christians find in Islam. But at least we will have been alerted to the danger of simplistic answers which either repel Muslims (because they convey such a negative view of Islam), or leave them confused (because they blur the distinctives of the two faiths). We may then be in a position to decide between the following four views, held by different Christians.

- However much truth there may be in the Qur'an, taken as a whole, it denies the deity of Christ, his crucifixion and his resurrection, and therefore takes the heart out of the gospel. It cannot therefore be regarded as being inspired by God in any sense, and must have been inspired by the devil.
- We should recognize everything in the Qur'an that is consistent with the revelation of God as we know it in the Bible and in Christ. We should be glad for the common ground there is

between the Christian faith and Islam, but help Muslims to see where the Muslim understanding of God differs from the Christian understanding of him.

- Muhammad should be regarded as a prophet in some sense. Since he enabled the Arabs to reject polytheism and idolatry and to accept monotheism, he must have received some genuine revelation from God. He can perhaps therefore be regarded as being comparable to Old Testament characters like Gideon or Elijah, even though he is not part of the biblical 'salvation history' and falls short of the revelation of God given in Christ. 'Could it not be', asks Christian Troll, 'that at that particular time and in that particular context Islam was entrusted with the task of prompting the Church to reform itself?'[4]

- Muhammad should be recognized as a genuine prophet for Muslims. In spite of the differences between the revelation of God in the Qur'an and the revelation of God in the Bible and in Christ, the Qur'an should be recognized as a revelation of God that was appropriate for the Arabs in its original context and is still appropriate for Muslims all over the world today.

Is Islam inspired by the devil?

Some Christians would never think in terms of demonic inspiration and would be embarrassed to think that Muslims might overhear Christians posing the question in such a blunt way. Others, however, feel compelled to ask the question at one time or another, because they need to explain the source of the error they perceive in Islam.

One possible starting point would be to take texts such as these from the letters of Paul.

- 'The god of this age has blinded the minds of unbelievers' (2 Cor. 4:4).
- 'Our struggle is ... against the powers of this dark world and against the spiritual forces of evil in the heavenly realms' (Eph. 6:12).
- 'Satan himself masquerades as an angel of light' (2 Cor. 11:14).

All these verses are no doubt thoroughly relevant to our thinking about all faiths and ideologies. There are several reasons, however, for suggesting that there can be real dangers in coming too easily and too quickly to the conclusion that Islam is a religion 'inspired by the devil'.

Why single out Islam for special mention? What about the godless humanism and materialism of the West today? What about some of the demonic forces at work in parts of the Christian world? When some Christians speak as if Islam is 'enemy number one' in the world today, there is a real danger of getting things out of proportion.

An overemphasis on the role of Satan in Islam can easily prevent Christians from facing up to the terrible record of the Christian church in its relations with Muhammad and his followers. Attributing every-thing we dislike or disagree with in Islam to demonic forces allows us to ignore the responsibility of the Christian church in much of what has happened. The very existence of Islam can be seen as a judgment on the Christian church, and the record of the church over fourteen cen-turies in its relations with Islam should leave us with a sense of shame.

In talking with Muslims we will, of course, want to disassociate ourselves from the Crusades, just as some Muslims have disassociated themselves from the actions of Islamists like Osama bin Laden. But resorting too quickly to the explanation that Islam is inspired by the devil may mean that we are letting ourselves off the hook too lightly, and that we never recognize the responsibility of the Christian church for much that has happened in the past.

If we teach that non-Christian religions are inspired by the devil, some Christians jump to the conclusion that people of these faiths must therefore by definition be possessed by evil powers. It is obvious that there are occult practices in some forms of folk Islam, and many Christians have no difficulty believing in demon possession (see chapter 36, 'Some issues facing Christians today'). But it is thoroughly unhelpful to suggest that Muslims – because of the nature of Islam – are in a special category of their own and therefore exposed to evil influences in a unique way.

We are probably influenced more than we realize by stereotypes of Islam that we have inherited from the past. It was not for purely biblical and theological reasons that our forefathers in the Eastern churches and in Europe thought of Islam in these terms. There were many other cultural, political and psychological factors at work not so far below the surface. This is how Jean-Marie Gaudeul makes the point, writing about the Middle Ages.

> Europe elaborated instinctively an image of everything it repudiated and projected this image on Islam, the symbol of all that was 'un-Christian' ... This was not deliberate, but instinctive: Europe had felt inferior to the Islamic civilization, it had received much from it: philosophy, the sciences, technology; unable as yet to express its own culture in positive terms, Europe rejected in Islam whatever seemed to threaten its Christian identity.[5]

Norman Daniels, in his book *Islam and the West: The Making of an Image*, shows that many of the popular images and stereotypes of Muslims and Islam in the minds of Europeans and Westerners today can be traced back to the writings of Christians in the Middle East and Europe in the Middle Ages.[6]

When Christians interpret the contemporary resurgence of Islam, especially in the Middle East, simply in terms of the work of Satan, they are probably guilty of resorting to a terrible oversimplification of complex issues. This revival is to some extent a response to centuries of European colonialism, and we cannot understand issues related to Iran, Iraq or Israel/Palestine if we do not appreciate the history of each of these areas. Simple explanations expressed in purely spiritual terms can easily prevent us from getting to grips with the complexities of history and politics.

Explaining Islam in terms of the demonic can sometimes simply be a way of recognizing what is culturally strange and foreign in Islam. Simple explanations of this kind seem to save us from the hard work of recognizing all the psychological, political and cultural factors which come into the equation.

If some Christians, then, refuse to answer the question 'Is Islam inspired by the devil?', others will answer with a simple 'Yes', because they can find no other way of explaining the fact that Islam seems to deny some of the most fundamental and essential Christian beliefs. But there will be others who will want to answer, 'Maybe, but...' These 'buts' will probably not turn the 'Maybe' to a 'No'. But they should at least make us recognize that simple categories cannot really help us in coming to terms with all that we find both in the religion of Islam and in the actual Muslims we meet.

26. THE ISLAMIC VIEW OF JESUS

'We believe in Jesus and all the prophets,' says the Muslim to the Christian. 'But what kind of Jesus do you believe in?' replies the Christian. 'What precisely is your picture of him?'

Ninety-three verses in fifteen different suras of the Qur'an speak about Jesus, and Christians and Muslims appear to have much in common regarding the important place they give to Jesus. But how significant are the differences in the way the two faiths think of Jesus? Does the amount of common ground make the differences seem minimal? Or are the differences so important that they point to fundamental differences between the two faiths? The Islamic view of Jesus is based primarily on the Qur'an, but has also been coloured by centuries of Islamic tradition.

Jesus in the Qur'an

The following are the main features in the picture of Jesus that emerges from the qur'anic verses about him. The quotations in this chapter are taken from Kenneth Cragg's translation, *Readings in the Qur'an.*[1]

Jesus is seen as one in the line of prophets sent by God who all taught the same message

> We have granted revelation to you [singular, i.e. Muhammad] as We gave revelation to Noah and the prophets who came after him. To Abraham also We gave revelation, and to Ishmael, Isaac, Jacob and the tribes, to Jesus and to Job, to Jonah, Aaron and Solomon. To David We brought the Psalms. (4:163)

> Say: 'We believe in God and in what He has revealed to us and His revelations to Abraham and Ishmael, to Isaac and Jacob and the tribes, and in what was brought to Moses, Jesus and the prophets, from their Lord. We do not discriminate between any of them and to God do we Surrender.' (3:84–85; cf. 2:136, 253)

Jesus was born of a virgin; his birth was announced to Mary by an angel

> To Mary the angel said: 'Mary, God gives you glad news of a word from Him. His name is the Messiah Jesus, son of Mary. Eminent will he be in this world and in the age to come, and he will have his place among those who are brought near to God's Throne. He will speak to men in the cradle and in his mature years, and he will be among the righteous.'

> Mary said: 'Lord, how shall I bear a son when no man has known me?' He replied: 'The will of God is so, for He creates as He wills. When His purpose is decreed He only says: "Be!" and it is. God will teach him the Scripture, the wisdom, the Torah and the Gospel, making him a messenger to the people of Israel.' (3:45–49)

He performed many miracles

> And to Jesus He will say: 'Jesus, son of Mary, remember My grace towards your mother when I aided you with the holy spirit, so that in your cradle and in your mature years you spoke to men. Remember how I gave you knowledge of the Book, and the wisdom, the Torah and the Gospel, and how by My leave you fashioned clay to the shape of the bird and when you breathed into it it became a bird by My leave, and how, by My leave too,

you healed those born blind and the lepers and how, by My leave again, you brought the dead to life once more.' (5:110)

It is blasphemy to elevate Jesus to the level of God

Truly they have lied against the truth who say: 'God, He is the Messiah, son of Mary.' Say: 'Who can arrogate sovereignty from God in anything? If God but wills it His power could annihilate the Messiah and his mother and every one else in the world. To God belongs the sovereignty of the heavens and of the earth and all that is within them and He is omnipotent over all.' (5:17)

They have ascribed invisible beings as partners to God, though He created them, and in their total ignorance they have attributed to Him sons and daughters. Glory to Him and exalted be He above what they allege. The very Creator of the heavens and of the earth, how could there be a 'son' to Him there never having been a 'spouse' to Him – He who created everything and who is omniscient over all things? (6:101–102)

While Jesus is not divine in any sense, he is unique among the prophets of God and is given titles such as 'Word' and 'Spirit' which are not given to any other human beings

People of the Book, do not go to unwarranted lengths in your religion and get involved in false utterances relating to God. Truly, Jesus, Mary's son, was the messenger of God and His word – the word which He imparted to Mary – and a spirit from Him. Believe, then, in God and His Messengers and do not talk of three gods. You are well advised to abandon such ideas. Truly God is one God. Glory be to Him and no 'son' to Him whose are all things in the heavens and the earth, their one and only guardian.

That He should be servant to God will never be disdained by the Messiah as beneath his dignity, nor indeed by the angels who dwell in the divine presence. Servants of His who take on arrogant airs and think themselves above serving – well, God will have them all summoned to answer for it. (4:171–172)

Jesus is to be thought of as similar to Adam in that they were both created by the word of God

God would have you think of Jesus as you think of Adam, created by God from the dust, saying to him 'Be' and into being he came. This is the truth from your Lord, so do not be among those who are dubious. (3:59–60; cf. 21:91)

Jesus was not crucified

As for their [the Christians'] claim that they [the Jews] killed the Messiah Jesus, son of Mary, the messenger of God, the truth is they did not kill him nor did they crucify him. They were under the illusion that they had. There is a lot of doubt about this matter among those who are at odds over it. They have no real knowledge but follow only surmise. Assuredly, they did not kill him. On the contrary, God raised him to Himself – God whose are all wisdom and power. And before they come to die, the people of the Book, to a man, will surely believe on him. On the Day of Resurrection he will be a witness against them. (4:157–159)

Jesus predicts the coming of Muhammad

And when Jesus, son of Mary, said: 'O Children of Israel, I am Allah's Messenger to you, confirming what came before me of the torah, and announcing the news of a Messenger who will come after me, whose name is Ahmad.' Then when he (Ahmad i.e. Mohammad) brought them the clear proofs, they said: 'This is manifest sorcery.' (61:6)

Jesus and Mary
The title 'son of Mary' is given to Jesus twenty-three times (e.g. 2:253; 3:45; 4:154). While Mary is an important person in her own right, these repeated references to Mary serve to underline the humanity of Jesus. He could not possibly be divine in any sense, because although he was conceived in a supernatural way, he was born to Mary in a very natural way and grew up like any ordinary person. According to Barbara Stowasser, Muslim scholars in the early centuries came to believe that the main purpose of all the revelations on Mary was 'divine clarification

of the true natures of Jesus and Mary in order that their creaturedom be but another sign of God's Oneness and Omnipotence'.[2]

The picture of Jesus that emerges from the Qur'an is summed up by M. Ali Merad, a Muslim scholar of Algerian origin, as follows.

> Prophet, Apostle of God, servant of God, these are titles which are applied in the Qur'an to many other prophetic figures. But Christ is more than that. Everything in the Qur'an inclines us to represent him as being above the common condition of men ... An exceptional divine work, an exceptional messenger, favoured in all things by God, Christ witnesses to an exceptional divine concern. Through all that the Qur'an has to say about Jesus, we cannot fail to recognize an unquestionable convergence: everything it gives leads to the declaration of Christ's surpassing greatness.[3]

The traditional Islamic interpretation of the death of Jesus is summed up by the same writer in this way:

> The Muslim's conviction is ... strengthened by everything he reads in the Qur'an, namely that God does not abandon His own: how then could He have abandoned Jesus, a being whom he produced miraculously, by His Kalima, a being whom He assisted by His Spirit, whom He had singularly favoured, conferring on him the remarkable power of giving life and of raising from the dead? God cannot hand over to the fury of some executioners a being with a nature like Jesus.
>
> Islam refuses to accept this tragic image of the Passion. Not simply because it has no place for the dogma of the Redemption, but because the Passion would imply in its eyes that God had failed.
>
> Islam rejects the idea of the death of Christ. This attitude safeguards at one and the same time the idea found in the Qur'an of God's honour and of man's dignity. For in Jesus mankind attains its supreme dignity, its consummation.[4]

Jesus in later Islamic tradition

Since Jesus in the Qur'an is such an enigmatic figure, Muslims after the time of Muhammad felt the need to explain the references to Jesus in the Qur'an in order to add to and fill out its picture of Jesus. In the traditions which were circulated, for example, in *The Tales of the Prophet* and in *hadith*, the main focus of interest was on four areas.

1. His miraculous powers

One story tells how he dyed ten garments in different colours in one single vat. Another story tells how he turned a group of children into pigs.

2. His asceticism

Jesus is described as wearing a robe of wool, which indicates that he lived very simply. He is quoted as saying, 'I have become worn out by my labours, and there is no poor person poorer than I am.' He has no human ties, except to his mother, and is known as 'the prince of wanderers'.

3. His saintliness

'The Sufis adopted Jesus', says Tarif Khalidi, 'as one of their major spiritual heroes,' and he became 'a patron saint of Muslim asceticism'.[5] Al-Ghazali described Jesus as 'Prophet of the Heart', and for Ibn-Arabi, who remembers that Muhammad is described in the Qur'an as 'the seal of the Prophets' (khatam al-anbiya), Jesus becomes 'the seal of the saints' (khatam al-awliya').

4. His role at the end of history when he comes to vindicate Islam

This is how traditional Islamic eschatology is summed up by Tha'alibi, a medieval writer, in Stories of the Prophets, quoting a reported saying of the Prophet Muhammad.

> Abu Salih Shu'ayb ibn Muhammad al-Bayhaqi has informed us with a chain of authorities back to Abu Hurayra how this latter related that the Messenger of God, upon whom be God's blessing and peace, said: 'The Prophets are brethren, though of different mothers, and their religion is one and the same. I am the nearest of mankind to Jesus son of Mary, on both of whom be peace, because there has been no Prophet between him and me. It will come to pass that the son of Mary will descend among you as a just ruler. He will descend to my community and be my deputy (or Caliph) over them, so when you see him give him recognition. He will be a man symmetrical in stature, of reddish-white (complexion), lank-haired, as though his hair were dripping perfume though it had not been moistened. He will come down in a greenish-yellow garment, will break crosses and kill swine, will put an end to the poll-tax (paid by non-Muslims under Islam), will raise the welcoming cry

from al-Rawha when he comes for the Greater and the Lesser Pilgrimage, undertaking them both with zeal. He will make war on behalf of Islam, until in his time he destroys all religions save that of Islam, and there will thenceforward be but one single prostration of obeisance, namely that to God, Lord of the Worlds. Also in his time God will destroy the Antichrist, the lying al-Dajjal ... Then he will die, and the Muslims will pray over him and bury him at Medina beside the grave of Umar.'[6]

The Ahmadiyya movement, which began in Pakistan in 1879, has taught that Jesus was taken down from the cross before he actually died, and later revived in the tomb. He then escaped from Jerusalem and travelled to Kashmir, where he died. Although the Ahmadis are a strong missionary group, they were officially declared non-Muslims by the government of Pakistan in 1973.

Early in this century Muslim apologists began to use the so-called Gospel of Barnabas, claiming that this is the only authentic account of the life of Jesus. It can easily be demonstrated, however, from its historical and geographical errors and from teaching which contradicts the Qur'an, that the book is a medieval forgery (see further chapter 22, 'A deeper look at the main Muslim objections').

If Muslims today know only the Jesus of the Qur'an and of later Muslim tradition, they insist that he was no more than a prophet and that he did not die on the cross. Many of them have little or no desire to read the Gospels or to explore Christian beliefs about him, because they think that all they need to know about him is revealed in the Qur'an. If they do read the Gospels and admire his teaching, they tend to regard it as hopelessly unrealistic. Although they are often impressed by his miraculous powers and may even be moved by the story of the crucifixion, they find it impossible to believe that God could have allowed it to happen, or to see Jesus as anything more than an ordinary man and a great prophet.

Christian responses

While some aspects of the qur'anic Jesus fit with the picture given in the New Testament (for instance, the virgin birth and some of the miracles), several other aspects appear to have come from unorthodox, if not heretical, Christian sources (such as the miracles performed during the childhood of Jesus, and the idea of a substitute who was crucified in place of Jesus), which 'reflect varying tendencies within Christianity – Gnostic, Monophysite and Nestorian'.[7] Christians have to recognize, however, that such an interpretation is totally unacceptable to Muslims who believe that the Qur'an was revealed directly by God to the mind of the Prophet, and that the contents of the Qur'an cannot therefore be traced back to human sources.

The basic reason why Jesus cannot be seen by the Qur'an as 'more than a prophet' is that he does not fit into the Islamic understanding of how God has revealed himself to the world. The contrast between the two faiths at this point is summed up vividly by Jens Christensen: 'Islam says: Book from God = revelation from God.' Christianity says: 'Christ from God = revelation of God.' Islam rules out the possibility of God revealing himself through an incarnation. For Muslims, therefore, however exalted Jesus may be, he cannot possibly be anything more than a person of 'surpassing greatness'.[8]

Christians feel compelled to point out to Muslims that the Jesus of the Qur'an is a very pale reflection of the Jesus of the New Testament. This feeling is expressed by Kenneth Cragg.

> This is the inward tragedy, from the Christian angle, of the rise of Islam, the genesis and dissemination of a new belief which claimed to displace what it had never effectively known. The state of being a stranger to the Christian's Christ has been intensified by further failures of love and loyalty on the part of institutional Christianity in the long and often bitter external relations of the two faiths through the centuries.
>
> It is for these reasons that the call of the minaret must always seem to the Christian a call to retrieval. He yearns to undo the alienation and to make amends for the past by as full a restitution as he can achieve of the Christ to Whom Islam is a stranger. The objective is not, as the Crusaders believed, the repossession of what Christendom has lost, but the restoration to Muslims of the Christ Whom they have missed.[9]

Jesus in the Qur'an and in later Islamic tradition becomes a thoroughly Islamic prophet. Co-opted within an Islamic world view, he is unique in certain respects, but merely one of the prophets, the last one before the final Prophet, Muhammad. In *The Muslim Jesus:*

Sayings and Stories in Islamic Literature, Tarif Khalidi sums up the Islamic Jesus as described in these sayings which he calls 'this gospel'.

> In its totality, this gospel is the story of a love affair between Islam and Jesus and is thus a unique record of how one world religion chose to adopt the central figure of another, coming to recognize him as constitutive of its own identity ... Jesus is always identified as a Muslim prophet ... for he is, after all, a figure moulded in an Islamic environment ... Here, then, is the true Jesus, 'cleansed' of the 'perversions' of his followers, a prophet truly obedient to his Maker and offered up as the true alternative to the Jesus of the Incarnation, Crucifixion, and Redemption.[10]

If we began this study hoping that the person of Jesus might be a bridge between the two faiths, this conclusion leaves us with the feeling that it may be a case of 'so near, and yet so far'. But however far apart we feel, the qur'anic picture of Jesus can still provide material for serious dialogue between Christians and Muslims. For, as Henri Michaud says in a study of Jesus in the Qur'an,

> After having tried to understand what the Qur'an says about Jesus, we shall ask our brothers of Islam with very great anxiety: 'Is this indeed what you believe about Jesus?' If there is a reply without ambiguity, then an irenical dialogue can begin.[11]

27. THE QUR'ANIC VIEW OF CHRISTIANS

The following verses from the Qur'an illustrate the variety of views about Christians which are expressed in the Qur'an – some very positive, some argumentative, and some highly hostile. We begin with the more positive verses and move along the spectrum to the more critical verses. The extracts are taken from a variety of English translations.

'They (Christians) have nothing to fear.'

> Lo! Those who believe (in that which is revealed unto thee, Muhammad), and those who are Jews and Christians, and Sabaeans – who ever believeth in Allah and the Last Day and doeth right – surely their reward is with their Lord, and there shall be no fear upon them neither shall they grieve. (2:62)

This verse, which is regarded as being from the late Medinan period, seems to suggest that Jews and Christians (together with Sabaeans, possibly identified with a group in South Yemen at the time) who accept the basic creed of Islam about God as Creator and Judge, and who live good lives, will have nothing to fear on the Day of Judgment and can be confident that they will enter Paradise. Because the reference to 'Sabaeans' is vague, the verse came to be used as a basis for extending toleration to Zoroastrians in Persia.

'They are closest to the Muslims in affection.'

> You shall find the most hostile people to the believers to be the Jews and the polytheists; and you will find the closest in affection to the believers those who say: 'We are Christians.' For among them are priests and monks, and they are not arrogant. And when they hear what we revealed to the Apostle, you see their eyes overflow with tears on account of the truth they recognize. They say: 'Our Lord, we believe, so write us down among the witnesses.' (5:82–83, Fakhry)

This verse is often quoted by Muslims as a proof-text to demonstrate a positive attitude towards Christians. The remainder of these verses, however, give the reasons for the positive assessment of Christians in this particular situation. The first reason that is given is that certain Christian leaders lead godly and humble lives. The second reason is that when these Christians hear the message of Islam proclaimed, they accept it with joy and enthusiasm and become Muslims.[1] Traditional Muslim commentators nearly always interpreted this verse as referring to Christians who converted to Islam. Since, according to Muslim commentaries, a verse of this kind was revealed in a very specific context, Muslims need to be careful about taking this as their main proof-text to express a positive attitude towards all Christians at all times.

'Let's agree on a formula about God that Muslims, Jews and Christians can all accept.'

> Say, 'O people of the Book, come to a just word, common between us and you that we worship no one except God: that we associate nothing with Him, and that we do not take one another as lords instead of God.' But if they turn their backs, say, 'Bear witness that we are Muslims.' (3:64, M. Ayoub)

This verse is sometimes quoted as an invitation to dialogue (in the modern sense). It is more accurate, however, to see it as an invitation to Jews and especially to Christians to accept an Islamic understanding of God. The thrust of the challenge is: 'Can we not agree on a formula in which we worship the One True God and refuse to elevate any human being to the level of God?'

'We Muslims believe the same as what was revealed to Jesus. We worship the same God as you.'

> Say (O Muhammad): We believe in Allah and that which is revealed unto us and that which was revealed unto Abraham and Ishmael and Isaac and Jacob and the tribes, and that which was vouchsafed unto Moses and Jesus and the Prophets from their Lord. We make no distinction between any of them, and unto Him we have surrendered. (3:84)

'Christians should not make exaggerated claims for Jesus.'

> People of the Book, go not beyond the bounds in your religion, and say not as to God but the truth. The Messiah, Jesus son of Mary, was only the Messenger of God, and His Word that he committed to Mary, and a Spirit from Him. So believe in God and His Messengers, and say not, 'Three.' Refrain; better is it for you. God is only One God. Glory be to Him – that He should have a son! To him belong all that is in the heavens and in the earth. God suffices for a guardian. (4:171, A. J. Arberry)

This verse is a challenge to Christians who, from the point of view of Islam, make exaggerated claims about Jesus. Other verses in the Qur'an (e.g. 5:116) suggest that the 'trinity' which is rejected was thought to consist of God the Father, the Virgin Mary and Jesus their son. While most Muslims would today admit that this is not the Trinity that Christians believe in, they would feel that verses of this kind exclude *both* heretical ideas of this kind *and* the traditional, orthodox understanding of the Trinity.

'Use wise exhortation to convince Christians to accept Islam.'

> Do not dispute with the people of the Book save in the fairest way; except for those who are evildoers. And say: 'We believe in what has

been sent down to us and what has been sent down to you. Our God
and your God are one and to Him we are submissive.' (29:46, Fakhry;
cf. 22:20)

Call to the Way of your Lord with wisdom and mild exhortation, and argue
with them in the best manner. Your Lord surely knows best those who
stray from His path, and He knows well those who are rightly guided.
(16:125, Fakhry)

'Don't make friends with Christians.'

O believers, do not take the Jews and the Christians as friends; some of
them are friends of each other. Whoever of you takes them as friends is
surely one of them. Allah indeed does not guide the wrongdoers ... O
believers, do not take as friends those who take your religion as a mockery
or a sport, be they from among those who received the Book before you,
or the unbelievers. Fear Allah if you are true believers. (5:51, 57; cf. 3:18;
4:144, Fakhry)

Ruqaiyya Waris Maqsood explains this injunction by referring to a
particular situation in the life of the Prophet.

This surah was revealed to deal with specific problems that arose from the
Treaty of Hudaybiyah when Muslims were allowed permission to fight
such Jews and Christians as broke their sworn treaty of loyalty to the
Islamic State of Madina, as well as any other enemies who attacked them
(Surah 9:29–31). It did not constitute an injunction against normal friendly
relations between Muslims and such Jews and Christians as were
well-disposed towards Muslims. The term *wali* has several shades of
meaning – ally, friend, helper, protector, etc.[2]

'Exalting Christ to the level of God is blasphemy.'

They do blaspheme who say: 'God is Christ the son of Mary.' But said
Christ: 'O Children of Israel! Worship God, my Lord and your Lord.'
Whoever joins other gods with God – God will forbid him the Garden,
and the fire will be his abode. There will for the wrongdoers be no one to
help. They do blaspheme who say: God is one of three in a Trinity: for

there is no god except God. If they desist not from their word (of blasphemy), verily a grievous penalty will befall the blasphemers among them. (5:72–73, Yusuf Ali)

The word for 'blaspheme' here (*kafara*) is a strong word which expresses the most serious kind of unbelief and speaking against God. It can be pointed out that Christians have no difficulty in saying 'Jesus is God' in the sense that the Gospel according to John says that 'the Word was God' (John 1:1). Most Christians, however, would hesitate to turn the sentence round and say 'God is Jesus'. If we were to say 'Allah is Jesus', we can perhaps begin to understand why a statement of this kind is so offensive to Muslims. And if we believe that God is a trinitarian God, when we use the word 'God' we are not only thinking of God the Father, but of the Father, the Son and the Spirit.

'Fight against them until they submit.'

Fight against those who do not believe in God nor in the last Day and who do not hold forbidden what God has prohibited and who do not adhere to the religion of truth, being among those to whom the Book was given. Do so until they pay the *Jizyah* (tax on tolerated communities) personally, once they have been reduced to submission. (9:29, Cragg)

The word for 'fight' (*qatilu*) is from the root *qatala*, which means 'to kill', and therefore has a strong meaning in Arabic. The phrase 'being among those to whom the Book was given' indicates that this verse is clearly speaking about Jews and Christians, since they are 'People of the Book'. In this verse, therefore, Muhammad and the Muslims are called to fight against Jews and Christians who (a) do not believe in God or the Day of Judgment, (b) do not accept the prohibitions contained in the Qur'an, and (c) refuse to become Muslims. They are to fight against them until they are 'reduced to submission' and pay the *jizya* tax as a token of their submission to Islamic rule. This verse recognizes that not all Jews and Christians are the same, and only calls on Muslims to fight certain kinds of Christians. They are not to be killed like the idolaters (9:5).

Principles of interpretation

There are two principles of qur'anic interpretation which are relevant to the discussion of all these verses.

- The insistence on knowing the context in which a particular verse was revealed (the *asbab al-nuzul*, the occasions of revelation; see chapter 8, 'The Qur'an') reminds Muslims of the need to find out the specific context in which *each* of these verses was revealed. Thus most commentators would say that many of the positive verses like the first ones quoted above were revealed during the Meccan period and were probably associated with the time when the Prophet sent some of his followers to seek asylum with the Negus, the Christian emperor of Abyssinia. It is hardly surprising therefore if qur'anic verses from this period reflect a positive view of Christians and Christianity, and that verses like the later ones reflect a period in Medina when attitudes towards Christians were not so positive.
- The second principle is that of Abrogation, which says that a later verse can sometimes abrogate or cancel an earlier verse (see chapter 8, 'The Qur'an'). If Muslims apply this principle to this set of verses, as some of them do, they conclude that the later, more critical verses abrogate the earlier, more tolerant verses. If, therefore, Muslims are looking to the Qur'an for guidance about how they should think about Christians today, many of them will look to the later verses rather than the earlier ones.

It soon becomes evident that these two principles can sometimes point in different directions. If Muslims are to follow the first principle, they will want to ask, 'Which of the various situations reflected in the Qur'an has most similarities with the situation in which we are living today?' Muslims in the West might answer that their situation has more in common with the situation of the early Muslims seeking refuge in Abyssinia than with the Islamic state in Medina. If they follow the second principle, however, they are likely to adopt a harsher attitude towards Christians. We need to conclude at the very least that Muslims have different ways of interpreting the Qur'an, and that it is not always easy to summarize in a few sentences 'the qur'anic view of Christians'.[3] Different verses give a different message, and different people interpret all these verses in slightly different ways.

28. CRUCIAL DIFFERENCES: THE PARTING OF THE WAYS

If some Christians concentrate on the differences between Christianity and Islam, others tend to emphasize the common ground without ever getting to grips with the areas of disagreement. Is it ever possible to strike the right balance between these two approaches? While attempting to be scrupulously fair and honest, is it possible to recognize and rejoice in what is common between the two faiths, and at the same time to articulate the fundamentally different assumptions behind the disagreements in other areas of belief?

In their discussions with one another Christians and Muslims often feel that, for part of their journey at least, they are walking together in the same direction along the same road. But then they come to a fork in the road and find themselves going in different directions. Where, then, are these forks in the road, and what are the issues over which Christians and Muslims discover that their paths diverge?

In this chapter we take six different subjects and attempt to summarize what most Muslims believe alongside what most Christians believe.

1. Revelation: Can God be known?

'Nothing is like unto Him' (42:11, Fakhry). God is therefore utterly transcendent, radically different from everything in the world.

God is transcendent; but because God made humankind in his image and likeness (Gen. 1:26–27), God cannot be totally other and different from human beings. The image of God in humankind means that there is a basic likeness between God and humankind which creates the possibility of a personal relationship with God, and of God revealing himself to humans.

The Qur'an teaches that humankind is God's representative (*khalifa*) on earth, his vice-gerent.

Similarly, in the creation story in Genesis, Adam and Eve are given responsibility for the earth: 'Be fruitful and increase in number.'

While the Qur'an uses expressions like 'seeking the face of God' (e.g. 2:272), orthodox Islamic theology has its own way of understanding anthropomorphic language and generally teaches that *God himself cannot be known*; only his will can be known.[1]

Christian theology teaches that *God can be known* because he has revealed himself – through the universe, through human conscience, through the Bible, and supremely through Jesus.

The 'names of God' reveal something of the character and attributes of God; but God is so 'wholly Other', so different from humans, that the meaning of these names when applied to God is not the same as when applied to people.

We need not be so uncertain about the meaning of such words. When God says, 'Be holy, for I am holy,' he defines the meaning he gives to the word 'holy' and does not leave it to humans to decide what it may mean.

God wants the human race to know
his will and has revealed it through
the Qur'an.

Jesus spoke about the possibility of
knowing God, and related this
possibility to his own coming into the
world (John 17:3).

The climax of God's revelation
comes *through a book*, with
Muhammad as the one who receives
the revelation, which is later written
down.

While God has spoken through his
prophets, the climax of God's
revelation comes *through a person*,
Jesus. The New Testament writers
interpret the meaning of who he was
and what he has achieved.

2. Inspiration: In what sense is Scripture 'the Word of God'?

The very words of the Qur'an were
revealed through Muhammad
(12:2–3).

The writers of the Bible were
inspired by the Holy Spirit: '...men
spoke from God' (2 Pet. 1:21). The
Bible is therefore *both* the Word of
God *and* the word of humankind.

Muhammad did not compose or
write the Qur'an, he simply received
it and recited it, so that his own
thoughts and ideas did not contribute
to the revelations in any way (7:157;
29:28).

The biblical writers were not passive
instruments used by God; they
thought about what they were doing
and wrote in their own individual
style.

Since the Qur'an is 100% from God,
it is unnecessary and wrong to try to
find the 'sources' of the Qur'an.

Although they were inspired, there is
no reason why we should not study
the Bible as we study other literature
and ask questions about the writers,
their sources and their way of writing.

Because the Qur'an was revealed in
Arabic, it is vital to read and recite it
in Arabic. Translations of the Qur'an
may or may not be permitted; but

The Old Testament was written
mostly in Hebrew, and the New
Testament writers wrote in Greek,
and used Greek translations of the

even when permitted, they do not have the same spiritual value or status as the original Arabic.

Old Testament. We encourage translations of the Bible because we believe God wants all people to understand it as best they can. A translation of the Bible is just as much 'the Bible' as the original Hebrew and Greek. The meaning of the original *can* be conveyed adequately in any language.

3. Human nature: What is the true diagnosis of the human condition?

According to the Qur'an, Satan (*Iblis*) was responsible for tempting Adam and Eve and therefore became the source and origin of evil among humankind. Adam and Eve sinned when they gave in to the temptation of Satan and ate from the forbidden tree. But their sin was a mistake rather than wilful disobedience.

Although Adam and Eve were tempted by the serpent (representing Satan), they were fully responsible for their action. The sin of Adam and Eve involved pride, disobedience to the will of God and a desire to be independent of God.

When Adam and Eve realized their mistake and prayed for forgiveness, they were forgiven and restored to the condition they were in before. God gave them the message of Islam, and Adam became the first prophet of Islam. There was no such thing as 'the fall'.

As a consequence of their sin, Adam and Eve were expelled from the garden of Eden. The basic meaning of 'the fall' is that their disobedience had serious consequences – both for themselves and for the whole human race. They were estranged from God and the relationship that they had previously enjoyed with God was spoiled. This is the situation for all people today.

Sin is an act of disobedience to God's law, a breaking of moral and social

Human beings are sinful by nature. The basic meaning of the idea of conventions. Although human beings are prone to evil (12:53), they are not sinful by nature; they are simply imperfect and fallible. They are ignorant, not knowing the will of God, forgetful and weak (4:28). There is no 'original sin'; sin is not hereditary, since every child who is born is in the same condition that Adam and Eve were in.

'original sin' is that human beings inherit the sinful human nature of their parents. While they are not responsible for their parents' sin, they inherit the tendency to sin.

Since there is no collective responsibility, no person can bear the sins of another person (6:14; 7:28).

When we forgive others for wrongs done to us, we are 'bearing their sin', suffering the consequences of their wrongs, and not taking revenge for what they have done to us.

Sin does not affect God personally, since he is so transcendent that he cannot be affected by the sins of his creatures.

Sin does affect God personally. It hurts him not only that his laws have been broken, but also that his relationship with people is broken.

Repentance means confessing our sins, turning from the wrong that we have done and seeking God's mercy and forgiveness.

Repentance needs to go deeper than the mere confession of sins and include the admission that there is something seriously wrong with our nature. The problem has to do with what we are, not just with our thoughts and actions.

---

4. God's provision for humankind: What has God done to deal with human sin?

God's response to the weakness of humankind is to provide guidance (*hidaya*) that will show people how to follow 'the straight path' (*al-sirat*

God's response to human sin is through the *incarnation* (in which God reveals himself supremely through Jesus); the *atonement* (in which he *al-mustaqim*); a model of how Muslims should live; and the Islamic community.

deals with the root of human sinfulness); the giving of *the Holy Spirit* to live in the lives of Jesus' followers; and *the church* to provide the community in which Christians support each other as they live in the world.

'The Islamic doctrine of salvation does not conceive of men and women as sinners who must be saved through spiritual regeneration. Rather it holds that since man is not dead in sin, he does not need spiritual rebirth ... The basic emphasis of Islamic salvation lies instead in the historical responsibility of its followers, namely the establishment of the ideal religio-political order with a worldwide membership of all those who believe in God and His revelation through Muhammad, upon whom be peace.' (Abdulaziz A. Sachedina)[2]

When Jesus died on the cross, he was 'bearing' the sins of the world, taking on himself the judgment that we deserve. This therefore was God's way of demonstrating his love and mercy to us and showing his forgiveness of sins.

'Guidance' is provided by the Qur'an and the example of the Prophet, which show clearly the moral standards by which Muslims are to live as individuals and as communities. The life of Muhammad, as described in *hadith*, provides a detailed model of how Muslims should live.

After the death and resurrection of Jesus, God sent his Holy Spirit into the hearts and minds of the disciples of Jesus. The Spirit of God lives in the followers of Jesus today, making the presence of Jesus real to them and enabling them to be more like Jesus in their lives.

When Muslims live together in the Muslim community (the *umma*) and practise the faith together, the cohesion of the community encourages and supports people who

The church is described as 'the body of Christ' and every Christian is a member of this worldwide body. Living together as members of the worldwide church encourages and might otherwise go astray. This context is provided ideally in the Islamic state where the laws are based on Islamic *shari'a*.

strengthens each individual in worship, learning, service to the world and witness to Jesus.

5. Forgiveness and salvation: How does divine forgiveness work? What is the meaning of salvation?

God is merciful and willing to forgive all who sincerely repent, believe and devote themselves to good works. God forgives simply by pronouncing forgiveness. Forgiveness depends simply on the justice and mercy of God and his declaration of forgiveness (4:106).

Since God is both Creator and Judge, both loving and holy, his forgiveness cannot simply be a declaration that we are forgiven. If the laws of God have been broken, a simple pardon would undermine his law. Something more is involved, since God can hardly remain just and holy while at the same time simply pardoning sinful people who turn their backs on him.

There is no need for any sacrifice or atonement. Each one of us individually is responsible before God, and no one can bear the sins of any other person. Since Jesus did not die on the cross, there is no justification for ideas about 'redemption' through his death or for linking divine forgiveness with his death.

In forgiveness on the human level between people, the greater the sin, the more it costs for a person to forgive another person who has wronged him/her. Forgiving a serious sin involves bearing the consequences of that sin and refusing to punish the other person. Similarly it must *cost something* for God to forgive. These are some of the basic ideas underlying sacrifice and atonement. As Jesus died on the cross he was bearing the judgment on all human sin and at the same time demonstrating God's self-giving, sacrificial love for all people. God's forgiveness does not depend on our good deeds, but on his love and grace demonstrated in the death of Jesus on the cross. No amount of good deeds that we perform can outweigh our wrong deeds or change our sinful nature. The cross expresses *the divine love that suffers.*

Many believe that the good deeds we do cancel the effects of bad deeds. Our good and bad deeds will be weighed in the balance by God on the Day of Judgment. We can hope that, if we live a good life, our good deeds will outweigh our bad deeds; but we cannot know until the Day itself (2:82). If God accepts us, we will be admitted to Paradise; if not, we go to Hell (7:40–46). Many believe that if they have even an atom of (Muslim) faith, they will enter Paradise. Most Muslims believe that they can trust the intercession of the Prophet to help them (24:62; 3:159). Some also believe in some kind of Purgatory through which they will pass before eventually entering Paradise.

Even in this life we can be sure of God's mercy and forgiveness. Part of the idea of 'salvation' is that if we trust in Jesus, we can be sure that we are forgiven and reconciled to God, and therefore have no need to fear condemnation and rejection on the Day of Judgment.

6. Politics and the state: What is the place of the state in the kingdom of God?

During the period in Mecca, Muhammad was simply a persecuted prophet. After the *hijra* he became both prophet and statesman. Not only did he receive the revelation

Jesus refused to use force to defend himself or to ensure the success of his movement. He told Pilate, 'My kingdom is not of this world. If it were, my servants would fight to from God in the Qur'an; he believed he was called to establish an Islamic society in Medina.

prevent my arrest by the Jews' (John 18:36). He refused to identify the kingdom of God with any one political system.

Muslims have generally found it difficult, if not impossible, to separate 'mosque' from 'state', 'the things that are Caesar's' from 'the things that are God's', the religious from the secular. 'The chief characteristic of Islam is that it makes no distinction between the spiritual and the secular in life.' (Sayyid Abul A'la Mawdudi)[3]

While church and state have been closely related in different ways and in different countries in the past, most Christians today are cautious about any close association between church and state. Faith cannot be forced on anyone. Truth is often corrupted by too close association with power. And in a pluralist society the majority faith has to allow for religious freedom.

Muslims usually believe that 'Islam must rule' and that the rule of God needs ideally to be embodied in an Islamic state. Islam ideally is both 'religion' and 'state' (din wa dawla).

At the same time there has been little agreement among Muslims about how these convictions should be worked out in practice. And historically there has nearly always been some kind of separation between religious leaders and political leaders. This is an area of tension today between Islamists and moderate Muslims, and between Sunnis and Shi'ites.

The separation of church and state does not mean that Christians have no role to play in making their voice heard in the media and in government. Jesus encourages his disciples to be 'salt' and 'light' in their society (Matt. 5:13–16).

Is there any common denominator in our discussion of these six issues? Where there has been a parting of the ways between Christians and Muslims, perhaps it is because we are faced ultimately with a choice between two ways of thinking which cannot be reconciled. *From the Christian perspective*, Islam is utterly rational and reasonable in each of these areas, but only by the standards of human reason.

Jesus had to rebuke Peter at Caesarea Philippi for his 'Islamic' thinking over the question of his suffering and death: 'You think as men think, not as God thinks' (Mark 8:33 NEB). Could we apply this to the thinking of Islam in these areas as well? *From the standpoint of the revelation of God in Christ*, Islam seems to be thinking as men think in each of the six areas considered in this chapter.

- Muhammad Hamidullah writes: 'There are several ways of establishing contact or communication between man and God. The best would have been incarnation; but Islam has rejected it.'[4] By ruling out the possibility of incarnation and by reducing Jesus to the level of a prophet, it claims to be able to tell God what he can and cannot do in revealing himself to the human race.
- In its concept of inspiration it is ruled by an almost mechanical view of divine communication through a book as the final and supreme disclosure of God and the only guarantee of a reliable revelation.
- Its diagnosis of human nature is too superficial and optimistic, and hardly touches the root of the problem, since it has little or nothing to say about its deep-seated corruption.
- Because its diagnosis of human sin is too optimistic, it refuses to believe that human beings need anything more than teaching, law and the community to change their hearts and their character.
- Its message about forgiveness generally seems to leave people at best in uncertainty or complacency, and at worst in abject fear of what to expect on the Day of Judgment, and refuses to see in the life, death and resurrection of Jesus a demonstration of God's love.
- By linking truth to power, it seems blind to the corruption that so often goes with political power, and in offering the world its vision of a society under Islamic law, it associates the kingdom of God too closely with what is Caesar's.

What we know of Peter after that decisive encounter with Jesus described in Mark 8 suggests that he must have accepted this stinging rebuke. He must have been able to change his thinking – at least gradually throughout the rest of his life – because of what he saw in Jesus.

29. THINKING BIBLICALLY ABOUT ISLAM

Are there ways in which we can use our own Scriptures to help us evaluate Islam? Our own thinking about Islam is coloured by historical, political and sociological factors (whether we live in the East or the West). Should we not be able to find in the Bible a more objective reference point that will challenge our prejudices and help us to think in a more deeply Christian way about Islam?

The attempt to 'think biblically' may turn out to be a new discipline that cannot be taught by textbooks and cannot be included under any one of the basic disciplines of traditional theological study. There will be little place for simply collecting proof-texts. We shall rather need to draw on all the resources of biblical scholarship at our disposal to help us understand the text in its proper historical context and then draw legitimate parallels with Islam.

Here are four ways in which Christians have tried to relate the biblical text to the teaching of the Qur'an.

'False prophets' and 'the Antichrist'

Many Christians turn instinctively to Matthew 24:23–27, believing that it provides the only truly biblical category for understanding Muhammad: 'False Christs and false prophets will appear.' They might also turn to 1 John 2:22–23: 'Who is the liar? It is whoever denies that Jesus is the Christ. Such a person is the antichrist – denying the Father and the Son. No-one who denies the Son has the Father; whoever acknowledges the Son has the Father also.'

There is a certain danger, however, in thinking that this is the beginning and end of thinking biblically about Islam. If we bind ourselves exclusively to these categories, we may find it impossible to enter sympathetically into the mind of Muslims. We will find it hard to appreciate the development of Muhammad's teaching, and we may fail to understand the true context and the real intention of Muhammad's denial of the divinity of Jesus.

Muhammad's public ministry did not begin with a rejection of Christian beliefs. It began with a passionate rejection of the idolatry of Mecca and a call to the worship of the one Creator God. Muhammad must have been in contact with individual Christians and groups of Christians at many stages of his life. But it was only later in his public ministry, when he came in closer contact with Christians at Medina and elsewhere, that he felt compelled to extend his denunciation of idolatry to include Christian beliefs about Jesus as the Son of God.

There are good reasons for believing, however, that Muhammad did not really understand the Christian claim that Jesus was the Son of God. He may have rejected what he thought was a Christian belief because it seemed to be as crude as the polytheistic beliefs of the Meccans. We do not know how Muhammad *would have* responded if he had been granted first-hand knowledge of the gospel and had understood how the Christian faith can be monotheistic and trinitarian at the same time. But if what he rejected as blasphemous was at best a distortion and at worst a travesty of Christian beliefs, are we really justified in thinking of Muhammad simply as a post-Christian heretic? Could it be that we are influenced too much by our historical sense, which tells us that since Muhammad lived centuries after Jesus, he must be considered simply as a false prophet who rejected the New Testament gospel about Jesus?

'Allah' – the God of Islam?

Christians often feel uneasy with the word 'Allah' because it sounds so foreign, and Allah is thought of simply as 'the God of Islam'. Since we have already discussed some of the theological issues involved here (see chapter 25, 'Theological questions'), our discussion here can focus on some of the words for God used in the Bible, particularly in the Old Testament.

We have seen that *Allah* in Arabic is probably the definite article, 'the' (*al-*), combined with the word 'god' (*illah*). *Allah* would therefore originally have meant something like 'the God', that is 'the High God', the highest deity at the head of the pantheon worshipped at Mecca at the time of Muhammad. The *Shahadah* (the Confession) uses both words: *la illaha* (there is no 'god') *ill-allah* (except 'God', *Allah*).

Arabic and Hebrew are both Semitic languages and have a great deal in common, just as Romance languages such as French and Spanish have much in common. The equivalent in Hebrew to the Arabic *Allah* is *ha-el* (or in its plural form *ha-elohim*), literally 'the God' of 'God'. The Hebrew *'el* is found with the article in verses like these: 'I am God [literally the God], the God of your fathers' (Gen. 46:3; cf., e.g., Gen. 31:13; 35:1; 2 Sam. 22:31, 33, 48; Pss. 68:20–21; 77:15).

The more common word for God in the Old Testament, however, is the plural form *'elohim*. It seems that *'el* was thought of as the High God of all the Semitic peoples of the Ancient Middle East. This is reflected in the account of Abraham's meeting with Melchizedek in Genesis 14. We are told that Melchizedek, the king of Salem, was 'priest of God Most High' (*'el-elyon*), and that he blessed Abraham with the words, 'Blessed be Abram by God Most High, Creator of heaven and earth. And blessed be God Most High, who delivered your enemies into your hand' (Gen. 14:19–20). Abraham did not assume that Melchizedek was worshipping a god who was totally different from the God he himself worshipped. He seemed to assume that they were worshipping one and the same God when he went on to say, 'I have raised my hand to the LORD, God Most High, Creator of heaven and earth' (Gen. 14:22).

If *'el* and *'elohim* are the Hebrew words for 'God', then 'Yahweh' is his *personal name*, the name that distinguishes him from the gods of other peoples, such as Baal and Astarte (Canaanites), Dagon (Philistines), Chemosh (Moabites and Ammonites) and Molech (Ammonites). According to Exodus 3 and 6, the name Yahweh was first revealed to Moses when God met him in the desert and commissioned him to lead the people of Israel out of Egypt: 'I am the LORD. I appeared to Abraham, to Isaac and to Jacob as God Almighty, but by my name the LORD [Yahweh] I did not make myself known to them' (Exod. 6:2–3).

If, however, the name Yahweh was first revealed to Moses, how are we to explain references to Yahweh before the time of Moses? How, for example, do we explain the sentence in Genesis 4:26, 'At that time men began to call on the name of the LORD'? The apparent inconsistency is removed if we understand that the writer of Genesis assumed that the God who had revealed himself more fully to Moses as Yahweh was the one God who had been worshipped since the beginning. The revelation of the name Yahweh did not introduce a *new* god to Moses and the people of Israel; rather, the one true God who had been worshipped from the beginning was now, through the experience of Moses, revealing more of himself and his nature as a holy and loving God who cares for his people.

This would also explain why Job is portrayed as someone who has personal dealings with Yahweh in spite of the fact that he is a foreigner from the land of Uz (perhaps Edom or Aram), living around the time of the patriarchs and with no connections to Israel. At the beginning of the book we are told that Job 'fears God ['elohim] and shuns evil' (Job 1:8). But at the end of the book it is *Yahweh*, the covenant God of Israel, who speaks to Job out of the storm (Job 38:1; 40:1; 42:1).

The message of the Old Testament, therefore, is that there is only one true God, and that this God has revealed himself in a unique way through the history of the people of Israel. The prophets constantly denounce the lower gods and goddesses, such as Baal and Astarte, who are worshipped by the surrounding peoples. They call people to the worship of the one and only God who has revealed himself in a special way to the people of Israel in order to reveal himself more fully to the nations. Since there is no God apart from him, the prophets feel secure in pouring scorn on the gods of the nations who are nothing but 'idols' (Ps. 96:5; Deut. 32:16–17; Isa. 44:9–20).

At this point we can recognize similarities between the work of some of the Old Testament prophets and Muhammad. Just as the prophets campaigned vigorously against idolatry in all its forms and called the people back to acknowledge the one God, so Muhammad called his people to worship Allah, the High God of the Arabs, who had become obscured by the 360 gods and goddesses who were worshipped by the people of Mecca.

There is also a parallel with what happened when the Christian gospel first came to western and northern Europe. Christian mission-aries used the words for the High God in the pantheon of different tribes, and it is from these that we get the words we use today for God – Gott, Dieu, and the like. As the Christian faith became more widely accepted, the other gods and goddesses lost much of the power that they had held in people's minds and eventually came to be remem-bered only, for example, in Norse mythology and in the English names of the days of the week (Tiw, Tuesday; Odin, Wednesday; Thor, Thursday; Frigga, Friday; Saturn, Saturday).

Much of the foreignness in the name *Allah* begins to disappear when we see how close it is linguistically to the Hebrew words for God. We should not, however, fall into the trap of saying that the God of the Bible is therefore the same as *Allah*, the God of Islam. But this study of the words for God in the Old Testament should at least clear the air and help us to tackle the bigger theological questions involved in discussions of this kind.

Gideon

The picture of Muhammad which emerges from the earliest Meccan suras of the Qur'an and from the earliest traditions is of a man who combined a strong protest against idolatry with an attempt to bring unity among the tribes around Mecca and further afield in the Arabian peninsula. When we remember the thoroughly degenerate state of Arabian religion at the time of Muhammad, as well as the continuous conflicts between the tribes, we cannot avoid feeling genuine amaze-ment and admiration for all that he achieved in his lifetime in both these areas.

This picture bears a striking resemblance to the picture of Gideon in the book of Judges. Here, too, is a man who combined a protest against idolatry ('Tear down your father's altar to Baal', Judg. 6:25ff.) with political and military action for his people ('Save Israel out of Midian's hand', Judg. 6:14).

If Muhammad's ministry began with the same fervour as Gideon's ministry, something certainly went wrong (from a Christian perspective) at a later stage. It is only right to remember that something also went wrong later in Gideon's life: 'Gideon made an idol from the gold and put it in his home town, Ophrah. All the Israelites abandoned God and went there to worship the idol. It was a trap for Gideon and his family' (Judg. 8:27–28 GNB).

Is it too dangerous to draw such a parallel between Muhammad and Gideon? It must be emphasized that we are saying only that the cases are similar, not identical. Moreover, while we can see how Gideon fits into the plan of biblical history from Abraham to Jesus, we cannot of course fit Muhammad into the same scheme. But if there is any parallel at all, it should help us at the very least to feel more sympathy for the vision with which Muhammad began his ministry – the vision of the Arabian tribes united as one people in the worship of the one true God.

Judaism and Islam

Muslims insist that the contents of the Qur'an came directly to Muhammad from God and not from any human source. It is therefore not acceptable to speak as if Muhammad derived any of these ideas and stories from any human sources around him. But since Christians cannot generally accept this understanding of the process of revelation, they feel that they cannot avoid studying the life of Muhammad in the context in which he lived, in order to try to understand what he may have learned from others and what was creative and new in the message of the Qur'an.

Following this kind of approach, we could say that from his early contact with Jews, particularly with the Jewish community in Medina after the *Hijra* in 622, Muhammad must have absorbed something of the spirit and ritual of Jewish worship, as well as many stories from the Old Testament and later rabbinic legends. This background should help us to understand not only the most obvious similarities between the doctrines of Judaism and Islam (such as their understanding of the oneness of God), but also some of the deeper similarities between the spirit of the two religions (such as their understanding of the role of the law). It should therefore make it easier for us to put ourselves in the place of Muslims and to see Jesus as they see him.

It requires effort and discipline, however, to read the Gospels in this way. We naturally tend to think of the disciples as Christian believers right from the start, instead of seeing them as devout, orthodox Jews. But what if we take off our 'Christian spectacles' for a moment and try to see Jesus against the background of Old Testament assumptions and several centuries of Jewish traditions? We then begin to realize that Muslims react to Christian claims about Jesus (if they have not misunderstood them) in the same way as the high priest reacted to Jesus' claims about himself: 'You have heard the blasphemy' (Mark 14:64). It is the same instinct, the same jealous concern for the oneness of God, that makes it unthinkable that a mere human being could be associated with God in anything other than a creature-Creator relationship. We begin to see also that there is an understandable logic behind Peter's objection to the idea that the Messiah must suffer and die: how could God let his representative on earth be so humiliated? Surely God must vindicate his servants the prophets in the eyes of the world?

This parallel between Judaism and Islam needs to be qualified at three points. In the first place, Muhammad was too much of a creative genius to be described as one who simply borrowed from Jewish sources. Everything that he absorbed was stamped with the imprint of his own creative mind, as we see in the distinctive thrust that is given to the story of Joseph (sura 12).

Second, some of Muhammad's teaching was influenced, if not actually determined, by the negative response he received from the Jews in Medina. His early openness soon turned to bitter hostility when he finally saw that he had no chance of winning them over as a community. Thus, for example, having earlier prayed with his face towards Jerusalem as the Jews did, he now began to pray facing Mecca. There had been nothing in the Old Testament or in rabbinic tradition which linked Abraham with Mecca. But Muhammad now claimed that Abraham and Ishmael had been associated with the building of the Ka'ba in Mecca. He claimed that Abraham was a Muslim, and in the words of Alfred Guillaume, 'thus at a stroke the primitive and apostolic character of Islam was established'.[1]

Any attempt to draw a parallel between Judaism and Islam, then, must take into account this torturous love-hate relationship between Muhammad and the Jews which has coloured relations between Muslims (particularly Arabs) and Jews ever since, not least in the twentieth and twenty-first centuries.

Third, in spite of the similarities between the two religions, the Jewish people had special privileges because of their place in God's plan of salvation: 'They are God's people ... he made his covenants with them and gave them the Law; they have the true worship; they have received God's promises; they are descended from the famous Hebrew ancestors; and Christ, as a human being, belongs to their race' (Rom. 9:4–5 GNB). This was Paul's understanding of the privileges of the Jewish people simply by virtue of being descended from Abraham through the line of Isaac, and can be applied to the Muslim people only in the sense that the covenant promises of God are now open to all who turn to Jesus, as Peter says on the day of Pentecost: 'God's promise was made to you and your children, and to all who are far away – all whom the Lord our God calls to himself' (Acts 2:39 GNB).

If, however, these qualifications are not serious enough to make us abandon the attempt to see Islam in the light of New Testament Judaism, this approach may also help us to come to terms with the bewildering variety of Christian responses to Islam. Is it a religion inspired by the devil, or a valid religion which offers valuable insights for all? Is it a Christian heresy like Jehovah's Witnesses, or can it sometimes be a genuine preparation for the gospel?

We find similar problems in the responses to Judaism in the pages of the New Testament. Paul's verdict about the Jews in his letter to the Thessalonians (written in about AD 50 or 51) sounds very harsh:

> The Jews ... killed the Lord Jesus and the prophets, and persecuted us. How displeasing they are to God! How hostile they are to everyone! They even tried to stop us from preaching to the Gentiles the message that would bring them salvation. In this way they have brought to completion all the sins they have always committed. And now God's anger has at last come down on them! (1 Thess. 2:14–16 GNB)

In his letter to the Romans (written in AD 57), however, he reveals how he actually prays for his fellow Jews:

> I am speaking the truth; I belong to Christ and I do not lie. My conscience, ruled by the Holy Spirit, also assures me that I am not lying when I say how great is my sorrow, how endless the pain in my heart for my people, my own flesh and blood! For their sake I could wish that I myself were under God's curse and separated from Christ. (Rom. 9:1–3 GNB)

In his travels in Asia Minor, Paul made it a matter of policy to go first to the synagogue in every city, believing that those who knew the Old Testament Scriptures would be the first to respond to the good news about Jesus. When we come to the book of Revelation (probably written some thirty years after Paul's death), however, the risen Lord's description of one particular synagogue in Asia Minor paints it in a very different light: 'I will make those of Satan's synagogue, who claim to be Jews but are lying frauds, come and fall down at your feet; and they shall know that you are my beloved people' (Rev. 3:9 NEB).

If we are confused by this ambivalence, we need to go back to the words of Jesus himself and ask how it was that he could say to one Jew, 'You are not far from the kingdom of God' (Mark 12:34), but on another occasion to a group of Jews, 'You are of your father the devil' (John 8:44 RSV). Part of the answer needs to be that there is a difference between Judaism and Jews – between the body of beliefs and traditions, and the people who hold them with varying degrees of conviction. We also need to be suspicious of sweeping generalizations and simple categories, whether they spring from an attitude that is excessively generous or one that is excessively negative.

If we base our understanding of Judaism only on the scribes and the Pharisees described in the New Testament, we may be incapable of recognizing a Nicodemus who has grown up in the same tradition but is reaching out for something more (John 3:1–13). If we think that all our Muslim friends are as dogmatic as Caiaphas (Mark 14:63–64), we will fail to notice those who are as open but as cautious as Gamaliel (Acts 5:33–39). If we think that all Muslims are in the same category as the members of the synagogue of Philadelphia (Rev. 3:9), we can hardly fail to rebuff any leader (such as Jairus) who comes with his deep personal need and a faith that reaches out to Jesus (Mark 5:22ff.). If the practice of Islam can make some Muslims as self-confident as the Pharisee (Luke 18:11ff.), can it not sometimes lead others to the

point where God can say to them, as he did to the God-fearing
proselyte Cornelius, 'God is pleased with your prayers and works
of charity, and is ready to answer you. And now send some men
to Joppa for a certain man whose full name is Simon Peter' (Acts
10:4–5 GNB)?

30. COUNTING THE COST OF CONVERSION

'Islam', in the words of Abul A'la Mawdudi, 'is a one-way door, you can enter through it but you cannot leave.'[1] A Christian response to this assumption is summed up just as sharply by Kenneth Cragg: 'A faith which you are not free to leave becomes a prison, and no self-respecting faith should be a prison for those within it.'[2]

It is a sad fact that in spite of Islam's tolerant attitudes in many areas, Muslims do not find it easy to accept the idea of fellow Muslims becoming Christians. Conversion to Christianity (or to any other religion) has generally been regarded as a betrayal of family and community, as tantamount to treason, and therefore as punishable by death.

While attitudes in some communities are becoming more liberal and tolerant, Muslims who express an interest in the Christian faith are often subject to strong pressures, and those who take the step of being baptized frequently experience opposition and hostility in the home, at work and in the wider community. Many converts in the past have had to leave their homes for safety, and some have been killed.

In trying to understand the attitudes of Muslims towards those who want to change their beliefs in any significant way, we need to understand, first, why Muslims have such strong views on the subject and, second, how to think through several specific issues that may need to be faced by those who want to be disciples of Jesus.

Apostasy in the Qur'an and *hadith*

The following are the main passages in the Qur'an which teach how Muslims should deal with those who renounce the faith of Islam.

> Whoso becometh a renegade and dieth in his disbelief: such are they whose works have fallen both in the world and the Hereafter. Such are rightful owners of the Fire: they will abide therein. (2:217)

> They long that ye should disbelieve even as they disbelieve, that ye may be on a level (with them). So choose not friends from them till they forsake their homes in the way of Allah; if they turn back (to enmity) then take them and kill them wherever ye find them, and choose no friend nor helper from among them. (4:89; cf. 4:137; 16:108)

> And whoso seeketh as religion other than the surrender (to Allah) [Islam] it will not be accepted from him, and he will be a loser in the Hereafter ... Lo! those who disbelieve after their (profession of) belief, and afterward grow violent in disbelief: their repentance will not be accepted. And such are those who are astray. Lo! those who disbelieve, and die in disbelief, the (whole) earth full of gold would not be accepted from such an one if it were offered as a ransom (for his soul). Theirs will be a painful doom and they will have no helpers. (3:85–91)

Maulvi Muhammad Ali's comment on 2:217 explains the context of these verses and points out that there is no suggestion of capital punishment for an apostate.

> The persons spoken of in this passage are the apostates, or those who 'turn from their religion'. A wrong impression exists among non-Muslims, and among some Muslims as well, that the Holy Qur'an requires those who apostatize from Islam to be put to death, but this is not true ... As the plain words of the Qur'an show, what is stated here is that the opponents of Islam exerted themselves to the utmost to turn back the Muslims from

their faith, by their cruel persecutions, and therefore if a Muslim actually went back to unbelief he would be a loser in this life as well as in the next, because the desertion of Islam would not only deprive him of the spiritual advantages which he could obtain by remaining a Muslim, but also of the physical advantages which must accrue to the Muslims through the triumph of Islam. And neither here nor anywhere else in the Qur'an is there even a hint of the infliction of capital or any other punishment on the apostate.[3]

It is important to note, therefore, that the death penalty for apostasy is not based on the Qur'an, but on sayings of the Prophet recorded in *hadith*. These are some of the relevant sayings.

It is related from Ikrimah that he said, 'Hypocrites were brought to Ali and he burnt them.' The news of that reached Ibn Abbas, and he said, 'If it had been I, I would not have burnt them, because of the prohibition of the Apostle of God: Do not punish with the punishment of God; but I would certainly have killed them according to the word of the Apostle: Whoever changes his religion, kill him.'

Slay (or behead) him who changes his religion.

The blood of a fellow Muslim should never be shed except in the case of the adulterer, the murderer and the person who abandons his religion and separates himself from the community.

The traditions differ, however, on whether or not apostates should be given an opportunity to repent. Some traditions say that God does not accept the repentance of an apostate, while others say that in some cases even the Prophet forgave apostates. According to Ruqaiyya Waris Maqsood, 'The Prophet only ever sentenced an apostate to death if the crimes of treason and murder had been committed.'[4] Al-Baidhawi, the famous commentator of the thirteenth century, gives a very strict interpretation in his comment on 4:89.

Whoever turns back from his belief (*irtadda*), openly or secretly, take him and kill him wheresoever ye find him, like any other infidel. Separate yourself from him altogether. Do not accept intercession in his regard.[5]

A study of Muslim commentaries shows that, in their original context, none of these verses is concerned with Muslims becoming Christians. Most of them deal with those who were known as 'hypocrites', that is, idolaters who made an insincere profession of Islam and later went back to their former way of life.

Apostasy in *shari'a*

The traditional response to apostasy in *shari'a* law is summed up by a Sudanese Islamic scholar, Abdullahi Ahmed An-Na'im, in these terms:

> On the basis of these Sunna, and standard commentaries on the Qur'an, traditional Islamic schools of jurisprudence are unanimous in holding that apostasy is punishable by death, although they differ on such questions as to whether to execute the sentence immediately or grant the apostate a reprieve of a few days in order to allow him time to reflect and reconsider his position in the hope that he may recant and reembrace Islam, thereby saving his life as well as his soul. There is also disagreement on whether a female apostate is to be killed or merely imprisoned until she returns to the faith. Her offense is not regarded by any school or jurist to be of less magnitude; the disagreement merely relates to whether the appropriate punishment is death or life imprisonment.[6]

The *Shorter Encyclopedia of Islam* describes the situation that has generally prevailed since the end of the nineteenth century.

> In former Turkish territory and Egypt as well as in Muslim lands under European rule since the middle of the nineteenth century, under European influence the execution of an apostate on a kadi's [judge's] sentence has been abolished, but we still have imprisonment and deportation; nevertheless renegades are not sure of their lives as their Muslim relatives endeavour secretly to dispose of them by poison or otherwise.[7]

Apostasy as understood by Muslims today

Muslim views today cover the same spectrum of positions that we have noted in the past. The strictest interpretation of the traditional view is given by Abul A'la Mawdudi.

To everyone acquainted with Islamic law it is no secret that according to
Islam the punishment for a Muslim who turns to *kufr* (infidelity,
blasphemy) is execution. Doubt about this matter first arose among
Muslims during the final portion of the nineteenth century as a result of
speculation. Otherwise, for the full twelve centuries prior to that time the
total Muslim community remained unanimous about it ... All these
collectively will assure you that from the time of the Prophet to the present
day one injunction only has been continuously and uninterruptedly
operative and that no room whatever remains to suggest that perhaps the
punishment of the apostate is not execution.[8]

The late Isma'il al-Faruqi, who was a professor of Islamic studies in
the USA, explains the original context of the relevant qur'anic verses
and suggests similarities to the situation of Muslims today. His view,
which relates his interpretation of the Islamic sources to the contemporary political context, probably sums up the attitude of most
orthodox, traditionalist Muslims today.

Islamic law does allow a person to exit from the Islamic state. However,
the Islamic state has, of course, to protect itself – and ... conversion so
often seems to be tantamount to subversion of Islamic values and
existence. This was the situation certainly which existed in the original
Islamic state in Madinah [Medina] during the prophet's life, where for a
person to convert out of Islam meant joining the polytheistic camp of
Makkah [Mecca] which was in a constant state of war against the Muslims.
Now obviously that was the situation in which, for political reasons,
legislation was formulated that conversion out of Islam is not to be
tolerated. When, later, Islam became dominant in Madinah and Makkah,
and subsequently built an empire for itself, this legislation continued to be
observed although you might argue that there was empirically no use for it;
conversion represented no threat at all to the security of the Muslim
community. But would you really consider revoking that legislation
altogether and grant unrestricted freedom to anyone to change his religion
according to the Islamic principle that everyone has the right to 'convince
and be convinced', when we have heard of what is happening in Indonesia?
What we have heard about the situation confronting Islam in Indonesia is
like a re-enactment of Madinah and Makkah. When politics get so
intermingled with Christian mission, what sort of situation would you

expect if total religious freedom were allowed? Give us the assurance that political involvement in mission will cease, and that power politics will no longer intrude, then the principles of religious freedom would be approved by every sensible Muslim on earth. We Muslims are at the receiving end of the line of injustice. We haven't emerged yet from two centuries of colonization.[9]

These traditional interpretations have, surprisingly, been challenged by Hasan al-Turabi, an Islamist who has been involved in politics in the Sudan for several decades.

The Prophet's saying about apostasy is a short statement pronounced within the context of war conditions. Muslims were greatly affected to see one of their companions desert his kith and join the ranks of disbelievers. They were not sure if they should kill him or spare his life because he was a Muslim once. The Prophet, peace be upon him, explained that one who abandons his religion and deserts his fellows should be killed. Regrettably, people of subsequent generations have taken the Prophet's saying out of its historical context and generalized it. In so doing they deny one of the basic truths of Islam: the freedom of faith. How can it be imagined by a rational person that Allah, Who has compelled none to believe, allows us the right to compel others and force them to believe? The Qur'anic verses that prohibit compulsion and coercion are numerous and so are the sayings and practice of the Prophet. That is why I do not hold the common view on the question of apostasy.[10]

This kind of more liberal interpretation of Islamic teaching on apostasy is explained in greater detail by Rafiq Zakaria, an Indian Muslim, showing how a committed Muslim today interprets the sources in the Qur'an and *hadith* on which the traditional ruling has been based.

For an apostate, or *murtadd*, 'one who turns back' from Islam, there is no punishment in the Qur'an. According to one verse: 'O true believers, whoever of you apostatizes from his religion, God will certainly bring other people to take his place, whom He will love and who will love Him, who shall be humble towards the believers, but severe to the unbelievers. They shall fight for the religion of God and shall not fear the obloquy of the detractor' (5:54). There are no recorded cases of the Prophet punishing those Muslims who renege on their faith. There is, however, misconception about the punishment for apostasy, which has distorted the image of Islam. It has arisen because of classical jurists who have opined that the punishment for apostasy in Islam is death. But Muslims subscribe to the concept of 'freedom of worship', and demand the right to convert non-Muslims. The Qur'an makes it clear that 'there is no compulsion in religion'; how then can it pronounce the death penalty on those who 'turn away' from Islam, or 'turn back' on it? On the contrary, the Qur'an mentions that in place of those who have given up the right path, God will bring better and more faithful ones ... It is true that if, during a war, some Muslims committed treason and went over to the other side, then they were put to death on being captured. But that was for being traitors, not apostates. This is clear from many traditions reported in Sahih al-Bukhari, the most reliable book of traditions. Unfortunately, there is one tradition – 'Whoever changes his religion shall be put to death' which contradicts the entire tenor of a mass of other traditions and, therefore, cannot be relied on. It also contradicts the verses in the Qur'an that speak of freedom of worship. Besides, it makes a general proposition and does not specifically refer to a change of religion by Muslims alone. The Encyclopedia of Islam has correctly pointed out: 'In the Qur'an, the apostate is threatened with punishment in the next world.' He can be killed if he joins the enemies of God and forsakes his religion, but that would not be merely for changing religion.[11]

Apostasy and human rights today

It needs to be pointed out that there is real tension, if not inconsistency, at this point between the traditional Islamic response to conversion and the UN Universal Declaration of Human Rights. This charter has been officially accepted by most countries, including many Islamic states and those in which Muslims are a majority. It allows the freedom not only to hold and practise, but also to change one's own religion. Article 18 states:

Everyone has the right to freedom of thought, conscience and religion; this right includes freedom to change his religion or belief, and freedom, either alone or in community with others and in public or private, to manifest his religion or belief in teaching, practice, worship and observance.

The inconsistency between this declaration and the practice of many Muslim states has been pointed out by Abdullahi Ahmed An-Na'im.

> The inescapable conclusion ... is that it is inconsistent with modern notions of religious freedom, an internationally acknowledged basic human right and generally accepted fundamental civil liberty guaranteed by most constitutions throughout the world.[12]

In recent years Muslims have drawn up their own statements on human rights, for example in the Universal Declaration of Human Rights produced in 1981 by the Islamic Council of Europe. This document has been described by Ali Merad as 'an important step towards reconciling Islamic tradition with the modern demand for freedom'. A later statement, The Declaration of Human Rights in Islam, came out of a convention of the Organization of the Islamic Conference in 1990. This was regarded by many Western commentators as a step backwards, since it fails to focus on the main conflict, remains ambiguous and tends to harmonize conflicts.[13]

While it needs to be recognized that many of these issues are complex and technical, no one can deny the seriousness of the dilemma facing many Muslims in these areas today. It is no exaggeration, therefore, for Mohammed Talbi to speak of 'a truly rending problem for devout Muslims'.[14] And Ann Elizabeth Mayer is very frank about the options facing Muslim governments when she writes, 'The stage seems to be set for efforts to mesh Islamic law and its attendant values with human rights. Whether the result will be a fruitful and constructive combination of the two or more official hypocrisy, only time will tell.'[15]

The most significant test of Muslim attitudes to conversion, however, is not the statements of jurists and theologians of the past and present but *what actually happens in practice*. However liberal and tolerant Muslim leaders can be, what really seems to count at the end of the day is the attitude of a particular family to one or more of their number who seem to be turning their back on their religion, and bringing shame and dishonour on the whole family.

Al-Faruqi explains that when this happens, 'we are not talking about an Islamic state acting under Islamic law, but a village group or a city group aroused by the idea that they have lost one of their fellow members so they go and kill him or put difficulties in his path. This is not an application of the Islamic law.' In many cases, however, it is hard to draw a clear dividing line between what happens in a local community and what is done by the group in the name of Islam. However charitable we want to be, we have to reckon with the fact that in the majority of cases, Muslims who want to become disciples of Christ are thought of, and treated as, apostates and outcasts from their family and community.

Arguments against the traditional Islamic teaching about apostasy

In their original context in the Qur'an, none of the verses about apostasy is concerned with Muslims becoming Christians.
Most of these verses deal with people who were known as 'hypocrites', that is, idolaters who made an insincere profession of Islam and later went back to their former way of life (see, e.g., 49:14). According to al-Baidhawi, 4:49 refers to members of an Arab tribe who declared that they were Muslims, but then returned to Mecca and joined the idolaters there in their struggle against Muhammad.

Killing an apostate goes against the verses supporting freedom of religion.
The most quoted verse is 'There is no compulsion in religion' (2:25). According to the commentator al-Tabari (died 923), the context for the revelation of this verse was the following incident: a Muslim in Mecca asked Muhammad what to do about his two sons who had become Christians through the influence of a Syrian merchant and wanted to go to Syria with him. It was in response to this question that Muhammad received the message 'There is no compulsion in religion'. Al-Tabari added that this verse is not abrogated by later verses calling for *jihad*.[16] Al-Razi made this additional comment: 'This means that God ... based it [faith] on free will and the ability to choose.'[17] Even the Islamist Sayyid Qutb supported this emphasis on freedom of religion in his commentary on the verse:

> The decision is left to him with regard to the matter of guidance and error in belief ... Freedom of belief is one of the primary rights of man; thus whoever deprives a human being of his freedom of belief, deprives him essentially of his humanity. Freedom of belief includes the freedom to

propagate one's faith. It includes also security against harm and sedition; otherwise it is freedom in name only, having no meaning in real life.[18]

There are several qur'anic verses which are frequently quoted to provide a basis for pluralism and co-existence.

You have your religion and I have mine. (109:5, Fakhry)

Had your Lord willed, everybody on earth would have believed. Will you then compel people to become believers? (10:99–100, Fakhry)

To each of you, We have laid down an ordinance and a clear path; and had Allah pleased, He would have made you one nation, but [He wanted] to test you concerning what He gave you. Be, then, forward, in good deeds . . . (5:48, Fakhry)

The death penalty for apostasy probably became established in Islamic tradition soon after the death of the Prophet as a result of the Wars of Apostasy.
Many tribes in Arabia refused to pay their *zakat* tax to the Muslim community after the death of Muhammad because they believed that, in accordance with Arab tradition, their loyalty to Muhammad ended with his death. In his correspondence with these tribes, Abu Bakr did not quote qur'anic verses about apostasy, which did not stipulate the death penalty. Instead he treated the tribes' refusal to pay the tax as treason, as rebellion against the Islamic community, and therefore as an action punishable by death. In a letter to 'Umar, who had questioned his tough policy towards the tribes, Abu Bakr replied, 'I solemnly declare that I will fight whoever differentiates between prayer and *zakat*, as *zakat* is the right to be taken from property. By God, if they refuse to pay even a ewe lamb they used to pay to God's people, I will fight them for withholding it.' As a result of this policy, *religious apostasy* (which did *not* carry the death penalty) became associated with *political treason* (which *did* carry the death penalty).

Issues facing Muslims who want to follow Christ

Many Christians today deliberately avoid expressions like 'becoming a Christian', because in the past they have given the impression that

Muslims who want to follow Christ have to reject everything in their Islamic faith and leave the Islamic community. In some situations today Muslims of this kind are finding ways to *remain within* their own communities and still be totally committed to Christ. But what are the practical questions that Muslims have to face when they feel themselves being drawn to the person of Christ? And how can Christians help them in thinking through the sensitive issues involved?

The following discussion material sets out some of these questions by pointing to a number of biblical passages and then raising questions about how these passages can be applied in this context today. It is important that we should understand the difficulty and the complexity of the questions, and recognize that there may be different ways of interpreting the passages in different contexts.

1. Is open confession essential?
The importance of confession. Read Matthew 10:32–33; Romans 10:9–10.

- What is the importance of confession for the new believer?
- Does the confession always have to be public?
- Must the convert always confess his/her faith openly before family and friends from the very beginning?

Being a 'secret disciple'. Read John 3:1–10; 7:50–52; 19:38–42; 12:42–43.

- Does the Gospel account imply any criticism of Nicodemus, Joseph and other Jews who believed, for being secret disciples?
- Did they in any way deny Jesus by hiding their commitment to him?
- Did their actions amount to a public confession of Jesus?
- Is there any reason why a Muslim convert should not in certain circumstances remain a secret disciple until the time is ripe to declare his/her faith openly?

2. What about relationships with the family and the community?
Christ and family loyalties. Read Luke 14:25–33; Matthew 10:16–23, 34–39; Mark 10:23–31.

- Will the family be tolerant, critical or hostile?

- Will the convert be able to remain within the family?
- Is the opposition likely to be such that he/she will have to leave his/her family for his/her own safety or peace of mind?

3. Do they have to change their culture?

Read Acts 15:1–35. The importance of this passage is that it shows how leaders of the church refused to insist that Gentiles who believed in Jesus had to become Jews and accept everything in Jewish culture and religion in order to follow Christ. They wrote to the new Gentile believers stating only a few basic requirements. One of these related to sexual morality, while the others expressed sensitivity to certain Jewish traditions.

- Although the situation today is not exactly the same, are there any general principles which can be applied to this issue today?
- How do we distinguish between the gospel and culture?

4. How should they relate to Christians and to the church?

Welcoming the new believer. Read Acts 9:10–19.

- How easy was it for Ananias to go to Saul and say, 'Saul, my brother...'?
- What were the fears and prejudices in Ananias's mind which had to be dealt with?
- What can we do to help the new Muslim believer to feel that he/she is fully accepted as a brother or sister?
- Should we parade them to give testimonies about their conversion in public?

5. What if there is no church or fellowship for them to join?

Meeting in the name of Jesus. Read Matthew 18:20; Acts 2:42–43.

- Jesus promises that he will be present whenever even 'two or three' meet together in his name. Could a meeting of this kind be the beginning of a fellowship that meets regularly in his name?

- The first group of believers – the first 'fellowship' or 'church' – used to meet regularly both in homes and in the temple courts in Jerusalem. Does this suggest how a group of believers could begin to meet together?

6. Is baptism essential?

The significance of baptism. Read Matthew 28:18–20; Mark 16:15–16. The Jews were familiar with the practice of ceremonial washing for purification. They also baptized proselytes, i.e. non-Jews who wanted to accept the faith of Judaism. At the time of Jesus, therefore, the practice of baptism was known, and it was already connected in people's minds with the idea of cleansing from sin. What Jesus did was to take a practice which was already known, and make it a once-and-for-all act of initiation, performed in his name. The Gentiles were not familiar with the practice of baptism, and it would have been entirely new to them. They would not bring to baptism any negative ideas or misunderstandings from their own background. To the Muslim, baptism means nothing more nor less than apostasy from Islam. It means that Muslims have cut themselves off from their family and society; they are renouncing their religion and community, accepting a new religion and joining a different community.

- Are we to say that every Muslim convert must be baptized? Or are there circumstances in which a Muslim convert might delay baptism – perhaps indefinitely – because he/she does not see baptism in the same light as his/her Muslim family?
- We want Jesus and the message of the cross, and not any secondary issues, to be the only stumbling block. Are there situations in which baptism creates an unnecessary stumbling block for the rest of the Muslim community, because it is seen not only as a sign of public confession of Jesus, but as a final repudiation of the Muslim community?
- If Jesus was simply adapting a ceremony already familiar to Jews, could we not on the same principle consider adapting a similar ceremony already known to the Muslim? Muslims practise a ceremonial washing before they say the *sala* five times a day. Is it conceivable that a ceremony similar to the ritual washing could be evolved in which, for example, Muslim

disciples of Jesus have water poured out for them as it would be
in the preparation for the ritual prayer? The significant thing in
this case, however, would be that the one who pours water for
them would do it 'in the name of Jesus' and in the presence of
the community of believers.

7. Is suffering inevitable?
The disciple and his master. Read Matthew 10:24–25.

- What kind of treatment does Jesus warn his disciples to expect?

Rejoicing in suffering. Read Acts 5:40–42.

- Why were the apostles being persecuted?
- How did they accept this persecution and suffering?

The shame of rejection. Read Hebrews 13:10–14; 1 Peter 2:18–25;
5:12–19.

- How can the example of Jesus help us when we find ourselves
  rejected by our own community and covered with shame in
  their eyes?

31. FACING THE POLITICAL CHALLENGE OF ISLAM

Writing in the 1960s, Jens Christensen said, 'The subject of politics is one of the most fundamental and difficult problems we have to contend with in coming to grips with Islam.'[1] The report of a conference on the theme of *Suffering and Power in Christian-Muslim Relations*, convened in Nigeria in 2000, explained why issues of power are so significant.

> Relations between Christianity and Islam are primarily a matter of relations between two communities, rather than between individual believers. Both faiths create a people, and make claims about God's rule of the whole of life. Their religious leaders are not individual mystics but leaders of communities. The issue of power is thus central to relations between them.[2]

We are therefore forced to ask questions such as these:

- Why does Islam seem to be such a political religion – so much more political than Christianity as we know it today seems to be?

- What is the Muslim vision for the world? Do all Muslims want or expect Islam to triumph? If so, is it to triumph through persuasion, or force, or both?
- How are Christian minorities perceived and treated in Islamic countries? How should they respond, for example, to different kinds of discrimination?

In order to begin to answer these questions, we need to begin with the life of the Prophet and trace the development of Islamic teaching and practice in these areas through the centuries, recognizing a variety of approaches in different contexts. Only against this background can we consider how Christians should respond to the political challenges of different kinds today.

Throughout this discussion, however, it will be taken for granted that when Christians are not the suffering minority, but are in the majority or in a position of power, they should be guided in all their thinking by the Golden Rule taught by Jesus in the Sermon on the Mount: 'So in everything, do to others what you would have them do to you, for this sums up the Law and the Prophets' (Matt. 7:12). This must mean, for example, that Christians in Western countries will ask themselves how they would like to be treated if they were members of a Christian minority living in an Islamic society. Their answer to this question should determine their basic attitude to minorities of other faiths living alongside them. They will want to extend to others the same rights which they expect for themselves. And if Christians expect Muslim authorities to respond to complaints about unfair discrimination against Christians, Western Christians should be especially sensitive and responsive to complaints about unfair discrimination against Muslims living alongside them.

The example of Muhammad

For the first twelve years of his ministry, Muhammad was essentially a prophet calling the people of Mecca to renounce idolatry and worship the one true God, and gathering around him a small group of disciples. The *Hijra*, the 'migration' of Muhammad and his followers from Mecca to Medina, however, marked a turning point in his life, since it meant that he now became both prophet and statesman. From then on, he led the Muslims into battle and claimed to receive from God all the detailed legislation required for the establishment of the Islamic community in Medina.

The Islamic concern for the life of the community, therefore, together with all the political interest that is part of that concern, springs ultimately from the example of the Prophet. This is how Kenneth Cragg sums up the significance of this 'progression from preaching to ruling'.

> So it was that he grew steadily more and more preoccupied with the ultimate issues of how his truth would succeed ... His life came to a watershed in what is the central issue of all religious history, namely the relation of truth to power. The city of Islamic origins, Mecca, is linked with another city of Islamic statehood, Medina ... The search for religious recognition became a quest for political power. The student is here at the heart of the deepest issue in the psyche of Muhammad. It used to be assumed, in some quarters, that his character underwent a certain declension and that an initial sincerity came to be undermined by baser motives. But this is to miss the real point. The real problem is deeper. The urge for power is more truly seen here, not as a lapse but a logic, not something now less sincere and idealist, but more so in a different guise. How is a prophet sincere if he becomes reconciled to non-success, or refuses to undertake what success requires when his words, long sustained, have failed of response? There may have been other factors in Muhammad's reach for power. There were economic and social motives. There was also that Arab 'manliness' and the tradition of battle in the picture. But, in the last analysis, Islam sees the militancy of Muhammad as the legitimate and appropriate progression from preaching to ruling, and all within the will of God.[3]

If Christians today have little sympathy with Muhammad's understanding of the use of power in the kingdom of God on earth, they need to remember that in the Christianity which Muhammad and the early Muslims knew in several of the countries surrounding Arabia, church and state were one. We might even have to say that Muhammad learned the model he followed from the Christians, since the code he established to regulate relations between Muslims and their non-Muslim subjects had close parallels with the codes adopted by the Christian Roman emperors Theodosius and Justinian for dealing with pagans, Jews and heretics. As Michael Nazir-Ali points out, 'In many parts of the world, Muslim rule succeeded theocratic Byzantine imperialism ... It is paradoxical that the Byzantine Church itself became subject to these provisions when they became part of the Muslim legislation on the *dhimma*.'[4]

The constitution of Medina

Soon after Muhammad settled in Medina, he drew up a document known as *The Constitution of Medina*. This document begins as follows.

> In the name of God, the Merciful, the Compassionate!
> This is the writing of Muhammad the Prophet, between the believers and the Muslims of the Quraysh [from Mecca] and from Yathrib [Medina] and those who fight with them.

It then lists forty-six different articles, of which these four are particularly significant.

- They are a single community (*umma*) distinct from other people.
- Whenever there is anything about which you differ, it is to be referred to God and to Muhammad (peace be upon him).
- The Jews bear expenses along with the believers so long as they continue at war.
- The Jews of Banu 'Awf are an *umma* along with the believers. To the Jews their religion and the Muslims their religion.[5]

Michael Nazir-Ali points out some aspects of this Constitution and its potential significance for Muslims today.

> Here a single umma or community is created which includes refugees from Mecca and their hosts in Medina, Muslims, Jews and even unbelievers, all bound together in terms of a solemn social contract, under the terms of which all are treated equally. The situation was extremely volatile, however, and the cordial relations with the Jews did not last long. The contract did not, therefore, endure but, for its time, it is a most remarkable document and ought to have greater influence in the development of Islamic polity

than it does. Today, there are many projects for an Islamic State in different parts of the world. The question is: would such a state be modelled on the Constitution of Medina; and if not, why not?[6]

Christians and Jews as *dhimmis* under Islam

Jews and Christians who refused to submit to Islam were allowed to continue to practise their own religion as 'People of the Book'. 'Idolaters' had no such privileges, and it seems that in the early years they were offered the simple choice between submission to Islam, slavery or death. Later, however, when Muslims found themselves ruling over large numbers of peoples of other faiths who refused to accept Islam, the protected status given to Jews and Christians was extended to include people such as Zoroastrians, Buddhists and Hindus.

This system was given the name *dhimma*, which means literally a contract or obligation. The assumption was that the Muslim community accepted responsibility for these Jews and Christians, who, as *dhimmis*, constituted tolerated and protected communities living under Muslim rule, and paid a special tax called *jizya* as a token of their submission. The word for this tax was taken from a qur'anic verse in which Muslims are instructed to fight against certain Christians who refuse to accept Islam, '. . . until they pay the *jizya* personally, once they have been reduced to submission' (9:29; see chapter 27, 'The qur'anic view of Christians'). A. Yusuf Ali comments on the word as follows.

> Jizya: the root meaning is compensation. The derived meaning, which became the technical meaning, was a poll-tax levied from those who did not accept Islam, but were willing to live under the protection of Islam, and were thus tacitly willing to submit themselves to its ideals being enforced in the Muslim State, saving only their personal liberty of conscience as regarded themselves. There was no amount fixed for it, and in any case it was merely symbolical – an acknowledgment that those whose religion was tolerated would in their turn not interfere with the preaching and progress of Islam.[7]

Early Muslim tradition records the text of treaties which Muhammad made with Jewish and Christian communities in Arabia. This, for example, was the agreement made with the Christian communities in Najran in the south of Arabia (modern Yemen).

> This is a letter from Muhammad the prophet, the Messenger of God, to the people of Najran ... Najran and their followers have protection of God and the *dhimmah* of Muhammad the prophet, the messenger of God, for themselves, their community, their land, and their goods, both those who are absent and those who are present, and for their churches and services (no bishop will be removed from his episcopate, no monk from his monastic position, and no church warden from his church-wardenship) and for all, great or little, that is under their hands ... On the terms stated in this document (they have) protection of God and *dhimmah* of the prophet for ever, until God comes with His command, if they are loyal and perform their obligations well, not being burdened by wrong.[8]

In spite of these agreements, however, the Christians and Jews were expelled from Arabia some years later during the time of the caliph 'Umar on the basis of a saying reported to have come from Muhammad himself. This is how these expulsions are recorded in *The Life of the Apostle of God* by Ibn Ishaq.

> When God took away His prophet, Abu Bakr continued the arrangements (with the Jews of Khaybar) until his death, and so did 'Umar for the beginning of his amirate. Then he heard that the apostle had said in his last illness, 'Two religions shall not remain together in the peninsula of the Arabs' and he made inquiries until he got confirmation. Then he sent to the Jews saying, 'God has given permission for you to emigrate,' quoting the apostle's words: 'If anyone has an agreement with the apostle let him bring it to me and I will carry it out; he who has no such agreement let him get ready to emigrate.' Thus 'Umar expelled those who had no agreement with the apostle.[9]

The Code, Ordinance or Pact of 'Umar

This is the name of a document which purports to be a response from 'Umar, who ruled as the second caliph between 634 and 644, to the Muslims who were demanding that the lands of Iraq and Syria (Palestine) should be shared among the Muslim conquerors. It is likely that the document is a compilation that reflects a later stage in the codification of Islamic law concerning conquered peoples. It is significant for our purposes, however, because it summarizes what came to be regarded as Islamic practice, if not law, concerning Jewish and Christian *dhimmis* for centuries.

The following letter, which reflects many of the details given in other versions of the Code, summarizes the obligations accepted by Christians in Syria when they submitted to Islamic rule under the caliph 'Umar.

> This is a letter to the servant of God 'Umar ... from the Christians of such-and-such a city. When you came against us, we asked you for safe-conduct for ourselves, our descendants, our property, and the people of our community, and we undertook the following obligations towards you:
>
> - We shall not build, in our cities or in their neighbourhood, new monasteries, churches, convents, or monks' cells, nor shall we repair, by day or by night, such of them as fall in ruins or are situated in the quarters of the Muslims ...
> - We shall not teach the Qur'an to our children.
> - We shall not manifest our religion publicly nor convert anyone to it. We shall not prevent any of our kin from entering Islam if they wish ...
> - We shall not mount on saddles, nor shall we gird swords nor bear any kind of arms nor carry them on our person ...
> - We shall always dress in the same way wherever we may be ...
> - We shall not display our crosses or our books in the roads or markets of the Muslims. We shall only use clappers in our churches very softly. We shall not raise our voices in our church services or in the presence of Muslims, nor shall we raise our voices when following the dead. We shall not show lights on any of the roads of the Muslims or in their markets. We shall not bury our dead near the Muslims ...
> - We shall not build our houses overtopping the houses of the Muslims ...
>
> We accept these conditions for ourselves and for the people of our community, and in return we receive safe-conduct. If in any way we violate these undertakings for which we ourselves stand surety, we forfeit our covenant (*dhimma*), and we become liable to the penalties for contumacy and sedition.[10]

Michael Nazir-Ali explains the legacy of the Code of 'Umar right up to the present time.

> Emancipation from the provisions of this pact came only gradually and often painfully, for the non-Muslim populations. It was not until the early years of this century [twentieth century] that the pact as such ceased to be operative in most Muslim lands. Vestiges of it survive, however, in the way expatriate non-Muslims are treated in the State of Saudi Arabia and in the Gulf. Even in the relatively tolerant parts of the Gulf States, church buildings have to be away from the centres of towns, many congregations must share one building (24 in one instance), no display of Christian symbols is allowed and the ringing of church bells is not permitted. In Saudi Arabia ... no church buildings are allowed at all and even services in the homes of Christians are liable to be broken up by the religious police.[11]

The concept of Islamic rule in Islamic law and theology

Jihad, which means literally 'effort', came to be a technical term referring to the effort of Muslim believers striving for the rule of God and the supremacy of Islam in the world. Many Muslims in recent times have distinguished between *jihad* in this sense and the more inward and spiritual struggle in which believers seek to overcome all that is unworthy within themselves. In spite of these more recent developments in the meaning of the word, however, we should be aware of how Muslim thinkers of the past have understood this concept. The following statement comes from Ibn Khaldun (1333–1406), the famous Arab historian.

> In the Muslim community, the holy war (*jihad*) is a religious duty, because of the universalism of the (Muslim) mission and (the obligation to) convert everybody to Islam either by persuasion or by force. Therefore, caliphate and royal authority are united (in Islam), so that the person in charge can devote the available strength to both of them (religion and politics) at the same time. The other religious groups did not have a universal mission, and the holy war was not a religious duty to them, save only for purposes of defence. It has thus come about that the person in charge of religious affairs (in other religious groups) is not concerned with power politics at all. (Among them) royal authority comes to those who have it, by accident

and in some way that has nothing to do with religion. It comes to them as the necessary result of group feeling, which by its nature seeks to obtain royal authority, as we have mentioned before, and not because they are under obligation to gain power over other nations, as is the case with Islam. They are merely required to establish their religion among their own people.

He names the main groups of Christians in his day and continues with this comment:

> We do not think that we should blacken the pages of this book with discussion of their dogmas of unbelief. In general, they are well known. All of them are unbelief. This is clearly stated in the noble Qur'an. (To) discuss or argue those things with them is not up to us. It is (for them to choose between) conversion to Islam, payment of the poll tax, or death.[12]

Such a statement needs to be understood in its fifteenth-century context. And Christians need to be aware that some Christians in the past have had similar aspirations about the supremacy of Christianity as a force in the world. But Ibn Khaldun's statement is particularly significant because of the way he underlines the *theological* reasons for the difference he perceives between Islamic and Christian ideas about political power. Many Muslims today would also share his negative views about the status of Christians and his estimate of Christian beliefs as 'unbelief'.

A variety of Islamic views about political power today

Views of Muslims today cover a wide spectrum – from those that are somewhat harsh in their approach to non-Muslims to those which are much more tolerant. This, for example, is a statement of how one Nigerian Muslim leader of the Qadiriyya Order has understood the concept of *jihad* in recent years.

> If you are living with a non-Muslim in your area and you want him to go, you simply call him and tax him. You tell him three times that he will live in your neighbourhood but only on condition that he pays tax … If he refuses to pay tax and still insists on living with you, on your own land, then you

have to advise him on three occasions that I will be coming at so, so, so date to wage a war against you. Only when he consistently proves obstinate are you allowed, in Islam, to wage war against him. The intention is to ensure that he is well prepared.

In particular countries (such as Pakistan) some Muslims have been calling for the Code of 'Umar to be reintroduced as the basis for dealing with non-Muslim minorities in Muslim states. On the other hand, Professor Mohammed Talbi, a Tunisian Muslim historian, believes that the *dhimma* system must be regarded by Muslims as a thing of the past.

> We face here an extremely complex history. In seeking to overcome this historically contentious question we need, today, to approach this problem with much realism, departing from our respective traditions and in accordance with our present aspirations. Today we live in a world where dhimmis no longer should exist. It has become imperative and absolutely indispensable to shelve this notion in the cupboard of history, something which from the point of view of Islam I deem absolutely possible. We face here an evolution which, according to my point of view, is part and parcel of the very meaning of Islam which today subscribes – with certain reserves – to human rights.[13]

In a book titled *The Struggle within Islam: The Conflict between Religion and Politics*, Rafiq Zakaria writes out of his experience of the Muslim community in India. The book traces 'the continuous fight between the holders of power and theologians', and is a sustained protest against the many different forms that fundamentalism has taken through the centuries. It commends the secularist approach as the only one that is true to the spirit of Islam and appropriate in the world today.

> In their muddled zeal the modern fundamentalists forget that it was not Hasan al-Banna, Mawdudi, and Sayyid Qutb who freed the Muslims from colonial exploitation and gave them a better and more secure future, but Ataturk, who despite his heresies, saved Turkey from the clutches of European power; Jinnah, a non-practising Muslim, who single-handedly created the most powerful Muslim state in the world; Nasser, who liberated

the Arabs from the foreign yoke and gave them new strength and hope; Sukarno, who brought freedom to more Muslims than any other leader and united the Indonesians under one banner; Tenko Abdul Rahman, who breathed new life to the Malaysian Muslims and made them a force in South-East Asia; Mujibur Rahman, an avowed secularist, who founded the second biggest Muslim state (Bangladesh) in the world; Qaddafi, whom the fundamentalists disown, but who challenged the might of America in North Africa; Boumedienne, who fought the imperialists and provided a socialist system to their people. These and many more in the secular mould were the real builders of modern Islam. Without them the Muslims would not have breathed the fresh air of liberty and equality; without them they would not have been able to hold their heads high in the comity of nations; without them they would have continued to be hewers of wood and drawers of water. These leaders might not have been pious and puritanical, orthodox and traditional; some of them might not have offered their prayers regularly; most of them did not fit into the straitjacket of scholastic theology; but they all brought Muslims out of the sloughs of despondency and despair and made them once again a power to reckon with ... Despite their lapses and faults they have taken Islam ahead and by their secular outlook ensured the future of nearly a billion Muslims all over the world.[14]

Christian responses

How, then, should Christians respond today to the wide variety of ways in which they experience the challenge of Islam on the political level? Much will depend on the local situation. But if there is an opportunity for Christians to stand back from their immediate situation, these are some of the most important principles that should determine their response. Taken together, they can at least provide a framework within which Christians can decide how to face difficulties in particular contexts.

1. Accurate information and responsible publicity

Part of our problem is that people in all communities are influenced by impressions, prejudices and stereotypes, especially as they are communicated by the media. Our information is often one-sided, misleading or hopelessly out of date. It is therefore essential that we are scrupulously accurate and honest in our reporting of what is happening in different countries. We need to avoid making generalizations, recognizing that no two countries are the same and that situations are constantly changing. There are a number of organizations today which are seeking to respond to this need.[15]

2. United local protest

In some situations where they have reason to be concerned, Christians of all denominations need to work together to make their voices heard. Emmanuel Gbonigi, the Anglican bishop of Akure in Nigeria, gives the following two examples of protests which led to positive results.

On one occasion in my home town of Akure, the Muslim deputy governor attempted to impose a Muslim head in a Christian-founded school. The governor was blackmailed into avoiding a meeting with church leaders at which they might have pressed their case. The churches called a press conference. The churches told the press that we were determined not to cheat Muslims and deny them their rights; but neither must Muslims be allowed to oppress Christians. The reality was that Christian students and teachers were in a majority even in the local Muslim schools.

The Chief Imam of Akure and his colleagues met members of the Christian council of Nigeria. They agreed that it was important to avoid religious conflict in the country. To promote harmony, they agreed that in Muslim-founded schools, there should be Muslim staff when available; in Christian-founded schools there should be Christian staff. But there will be no mosques in Christian schools nor chapels in Muslim schools.

By frank discussion and friendly personal contacts, Christian and Muslim leaders were able to avert a crisis and find a just way forward.

Already during Banbangida's time, when Nigeria applied for membership of the Organization of Islamic States, an event occurred which shows how reconciliation is possible even when such a sour atmosphere exists. Chief Abiola, a wealthy Muslim political leader and the owner of a newspaper, supported Nigeria's application for OIC membership and used his paper to campaign for it. As chairman of the Christian Association of Nigeria, I rejected the idea and encouraged Christians to boycott Chief Abiola's newspaper. Abiola and a large entourage came to visit me in my office to discuss the matter. When we met I was able to raise various issues besides the boycott; such as the way that Christians were refused access to advertising in his paper. Abiola was open and honest enough to recognize the justice of these complaints. This was the start of an ongoing dialogue between him and me. We organized a joint discussion group of Muslim and Christian leaders to defuse national tensions. I encapsulated the objective of these discussions in five points: *mutual knowledge, mutual understanding, mutual respect, mutual love, mutual cooperation.*[16]

3. Protest from governments and international bodies

Whether or not the Christians in any situation are able to say anything publicly about that situation, there is often a need for the protest to come from governments of other countries and international bodies outside the country. Kaleem John describes how this has worked in relation to the Blasphemy Laws which have created serious problems for Christians and others in Pakistan.

Many human rights organizations including Amnesty International (AI) and the Human Rights Commission of Pakistan (HRCP), as well as the US State Department have highlighted the harshness and unsuitability of the Pakistan penal code Section 295-C. HRCP and AI have strongly requested the government honestly to re-examine the Blasphemy Laws and to ensure that the law against blasphemy is not abused to imprison prisoners of conscience and that no one is sentenced to death.

It has been noticed that the Blasphemy Law is even misused against Muslims by their Muslim enemies. Consequently, some Pakistani Muslims agitate against the Blasphemy Laws, because the laws are apt to be misused and abused for purely personal and *mala fide* purposes. These Muslim opponents of the laws include some 'religious activists' and 'fundamentalists', because the laws which threaten and punish minorities, especially 295-C, have also been used against rival fundamentalists and religious activists.

However, it is minorities such as Christians which are most under threat...[17]

4. Turning the other cheek

It is often suggested by Christians and others that true Christian obedience to the teaching of Jesus in the Sermon on the Mount demands passive acceptance of every insult and injustice. The

following extract from John Stott's exposition of these verses,
however, suggests that this can hardly have been the real intention
of Jesus.

> Jesus' illustrations and personal example depict not the weakling who
> offers no resistance ... They depict rather the strong man whose control of
> himself and love for others are so powerful that he rejects absolutely every
> conceivable form of retaliation ... So the command of Jesus not to resist
> evil should not properly be used to justify either temperamental weakness
> or moral compromise or political anarchy or even total pacifism. Instead,
> what Jesus here demands of all his followers is a personal attitude to
> evildoers which is prompted by mercy not justice, which renounces
> retaliation so completely as to risk further costly suffering, which is
> governed never by the desire to cause them harm but always by the
> determination to serve their highest good.[18]

The report on *Suffering and Power in Christian-Muslim Relations* makes the
following comments about interreligious violence and injustice and
the practical application of Jesus' teaching:

> Sometimes it is largely ethnically or politically based, but at other times it
> arises from an Islamic theological assessment of Christians. We affirm that
> Matthew 5:38–48 (*'Turn the other cheek ... Love your enemies'*) is relevant in all
> cases, insofar as Christians should never nurture vengeful attitudes, and
> should always respond out of love and prayer for the welfare of any
> opponents. However, injustice should be resisted, and some feel that they
> have turned both cheeks several times and 'have no third cheek to turn'.
> We believe that there are cases when Christians are called upon to organize
> themselves and their sympathizers in the face of oppression, and to take
> action such as demonstrations, strikes and boycotts to protest against
> unjust treatment.[19]

5. Appealing to Islamic principles

The following extracts are taken from a paper by Michael Nazir-Ali,
written while he was living in Pakistan, in response to a request for
advice from a Christian member of parliament who was serving on the
Parliamentary Constitution Committee in Pakistan. It is a good
example of a Christian response from within the situation to political

questions about the place of Christians and other minorities within an Islamic state, based on the principle of working for the good of the entire nation.

> The Christian minority in Pakistan does not wish to become a disenfranchised, segregated group which has little or nothing to contribute to national life ... We would continue to wish to be treated as equal citizens with freedom of worship and proclamation; free to build, maintain and manage our own institutions. In particular, any move to reinforce the so-called 'Ordinance of 'Umar' is to be resisted.
>
> We would hope that in any future polity, our country would acknowledge the ultimate sovereignty of God which is exercised through the people ... Granted that the polity of Pakistan will be in accordance with Islamic ideals and aspirations, the basis of such a polity should then be the Qur'anic conception of human beings as vice-regents of God fulfilling the trust which they have undertaken. Only in such a broad and liberal system would the minorities feel at home ... Which nomenclature we use for our polity is of secondary importance. What is important is to safeguard the principle of popular, representative government and enfranchise all sections of the population.
>
> We must beware of serving only our own community interest. We must work for the good of the entire nation and especially of the poor, the weak and the oppressed.[20]

6. A Christian appreciation of power and an acceptance of suffering in the name of Christ

When all the protests have been made and there is no other 'Caesar' to appeal to for justice, Christians need to recognize that their attitudes to power and its use must be assessed in the light of the experience of Christ. The Report on *Suffering and Power in Christian-Muslim Relations* emphasizes what is distinctive about Christian attitudes, and shows how these have worked out in practice in difficult circumstances in Nigeria.

> Christians' motivation, ethics and way of life are determined by Christ's suffering for us. He could have exercised his power to overthrow the Roman government and Jewish leadership. Instead, he came into the world to reveal the Father to us. He accepted death on the cross to take upon

himself the punishment for our sin, and he called us to discipleship. By the force of his words and by his chosen meekness before the Sanhedrin, King Herod and Governor Pilate he demonstrated his ultimate power. In his willingness to walk the way of the cross he set Christians an example, showing that far more is achieved for the kingdom of God through suffering than through powerful control...

In the midst of suffering we often see the power of the gospel as Christians become stronger disciples, and as persecutors are so challenged by the love of Christ demonstrated in the Christians' meekness that they grasp the gospel for themselves. We were given a practical example of suffering, power, witness and the intervention of God. In 1987 Muslim mobs burned down 120 churches in Kaduna State, but Christians did not retaliate. They saw themselves as the chosen people of God, whose future witness would be compromised by retaliation. Instead, they went to worship in the ruins of their burnt churches. Many Muslims were challenged by this spirit of meekness and started to see the power of love. Muslims also noted that for 13 weeks it rained for six days a week, but never on Sunday: which was taken to be God's provision so that Christians could worship without getting soaked. We were challenge by this testimony to the courage of the Nigerian Church.[21]

It is, of course, far easier to state these principles than to know how to apply them in every situation. It requires serious study of the Bible, of Christian and Islamic history, and of national and international politics. Christians need to be thoroughly informed of the facts and aware of the particular issues involved.

Those who look on from outside the situation have a special responsibility to stand by their fellow Christians who have to live with all the pressures. If there is any sense in which Islam wants to win the world, Christians all over the world will need to work out how to respond to the political challenge – and to do so in ways that are not Islamic but distinctively Christian (see further chapter 36, 'Some issues facing Christians today').

PART FIVE

BEARING WITNESS TO JESUS

We need the song note in our message to the Muslims ... not the dry cracked note of disputation, but the song of joyous witness, tender invitation.
Temple Gairdner[1]

We believe not in words, but in the Word made flesh, a Word which only the Spirit of God can interpret to us. To argue is to turn it to mere words.
Roger Hooker[2]

If Christ is what Christ is, he must be uttered. If Islam is what Islam is, that 'must' is irresistible. Wherever there is misconception, witness must penetrate; wherever there is the obscuring of the beauty of the Cross, it must be unveiled; wherever persons have missed God in Christ, he must be brought to them again ... In such a situation as Islam presents, the Church has no option but to present Christ.
Kenneth Cragg[3]

Muslims are familiar with the idea of 'bearing witness', since the first pillar of Islam is *shahadah*, bearing witness to the basic creed of Islam. Christians are also familiar with the idea because of the words of Jesus to his disciples after the resurrection, '... you will be my witnesses ...' (Acts 1:8).

It can hardly be emphasized too strongly that the most effective Christian witness usually arises naturally in situations where Christians and Muslims are meeting or living together, and where the testimony of Christians is lived out in a lifestyle that is genuinely Christian. The following chapters offer several different models of how Christians can bear witness to their beliefs about Jesus and their experience of him. None of them is offered as a blueprint, and there are no simple techniques that are bound to make our witness easy or effective. All we can do here is try to learn from the experience of others, noting what they have found to be appropriate ways of making the Christian message about Jesus intelligible and relevant to Muslims. The last chapter describes some specific challenges faced by Christians in different situations in their relations with Muslims.

32. NATURAL OPENINGS IN EVERYDAY LIFE

A typical situation

It is seldom possible, of course, for us to prepare in advance what we should say in different situations. It may be helpful, however, to begin to reflect on the kind of situations in which there will be opportunities for Muslims and Christians to speak together about the practices and beliefs of the two faiths. The following conversation, for example, is taken from the book *What Shall I Say to My Muslim Friends?* by Margaret Burness, and is the kind of conversation that could easily take place at the time of Id, or Idul Adha, the Muslim feast celebrating Abraham's sacrifice of a ram in place of his son (whom Muslims believe was Ishmael, not Isaac). The celebration of this festival has several similarities with Christmas as it is celebrated in the West and in certain other parts of the world; for example, it is a public holiday in Muslim countries, and there are family parties, greetings cards and presents. The typical greeting between Muslims is *Id mubarak* ('May this feast be blessed').

*There is a knock on Elizabeth's door; and when she opens it, she sees her neighbour's
daughter Fatima with a bag of cakes.*

ELIZABETH: Hello, Fatima. Come in.

FATIMA: Thank you, Mrs Twining, but I can't stay. I have to go and help
mother – she's very busy preparing food for all our guests tomorrow. She
sent me to bring you these special cakes – she would be very glad if you
and Mary could come to see us tomorrow evening, and my father would be
glad to welcome your husband – it's our *Id*.

ELIZABETH: Thank you very much. We'll come tomorrow if we can.
What does *Id* mean?

FATIMA: It's a festival – people come from miles away to greet their
families and friends. We exchange special greeting cards and presents. We
dress up in our best clothes and eat special food. It's not as good as it was
at home, though. We're not allowed to kill a ram here – you have some law
against it, I think. It's just like your Christmas, no difference.[1]

What is Elizabeth to say to Fatima? How appropriate are the
following possible responses?

- 'Of course there's a difference – we don't kill rams!'
- 'It does sound like Christmas. I hope you have a very happy day
  tomorrow with your family and friends!'
- 'There is something more to Christmas than turkeys and
  presents – we are celebrating a very special present God has
  given to us all, Jesus Christ our Lord and Saviour. It's his
  birthday we remember at Christmas. I would love to hear
  sometime what you are celebrating tomorrow – but it's not the
  same thing, is it?'
- 'Yes, the cards, presents and family parties are much the same,
  but there is another connection too. We Christians remember,
  like you, how Abraham was prepared to sacrifice his son, and
  how God made a greater sacrifice. Jesus Christ, the Lamb of
  God, died to take away the sins of all the world. At Christmas
  we celebrate the birthday of Jesus, the Lamb of God.'

Thinking through the strengths and weaknesses of each of these
responses can help Christians to know what responses are most

appropriate and helpful in situations of this kind and which responses to avoid.

Christian responses to folk Islam

Several aspects of folk or popular Islam have been described in chapter 12. If Christians can appreciate the ways in which genuinely felt needs are being met through folk Islam, they may have opportunities to show how these same felt needs can be met in a more deeply satisfying way in Christ.

Figure 32.1 by Bill Musk indicates (in the column on the left) the felt needs that underlie the different practices of popular Islam, and (in the column on the right) ways in which these needs can be met in Christ.[2]

The following story of a woman in one of the Russian republics is a recent example of how some of these principles have worked out in practice.

Sayora and her husband Makhmoud have a disabled son and a daughter, and live in one of the Central Asian republics. Some years ago Sayora met Nicole and some of the other foreign Christians who live and work in the area, and they call them 'Muslims' – not because they belong to the religion of Islam but because in their eyes the term describes 'a good person'. Sayora has seen in Nicole and her colleagues something that confirms that their words about Jesus are true.

It took Sayora several years to trust Nicole and her co-workers enough to explain their belief that physical handicaps are the result of a curse. In their upbringing they learned that the 'European' (Russian) doctors don't believe in such things and don't want to hear about them. But for these women the spirit world is a regular part of daily life, and these beliefs are part and parcel of their world view, in spite of half a century of communist rule. In fact only one of the new believers was known to have got rid of her amulets when she was baptized, and one household gave back to their mother a valuable hundred-year-old book of charms rather than destroy it.

Sayora enjoyed attending a weekly meeting for women who follow Jesus at which they sing songs to the folk tunes that they knew. But there were other issues that soon came to the surface apart from charms and the occult. A few months after starting to follow Jesus, Sayora's husband,

Felt needs in popular Islam	Popular-level answers to felt needs			Spiritual crisis	Felt needs met by Jesus Christ
	More animistic → Less animistic				
Fear of the unknown	Idolatry, stone worship	Fetishes, talismans, charms	Super-stition	POWER ENCOUNTER WITH JESUS CHRIST	Security in Christ as keeper, guide
Fear of evil spirits	Witch-craft	Amulets, knots	Exorcism		Exorcism by Christ; power over spirits
Power-lessness before power of shaman	Sorcery	Prophy-laxes	Prophy-laxes		Protection from attack; offensive weapon for spiritual warfare
Fear of the future	Angel worship	Divination spells	Fatalism, fanaticism		Trust in Christ as Lord of the future
Shame of not being in the in-group	Curse	Hair/nail trimmings			Acceptance in the fellowship of believers
Disequi-librium	Magic	Divination			Restoration and answered prayer
Sickness	Tree/ saint worship	Healing magic			Divine healing in Christ's power
Helpless-ness in crisis	Magic	Vows	Inter-cession of saint		Christ answering prayer directly
Meaning-lessness of life		Turning to spirit world			Purpose in life as God's child; using gifts, abilities
Vulner-ability of women	Occult influence	Zâr-type ceremony	Practices at birth etc.		Security in Christ; influence as prayer warriors

Figure 32.1

Makhmud, returned from ten months away in Russia where he worked on a construction site. Their marriage had been arranged by their parents ten years earlier, and they lived with his family for the first seven years. When they had the chance to move into their own home, the only way they could afford it was for him to become a migrant worker and be away from home for long periods. So she hardly knew him, and it was duty, not love, that was the main feeling she had towards him – duty mixed with shame, since she had given no 'real' child to him and his family, only a disabled son and a girl.

One day when Sayora was reading the Bible with Nicole, she asked, 'Do you read the Bible and pray every day – even when you are ... unclean?' Nicole suddenly realized why, at certain times of the month, Sayora seemed particularly uninterested in prayer or reading the Bible. Even in the superficial form of Islamic practice she had known as she grew up, it was ingrained in Sayora's mind that only those who are *clean* can pray or should touch a holy book – and for women, that ruled out several days in each month. Nicole therefore read the story in Mark 5 about the woman who had been ill for so many years. Suddenly both Sayora and Nicole understood as never before that Jesus loves women, even unclean women!

Nicole learned that a systematic Bible study approach sparked little interest, but linking day-to-day issues to faith became very important to her. So, for example, they began praying for the safe delivery of a calf, and when God answered their prayers Sayora had something she could confidently share with her husband about her new faith: 'Don't we have a beautiful calf? And the birth was so easy – Nicole and I prayed for this!' Makhmud was a bit surprised, since he was not religious and didn't know about his wife's new interests.

The next time Nicole came to visit their home, he was at home, rather than out with his work and drinking friends. He had a quick look at the Injil Nicole brought along, and asked 'Isn't this fundamentalism? Isn't the state against this?' 'No,' Sayora answered, 'this book teaches us to pray for the government and our enemies. Sometimes the police do not understand the differences – but there is nothing bad in the Injil.'

Nicole invited him to a Christmas celebration to which she and the expatriate team invited all their friends and neighbours. Makhmud came, but was still wondering about things when he left for his work in Russia again a few weeks later. Nicole asked him if he would agree to Sayora meeting occasionally in their house with three or four other ladies from their village who had also started to read the Injil, and he agreed. Since it would be like a normal women's group that any neighbourhood has, he readily gave his consent.

Nicole was amazed to see the women's eagerness to make this small house meeting work, and pleasantly surprised to see how well it worked when their enthusiasm had been weak for the regular Friday meeting with other believers. The women already knew each other, trusted each other and had the same problems in their daily village life. Also they had natural meetings anyway – for example on birthdays and the anniversaries of the deaths of relatives and neighbours. Whenever they meet now they read their Bibles and invite other guests to join in with them.

33. USING THE BIBLE

This chapter explains three different ways in which Muslims can be introduced to the text of the Bible.

The prodigal son (or the two lost sons)

The text of this parable in English or in Arabic, together with an appropriate explanation, can be obtained from Tvaerkulturelt Center, Ryesgade 68C, 2100 Copenhagen, Denmark (info@tvaerkulturelt-center.dk) or downloaded from www.ivpbooks.com/crossandcrescent, or www.colingchapman.org.

What is so unique about the parable of the prodigal son (or the two lost sons) in the context of Christian witness to Muslims? There are at least five reasons why it can be especially valuable as a way of introducing them to the message of Jesus.

1. It is a story told by Jesus himself
Whatever Muslims believe about the corruption of the Bible, many of them are curious to know what the Christian version of the *Injil* actually says. We can tell them that this story is given in the *Injil* as a

story told by Jesus, and that it summarizes much of what was unique in his teaching.

2. It presents the message of Jesus in the form of a story

Those of us in the habit of trying to share the gospel by explaining a series of abstract theological propositions (such as 'All people are sinners; Christ died for our sins') may get further if we can learn the art of telling stories. A story is something that can be told, elaborated and dramatized. A series of pictures will be printed on the minds of those who hear it. Their imagination will be stirred, and there will be something that we can discuss together. Long after they have forgotten us and what we have said, they may remember this vivid story.

3. The parable teaches the essence of the good news proclaimed by Jesus

In his study of the parables of Jesus, Kenneth Bailey suggests that Jesus' basic message can be summed up as 'the costly demonstration of unexpected love'.[1] Each word in this phrase is significant.

- God *loves* all people.
- His love is *unexpected*, since we would not expect him to love his rebellious and sinful creatures.
- Not only does he proclaim his love, he actually *demonstrates* his love in action.
- This demonstration of his unexpected love is *costly* for him, since in a sense he suffers in the process of forgiving sins.

The parable of the prodigal son expresses all these points with special force. The father loves his sons – both the rebellious one who wants to leave home and the older one who has such a cold and formal relationship with him – and goes on loving them even when we might expect him to want to punish and reject them. He demonstrates his love to both of them in ways that would have been considered surprising, if not shocking, to his original hearers. And the father suffers in the process of demonstrating his love for them.

Bailey summarizes the significance of the prodigal's homecoming as follows.

On his return, the prodigal is overwhelmed by an unexpected visible demonstration of love in humiliation. He is shattered by the offer of grace, confesses unworthiness, and accepts restoration to sonship in genuine humility. Sin is now a broken relationship which he cannot restore. Repentance is now understood as acceptance of grace and confession of unworthiness. The community rejoices together. The visible demonstration of love in humiliation is seen to have clear overtones of the atoning work of Christ.[2]

4. The parable comes out of a culture that is similar to the culture of much of the Muslim world

The strong emphasis in Islam on the unity of the family and family loyalties, and the fact that most of the Muslim world is in Africa, the Middle East and Asia, should make it easy for Muslims to understand what is happening in the story. In these cultures, who could imagine a younger son asking for his share of the inheritance while his father is still alive? Should a father not punish his sons when they dishonour the name of the family? Has an elder brother got to swallow his pride and welcome home a younger brother who has disgraced himself?

5. The teaching of the parable is especially appropriate for Muslim readers

Muslims are taught to think of themselves as 'servants' who relate to God as their Master. When the prodigal thinks of coming home, his face-saving plan is that he will ask his father to accept him back as a servant or slave so that he can earn his wages and at least have something to pay back to his father. Such a solution, however, is unthinkable to his father, who wants to welcome him home as a son. Jesus, who spoke of himself as 'the Son' and enjoyed an especially intimate relationship with God as Father, brought the good news that all his disciples can approach God as Father and have all the privileges and responsibilities of being full members of God's family, and not just servants.

One surprising thing about the parable is that it does not have an ending. Perhaps this is because Jesus wanted his listeners to put themselves in the shoes of the elder brother and ask, 'What would I do if I were in his place? Would I listen to my father's pleading and join in the party to welcome my brother home? Or would I be so angry with him that I would take the nearest stick and beat him in full view of all the guests? And if God is like the father, and wants me to know and love him as a Father, how am I going to respond to his love?'

If the parable can be used in a context in which there can be genuine discussion, it can be followed up with gently probing questions such as these:

- What is your picture of what God is like?
- Do you find it difficult, if not impossible, to believe that God is like a loving Father?
- Do you believe that God loves you and loves all people – even when we sin?
- Do you think there is any difference between saying 'God is merciful' and saying 'God is loving' or 'God is love'?
- How do you think God shows his mercy or his love to us?

The Gospel according to Luke

We have already seen (in chapter 21, 'Guidelines in discussion with Muslims') that the Gospel of Luke is perhaps the most appropriate of the four Gospels for Muslim readers. There are three further reasons for choosing Luke's Gospel.

1. The Christology of Luke may be a little easier for Muslims to appreciate than that of the other Gospels
In Luke 1:32, for example, 'Son of God' is associated with the idea of Jesus as a descendant of David, and in Luke 1:35 with the Holy Spirit coming on Mary. As in the other synoptic Gospels, it is only very gradually that the disciples come to realize that Jesus is 'more than a prophet' (Luke 7:26).

2. The fuller birth narratives may be of special interest to Muslims, showing that there is some common ground between the Qur'an and the New Testament
They will certainly, however, become aware of some significant differences between the two accounts.

3. It makes a great deal of sense for Muslim readers to go on to read Acts after the Gospel, if, as is likely, Luke was the author of the Acts of the Apostles as well as his Gospel

The Gospel is about 'all that Jesus began to do and to teach' (Acts 1:1), while Acts records what Jesus continued to do and teach through the church. Muslim tradition has much to say not only about the life of Muhammad, but also about his immediate successors (the caliphs), who played a significant role in the history of Islam (see chapter 13, 'The spread and development of Islam'). Christians similarly attach a great deal of importance to the life of the early church as recorded in Acts. Thoughtful Muslims can hardly fail to notice the contrast between the way in which Christianity spread in the early years after the ministry of Jesus and the way in which Islam spread immediately after the death of the Prophet.

One particularly helpful edition of the Gospel of Luke is the 'Study Edition' published by the United Bible Societies, which explains words, customs and ideas that may need some clearer explanation for Muslim readers. It is available from The Bible Society, Stonehill Green, Westlea, Swindon SN5 7DG, UK.

The Message of the Tawrat, the Zabur and the Injil

In 1981 the Bible Society in Lebanon published a folder of selected Bible passages especially chosen for Muslim readers, under the title *The Message of the Tawrat, the Zabur and the Injil*. The text can be downloaded from www.ivpbooks.com/crossandcrescent, or from www.colingchapman.org.

It was initially distributed in Arabic, French and English, and since then has been translated into other languages in the Muslim world. The following are the main ideas which lie behind these selections.

The title

The title uses the qur'anic names of the three main Scriptures which Muslims believe were revealed before the Qur'an: the *Tawrat* revealed to Moses, the *Zabur* to David, and the *Injil* to Jesus (see chapter 8, 'The Qur'an'). In the Qur'an God says that the message revealed to Muhammad contains the same message as that revealed in the previous Scriptures. Jews and Christians are invited to believe Muhammad's message because it is no different from the message contained in the Scriptures that they have in their possession.

The title is therefore intended to convey something like this to the Muslim reader: 'You believe that these are Scriptures which were revealed by God to the Jews and Christians, and that the Qur'an was simply confirming the message that was contained in their Scriptures. But do you know what these Scriptures contain? The following passages give an idea of the central message of these Scriptures which are in the same form today as those in the hands of Jews and Christians in the time of Muhammad.'

The introduction

The introduction explains briefly what the Bible is. Since the Qur'an for Muslims consists of what God revealed to one man in the course of twenty-three years, it is not easy for them to grasp the idea that the Bible is like a library of books containing history, stories, prayers, letters and visions written by many different writers over a period of up to two thousand years. For the same reason each passage has an introduction to explain what it is that we are about to read. Is it history? Is it a letter? Who recorded these words? Whom was he or she addressing? And what is the main point of what is said in this passage?

We need to avoid controversy as much as possible

Thus, for example, the word 'Trinity' is not mentioned, although the claims that Jesus made about himself are clearly presented. We avoid any special emphasis on Jesus as the Son of God because of possible misunderstanding in the mind of Muslims, and because it is possible to draw attention to the claims of Jesus in different ways.

We start on common ground

The first studies therefore deal with God as Creator and human beings as creatures, and with God who reveals his laws to them. In this way we are trying to build bridges with Muslims by studying truths which they also believe, even if they express them in a slightly different way. We are also trying to lay foundations for the later studies. Thus long before we come to the delicate question of the crucifixion, we have

tried to prepare the way by looking at sacrifice and forgiveness in the
Old Testament, and the tension between the holiness and the love of
God. The terminology needs to be as Islamic as possible, provided
there is no compromise of Christian belief. For this reason we use
the qur'anic names for Jesus (*'Isa*), John the Baptist (*Yahya*) and the
devil (*Shaitan*).

*The most important theological assumption made in the studies is that we can
present the gospel in the way that is unfolded in Paul's letter to the Romans*
Law must come before grace. We need to know that we are sinners
under the judgment of God before we can see Jesus as God's answer to
our need. When, by the application of the law, sin has been shown
to be sin (Rom. 7:13), we are compelled to turn to the one through
whom God has done something to deal with that sin. In this respect
the approach differs significantly from that which underlies the parable
of the prodigal son. There, and in other parables of Jesus, as Kenneth
Bailey has pointed out, the emphasis is on God demonstrating his
unexpected love in costly ways. Sinners turn to God in repentance and
faith *in response to this unexpected demonstration of his love.* They become fully
aware of their sin *after* they have seen how much God loves them and
how much he has done for them to win their love.

The passages are grouped under ten themes, with each one on a separate paper
Christians who are able to study the passages with interested Muslims
should proceed slowly and take one subject at a time. Each study ends
with a prayer from the Bible, which can be read aloud together. This is
intended so that even if there is discussion or controversy in the study
of the passages, it is possible to end in a spirit of prayer and worship
rather than of controversy. It would be wrong to put words into the
mouths of Muslims that they cannot in all honesty say. But in most
cases there is nothing in the prayer that is likely to offend Muslims and
which they could not say with complete conviction.

34. STARTING FROM THE QUR'AN

Whenever there is resistance to the gospel among Muslims, it is easy to find reasons *on their side* for such rejection. But what if some of the responsibility is *on our side*? If the Christian church has contributed to the misunderstanding and rejection, we have an obligation to look again more carefully at the way we articulate our message.

The three studies in this chapter attempt to take up this challenge by studying an important theme in the Qur'an before turning to see how that same theme is developed in the Bible. The value of this method is that it forces us to understand the mind of well-taught Muslims. Instead of simply restating Christian doctrines in a traditional way, we will first have to understand what the Qur'an teaches on these themes and only then turn to the Bible. Our restatement of Christian teaching after such a study of the Qur'an should then be more intelligible to the Muslim mind.

God and his prophets

Here is a theme that is fundamental to Islam: God responds to human ignorance by sending prophets and messengers or apostles. As we explore how Muslims think about these prophets, we will want to recognize all the common ground we can find between the two faiths, working within that area where the two overlap (see chapter 24, 'Exploring dialogue'). Or, to change the metaphor, we will want to see how far we can walk along the same road with the Muslims before we come to the fork where our paths diverge.

When after this we turn to the Scriptures, we will be trying to look in a fresh way at how they describe the relationship between God and his prophets. We will want to see if we can correct Muslim misunderstandings of Christian beliefs and find ways of restating the gospel that engage the Muslim mind.

Here we will use Jeremiah as our example of a biblical prophet. He is not entirely unknown to Muslims, although he is not mentioned in the Qur'an. Sura 2:259 speaks of a doubting man who passes by a ruined town and exclaims, 'How shall Allah give this township life after its death?' Allah's response is to cause him to be dead for a hundred years and then bring him back to life. Some of the early commentaries on the Qur'an identify this man with various Old Testament characters, including Jeremiah.

We know more about the life and personality of Jeremiah than about almost any other prophet in the Old Testament. Just as 2 Corinthians lays bare the heart of Paul and reveals much of his thinking and feeling, so the book of Jeremiah reveals much about him as a man and as a prophet, and in particular about the inner agonies that he faces in his ministry. Since Jeremiah stands halfway between Moses and Jesus, he may have something to say to those who cannot make such a huge leap immediately from the prophet on Mount Sinai to the Prophet in the garden of Gethsemane.

God and his prophets in Islam

The following summary of Islamic teaching is based largely on a chapter by a Kenyan Muslim writer, B. D. Kateregga, in *Islam and Christianity: A Muslim and a Christian in Dialogue.*[1]

A messenger/apostle (*rasul*) is sent with divine Scripture to guide and reform humankind. The four most important are those through whom Scriptures were revealed: Moses, David, Jesus and Muhammad. A prophet (*nabi*) carries information or proclaims God's message, but is not given books like the messengers. Thus all messengers are prophets, but not all prophets are messengers.

Both prophets and messengers are given a message by God through revelation (*wahy*) for the guidance of a group or nation. They all bring essentially the same message – the message of Islam. Almost every nation has had its messenger or prophet. Twenty-five are mentioned in the Qur'an (16:36; 2:136) and 124,000 in tradition.

All God's prophets are trustworthy, knowledgeable and obedient to God. They are the best examples of moral trust – human beings, but protected by God from serious sin and bad diseases. They set very good examples with their own lives, although (according to strictly orthodox teaching) they are not sinless.

We must accept all God's prophets and messengers. Denying any one of them, therefore, constitutes unbelief (4:150–151). Some prophets are more highly endowed than others (especially Moses and Jesus, 2:253), but it is sinful to elevate any one prophet and put him on a higher level than the others.

Many prophets are mocked and rejected (15:11; 17:94). Some prophets are delivered by God, such as Noah (21:76; 26:118; 29:15; 37:76), Lot (21:71, 74; 26:170) and Moses (28:20–22; 26:65). It is worth noting that in several of these passages the word used is *najjainahu* ('we delivered him'), where the verb is the same as that used in the Arabic Lord's Prayer for 'deliver us' (*najjina*). It seems to be understood that God is in some way obliged to rescue his prophets; he must intervene to save them from the hands of those who want to destroy them: 'Then shall We save Our Messenger and the believers, in like manner (as of old). It is incumbent on Us to save believers' (10:104). 'Allah delivereth those who ward off (evil), because of their deserts. Evil toucheth them not, nor do they grieve' (39:61). 'They said: In Allah we put trust ... of Thy mercy, save us from the folk that disbelieve' (10:86–87).

Some of the prophets are killed 'wrongfully' (for instance, Abel, Zecharias and Yahya; 2:61, 87, 91; 3:21, 112; 4:155; 5:70). Those responsible for killing the prophets are later punished by God (2:61; 3:21).

Muhammad is 'the seal of the prophets' (33:40). In receiving what was revealed to him, he recites the stories of the previous prophets, partly as a warning to unbelievers (46:30–34) and partly as an encouragement to himself to persevere with patience in the face of opposition (46:35).

A study in the life of Jeremiah

Here we can note briefly some of the main characteristics of the ministry of Jeremiah, observing where there is anything similar or significantly different in the ministry of Muhammad.

The prophet has a clear call from God at the beginning of his ministry (Jer. 1:1–19), in which he feels that God has laid his hand on him (v. 5). God promises to give him the words to speak (v. 7) and to rescue him from enemies (v. 8). Later in his ministry, when experiencing hostility from the people, Jeremiah questions several elements in the original call he received (Jer. 15:11–18). It is interesting to compare this language about Jeremiah's call with that of the Qur'an and the early accounts of the call of Muhammad in the early *siras* (Lives of the Prophet) and in *hadith*, some of which speak of a nocturnal vision in a dark cave, while another speaks of a vision received in clear daylight.

Jeremiah receives God's message in different ways, and there is considerable variety in the language used to describe the process of revelation. Sometimes he is said to recite the words that are given to him by God (Jer. 1:7). Elsewhere the reception of the message is compared to drinking (Jer. 23:9). In another place he listens to the words he is to convey (Jer. 23:18). In one case he receives the message during a dream (Jer. 31:23–26; but contrast 23:29).

This language is of special interest when we appreciate how Muslims think of the process of revelation and inspiration. Muhammad is simply the human vehicle through which an eternal message is delivered to humankind. He is almost like a typewriter used by God to deliver his word, or a pipe through which words are conveyed like liquid.

Jeremiah declares the judgment of God which will fall on a stiff-necked, stubborn and disobedient people (Jer. 11:9–17; 19:15). Similarly Muhammad speaks of the imminent judgment of God and tells many stories of God's judgment on sinful people in the past.

The prophet calls for repentance (Jer. 11:1–8). Muhammad likewise has a message of judgment to proclaim. But whereas Jeremiah is recalling his people to obedience to a law revealed centuries before through Moses, Muhammad claims to bring a new revelation for the Arabs, which is basically the same as that revealed through previous prophets.

The prophet Jeremiah is identified with his people, and because of his identification with them he confesses their sins and prays for them (Jer. 8:18 – 9:1; 14:7–9; cf. Lam. 3:1–52, especially vv. 40–47).

At the same time the prophet shares the anguish of God over his sinful people (Jer. 6:9–12; 14:17–18). It is not always clear whether the 'I' refers to God or the prophet. The Qur'an never uses language of this kind to describe God's response to evil; anguish is far too human an emotion to be ascribed to God. It is therefore inconceivable that Muhammad as prophet should identify himself with God in this way.

Jeremiah's message is rejected, and he is rejected (Jer. 11:18–23; 12:6). Gerhard von Rad makes the significant comment that in Jeremiah we see 'a shift in the centre of interest from the message to the messenger'. As a result he suffers great indignities and is treated cruelly. For example, he is put in the stocks (20:2), imprisoned (32), left in a muddy cistern, ignored by the leaders and humiliated by the king (38). Finally he is bound and taken to Babylon, but later freed (40). In his agony he pours out his complaint to God (Jer. 15:10–18; 20:7–18), asking for judgment and vengeance on his enemies (20:12; cf. Lam. 3:58).

When Muhammad is persecuted, he is given in the Qur'an examples of prophets who have been patient in their sufferings before him. Richard Bell, an Islamic scholar, believed that the example of Moses leading his people out of bondage and suffering in Egypt may have made a strong impression on Muhammad. The idea would therefore be that if God brought his people out of Egypt, surely he can also deliver the Prophet and the Muslim community; in this way the pattern of the exodus is repeated in the *Hijra*, the migration from Mecca to Medina.

Jeremiah has a message of hope – but only after judgment (Jer. 30 – 33, especially 30:3, 18; 31:2, 16–17). He is even told to buy a field to demonstrate the certainty that there will be a future for the people in the land (32). His life ends, however, in misery and shame, as he is taken down to Egypt (Jer. 43:1–13, especially vv. 4–7). At the end of the book we are left asking, 'Did God keep his original promise to deliver Jeremiah?'

Jeremiah can be compared with Jesus. Whereas Jeremiah is called to take the cup of the wrath of God and make all the nations drink it (Jer. 25:15–31), Jesus in the garden of Gethsemane finds that *he himself* is being called to drink the cup of wrath. What makes the prospect of his coming death so much more intolerable is that he knows that those who should drink the cup are 'all the wicked of the earth' (Ps. 75:8).

Jeremiah can be compared with Paul. In Luke's account of the conversion of Paul, there are clear echoes of the call of Jeremiah (Acts 9:15). When Paul writes about his own conversion, he uses language similar to Jeremiah's account of his call (Gal. 1:15–16).

In such ways as these the story of how God dealt with this particular prophet in the Old Testament and how the people treated him may give some clues about the Christian understanding of prophethood. It may offer the opportunity to put to Muslims questions such as these:

- Do you as Muslims take seriously enough the perversity of humans in their rejection of the Word of God? You say that people are created 'weak' and suggest that all we need is law and admonition, combined with the example of the Prophet. But look at the way the people of Judah treated the prophet Jeremiah! Is there not something more seriously wrong with human nature than mere weakness, ignorance and forgetfulness?
- What do you understand about the inner experience of the prophet or of any prophet? In the light of the experience of Jeremiah, do you accept that suffering may be a necessary part of the prophetic experience? And how do you explain the fact that God does not always seem to deliver his prophets?
- What does it mean if the prophet is willing to suffer? Could it not say something about how God deals with evil? Could it not suggest that judgment is not the only response God can make to evil? If this can be so, the prophet's suffering can become a kind of mirror of the suffering of God himself. The prophet's suffering can indicate the way that God himself suffers as he bears with his people and forgives them.
- How do you understand God's involvement in this prophet? Is there not a sense in which the honour of God is tied up with his

prophet, so that what the people do to him, they are doing to God? If so, is God bound to deliver his prophet? If he is bound, why the exceptions? Why did he allow some to be humiliated and killed? What does it say about God that when the preaching of his Word draws out the worst in human nature, he does not rescue his servant, but allows him to suffer?

These questions can be answered only by Christians when they have been with Jesus in Gethsemane and begun to understand that 'God was in Christ' (2 Cor. 5:19). But if the followers of the Prophet can see Jeremiah as being half way between Moses and Jesus, perhaps they can catch a glimpse of what the fuller answers to these questions can be in Jesus.

God and his Word

Jesus is given the title 'Word' in both the New Testament and the Qur'an.

> In the beginning was the Word, and the Word was with God, and the Word was God. (John 1:1)

> The Messiah, Jesus son of Mary, was only a messenger of Allah and His Word which he conveyed unto Mary, and a spirit from Him. (4:171)

Although we have here some obvious common ground, the same title is interpreted differently in the two communities. Do we therefore simply have to accept that we are poles apart, or is there any possibility of building bridges?

Jesus as 'Word' in the Qur'an
The following verse describes the annunciation of the birth of Jesus to Mary.

> (And remember) when the angels said: O Mary! Lo! Allah giveth thee glad tidings of a word from Him, whose name is Messiah, Jesus, son of Mary ... (3:45)

Another important verse in which Jesus is spoken of as God's Word comes in the context of an appeal to Christians not to exalt Jesus too highly.

> O People of the Scripture! Do not exaggerate in your religion nor utter aught concerning Allah save the truth. The Messiah, Jesus son of Mary, was only a messenger of Allah, and His Word which he conveyed unto Mary, and a spirit from Him. So believe in Allah and His messengers, and say not 'Three' – Cease! (it is) better for you! – Allah is only One God. (4:171)

If we go on to ask how the title 'Word' is interpreted in the Qur'an, a verse in sura 3 gives the answer.

> Lo! The likeness of Jesus with Allah is as the likeness of Adam. He created him of dust, then He said unto him: Be! and he is. (3:59)

The traditional Muslim interpretation of the title has therefore been that Jesus is the Word of God in the sense that he was *created by the Word of God*. Thus the thirteenth-century qur'anic commentator al-Baidhawi says, 'Jesus is called "a word", because he came into existence by God's command without a father, so that he resembled the new creations.'[2] Another commentator, al-Razi, gives a different explanation: Jesus is called 'a word' because he was the fulfilment of the word spoken by the prophets.[3] Yusuf Ali's comment on 3:39 is: 'Notice: "a Word from God", not "the Word of God", the epithet that mystical Christianity uses for Jesus ... Jesus was created by a miracle, by God's word "Be", and he was.'[4]

Christian responses

One natural response on our part is to investigate sources and ask where Muhammad might have heard these ideas. Although the title is found in only five verses in the New Testament (John 1:1, 14; 1 John 1:1, 10; Rev. 19:13), the idea of Jesus as the eternal Word of God was developed by theologians between the second and fourth centuries, notably by Clement of Alexandria.

It is significant, however, that the title was used much less after this time, and was left out of the major creeds. Geoffrey Parrinder suggests this may have been because the *Logos* idea had also been used by various Gnostic sects. The example he gives is the apocryphal Acts of John, written about the second century AD, which describes the disciples taking part in a dance, 'going round in a ring', and saying to Jesus, 'Glory be to thee, Lord: Glory be to thee, Grace: Glory be to thee, Spirit.'[5] This same document says that Jesus was crucified in appearance only (compare the qur'anic verse, 'They slew him not nor crucified, but it appeared so unto them', 4:157). Muhammad may well have found the title 'Word' and the qur'anic idea of the crucifixion in heretical or less orthodox Christian sources like these.

This kind of enquiry about sources makes sense to many, because it helps us to understand how Muhammad may have come into contact with these ideas in either Arabia or Syria. It needs to be recognized, however, that such a suggestion is anathema to Muslims. They believe that the words of the Qur'an were revealed directly from God, which rules out the possibility that what is recorded in the Qur'an could have come to Muhammad from any human source.

Another response to Islamic interpretations of Jesus as 'Word of God' comes from the seventh-century treatise *On Heresies* by John of Damascus (see chapter 23, 'Learning from the controversies of the past'). He speaks of Islam as 'the heresy of the Ishmaelites' and gives a clear idea of how he must have engaged in discussion with Muslims in Damascus less than one hundred years after the death of the Prophet. He suggests that when Muslims accuse Christians of *shirk* (associating a created being with God the Creator), Christians should reply that Muslims appear guilty of mutilating God by refusing to believe that the Word of God is fully divine.

> Since you say that Christ is Word of God and Spirit, how is it that you revile us as *Hetairiastai* (Associators)? For the Word and the Spirit are not separated from the one in whom they are by nature. If therefore His Word is in God, it is evident that the Word is also God. But if the Word is outside of God, then according to you God is without reason and without life. And so, fearing to provide an Associator for God, you have mutilated Him. It were better for you to say that He has an Associate than to mutilate Him, and to treat Him as stone, or wood, or some insensible thing. Wherefore you speak falsely of us when you call us '*Hetairiastai*' but we call you '*Koptai*' (Mutilators) of God.[6]

Whether or not these two responses bring us any nearer together, our main desire should be to come back to the Gospels to see what light they shed on the title 'Word'. We want to say to the Muslim, 'We understand what you mean when you say that Jesus is the Word of God or a Word of God. But will you allow us to explain what Christians understand by the title?'

Jesus as the Word in the Gospel of John

Any explanation of the concept of Jesus as 'the Word' must begin with the prologue to John's Gospel, and take into account the background of ideas that must have influenced him. Greek philosophers centuries before him had thought of the *logos*, word or reason, as the rational principle by which the universe is sustained. And the Jews, probably under the influence of Greek philosophy, had reflected on the role of the creative Word of God in Genesis 1 and of the Wisdom of God described in Proverbs 8:22–31. When John spoke of Jesus as 'the Word', most of his readers would have connected the title with one or both of these ideas, which were common in the first century. But they would not fail also to take note of John's incredibly bold claim that the eternal *Logos* of God 'was God' (John 1:1), and that he 'became flesh and made his dwelling among us' (John 1:14).

Words of command can 'get things done' and achieve certain ends. Thus when John speaks of Jesus as the Word of God, he means that it was through Jesus that the universe was created: 'Through him all things were made; without him nothing was made that has been made' (John 1:3). Whereas the Qur'an speaks of Jesus as created by the Word of God, John believes that God created the universe through Jesus the eternal Word.

But words also reveal a person's mind and character. So when John thinks of Jesus as the Word of God, he also means that Jesus reveals God in the fullest possible way: 'No one has ever seen God, but God the One and Only, who is at the Father's side, has made him known' (John 1:18; *exegesato*, literally 'has given us an exegesis of him').

If, then, the title is used by only one writer in the New Testament, and this is what he seems to understand by it, where else do we need to look? Much can be gained from looking at the synoptic Gospels, which give us a different kind of account of the life and teaching of Jesus. We may then see how the apostle John, writing in the

AD 90s and reflecting on all that he and the other apostles had seen and heard of Jesus of Nazareth, could have come to think of him as the eternal Word of God. We look first at the so-called 'nature miracles', second at the healing miracles, and third at his announcement of forgiveness, noting in particular the words of Jesus associated with these actions.

The nature miracles

- He calms the storm: 'Quiet! Be still!' (Mark 4:35–41)
- He feeds the five thousand after giving thanks (Mark 6:30–44).

The feeding of the five thousand (Mark 6:30–44) is of special significance, since it may be referred to in the Qur'an. In the sura titled *The Table Spread*, the disciples are reported as praying, 'Send down for us a table spread with food from heaven' (5:112–115). It is also helpful to notice the verse in the Qur'an in which Jesus speaks of his miracles: 'I fashion [*akhluqu*, create] for you out of clay the likeness of a bird and breathe into it and it is a bird, by Allah's leave' (3:49). One Muslim's pilgrimage to faith in Jesus began when he thought about the implications of the word 'fashion' or 'create': surely only God can create; so how can Jesus here speak of himself creating something?

The healing miracles

- A man possessed by evil spirits: 'Be quiet! Come out of him!' (Mark 1:21–23)
- A man with leprosy: 'Be clean!' (Mark 1:40–45; cf. the Qur'an: 'I heal ... the leper', 3:49)
- A paralysed man: 'Your sins are forgiven' (Mark 2:1–12).
- Legion: 'Come out of this man, you evil spirit!' (Mark 5:1–13)
- A sick woman: 'Go in peace and be freed from your suffering' (Mark 5:25–34).
- A dead girl: '*Talitha koum*! Little girl ... get up!' (Mark 5:21–24, 35–43; cf. in the Qur'an, 'I raise the dead, by Allah's leave', 3:49)
- A deaf and mute man: '*Ephphatha*! Be opened!' (Mark 7:31–37)

- A boy with an evil spirit: 'You deaf and mute spirit, I command you, come out of him and never enter him again' (Mark 9:14–32).
- Blind Bartimaeus: 'Your faith has healed you' (Mark 10:46–52; cf. in the Qur'an, 'I heal ... him who was born blind', 3:49).

Words of forgiveness

- A paralysed man: 'Son, your sins are forgiven' (Mark 2:5).

One reaction of the Pharisees to Jesus pronouncing forgiveness to a paralysed man ('He's blaspheming! Who can forgive sins but God alone?', Mark 2:7) is exactly the same as that of the orthodox Muslim who knows that the Qur'an says, 'Who forgiveth sins save Allah only?' (3:135)

With the memory of Jesus' words and miracles indelibly printed on his mind, the apostle John recognizes that the words of Jesus have power to still storms – something only God can do ('He stilled the storm to a whisper', Ps. 107:29) – and bring healing and forgiveness, which once again is the prerogative of God himself (he 'forgives all your sins and heals all your diseases', Ps. 103:3). If, therefore, the words of Jesus have the power to do things that only God can do, Jesus must be the one through whom God has spoken and acted in a special way.

The title 'Word', which John gives to Jesus, is therefore firmly grounded in all that John remembers of Jesus. For if the words of Jesus were in effect the words of God in these different situations, is it not natural to think that Jesus is himself the Word of God? And if the historical Jesus spoke and acted in this way, speaking the creating, healing and forgiving Word of God, then the risen and ascended Jesus can still speak these words to us today. The Word of God cannot be less than, or other than, God himself.

God and his mercy

'In the name of God, the Merciful, the Compassionate,' says the Muslim in the *Fatiha*. 'How can I find a merciful God?' cried Luther in his despair. It is one thing to proclaim the mercy of God, but another to be sure of experiencing that mercy. Thinking about the mercy of God, therefore, brings us nearer to the heart of the matter. For how do we benefit from God's prophets and his Word unless they communicate not only teaching about God's mercy, but an experience of that mercy?

God and his mercy in the Qur'an
The Qur'an's teaching about mercy can be summarized in the following way.

- God is merciful and forgiving (*rahman, rahim, ghafur*). 'Your Lord is a Lord of all-embracing mercy, and His wrath will never be withdrawn from guilty folk' (6:148). 'Despair not of the Mercy of Allah, who forgiveth all sins. Lo! He is the Forgiving, the Merciful' (39:53; cf. 23:118).
- God loves certain kinds of people: those who do right (3:134, 148; 5:13, 93), those who turn to him (2:222), the pure (2:222), the God-fearing (3:76; 9:4, 7), the patient (3:146), the trusting (3:159), the equitable (5:42; 49:9; 60:8) and those who do battle for his cause (61:4).
- God does not love certain other kinds of people: aggressors (2:190), the corrupt (5:64; 28:77), the evil unbelievers (2:276), the ungrateful (22:38), the braggart boasters (31:18), the prodigals (6:142; 7:31), the proud and boastful (4:36), the unbelievers (30:45), the wrongdoers (3:57, 140; 42:40), the treacherous (4:107; 8:58; 22:38), those of harsh speech (4:148), the transgressors (5:87).
- Forgiveness is associated with obedience to God and his Prophet. 'Say (O Muhammad, to mankind): If you love Allah, follow me; Allah will love you and forgive you your sins. Allah is forgiving, Merciful' (3:31; cf. 8:29; 20:73; 46:31; 57:28; 61:11–12; 71:3–4).
- God's forgiveness is inscrutable; he forgives whom he wills. 'He [Allah] will forgive whom He will and He will punish whom He will' (2:284; cf. 3:129; 5:18). 'Knowest thou not that unto Allah belongeth the Sovereignty of the heavens and the earth? He punisheth whom He will, and forgiveth whom He will. Allah is able to do all things' (5:40; cf. 48:14).

- We cannot be sure of forgiveness; God will show mercy on the Day of Judgment. 'We ardently hope that our Lord will forgive us our sins because we are the first of the believers' (26:51); '...and who, I ardently hope, will forgive me my sins on the Day of Judgment' (26:82; cf. 14:41; 66:8).
- There is no forgiveness for certain sins, such as *shirk* (association). 'Allah pardoneth not that partners should be ascribed unto Him. He pardoneth all save that to whom He will' (4:116; cf. 4:48, 137, 168; 9:80; 47:34).

God and his mercy in the teaching of Jesus

One of the clearest expressions of the teaching of Jesus about the mercy of God is found in the parable of the two lost sons (also known as the parable of the prodigal son; see chapter 33, 'Using the Bible'). If we put the teaching of the parable alongside the teaching of the Qur'an, we can note how the teaching of Jesus compares with each point of the summary of the Qur'an's teaching given above.

- The message of this parable is that God is merciful and forgiving. In this respect there is no difference between the parable's and the Qur'an's presentation of God's mercy.
- God loves not only those who love him. The father in the parable loves both sons and shows the same kind of forgiving love to both of them.
- God's forgiveness is associated with the one who proclaims and declares that forgiveness to people. The father himself welcomes his son and reinstates him in the family. When Jesus declares, 'Your sins are forgiven,' it is because he speaks with the authority of God himself. So what Jesus does, God does; and what God does, Jesus does.
- God does indeed show mercy on whom he wills (Rom. 9:18); but we *can* know where we stand before him. The way the father expresses his love for both his sons shows how God's love extends to us all. It also shows how he takes the initiative, and comes to meet us and welcome us home.
- We can be sure of God's mercy and forgiveness. We do not have to wait until the Day of Judgment before we know how we stand before him. The prodigal knows that he is forgiven,

because his father goes out of his way to show that the wrongs of the past are forgiven and forgotten.

- The only unforgivable sin in the teaching of Jesus is what he calls 'the sin against the Holy Spirit' (Mark 3:23–30), that is, attributing the work of God to Satan and calling what is good evil. If the older son in the parable refuses in the end to accept the mercy shown to him by his father, he is spurning his father's love, and the breach in their relationship looks as if it must be final. But this is only after the father has demonstrated his love for his son in a way that is beyond all doubt.

The teaching of Jesus therefore reveals an understanding of the mercy of God which, while it has something in common with the teaching of the Qur'an, is distinctively different. Daoud Rahbar has had to grapple with the similarities and differences in his own experience. Writing in 1960 as a well-known Muslim scholar, he made a thorough study of the justice of God in a book called *God of Justice*.[7] Some years later, he explained his conversion to the Christian faith, pointing out that the distinctive thing about the New Testament is the way God's love is related to his justice.

> To sane human intellect anywhere in the world certainly justice is a necessary attribute of the Sovereign Creator. But what should truly divine justice mean?
>   Think of the Creator-God in two ways:
>
> - The Creator says to Himself: 'I am going to create mankind; on earth they will have sickness, anxiety, fear, social wrongs, infidelities of fortunes and fellow-beings, deaths of loved ones, disappointments, toils, and then when they die [I] shall reward and punish them strictly. This is my justice.'
> - Think of the Creator-God in another way: He says to Himself, 'I am going to create the world that I may have fellowship with man. Men will live their *finite* lives of suffering *whereas my own suffering is eternal*. To make my eternally suffering disposition manifest to man I shall myself go and live a span of earthly human life and disclose directly to men that I am with them in their suffering. In that earthly life I shall suffer literally the *worst* of suffering by dying the worst death of human violence ... '

God created the heavens and the earth because He has an eternal yearning for loving purely. The motive of the divine act of creation is not the desire to be obeyed by creatures. The motive of that act is to have objects of infinite and pure suffering love, the eternal attribute of God. When I read the New Testament and discovered how Jesus loved and forgave His killers from the cross, I could not fail to recognize that the love He had for men is the only kind of love worthy of the Eternal God ... If the innocent Jesus, who forgave and loved His crucifiers from the cross, was not the Creator-God Himself, then the Creator-God is proven to be inferior to Jesus. And this cannot be. The Creator-God and Jesus are one and the same Being. May all men know that truly divine love.[8]

35. EXPLAINING CHRISTIAN BELIEFS ABOUT JESUS

Muslims have great difficulty with the title 'Son of God' as applied to Jesus, largely because they believe that the Qur'an's condemnation of the idea of God having sons and daughters applies not only to the pagan beliefs of the Meccans, but also to the beliefs of Christians about Jesus. In this situation the first thing that Christians need to do is to attempt to remove misunderstandings. The idea that Jesus became 'the Son of God' through some kind of physical begetting is as blasphemous to Christians as it is to Muslims. If Muslims can accept that Christians do not hold ideas of this kind and think of themselves as genuine monotheists, is there any way of helping them to understand more positively what Christians do believe about Jesus?

This chapter attempts to explain how the first disciples of Jesus came to believe that he was 'more than a prophet'. Although the phrase 'more than a prophet' is related in its original context in the accounts of the life of Jesus to John the Baptist (Luke 7:26), it can also be a helpful starting point for explaining what Christians believe about Jesus. We share with Muslims the belief that Jesus is a prophet. But for us he is a great deal *more than a prophet*. But at least Christians and Muslims can start with common ground in declaring *together* their belief that Jesus is a prophet, sent by God, with a message for the human race.

In what follows we trace how the ideas of the disciples and early Christians about Jesus developed gradually during the three years of his public ministry, after his death and in the next three centuries. This may be helpful because Jewish ideas about God – and especially about the oneness of God – at the time of Jesus were very close to Muslim ideas about God. Both Jews and Muslims insist that God is One. In the Torah Moses says, 'Hear, O Israel: The LORD [*Yahweh*] our God, the LORD is one...' (Deut. 6:4). Muslims in their *shahadah* say, 'There is no god but God [*Allah*]...' and speak of God as *ahad* (One). The well-known *Surat al-Ikhlas*, for example, begins, 'Say, "He is Allah, the only One, Allah, the Everlasting"' (112:1–2, Fakhry).

The starting point: a Jewish understanding of the oneness of God

We could say therefore that the Jewish disciples of Jesus start with *a very Islamic understanding of God.* They follow Jesus in the beginning as a religious teacher, a rabbi. But as they spend time with him, seeing all the things he does and hearing the things he says about himself, their ideas develop and change. The main thrust of his message is about 'the kingdom of God', that is, about the coming of the kingly rule of God in the world. Mark, the earliest of the four Gospels which, according to an early tradition, is based on the testimony of the apostle Peter, summarizes the message of Jesus in these words: 'The time [i.e. the time spoken of by the prophets] has come... The kingdom of God is near. Repent and believe the good news!' (Mark 1:15). Many of the parables of Jesus are about the coming of the kingdom and speak about what happens when God establishes his rule in the world. But they do so in indirect and enigmatic ways that force his hearers to think deeply about their meaning.

The miracles and teaching of Jesus

In the context of Jesus' teaching about the coming of God's kingdom, the miracles performed by him have special significance and force the disciples to think about his identity. So, for example, when he calms a storm on the Lake of Galilee, the disciples say, 'What kind of man is this? Even the winds and the waves obey him!' (Matt. 8:27). He feeds the five thousand – a miracle which is referred to in the Qur'an (5:112–115). He heals the blind, the deaf and the lame, and raises people from the dead – miracles of healing which are also described in the Qur'an (5:110). And he turns water into wine (John 2:1–11).

In the Qur'an the miracles of Jesus are performed by divine permission ('by my permission', *bi'idhni*, 5:110). But in the Gospels the disciples see them as signs of the coming of the kingdom of God. Jesus is doing things that only God the Creator can do and therefore seems to be God's agent in bringing in the kingdom. So the disciples are forced to ask the question, 'How is this man Jesus related to Almighty God, to Yahweh, the Creator of the universe?'

When these miracles and the teaching about the kingdom of God are combined with the things that Jesus *says about himself*, the mystery begins to deepen.

He claims to be able to forgive sins
When he heals the paralysed man, who has been let down through the roof by his friends, he says, 'Son, your sins are forgiven.' The teachers of the law who are present, who are orthodox Jews, are shocked, 'thinking to themselves, "Why does this fellow talk like that? He's blaspheming! Who can forgive sins but God alone?"' (Mark 2:1–12)

He claims to teach with authority
He is not constantly quoting other authorities as other Jewish teachers do: 'Rabbi *x* says this and Rabbi *y* says that . . .' Instead he says, 'Truly . . . I say to you . . .' And in the Sermon on the Mount, he says, 'You have heard that it was said to you . . .' (referring sometimes to the Old Testament and sometimes to the teaching of the rabbis), and then goes on to say, 'But I say to you . . .' (Matt. 5:21–22). We might say that there is something strangely self-centred about the teaching of Jesus. He says, for example, 'Come to me, all you who are weary and burdened, and I will give you rest. Take my yoke upon you and learn from me . . . and you will find rest for your souls' (Matt. 11:28–29). 'Taking the yoke of the law' was a common expression at the time, describing people who committed themselves to the study of the

Torah and to living a godly life. Jesus therefore is saying, 'Instead of taking the yoke of the law, I invite you to take *my* yoke and learn *from me* rather than from the Torah.'

He claims that he will one day judge the world

In the parable of the sheep and goats, he says, 'When the Son of Man comes in his glory, and all the angels with him, he will sit on his throne in heavenly glory. All the nations will be gathered before him, and he will separate the people one from another...' (Matt. 25:31–33). One of the surprising things here is that the criterion by which people will be judged on the Day of Judgment is the way they have responded *to him*: 'Whatever you did for one of the least of these brothers of mine, you did for me' (Matt. 25:40).

In his miracles, therefore, Jesus is doing things that only God can do, and in speaking about himself he claims to be able to do things that Jewish people would associate only with God. This inevitably creates an enormous problem for the disciples. They know that he is a human being, because they are living with him and observing him every day, and they know that God is One. But Jesus seems to enjoy an especially close relationship to God. He is a man like us, but he seems to be acting on behalf of God.

At the same time there is something very indirect about the way Jesus speaks about himself. He never says, 'I am God; I am divine.' Instead he uses enigmatic titles for himself, which are all taken from the Old Testament.

His favourite title for referring to himself is 'Son of Man'

On the surface this emphasizes his humanity, and this is what is implied in some verses where the expression is used in the Old Testament (e.g. Ps. 8:4; Ezek. 2:1). But there is one key passage, in Daniel 7, where the Son of Man is a figure that Daniel sees in a dream.

> In my vision at night I looked, and there before me was one like a son of man, coming with the clouds of heaven. He approached the Ancient of Days and was led into his presence. He was given authority, glory and sovereign power; all peoples, nations and men of every language worshipped him... (Dan. 7:13–14)

The Son of Man in Daniel's vision is clearly an individual, but he is also a corporate figure who represents 'the saints of the Most High', that is, all the people of God (Dan. 7:18, 22, 25, 27). It must have sounded very strange in a Jewish context that this Son of Man actually receives worship from 'all peoples, nations and men of every language'.

Jesus speaks of himself as 'the Son' who knows God as 'the Father'
'All things have been committed to me by my Father. No one knows the Son except the Father, and no one knows the Father except the Son and those to whom the Son chooses to reveal him' (Matt. 11:27). The problem with this title is that when we use it today, we read into it the ideas that were expressed later in the creeds – about the Son being eternal, 'the only begotten Son of God'. But in the Jewish context of the life of Jesus, the 'Son of God' is a title taken from the Old Testament that is applied to the whole people. Moses, for example, is told by God to say to Pharaoh, 'This is what the LORD says: Israel is my firstborn son ... Let my son go, so that he may worship me...' (Exod. 4:22–23). And speaking through the prophet Hosea, in a reference to the exodus from Egypt, God says, 'When Israel was a child, I loved him, and out of Egypt I called my son' (Hos. 11:1). At other times, however, it is the king, as the representative of the whole people, who is spoken of as 'the Son'. Thus in one of the psalms, King David writes, 'I will proclaim the decree of the LORD: He said to me, "You are my Son; today I have become your Father"' (Ps. 2:7). In the Old Testament, therefore, 'the Son' is sometimes the Children of Israel, the whole people of God, and at other times it is a title for the king who represents the people before God. It is important to notice, however, that in every case this father-son relationship is never understood in a literal way, but only as a metaphor.

There are two very significant occasions in the life of Jesus when he is described as 'the Son', and in both of these instances he hears a voice from heaven in which God addresses him as 'my Son', using the same kind of language which we have already seen applied to the Davidic king in the Old Testament. When Jesus is baptized in the River Jordan, he hears a voice from heaven which says to him, 'You are my Son, whom I love...' (Mark 1:11). Then at the transfiguration he hears the words, 'This is my Son, whom I love...' (Mark 9:7). Because this is a familiar term in the Old Testament, we need to understand it in these terms and relate it to Jewish hopes about the one who would fulfil the promises made to David, rather than reading into it the ideas that were developed later by Christian theologians after New Testament times.

Jesus identifies himself with the figure of 'the Servant of the Lord (Yahweh)'
This figure is described in a series of passages known as 'the Servant Songs' in the book of Isaiah (Isa. 43:1–4; 49:1–6; 50:4–9; 52:13 – 53:12). In some of these passages the Servant represents the whole people of Israel; at other times he is the faithful remnant; and sometimes again he is the prophet himself. In one very significant passage in Isaiah 52:13 – 53:12, the Servant experiences great injustice and suffering, and in his death bears the sins of others.

> Surely he took up our infirmities
>   and carried our sorrows,
> yet we considered him stricken by God,
>   smitten by him, and afflicted.
> But he was pierced for our transgressions,
>   he was crushed for our iniquities;
> the punishment that brought us peace was upon him,
>   and by his wounds we are healed.
> We all, like sheep, have gone astray,
>   each of us has turned to his own way;
> and the LORD has laid on him
>   the iniquity of us all.
> (Isa. 53:4–6)

So when Jesus says, 'The Son of Man did not come to be served, but to serve, and to give his life as a ransom for many' (Matt. 20:28), he is saying in effect, '*I am the Suffering Servant* described by the prophet Isaiah, and his words indicate something about the meaning of my death.'

In addition to these titles used by Jesus himself, he is described by the disciples as 'the Messiah' (the Christ)
This is an especially important title, since the Qur'an also describes Jesus as 'the Messiah', although it gives no indication of the meaning

of the word and the concept behind it. In the Qur'an, for example, at the annunciation of the birth of Jesus, the angels announce the birth in these words: 'O Mary, Allah bids you rejoice in a word from Him, whose name is the Messiah, Jesus, son of Mary. He shall be prominent in this world and the next and shall be near to God' (3:45, Fakhry).

To understand the meaning of the title 'Messiah' in the New Testament, we need to understand its Jewish background. In the Old Testament kings and priests were anointed with oil as a public sign that they were being set apart for their special work, appointed and commissioned by God. And over the centuries of the history of the Children of Israel the idea gradually developed that God himself would one day intervene in the history of his people to establish his kingly authority on earth through a descendant of King David, who would be God's special agent, his 'Messiah'.

During the public ministry of Jesus, one crucial conversation takes place at Caesarea Philippi, on the slopes of Mount Hermon, when Jesus asks his disciples, 'Who do people say I am?' The disciples reply, 'Some say John the Baptist; others say Elijah; and still others, one of the prophets.' And then Jesus asks them, 'But what about you? ... Who do you say I am?' Peter answers, 'You are the Christ' (i.e. 'the Messiah'; Mark 8:27–30). Peter is saying, therefore, 'You are God's anointed servant, his appointed agent to bring in the kingdom of God.' And in Matthew's version, he adds, 'the Son of the living God' (Matt. 16:16). But again, in the context of Jewish beliefs at the time, he simply means, 'You, Jesus, are the Messiah, God's anointed agent, the descendant of David who was to sit on David's throne.'

Although Peter and the disciples recognize Jesus as the Messiah, Jesus himself does not refer to himself as 'the Messiah'. The reason for this is probably that he is aware that the Jewish people at the time think of the Messiah mainly as a political or military figure, and Jesus' own understanding of the role of Messiah is very different from this. When at his trial the chief priest challenges Jesus directly with the question, 'Are you the Christ, the Son of the Blessed One?' Jesus replies, 'I am.' But he goes on immediately to speak of himself as the Son of Man in a way that echoes Daniel's vision (Mark 14:61–62). So the disciples, these very orthodox Jews, still see Jesus in his Jewish context, and the names and titles that are used to describe him are all drawn from Jewish scriptures. There is absolutely no compromise with the oneness of God.

Implications of the resurrection and Pentecost

The next important stage in the development of the disciples' understanding of Jesus comes after the resurrection. When he is crucified, the disciples cannot understand how God could have allowed his anointed representative to suffer such a shameful death. But when they see the empty tomb and meet the risen Jesus personally, they begin to see the resurrection as God's way of vindicating Jesus and affirming that he really is the person he claimed to be.

The highest point in the faith of the disciples, therefore, comes after the resurrection, when Thomas sees the risen Jesus and exclaims, 'My Lord and my God!' (John 20:28). This story is recorded in the Gospel according to St John, which was probably written about fifty or sixty years after the resurrection. John is not just recording the actions and teaching of Jesus like a journalist. He has had time to reflect on the significance of who Jesus is and what he has achieved. His Gospel is therefore different from the other three Gospels, which are called 'the synoptic Gospels'.

Seven weeks after the resurrection, on the day of Pentecost, the Spirit of God, the Holy Spirit, comes into the disciples in a new and dramatic way (Acts 2:1–13). So they come to believe that the same Jesus who had lived with them for three years is now living in them through the Holy Spirit, the Spirit of God himself.

Later reflection on Jesus as 'the Word of God'

In the Gospel according to John, the Word of God is not a being who is created at a particular time in the womb of Mary. The prologue at the beginning of the Gospel describes Jesus as the Word in the sense that he is the Word of God himself and therefore fully divine.

> In the beginning was the Word, and the Word was with God, and the Word was God. He was with God in the beginning ... The Word became flesh and made his dwelling among us. We have seen his glory, the glory of the One and Only, who came from the Father, full of grace and truth ...

No one has ever seen God, but God the One and Only, who is at the
Father's side, has made him known. (John 1:1–2, 14, 18)

In John's mind, therefore, Jesus is not a creature created by the Word
of God. Just as a person's words reveal the mind of that person, so
Jesus as the Word of God is himself fully divine and reveals through
his life in a human body the mind and the heart of God. The Gospel
according to John therefore reflects a further stage in the development
of the disciples' understanding of who Jesus is, a development that
takes place after the resurrection and that works out the implications
of what the disciples have seen and heard while Jesus was with them.

It seems that their thinking may have developed something like
this: 'If Jesus is the one through whom the kingdom of God has begun
to come on earth, he must have the authority of the king himself in
order to be his representative on earth. If Jesus spoke of himself as
"the Son", he is not just the Messiah in the sense that he is the
anointed descendant of David. If he claimed to know God as
"Father", he must have an especially close relationship to him. If he
could calm the storm, heal the sick and turn water into wine, he was
doing things in the material world that only God the Creator can do.
And if he could forgive sins and claim that he would one day judge the
world, he must be *more than a prophet* with a message from God. He
must somehow be identified with God in a way that no other human
being is. He is fully human, but does things that only God can do.'

Here again, however, it is important to emphasize that the disciples
are orthodox Jews, and that all of this thinking takes place in a Jewish
context, not a pagan context. The disciples do not reject their belief in
the oneness of God. They are forced by the evidence of their eyes and
ears to conclude that Jesus *comes from God*, and that *he must – in some sense
– be God*. And if they do not say bluntly that 'Jesus is God', it is largely
because they still believe in Yahweh, the God revealed in the Old
Testament, and are still convinced about the oneness of God. At the
same time they are beginning to understand that the oneness of God
must involve a more complex kind of unity within the Godhead than
they had ever imagined. They have known Yahweh as the God of the
Old Testament. They have lived with Jesus and come to see him as
'the Son of God' in a unique sense. And they have experienced the
coming of the Holy Spirit of God into their lives. So for some years

they are in the process of re-interpreting their idea of the oneness of God. It is no longer a simple mathematical oneness; it is a much more profound kind of oneness in which the Father, the Son and the Spirit are related to each other in a relationship of love (see John 17:5, 24).

Christian leaders were forced to define more carefully what they believed about Jesus, because in the three centuries after Christ there were many who challenged the consensus that was developing. One particular idea, known as 'adoptionism', suggested that Jesus became the Son of God at the time of his baptism when God 'adopted' him as his Son. Another highly significant challenge was presented by Arius, an Egyptian priest and theologian who taught that Jesus was not the eternal Son of God, but was created in the womb of Mary. Both these and other ideas were strongly rejected at the Council of Nicaea in AD 325 and at Chalcedon in 451, when the creeds that were accepted affirmed that Jesus was both fully human and fully divine.

When Jesus is described as 'the only begotten Son of God', Christian theologians were merely developing an idea that was already there in the Gospel according to St John: 'No one has ever seen God, but God the One and Only [or the Only Begotten], who is at the Father's side, has made him known.' When they used the phrase 'only begotten', they were explicitly rejecting the idea that Jesus was *created* by God. The father-son metaphor is therefore not used to describe the *origin* of the Son, where he comes from, but to describe his eternal *relationship* with God.

A summary of the gradual development in the understanding of Jesus

We can therefore attempt to summarize these different stages as follows.

- When the disciples begin to follow Jesus, they see him simply as an ordinary rabbi, a Jewish religious teacher.
- They hear the message of Jesus, which is about the coming of the kingdom of God, and begin to see that his parables, his miracles and the titles he uses for himself point to the special role that Jesus himself plays in the coming of the kingdom.

- Peter is the first of the disciples to put into words the disciples' belief, which develops gradually, that Jesus is 'the Christ, the Son of the living God'. But these ideas are still understood in their Jewish, Old Testament context.
- The disciples see the resurrection as God's way of vindicating Jesus as his Messiah, his representative, his agent in bringing in the kingdom of God on earth.
- In the years after the resurrection and the coming of the Holy Spirit at Pentecost, further reflection on the life of Jesus, his character, his miracles, his teaching and his claims about himself leads the disciples to believe that Jesus is the Son *not only* in the sense that he is the Davidic Messiah, *but also* in the sense that he is the eternal Son who knows God the Father and has been with God from eternity.
- At the end of this process the disciples still believe that God is one; but they now understand that there is an eternal relationship of love within the Godhead between the Father, the Son/the Word and the Holy Spirit.
- The creeds of the church which were formulated in the fourth and fifth centuries at Nicaea and Chalcedon did not introduce new ideas about Jesus, but simply affirmed that he was fully human and fully divine (at the Council of Nicaea), and attempted to define the relationship between his human nature and the divine nature (at the Council of Chalcedon).

Answering Muslim objections

If this is how the faith of the disciples develops during and after the life of Jesus, we can begin to see how to answer some of the arguments put forward by Muslims to challenge Christian beliefs about Jesus.

'It was Paul who elevated Jesus and put him on a level with God. This was a later development and Paul was largely responsible.'
Christians would want to answer that there is enough evidence in the Gospels to suggest that even during the lifetime of Jesus the disciples were beginning to see that Jesus is more than a prophet. Jesus' claim to be able to forgive sins, for example, contains within it the implicit claim that he is divine.

'Christians were influenced by pagan ideas about many gods. In Greek and Roman religion there are plenty of gods and goddesses who get together to produce sons and daughters. So "Son of God" is a pagan idea that is incorporated into Christianity.'
Here again Christians will respond that the crucial developments take place in a thoroughly Jewish context. Christianity later moves out into the pagan world; but in the formative years it is in a purely Jewish context, where polytheism and idolatry are totally rejected. It is inconceivable that the disciples of Jesus, as orthodox Jews, would have tolerated pagan ideas that would have compromised the oneness of God. These would have been rejected by every Jew as totally blasphemous.

'It was the church which elevated Jesus several centuries later in its creeds. The Emperor Constantine made Jesus divine at the Council of Nicaea in 325.'
The first disciples of Jesus spoke Aramaic as their mother tongue. As Christianity spread out of Palestine into the rest of the Greco-Roman world, Christians were speaking other languages and had to respond to attacks not only from Jews, but also from pagan religions and from Greek philosophy. They had to redefine what they believed about Jesus in a way that made sense not only to Jews, but also to Gentiles, who knew nothing about the Old Testament. But in formulating their beliefs about Jesus in a more systematic way, they were not inventing new ideas which totally transformed the very Jewish message of Jesus. They could not think and speak about him only in Aramaic, but had to articulate these beliefs both in Greek and Latin, and therefore had to use Greek words (like *phusis*, 'nature', and *homoousios*, 'of one essence') and Latin words (like *persona*, 'person', and *trinitas*, 'trinity'), in order to explain the relationship between the Father, the Son and the Spirit. But they did not invent the idea of the Trinity. The *word itself* was a Latin word, which the Jewish disciples would never have known. But the *idea* of the Trinity was not new. It was simply used to formulate in a more systematic way and in the new language of Latin what Christians had come to believe about the nature of the One God.

If, therefore, the Gospels are a substantially reliable account of the life of Jesus, the crucial developments in the disciples' ideas about Jesus take place during his lifetime. Once again we notice that this is *a gradual development*, that it takes place *in a Jewish context*, and that it is done *through Old Testament ideas and categories*. Jewish ideas about the oneness of God are not rejected, but redefined. The disciples continue to believe that God is one. But what Jesus says and does convinces them that, while he is fully human, he comes from God. He is *both* fully human *and* fully divine. He is the clearest possible revelation of God that we could ever have – a revelation of God in the life of a human being. And the resurrection is the final vindication of Jesus and his claims about himself. By raising him from death in such a dramatic and unique way, God demonstrated that Jesus was very much more than a prophet.

So Jesus is certainly a prophet sent by God with a message to deliver in words. Two of the disciples describe him immediately after the resurrection as 'a prophet, powerful in word and deed before God and all the people' (Luke 24:19). But he is *more than a prophet* who communicates a verbal message. In a profound sense, *he himself is the message*. His character, his life, his death and resurrection reveal the character of God and communicate the love and forgiveness of God in a unique way. The message of the New Testament therefore is, '*If you want to know what God is like, look at Jesus.*' In the words of the Gospel according to St John, 'No one has ever seen God, but God the One and Only, who is at the Father's side, has made him known' (John 1:18). John believes that the unseen, eternal, almighty God has revealed himself and made himself known to us in Jesus. Jesus, the eternal Son of God, the Word of God, became a human being in the womb of Mary in order to communicate the love, mercy and forgiveness of God to humankind.

How, then, do Christians want to respond to the question that Muslims often put to Christians: 'We Muslims recognize Jesus as a prophet. Why can't you return the favour and recognize Muhammad as a prophet?' Christians understand well how Muslims think about the Prophet Muhammad and the revelation that they believe came to him from God, and can appreciate why they want to challenge Christians in this way. But the Christian answer has to be that since we see Jesus as 'more than a prophet', as the revelation of God in the form of a human being, and since Muhammad came six hundred years *after* Jesus, it is hard for us to believe that there could be *any new or additional revelation from God* through a prophet who comes after Jesus and who simply delivers a message in words.

So we rejoice to find in the Qur'an many truths about God which we believe had already been revealed through the Old Testament prophets and supremely in Jesus. But if Jesus really is the eternal Word of God who became a human being in the womb of Mary in order to reveal God to the world and to reconcile human beings to God, it is hard for us to believe that God has *anything more* to communicate to the human race through another prophet who comes later. As we asked earlier in the book, would you light a candle when the sun is shining?

36. SOME ISSUES FACING CHRISTIANS TODAY

The following case studies – from Europe, Africa, the Middle East and Central Asia – illustrate some of the issues faced today by Christians who are living alongside Muslims and interacting with them. They all describe real situations, and are written by people with first-hand knowledge. These are some of the difficult contexts in which Christians have to show their understanding and respect for Islam and a genuine respect and love for their Muslim neighbours.

Should Christians support 'faith schools' in the UK?

At one time, the state only funded Christian and Jewish faith schools. That is no longer the case and, although there are still only a few state-funded Muslim schools, there has been a shift in government policy to encourage faith schools, of various religions, within the state sector. Islamist terrorism has been one of many issues that have called into question how British society can appropriately reflect the diverse religions and cultures of the nation. There has been a growth in Muslim schools outside the state system and this has been viewed with concern in some quarters. It is widely acknowledged that we can no longer think of Britain as a Christian country, but the growth of Muslim schools poses serious questions about British identity and heritage, equality and diversity.

Suggested advantages of Muslim schools

- The Golden Rule suggests that we should extend to others the same privileges that we expect for ourselves. There is nothing except tradition and prejudice to prevent us from having Muslim schools.
- Financing Anglican, Catholic, Methodist and Jewish schools has not turned the surrounding communities into inward-looking, self-contained communities of a particular faith, and extending the number of Muslim schools within the state sector ought to be supported.
- While Muslim schools are brought within the state system, there is more opportunity for a mixed intake that will add to community cohesion, avoid isolationism, and avoid creating a potential breeding ground for extremism.
- Muslim schools have greater potential for working with Muslim parents to ensure that high educational attainment is valued.

Suggested disadvantages of Muslim schools

- In most cases only a few Muslim leaders are making requests for greater numbers of Muslim schools. The majority of the Muslim community would prefer their children to go to existing state schools, whether church schools or not.
- Encouraging Muslim schools would make Muslim communities even more inward-looking and self-contained than they already are. They would become more and more like ghettos, since children in Muslim schools would have little or no contact with non-Muslims.
- While state-funded Muslim schools are obliged to teach about other faiths, private Muslim schools would teach only Islam and see their purpose as proselytism for the Muslim faith.

- Muslim schools are more likely to teach in ways that undermine Western values of gender and sex equality and promote ideas such as creationism.

Our response as Christians to the existence and encouragement of Muslim schools forces us to reflect deeply on our own attitude to faith and education. As with all interfaith encounters, these are areas for challenge and learning within the church. The Christian-Muslim encounter in Britain, and globally, does not happen in isolation. It also encompasses the challenge of our secular neighbours who are fearful of extremism, abuse and injustice from all religious communities. Reflecting on the various responses to Muslim schools, we might like to put the following questions to fellow Christians about our Christian approach to education.

- How can Christian schools be places of distinctiveness and also inclusion? In practical terms, what does it mean to be a Christian school, and how can these be places where those of other faiths and none are made to feel equally valuable?
- How can Christian schools avoid the creation of white Christian ghettos and more properly reflect the racial, social and religious mix of an area?
- Where a Christian school is in a monocultural area, how can the school intentionally break down barriers of ignorance and encourage relationships across social and religious divides?
- How should Christian worship be modelled in a school including all faiths and none in such a way that core values of grace and choice are fostered and respect for the faith communities and priorities of parents are established?

Is it appropriate for a secular government in France to ban the wearing of the veil?

France has a Muslim population of around 4 million, approximately 6.6% of the total population of 60 million, most of whom are from families which came originally from North Africa. Some French Muslims have argued that traditional Islamic teaching should be revised in response to the new challenges facing Muslims, and have encouraged assimilation into French society. Others, however, contend that, in an increasingly global and secular world, the only way for Muslims to survive and for Islam to make progress in non-Islamic societies is for Muslims to hold on to their beliefs and practices whatever the cost. They argue that since Muslims are expected to dress modestly, Muslim women in public should cover their entire body except their face and their hands.

In recent years more and more Muslim women in France – including young girls attending secondary and even primary schools – have been wearing the *hijab* or headscarf as a way of asserting their distinctive Islamic identity in what is, by and large, a secular and materialistic society. As a result, although school attendance is compulsory under French law for children up to sixteen, many girls were being excluded from school on the ground that government schools are supposed to remain neutral in terms of their pupils' religious or political persuasion.

When these problems stirred up a widespread and passionate debate throughout the country, the government appointed a special committee to look into the issue and come up with proposals aimed at making it easier for Muslims to feel at home within French society. Among other things, the report suggested that school pupils should not wear any distinctive object which would reveal their religious background. In 2004 the French parliament therefore passed a bill which ruled that no pupils attending government schools should be allowed to display any ostentatious religious mark such as a headscarf or a cross.

The intention of the French law is to protect schoolchildren from divisive political debates and to make the school a haven where all pupils are offered the same education in a context that is naturally conducive to learning. As France is a secular state, religious education is not part of the curriculum, and the state seeks to deal with all its citizens as individuals and as equals without any regard to the religious community to which they belong. Muslims should therefore be willing to compromise over this issue, or, if they insist on Muslim girls wearing the veil in school, should send them to private Muslim (or possibly Catholic) schools.

The argument against the government's legislation was that this law was a serious violation of people's right to religious freedom, and that it expressed a kind of secular fundamentalism. Some Muslims and non-Muslims in France have argued that the understanding of *laïcité* (secularity) should be more inclusive. Thus instead of trying to ignore the fact that religious communities are an integral part of French society, the state should acknowledge them and enhance their positive role in society, without discriminating against them.

Since this legislation was passed, there seem to have been fewer problems in French schools and many girls and their parents have reluctantly accepted the new legislation. However, the broader issue of integration into wider society remains a real challenge, and the controversy about the wearing of the veil has been somewhat overshadowed by the violence which erupted in many French cities in 2005, when immigrants burned cars and attacked the police. While some observers believe that the fact that many of those involved in the violence were Muslims is highly significant, others believe that the religious dimension of the conflict is insignificant, and that the main reasons for these expressions of anger were related to social factors like unemployment, poor social services and the difficulties in being fully accepted and integrated within French society.

What happens when there is a conflict between freedom of speech and the obligation of respect?

In September 2005 a Danish newspaper, *Jyllands-Posten*, published twelve cartoons of Muhammad which they had commissioned as a test of freedom of speech, having asked cartoonists to send in satirical drawings of the Prophet. According to the editor, this was a reaction to the increasing number of times when artists had been known to censor themselves out of fear of radical Islamists. When Danish Muslims protested, they did not feel that they were taken seriously. As a result a group of Danish imams and Muslim leaders travelled to the Middle East carrying with them not only the published cartoons, but also some other drawings which were even more offensive, sent to them by Danish citizens. The most offensive of the cartoons depicted the Prophet Muhammad as a terrorist wearing a bomb-shaped turban. In another cartoon he told suicide bombers that there were no more virgins left for them in Paradise. In February 2006 Muslims took to the streets in many places all round the world to express their outrage over the Danish cartoons. Some of these demonstrations were violent and more than 130 people were killed. Danish embassies in Damascus and Beirut were attacked, Danish flags were burned, Danish goods were boycotted, and posters in London called for the killing of the cartoonists.

The number of Muslim immigrants and refugees in Denmark has increased in the last three decades from no more than 30,000 in 1975 to just under 200,000 in 2006, in a population of 5.3 million. Many have given up their first nationality and acquired Danish citizenship. It was some of these Muslim 'New Danes' who alerted Arab and Islamic media to the cartoons. Because Denmark used to be a relatively homogenous society where most people would describe themselves as cultural Christians (Lutherans), many Danes have found it hard to respond to the challenge of living in a changing society which is gradually becoming increasingly multi-ethnic and multi-faith. Initially the Danish prime minister refused even to meet with the ten Muslim ambassadors who asked for a meeting back in October 2005, on the ground that the press in Denmark is not controlled by the government and that all citizens have a right to freedom of speech. The fact that since 2003 the Danish government has repeatedly introduced tighter legislation on asylum and immigration which is deemed unfair by many people added to the sense of grievance within the Muslim community. Interestingly, most Danes consider it unthinkable that a Danish newspaper would have dared to publish similar cartoons depicting other minority groups such as Jews, Greenlanders or Jehovah's Witnesses.

Islamic rage over these issues in Denmark and elsewhere has undoubtedly been fuelled by different parties (both Western and non-Western) who have exploited it for their own ends. The vehement reactions of Muslims worldwide, however, have demonstrated that Muslim societies remain profoundly religious despite the pervasive influence of Western secular culture. Islam teaches that all God's prophets were sinless either at birth or from the time they started their prophetic mission, and that as God's representatives on earth they must be respected and honoured. Since Muhammad was not just the last prophet but the greatest of all, any attack on him is felt as an attack on the God who sent him and on his community. This controversy has shown that Muslims in general are passionate people, and that when they feel their religion is being attacked or ridiculed, they are willing to defend their faith and the honour of their Prophet. In Denmark someone commented that while most Danes consider religion (of any kind if it is taken seriously) to be a threat, Muslims feel that it is their religion which is under threat.

While Muslim leaders have deplored the violence of Muslim protesters in some of the demonstrations, they condemned the publication of the cartoons as insensitive, offensive and provocative. They have argued that even in Western countries there are limits to freedom of expression, and that in most European countries those who incite racial or religious hatred can be prosecuted. They believe that since the government represents all citizens in the country, it has an obligation, for the sake of social harmony and public order, to ensure that no group is exposed to public slander or ridicule. In other words, the right of the Muslim community to be respected in its core beliefs should override the right to freedom of speech. In Denmark this point of view was supported by pastors from international churches and Christian immigrants and refugees with experience of living in multi-faith societies around the world.

In most Western societies, however, the right to freedom of expression is regarded as an absolute right which takes priority over all other rights. This means that people are free to criticize ideas, ideologies or religions however they wish, and everyone therefore has to learn to accept criticism and even ridicule from others. If Christians have had to learn to live with this kind of situation, why can Muslims not do the same? Individuals may choose to practise a kind of self-censorship out of respect for others, but are not under any obligation to do so, since any curtailing of freedom of speech is seen as a step towards excessive state control.

The controversy over the cartoons has highlighted the tension in a pluralist and secular society between the right to freedom of speech and the need to respect the beliefs of others, between individual rights and responsibility towards others. Does tolerance mean that *others* should accept *my right* to express my views freely? Or does it mean that *I* have a duty to respect the sensitivity of *others* – whatever I think about their beliefs? Conflicts of this kind are bound to arise when Muslims, who want God to be honoured not only in their private lives but also in the public sphere, find themselves living in secular societies where the majority want to keep God and religion out of the public sphere.

How should Christians respond to the reintroduction of *shari'a* law in Nigeria?

Islam first came to West Africa in the tenth century, and there were several Muslim states in the area of the present northern Nigeria which lasted for centuries. Islam strengthened its hold as a result of the Jihad Wars in the nineteenth century under leaders such as Usman Dan Fodio.

Under British rule from 1903, the power of *shari'a* courts was reduced so that they covered only family and divorce laws, and only for Muslims, and the traditional Islamic punishments for theft and adultery (known as the *hadd* punishments) were modified. When Nigeria gained its independence in 1960, it was established as a secular state, guaranteeing freedom of religion, including the right to practise, propagate and change one's religion. A penal code was introduced for the whole country, which was a synthesis of English and Islamic law. The present population is around 120 million, with 49% Christian, 45% Muslim and 6% of tribal religions.

In 1999 the twelve northern states, where the majority are Muslims, reintroduced *shari'a* law, and the jurisdiction of *shari'a* courts of appeal was extended in each state. All kinds of criminal offences involving Muslims have been dealt with in these courts, and in some states an additional *shari'a* police force was set up alongside the existing state/federal police. There were demands for a federal *shari'a* court to be set up to hear appeals from state *shari'a* courts, but this was always rejected. These developments coincided with the resurgence of Islam in countries like Iran and the Middle East and the growth of Islamism in many other countries.

In 1986 the government stirred up heated controversy when it was discovered that it had secretly negotiated Nigeria's membership of the Organization of the Islamic Conference (OIC). As a result of strong protest from Christians, the government withdrew its membership in 1992. In 2001 and 2002 the cases of Safiya Hussaini and Amina Lawal, women who had been raped but were sentenced to death by stoning for adultery, attracted media coverage across the world. These cases were eventually dismissed on appeal to the states' *shari'a* courts of appeal.

As a result of tensions between the two communities and personal, local conflicts, both Christians and Muslims have used violence against each other at different times, and many thousands of people have been killed. Both churches and mosques have been burned down.

The argument of many Muslims is that Nigerian law as it stands still contains too many foreign elements and should be made much more consistently Islamic. They see this as a way of affirming their Islamic identity and stemming the moral decline of the country. They claim that *shari'a* applies only to Muslims, and that its application is tolerant.

There has been strong resistance from Christians and others to the reintroduction of *shari'a* for the following reasons:

- Muslims themselves are not unanimous in their demand for *shari'a*. Some who are more liberal see it as an unnecessary intrusion into people's lives, or feel that it should only be introduced gradually and after being thoroughly tested. Even among Islamist radicals there are differences of opinion.
- Since Christians and Muslims live side by side and are constantly interacting with each other, it is difficult to have laws which apply to one community and not the other. For example, a law banning motorcyclists from carrying female passengers created serious problems for Christian women. Regulations about appropriate dress inevitably affect Christians who are expected to dress like Muslims.
- *Shari'a* law has frequently been used by individuals for personal or political purposes and to discriminate against minorities – e.g. by restricting access to the media and the building of new churches. It has also been applied selectively, so that, for example, in cases of adultery only the woman is punished and the man goes free.
- *Shari'a* allows Muslims to kill an apostate with impunity, and many argue that *shari'a* is being used to promote the Islamization of Nigeria. Any further extension of *shari'a* law – e.g. by the creation of a federal *shari'a* court – would raise serious questions about the federation of Nigeria as a secular state.

- It is pointed out that *shari'a* is unable to deal with one of the greatest problems in the country, which is corruption, because in traditional Islamic law there is no punishment that can be prescribed. This illustrates the inability of *shari'a* to adapt to changing situations and needs.

Christians in Nigeria in recent years have become much more united as a result of these conflicts, and have realized that they need to be involved in politics at every level. They have also agonized over the interpretation of Jesus' command to 'turn the other cheek' (Matt. 5:39), with the result that some have become more militant and resorted to violence – not only to defend themselves, but also to attack Muslims. When they can overcome the tendency to demonize Muslims and Islam, however, they can usually find ways to negotiate with Muslims to work out solutions which are consistent with the secular nature of the Nigerian Federation and enable both communities to live side by side in peace.

How should Christians respond to Islamization in Malaysia?

Based on the 2000 census, 'Bumiputera' (Malays and other indigenous people) make up 65.1% of the total population of 23.27 million; 26% are of Chinese descent and 7.7% are Indians originally from India; 60.5% of the total population are Muslims, and 9.1% are Christians. The Christians are found mostly in the urban centres, mainly Chinese and Indians, with the English language as the main medium in churches. There are also ethnic churches using Mandarin and the Chinese dialects and the Tamil language. A larger percentage of the Christian population is found among the tribal people in East Malaysia. Only a handful of Malays have openly declared themselves as Christian believers, and these have gone through the 'legal' process of renouncing their former religion.

Since Malaya gained its independence in 1957 and the state of Malaysia was established in 1963, race, religion and economics have been intertwined. For example, the constitution defines an ethnic Malay as one who professes to be a Muslim, and it requires the government to protect the rights and privileges of the Malays. The constitution also stipulates Islam as the official religion, while it allows freedom of religion. However, state and federal laws control and restrict the propagation of religion among Muslims. In the mid-1980s, certain Muslims expressed the desire to integrate the *shari'a* court and the civil court. From then on, the Islamization process increased in pace and the government established institutions such as the Islamic University (1982), the Islamic Bank (1983) and the Institute of Islamic Research (1987). In September 2001, the then prime minister, Dr Mahathir, declared that Malaysia was 'already' an Islamic country.

All non-Muslims, and not just Christians, are worried about the Islamization process in Malaysia. It is being introduced gradually and subtly, and is always presented in terms of the common good. Open resistance is not possible since the government threatens to employ the Internal Security Act on those who disturb the 'peace' of the country by raising 'sensitive issues'. Therefore, regardless of the claim concerning the practice of religious freedom in Malaysia, Malay Muslims are not willing to give up their privileged position which allows them to interpret how society should function and how persons should live. Non-Muslims are expected to accept the fact that they are essentially 'second-class citizens' in an Islamic state.

Christians are not openly persecuted, but there is evidence of systematic efforts to restrict the spread of Christianity. For example, though Bahasa Melayu is the national language, the 'Malay Bible' is not to be circulated freely and may be sold only in designated venues. At one time even the 'Iban Bible' meant for the Iban people in East Malaysia was banned. Certain state governments have also published a list of 'religious terms' that Christians may not use. For example, the name *Allah* is reserved for Islam, and Christians are to us the term *Tuhan*, which is a generic word for deity. Evangelism among Malays is strictly forbidden, and Malays who convert will need to go through a rehabilitation process. Often, a Malay believer has to go through a lengthy court case to have his/her conversion recognized. In a well publicized case which has recently been resolved, a Malay believer has been denied the right to marry a Christian.

How should Christians live in the Malaysian situation? Most Christians believe they must follow the counsel of the prophet Jeremiah to the exiles in Babylon, to 'seek the peace and prosperity' of the country (Jer. 29:7). Such a commitment includes an active involvement in as much of the nation's life as is possible. Christians should give up a 'survival mentality' and cultivate a 'good neighbour mentality' instead; that is, doing all they can to encourage harmony, well-being and development of the nation. Christians in Malaysia are especially involved in areas often ignored or neglected, for example in drug rehabilitation work and among AIDS victims, and also in times of disaster. Thus a Christian response to Islamization would be for Christians to demonstrate that the Triune God is working through them to love and bless even the Muslim Malay community.

What are the limits of contextualization?

In many situations in the past, when Muslims have wanted to become Christians, they have had to leave their families and try to become members of a Christian community. This process has often been extremely painful, with individuals struggling to establish a new life and find a new identity.

Since the 1970s, missionaries working among Muslims have been aware that traditional methods have simply 'extracted' converts from their community and expected them to settle in a very different kind of culture. They have therefore asked themselves whether conversion to Christ should always result in such severe dislocation. Is it not possible to communicate the good news about Jesus in language that is easier for Muslims to understand? Is it not possible for them to come to faith in families, not just as individuals, and remain in their family and community as fully as possible? And when a group of new believers is formed, is it not possible for them to worship and express their faith in ways that are culturally appropriate?

This approach, which is known as 'contextualization', has been pioneered in countries like Bangladesh and is now being practised in a variety of different contexts all round the world. Christians working in this way have recognized that there is a whole spectrum of approaches that have been adopted with new believers from Muslim backgrounds and have developed the following model, in which C1 represents the minimum of contextualization and C6 the maximum possible contextualization.

C1 New believers join an existing church which uses the language of the Christian community. In most cases these will be traditional churches which reflect a Western style of worship.

C2 New believers join existing churches, but use vocabulary which is more familiar to them as Muslims.

C3 New believers form new Christian fellowships and/or churches and use language, music and art forms with which they are familiar.

C4 Believers worship and organize themselves in a way that reflects the culture from which they come. For example, they pray standing and with hands raised, and place the Bible on a Qur'an stool to keep it off the floor.

C5 These believers think of themselves as 'messianic Muslims'; they worship Jesus as Saviour and Lord, but do not feel that they have left the Muslim community.

C6 New believers meet with each other secretly and are unable to declare openly that they are disciples of Jesus.

Many of those who are committed to the principles of contextualization go as far as the C4 position, and feel that those who go further are in danger of moving into syncretism, where Christian and Muslim ideas and practices are mixed together in such a way that the distinctives of the Christian faith are lost. These are some of the issues which are being discussed at the present time:

- Is it appropriate for new believers and for Christians working among them to continue to call themselves 'Muslims'? Many feel that this approach goes too far, because it is not using the word 'Muslim' in the way that Muslims understand it, and is in danger of introducing an element of deception and dishonesty.

- Is it possible for a Muslim disciple of Jesus, when challenged by Muslims, to say the *shahadah* ('There is no god but God, and Muhammad is the Apostle of God')? Christians generally have no difficulty with the first part of the sentence, but most find it difficult, if not impossible, to say the second part. Can a Muslim who believes in Jesus continue to say that Muhammad is *in some sense* 'the Apostle of God'?

- Is it possible to find an alternative to 'Son of God' as a title for Jesus? Because this term is so offensive to Muslims, Christians often speak of Jesus as 'the Word of God', using an expression that is found in the Qur'an (see chapter 34, 'Starting from the Qu'ran'). But is it possible to go further and translate 'Son of God' with qur'anic terms like *khalifat-ullah*, using the term that is given to Adam as the 'vice-gerent', 'vice-regent', 'steward' of God? Is it possible to translate 'the Christ' as 'the Mahdi', referring to the figure in Islamic eschatology who will return before the end of the world? Many feel that attempts of this kind go too far, because the Islamic content in these terms is so clear and strong that they cannot be made to carry a Christian meaning.

The dilemma can therefore be summed up as follows. How do we draw the line between appropriate contextualization and inappropriate syncretism? How do we decide what Islamic language and forms *are* capable of carrying a Christian content and meaning, and which are *not*?

Is it ever appropriate for Christians to engage in polemics?

'Polemics', 'apologetics' and 'dialogue' – all of which are derived from Greek words – are three very different ways in which Christians and Muslims have engaged with each other over the past fourteen centuries. 'Polemics' (from *polemos*, 'war') means attacking Islam with a view to discrediting it. 'Apologetics' (from *apologia*, 'defence') means giving a reasoned defence of Christian beliefs and challenging Islamic beliefs when appropriate. 'Dialogue' means engaging in an open-ended discussion with a view to defining what each party believes without criticism of the other and reaching a real meeting of minds and hearts.

Chapter 23 is a survey of how these different approaches have been practised in the past, and chapter 24 explores the practice of dialogue today. While most Christians will have no difficulty with the need for apologetics and dialogue, many will have reservations about polemics. These are some of the arguments that have been put forward for and against the use of polemics in the context of Christians meeting with Muslims.

Arguments in favour of polemics

- Polemics are culturally appropriate. Muslims who come from the Middle East, the Indian subcontinent and Asia are used to engaging in heated discussion with each other. Polite, restrained and rational debating may be a culturally acceptable way of operating in the West, but it is culturally foreign to most Muslims.
- Polemics force Muslims to think about difficult issues related to their scriptures, their beliefs and their history. If they have been accustomed to accept the Qur'an and Islamic beliefs without question, asking hard questions compels them to face up to difficult issues related to their faith in a way that they have never done before. They may even begin to doubt their own faith, and questioning can sometimes lead to Christian faith.
- Polemics directed at Muslims and Islam can be an encouragement to Christians who live as minorities in Muslim societies and who have little freedom to express what they really believe among Muslims. Since they are likely to get into trouble with the police if they say anything remotely critical of Islam, they feel confirmed and strengthened in their own faith when they hear Christians saying openly things about Islam which they think privately but would never dare to say in public.
- Polemics have produced some positive fruits. A number of Muslims have been forced to question their faith and have ultimately come to believe in Jesus.

Arguments against polemics

- Studies of the history of Christian-Muslim relations, such as Jean-Marie Gaudeul's *Encounters and Clashes*, suggest that polemics have led to a dead end, with Christians and Muslims attacking each other's beliefs and practices for centuries. In many cases they have misrepresented each other's faith, and polemics have led to centuries of mutual misunderstanding, contempt, ridicule, distrust and increased hostility.

- Polemics directed against Islam invite polemics against Christianity. The more we attack them, the more they want to attack us. It is basic psychology that attacking people and their beliefs makes them defensive, and encourages them to respond in kind. This could be the kind of situation that Jesus had in mind in these words in the Sermon on the Mount: 'Do not judge, or you too will be judged. For in the same way as you judge others, you will be judged, and with the measure you use, it will be measured to you. Why do you look at the speck of sawdust in your brother's eye and pay no attention to the plank in your own eye...?' (Matt. 7:1–3)
- There may be a fine line between 'challenging' (in apologetics) and 'attacking' (in polemics), but Muslims are probably very aware of the difference, which has something to do with respect. If they feel that we understand and respect their beliefs, they are more likely to be willing to listen to our challenge. But if they feel that their beliefs are being attacked, they are more likely to feel that we have little respect for their beliefs or for them as people, and make it difficult, if not impossible, to have any genuine dialogue.
- If polemics have sometimes produced good results, they more often lead to negative results. For example, the so-called debates staged by Ahmad Deedat, the South African apologist, between the 1960s and 1990s were staged like boxing matches in which he went all out to attack Christian beliefs and make his Christian opponent look foolish.
- In the context of polemics it is hard to separate discussion about beliefs from all the other cultural, social and political factors which affect Christian-Muslim relations in different situations. Instead of attacking each other's beliefs, it is probably more profitable in the long run for Christians and Muslims to meet as people, as individuals and communities, aware of the realities of the context in which they are living, and to engage in frank and open discussion about issues that concern them, as well as to discuss what they believe. If in these contexts Muslims begin to ask the hard questions, Christians need to be prepared to answer them, and to ask the hard questions of the Muslims.

How can Christians respond to the occult in an Islamic context?

Fatima's problems began when she was only twelve years old, growing up in a slum in Cairo. Somehow she had found the courage to refuse to marry a cousin to whom she had been betrothed. Enraged by this refusal, the spurned man's mother stole some of Fatima's clothes, smeared them with the blood of a rabbit, and cursed Fatima as she secretly buried them near her family's door. From that point on demons controlled the girl, not in the outward form of seizures and strange behaviour, but, as Fatima herself described it, living within her and at times making terrorizing appearances in the form of dark-skinned Nubians of southern Egypt.

Five years later Fatima married of her own choice. She and her new husband found a small flat in a five-storey building housing eight families in a sewage-stained street. Since water was only available at night, Fatima had to wake from her sleep to fill the family water bottles. But unless her husband accompanied her to calm her fears and protect her, the demons who had harassed her since adolescence would beat her or burn her with cigarettes. When she became pregnant with her first child, the demons promised to kill the baby. The child died three days after birth from the common infection of toxoplasmosis, but the demons cruelly claimed the credit.

During these years the young couple and their neighbours had been surprised when a European family moved into an empty flat in their building. Soon Fatima and Helen had developed a close relationship, and Fatima found herself confiding about her spiritual bondage with her European friend.

Over the years the two spent long hours speaking of faith and discussing the Bible. Gradually Fatima's interest grew until she was ready to pray to Jesus, at least in order to get rid of the demons. Eventually, Joseph and Helen asked another couple with greater experience in demonic encounter to help them, and through their prayers Fatima was set free from the demons and trusted in Jesus as her Saviour.

Helen thought that Fatima had been truly delivered, and indeed things went well for some months. And then one day as they prayed together, Fatima suddenly screamed because she had seen a demon hovering over Helen's baby. Later, as Fatima went down the stairs, a demon tried to trip her. She rebuked him in the name of Jesus and he left. Somehow the evil forces were again demonstrating their influence, even if at times apparently from the outside.

About this time Helen and her husband left the country. Mary, another European, continued the relationship with Fatima, who, in time, gave birth to a second, healthy child. As Mary arrived one day to chat, drink tea and pray, she was disturbed to find Fatima trembling. Fatima was eventually able to explain her condition: the demons had appeared and threatened to kill the child if she maintained contact with Mary. Despite this, the two continued to meet, although Fatima would often seemingly fall asleep, or her eyes would glaze over, when Mary began to speak of Jesus or read the Bible.

Mary and another co-worker did all that they knew to do to help Fatima by fasting, praying, and even attempting to cleanse her house of evil influences in Jesus' name. Since none of this brought her relief, they concluded that they must wait until Fatima came of her own free will to ask for help.

Six years went by and Fatima had not grown in her faith and was still bothered by the demons. Eventually desperation drove her to reveal her past to Mary in greater detail. On Mary's request she drew up a list of the various occult practices of Egypt's folk Islam, and then acknowledged the practices she herself had carried out. This exercise unlocked the door to her final deliverance.

Several years earlier, when Fatima was initially delivered, she knew that all of the demons had left her except one. She had attended a *zar* ceremony of the kind that hundreds of thousands of women take part in throughout the Middle East in an attempt to live at peace with the evil spirit that they know lives within them. They dance until they are almost in a trance and then a friend slaughters a chicken over their head, covering them in blood. In this attempt to appease the spirit, the women open themselves to even greater control by the demonic spirits they have contacted through the ceremony.

On the occasion when Fatima had attended the *zar* ceremony, she made a pact with a demon, which enabled two other demons to take control of her. Fatima had known this for those seven additional years of misery. But, although she knew the demons by name and even the parts of her body they occupied, she had never spoken of their presence or control to any of her Christian friends.

Mary responded by again teaching Fatima from the Bible about the power of Jesus and his victory over demonic powers. In particular, they taught her that she should repent of her sinful pact with the demon and that through this the demons would lose their right to dominate and oppress her. In this way Fatima found lasting deliverance. She repented of her sin, renounced in Jesus' name her pact with the demons, and told them to leave. And, without a great display, they left. She knew they had left because she watched them go.

Fatima's life has been significantly different since her deliverance. Her family is still poor and there are challenges from her relatives who know of her faith in *'Isa al Masih*. But the demons that terrorized her for seventeen years are gone. Her love for and faith in Jesus are vibrant despite the difficulties she faces.

CONCLUSION

We set out to reflect on relationships between Christians and Muslims and between Christianity and Islam. So now that we have explored the origins of Islam, its scriptures and traditions, its history, beliefs and practices, and have surveyed some of the most significant aspects of Christian-Muslim relationships over the centuries, are we in a better position to suggest how Christians can respond today to the different kinds of challenges presented by Islam which were outlined in the Introduction?

Those who are concerned about *numbers* and the growth and spread of Islam today may need to be reminded that the writers of the Bible were seldom preoccupied with numbers. Christians living as minorities in Islamic countries can therefore take comfort from the promise that Abraham's offspring (both physical and spiritual) will be as numerous as the dust of the earth and the stars in the sky (Gen. 13:16; 15:5), and from the apostle John's vision of heaven where he sees 'a great multitude that no one could count' (Rev. 7:9). They can also take note of the many times in the Bible that God encourages people with the words 'Do not be afraid' (e.g. Gen. 15:1; 21:17; Luke 1:13; 2:10; 12:32). When Christians are inclined to speculate about the salvation of others, they may need to notice that when Jesus is asked, 'Will only a few be saved?' he refuses to answer the question in terms of numbers, and simply urges every one of his hearers to 'make every effort to enter through the narrow door' (Luke 13:23–24). When numbers, however, are translated into power, and this power creates restrictions and difficulties for Christians, we are brought face to face with the political issues concerning Islam which seem to grow more significant every year.

When it comes to the *cultural* issues, it is clear that in spite of major differences of cultures across the world, there are certain values which are distinctly Islamic and are therefore part of the culture of most Muslims simply because they are based on the example of the Prophet as described in tradition. When Christians understand these core values and are sensitized to cultural differences, there should be nothing to hold them back from relating to Muslims both on a human level and as people of faith, and developing genuine friendships. Christians need to see Muslims as neighbours to be loved and not as people to be avoided because their culture is different (Matt. 22:39). While some aspects of the culture of Muslims will always remain difficult and foreign, if we can put aside our ethnocentricity, which makes us feel that *our* culture is always bound to be best and therefore the norm, we are sure to discover aspects of *their* culture which will put us to shame.

In recent years it has been the *political* issues that have raised the profile of Islam throughout the world. Because of the war which Muslims believe is being waged against Islam by the West, protests against perceived insults to the Prophet, terrorist acts carried out by Muslims, or demands for equal rights for Muslims, it should be obvious that Islam is not only interested in teaching people how to pray, but in seeing the kingdom of God established in the world in a very public way. In responding to the whole range of political issues, one of the crucial questions revolves around the relative importance of history and politics on the one hand and scripture and theology on the other. To what extent are events like 9/11 a reaction on the part of a number of Muslims to what the West (which is still often perceived by Muslims as 'Christian') has done to the world of Islam in the last three centuries, and to what extent are they to be explained in terms of Islamic scripture and beliefs?

Two significantly different responses have emerged among Christians in recent years. The first has been to recognize that Muslims have good reason to be angry because of the foreign policies of Western governments, and that 'Islamic terrorism' needs to be seen (partly if not largely) as a violent and angry response to injustices that have been done to the Muslim world. The second approach seeks to minimize the importance of the political issues and put the main emphasis on those elements of Islamic scripture and tradition which call for a robust, if not aggressive, approach towards non-Muslims. Those who take this approach are likely to argue that the root of the problems associated with Islamic extremism lies in the scriptures and theology of Islam, and that it is not the West, but Muslims, who need to change or modify their beliefs – such as the idea of *jihad*, for example. Those who take the first approach would insist that the political issues that have provoked the world of Islam are just as significant as the theological questions about the interpretation of the Qur'an. If Muslims, therefore, are called on to rethink and restate their beliefs, then the West is also required to face up to the implications of its actions in relation to the Muslim world.

The political issues that we are talking about, however, go far beyond the question of terrorism carried out in the name of Islam and are related to the dreams that many Muslims have for the rest of the world. Christians should have no objection to the fact that Islam is a missionary religion, since both religions are unashamedly missionary religions with a message they want to share with the world. But for many Muslims there is a clear political agenda that goes along with the missionary goal. Because of the example of the Prophet in establishing the first Islamic state in Medina, and because of the conviction that 'Islam must rule', Islamic faith needs ideally to be linked with power, and creating an Islamic society is the surest way to change human behaviour for the better. These goals create real concerns for non-Muslims who perceive that some (if not many) Muslims are not just talking about living their own lives in accordance with Islam, but extending the power of Islam over others who are not Muslims.

Christians will see many similarities between the theocratic model of Islam and the world of the Old Testament, where the whole community of Israel accepts the lordship of God and orders its communal life in accordance with the divine law revealed through Moses. But with the coming of Jesus we enter a different world, where the kingdom of God comes in and through the life of Jesus, and can be entered and experienced by individuals and communities not only in a theocratic community, but also in every conceivable kind of political context.

The fundamental difference between the understanding of the kingdom of God in Islam and in Christianity must ultimately be traced back to the lives of Jesus and Muhammad. The one renounces the use of force and is willing to go to the cross, establishing a new kind of multi-cultural community based on personal allegiance to Jesus and inward transformation, and embodying the imperatives of the Sermon on the Mount, such as justice and peacemaking. For three hundred years after the death of Jesus, Christian communities in the Mediterranean world continue to be powerless and often persecuted minorities. Then everything changes when Constantine, for a mixture of personal and political reasons, makes Christianity the religion of the Roman Empire. The Prophet of Islam, by contrast, starts his ministry as a persecuted Prophet and migrates to Medina to create an Islamic state which is based not on tribal loyalties, but on allegiance to the Prophet and to Islam. This state soon becomes an empire stretching from the Atlantic to the borders of China and India. Because Muhammad has effectively become his own Constantine, therefore, Islam seems to be most true to itself when it has power – which inevitably means power over both Muslims and non-Muslims.

Christians today have profoundly ambivalent feelings about Constantine and the concepts of 'the Holy Roman Empire' and 'Christendom'. But since they cannot unscramble the egg, they simply have to live today with both the positive and the negative aspects of a legacy which seems far removed from the experience of Christians in the first three centuries. In coming to terms with the political challenge of Islam at the present time, therefore, Christians need to be careful that they do not respond to what they perceive as *Islamic jihad* to conquer the world with their own corresponding kind of *Christian jihad*. When they face discrimination and persecution, they may often be able, like the apostle Paul, to 'appeal to Caesar' (Acts 25:11–12) – which in today's terms means appealing to the law of the land, to international law, and to widely accepted concepts of human rights. But they need to give up all hope of ever returning to the Constantinian model, and have to work out how to respond to every kind of problem with pragmatic solutions which are faithful to the Spirit of Christ and genuinely seek the common good (Jer. 29:1–9). And since they follow a crucified Messiah, it will not be altogether surprising if they find that some kinds of suffering are inevitable (1 Pet. 4:12–19).

The *ideological* challenge of Islam is, of course, closely tied up with the political. There is no justification for reducing everything to the simple formula of 'a clash of civilizations' or 'Islam against the West' and 'the West against Islam'. But there can be no mistaking the bold claim of many Muslims that Islam can and will fill the vacuum created in the West by centuries of doubt and provide alternatives to all the 'gods' that have failed – capitalism, communism, socialism, materialism and nationalism. One of the major problems here, however, is that since the link between religion and government, between church and state, in all Western countries has either been totally severed or become almost meaningless, Western governments find themselves at a loss in dealing with Muslims and Islam. Here are people who refuse to rule God out of the public sphere and want religion to play a role not only within the life of the Muslim community, but also in the life of the nation and the world. Secular politicians can take strong measures to safeguard the rights of every community and to protect their countries from terrorism carried out in the name of Islam. But they simply do not have the world view or the language to enable them to engage in a meaningful dialogue with Muslims who want to bring God into everything that they say and do.

Western Christians who have accepted the privatization of religion too easily may find themselves deeply challenged by Muslims who are sometimes saying the kind of things that Christians ought to be saying. But they may also have a very significant role as interpreters, because they ought to be able to understand and have considerable sympathy with both sides – with God-fearing Muslims on the one hand and secular Westerners on the other. There should be no place for a craven and apologetic spirit which gives in to every request or demand from Muslims and to every expression of secular political correctness. And if there is genuine trust between Christians and Muslims, Christians may be able to be real peacemakers and bridge-builders.

Unlike secular humanists, Christians *do* (or at least *ought to*) have the world view and the language to enable them to engage in serious dialogue with Muslims, not only about theology, but also about personal, social and political issues. This, therefore, might be the kind of contribution that Christians should be able to make to the dialogue: 'As Christians we understand your desire to see the whole world under Islam, because we would like to see every person in the world respond to the love of God as revealed in Jesus. Many of us also understand the pain and anger of Muslims because of all that the West has been doing for centuries to the world of Islam, and we acknowledge the role of this anger in much of the confrontation that is taking place today. But many of us have real concerns about the language and methods of *some* Muslims who are working for the spread of Islam with clear political agendas. Some of the fears of non-Muslims may be unjustified, because in pluralist democracies all religions have to play, as it were, on a level playing field and Islam, like every other religion, cannot use any means other than persuasion to win converts and change society. But the rhetoric of some Muslims inevitably creates fear, and we sense that many of you are struggling with the serious tension between moderates and extremists in the Muslim community worldwide. We hope that Muslims will take as much trouble to understand both the Christian faith and the secular West as we feel many Christians have taken to understand Islam. Christians and Muslims live side by side in a pluralist world, and we want to see much more serious dialogue between Christians, Muslims and people of other faiths or of none as we work for the common good in our society.'

We have seen that the *theological* challenge of Islam to Christianity centres, first, round the claim that the Bible has been corrupted and therefore superseded by the Qur'an and, second, by its repudiation of the deity and crucifixion of Christ and of the Trinity. Christians have far more in common with Muslims than they do with Hindus or Buddhists, because they share basic convictions about the One God and his created universe. But by denying the incarnation and the atonement, Islam is challenging some of the most fundamental beliefs of Christians and therefore seems to cut the nerve of the gospel.

The difficulties that Muslims find in the cross take us to the heart of the theological differences between the two faiths. It did not help matters that the Crusaders wore crosses emblazoned on their chests and backs as they launched a holy war to recover their holy places from Islam. This certainly increased antipathy towards the Christians and their beliefs, and protests about 'Western Crusaders' has continued to be part of some Islamist rhetoric until today. But the theological problems surrounding the cross were there long before the Crusades. What kind of a weak God is this, Muslims have asked, who stands by and does nothing to rescue his representative from the clutches of people who want to kill him? Since death by crucifixion involves such extreme shame and humiliation, it is unthinkable that the all-powerful God would ever allow his Messenger to die this kind of death. Success and victory are proof of divine approval, and God is bound to vindicate his Messenger in the eyes of the world.

Muslims make their protest against the cross for the best of reasons: they deny the incarnation because they want to protect the transcendence of Almighty God, who is totally different from his creatures; and they deny that God could have allowed the crucifixion because they want to protect the honour of God, and because divine forgiveness needs nothing more than human repentance and a pardon that is pronounced in words. But this means that Muslims are in effect telling God what he can and cannot do. They are also ruling out the possibility that there might be a deeper logic which connects forgiveness with suffering and points to the divine love which suffers in the process of confronting evil and declaring forgiveness. Starting from the assumption that human beings are basically good, they believe that all they need to put them on the right path is Islamic law, the example of the Prophet and the security of belonging to the House of Islam. The death of Jesus on the cross is therefore not only unthinkable for Muslims, but also unnecessary.

The cross is such an important symbol for Christians because part of its message is that the holy and just God forgives human beings by taking on himself the consequences of all their wrongdoing. Instead of condemning and punishing us as we deserve, by allowing Jesus to die on the cross the eternal God passes his final judgment on all evil and at the same time demonstrates the love and forgiveness which he now offers to all who turn to him in repentance and faith. In this way God once and for all breaks the cycle of wrongdoing and judgment, retribution and revenge. The incarnation of the eternal Son of God, his death and resurrection, and the release of the Holy Spirit into the hearts of all believers who form a new kind of community in the world – these together make up God's response to human evil and to all that is wrong in human nature, and create the possibility of the transformation of individuals and communities.

When Christians have done their utmost to understand Islam as sympathetically as possible, this, therefore, is the message that they want to share with Muslims. If they can see Muslims as people to be loved as neighbours and not as people whose religion is to be feared, they are called upon to bear witness to this message by word and deed in every situation in the world where they live alongside Muslims. After 9/11 there can no longer be any escape from the big questions about the place of Islam in the world. But whenever we speak about 'Islam' and 'Christianity', we need to recognize the absolute priority of personal relationships and return to the point at which we began in Part One. So we are not talking about two religions or systems interacting with each other. We are talking about 'Muslims' and 'Christians' – human beings relating to each other face to face wherever they are in the world and sharing heart to heart. And every committed Christian and Muslim will be wanting to say, 'Let God be God!'

NOTES

Part One title page

1 Roger Hooker, *Uncharted Journey*, Church Missionary Society, 1973, p. 22.

Chapter 1: Meeting face to face

1 Hooker, *Uncharted Journey*, p. 21.

Chapter 2: Appreciating Islamic culture

1 *Islam: A Brief Guide*, The Muslim Educational Trust, 130 Stroud Green Road, London, N4 3RZ.

2 Ruqaiyyah Waris Maqsood, *Teach Yourself Islam*, Hodder & Stoughton, 2006, p. 186.

3 Nawal al-Saadawi, *The Hidden Face of Eve*, Sherif Hetata, tr., Zed Press, 1980.

Chapter 3: Examining our attitudes

1 Christian W. Troll, SJ, *Muslims Ask, Christians Answer*, Gujarat Sahitya Prakash, Gujarat, 2005, p. 121.

2 For example, The Barnabas Fund, Christian Solidarity International, Open Doors and Middle East Concern.

3 See A. Guillaume, tr., *The Life of Muhammad: A Translation of Ibn Ishaq's Sirat Rasul Allah*, Oxford University Press, 1996.

4 Peter G. Riddell and Peter Cotterell, *Islam in Conflict: Past, Present and Future*, IVP, 2003, p. 212.

5 See my *Whose Promised Land?*, Lion, 2002, chapter 3.3, 'The conquest of the land', pp. 126–134.

6 See my *Islam and the West: Conflict, Co-existence or Conversion?*, Paternoster, 1998, chapter 8, 'Islamic mission today: is the West ripe for conversion?', pp. 57–81.

7 Bilquis Sheikh with Richard Schneider, *I Dared to Call Him Father*, Kingsway, 1979.

Part Two title page

1 Hooker, *Uncharted Journey*, p. 26.

2 Jens Christensen, *The Practical Approach to Muslims*, North Africa Mission, 1977, p. 369.

3 Ninian Smart, *The Religious Experience of Mankind*, Collins Fount, 1982, p. 12.

4 Muhammad Iqbal, quoted in H. A. R. Gibb, *Modern Trends in Islam*, Librarie du Liban, 1975, p. 78.

Chapter 4: What is Islam?

1 Ishtieq Ahmad, quoted in Peter G. Riddell, *Christians and Muslims: Pressures and Potential in a Post 9/11 World*, IVP, 2004, p. 18.

Chapter 6: Muslims at prayer

1 Constance Padwick, *Muslim Devotions: A Study of Prayer Manuals in Common Use*, SPCK, 1961, pp. xi, xiii.
2 Kenneth Cragg, *The Event of the Qur'an*, George Allen and Unwin, 1971, p. 74.
3 M. M. Pickthall, *The Meaning of the Glorious Koran*, Mentor, n.d., p. 31.
4 William Montgomery Watt, *Companion to the Qur'an*, George Allen and Unwin, 1967, p. 13.
5 Ahmad Kamal, *The Second Journey*, Allen and Unwin, 1964, pp. 69–81.
6 Ghulam Sarwar, *Islam: Beliefs and Teachings*, The Muslim Educational Trust, 2003, p. 12.

Chapter 7: The life of Muhammad

1 Al-Bukhari, *Sahih*, vol. 9, LXXXVII, The Book of Interpretation of Dreams, pp. 92–93.
2 Tarif Khalidi, ed. and tr., *The Muslim Jesus: Sayings and Stories in Islamic Literature*, Harvard University Press, 2003, p. 7.
3 Quoted in Richard Bell, *The Origin of Islam in its Christian Environment*, Macmillan, 1926, p. 166.
4 William Montgomery Watt, *Muhammad, Prophet and Statesman*, Oxford University Press, 1975.
5 See the writings of Muhammad Taha (1909–1986).
6 See my *Whose Promised Land?*, chapter 6.4, 'Zionism and Islam', pp. 289–298.
7 Colin Turner, *Islam: The Basics*, Routledge, 2006, p. 37.
8 Andrew Rippin, *Muslims: Their Religious Beliefs and Practices*, Routledge, 2005, pp. 54–55.

Chapter 8: The Qur'an

1 Wilfred Cantwell Smith, *Islam in Modern History*, Princeton University Press, 1957, pp. 17–18.
2 Bell, *The Origin of Islam in its Christian Environment*, pp. 90–91.
3 Al-Bukhari, *Sahih*, vol. 6, The Excellencies of the Qur'an, p. 479.
4 William Montgomery Watt, *Bell's Introduction to the Qur'an*, Edinburgh University Press, 1977, p. 55.
5 Rippin, *Muslims: Their Religious Beliefs and Practices*, p. 36. For further examples see Arthur Jeffreys, *Materials for the History of the Text of the Qur'an: The Old Codices*, Brill, 1937.
6 Turner, *Islam: The Basics*, p. 53.
7 Kenneth Cragg, *The Call of the Minaret*, Oxford University Press, 1964, p. 66.

8   Chawkat Moucarry, *Faith to Faith: Christianity and Islam in Dialogue*, IVP, 2001, p. 226.

9   Jan Slomp, 'To Understand the Muslim Approach to Scripture', unpublished paper, United Bible Societies seminar, Holland, January 1993.

10 Reza Aslan, *No God but God: The Origins, Evolution and Future of Islam*, Arrow Books, 2006, p. 159.

11 Guillaume, *The Life of Muhammad*, p. 159.

12 Watt, *Bell's Introduction to the Qur'an*, pp. 87–88.

13 Rippin, *Muslims: Their Religious Beliefs and Practices*, p. 2.

Chapter 9: Tradition (*hadith* and *sunna*)

1   Kenneth Cragg, in W. Foy, ed., *Man's Religious Quest*, Croom Helm/Open University Press, 1982, p. 512.

2   Alfred Guillaume, *The Traditions of Islam*, Oxford University Press, 1924, p. 15.

3   Turner, *Islam: The Basics*, p. 10.

4   Moucarry, *Faith to Faith: Christianity and Islam in Dialogue*, pp. 55–56.

5   Gai Eaton, *Islam and the Destiny of Man*, Allen and Unwin, 1985, pp. 186–187.

6   Rippin, *Muslims: Their Religious Beliefs and Practices*, p. 89.

Chapter 10: Law (*shari'a*) and theology (*kalam*)

1   Joseph Schacht, *Introduction to Islamic Law*, Clarendon Press, 1964, p. 1.

2   Kenneth Cragg, *Islam and the Muslim*, Open University Press, 1978, p. 49.

3   Rippin, *Muslims: Their Religious Beliefs and Practices*, p. 88.

4   Trevor Ling, *A History of Religion: East and West*, Macmillan, 1982, pp. 292–293.

5   H. A. R. Gibb, in *The Hutchinson Encyclopedia of Living Faiths*, Hutchinson, 1988, p. 196.

6   Michael Nazir-Ali, *Islam: A Christian Perspective*, Paternoster, 1983, p. 50.

7   E. Ustaz, 5 *Islamic Software*, Purification: Sunnah of the Body, Fiqh_us_Sunnah 1:22-a,16:38, Ij:37PF3.

8   Abdur Rahman I. Doi, *Shari'ah: The Islamic Law*, Ta Ha Publishers, 1984, pp. 134–135.

9   Doi, *Shari'ah: The Islamic Law*, p. 265.

10 Al-Ghazali, *The Ninety-Nine Beautiful Names of God*, trans. David B. Burrell and Nazih Daher, Islamic Texts Society of Cambridge, 1992, pp. 35–41.

11 William Montgomery Watt, *Islamic Creeds: A Selection*, Edinburgh University Press, 1994, pp. 42–45.

12 Al-Jaza'iri in *Islam From Within: Anthology of Religion*, Kenneth Cragg and Marston Speight, Wadsworth, 1980, pp. 135–144.

Chapter 11: Sufism

1   Gibb, in *The Hutchinson Encyclopedia of Living Faiths*, p. 190.

2   Turner, *Islam: The Basics*, pp. 140–145.

3   Ibid., p. 148.

4   Gibb, *The Hutchinson Encyclopedia of Living Faiths*, p. 194.

5   Michael Nazir-Ali, *Conviction and Conflict: Islam, Christianity and World Order*,
    Continuum, 2006, p. 12.

6   Shaykh al-'Alawi, in *Man's Religious Quest*, p. 520.

7   Ibid., p. 74.

8   Cragg, *Islam and the Muslim*, p. 75.

9   Turner, *Islam: the Basics*, p. 142.

10 Smart, *The Religious Experience of Mankind*, p. 520.

11 Article on Rabi'a al-'Adawiyya in *Shorter Encyclopedia of Islam*, Brill, 193?, p. 355.

12 Ibid., p. 355.

13 From Margaret Smith, *Rabia*, One World, 1997, p. 27.

14 Al-Ghazali, *Deliverance from Error and Attachment to the Lord of Might and Majesty*,
    in William Montgomery Watt, *The Faith and Practice of al-Ghazali*, Allen and
    Unwin, 1967, p. 132.

15 Jalal ud-Din Rumi, quoted in Maqsood, *Teach Yourself Islam*, pp. 267–268.

16 Ibid., p. 268.

17 Kenneth Cragg, in *Man's Religious Quest*, p. 521.

Chapter 12: Folk Islam or popular Islam

1   Maqsood, *Teach Yourself Islam*, pp. 45–46.

2   Paul Hiebert, 'Power Encounter and Folk Islam', in *Muslims and Christians on
    the Emmaus Road*, ed. Dudley J. Woodberry, MARC, 1989, from pp. 45–61.

3   Al-Bushiri, in James McL. Ritchie, 'The Prophet's Mantle (Qasidatu l Burda):
    Translation and Presentation', *Encounter*, Pontifical Institute for Arabic and
    Islamic Studies, 171–173 (January–February 1991), pp. 3–16.

Chapter 13: The spread and development of Islam

1   Nazir-Ali, *Islam: A Christian Perspective*, p. 35.

2   William Montgomery Watt, *Islamic Political Thought: The Basic Concepts*,
    Edinburgh University Press, 1968, pp. 16–17.

3   Quoted in Muhammad Husayn Haykal, *The Life of Muhammad*, North
    American Trust Publications, 1976, p. 364.

4   Antonie Wessels, 'The Significance of Jerusalem for Muslims', in *Jerusalem:
    What Makes for Peace: A Palestinian Christian Contribution to Peacemaking*,
    N. Ateek, C. Buaybis, M. Schrader, eds., Melisende, 1997, p. 48.

5   John Taylor, *Introducing Islam*, Lutterworth, 1971, p. 33.

6   Rippin, *Muslims: Their Religious Beliefs and Practices*, pp. 65–66.

7   Jacques Jomier, *How to Understand Islam*, SCM, 1989, p. 31.

8   See my *Islam and the West: Conflict, Co-existence or Conversion?*, chapter 2, 'Islamic
    mission in the past: persuasion without compulsion?', pp. 29–56.

9   Jomier, *How to Understand Islam*, p. 31.

10 Ibid., p. 37.

11 Fazlur Rahman, 'Non-Muslim Minorities in an Islamic State', *Journal of the
    Institute of Muslim Minority Affairs*, vol. 7, 1986, pp. 22–23.

12 See John Azumah *The Legacy of Arab-Islam in Africa: A Quest for Inter-religious Dialogue*, One World, 2001.

13 See Albert Hourani, *Europe and the Middle East*, Macmillan, 1980, p. 4.

14 James Reston, *Warriors of God: Richard the Lionheart and Saladin in the Third Crusade*, Anchor, 2002, p. xviii.

15 Turner, *Islam: The Basics*, pp. 176–177.

16 Ibid., p. 164.

17 Cragg, *Islam and the Muslim*, pp. 78–79.

18 Turner, *Islam: The Basics*, p. 172.

19 Rippin, *Muslims: Their Religious Beliefs and Practices*, p. 182.

20 See my *Whose Promised Land?*, chapter 6.4, 'Zionism and Islam', pp. 289–298.

21 Ling, *A History of Religion: East and West*, p. 300.

Chapter 14: Branches and movements within Islam

1 Philip Lewis, *Cross and Crescent Workbook*, CMS, 2003, p. 5.

2 See further Philip Lewis, *Islamic Britain: Religion, Politics and Identity among British Muslims*, I. B. Tauris, 2002.

Chapter 15: Issues facing Muslims today

1 Zaki Badawi, *Islam in Britain*, Ta Ha Publishers, 1981, pp. 26–27.

2 Paul Grieve, *Islam: History, Faith and Politics: The Complete Introduction*, Robinson, 2006, p. 260.

3 Cragg, *The Call of the Minaret*, p. 19.

4 Wilfred Cantwell Smith, *Questions of Religious Truth*, Gollancz, 1967, pp. 48–49.

5 See Fazlur Rahman, *Islam*, University of Chicago Press, 1979, chapter 2, 'The Qur'an', pp. 30–42.

6 Gibb, *Modern Trends in Islam*, p. 127.

7 Rafiq Zakaria, *The Struggle Within Islam: The Conflict Between Religion and Politics*, Penguin, 1968, p. 295.

8 Cragg, *The Call of the Minaret*, p. 24.

9 Ronald Nettler, *Islam and the Minorities: Background to the Arab-Israeli Conflict*, Israel Academic Committee on the Middle East, 1978, p. 11.

10 See my *Whose Promised Land?*, chapter 6.4, 'Zionism and Islam', pp. 289–298, and *Whose Holy City? Jerusalem and the Israeli-Palestinian Conflict*, chapter 5, 'Islamic Jerusalem', pp. 89–107.

11 See my *Islam and the West*, chapter 5, 'Human rights: a conflict between secular and Islamic concepts?', pp. 113–150.

12 Paul Grieve, *Islam: History, Faith and Politics: The Complete Introduction*, p. 333.

13 Abul A'la Mawdudi, *The Road to Peace and Salvation*, p. 14.

14 Mumtaz Ahmad, *State Politics and Islam*, American Trust Publications, 1986, p. 9.

15 Riddell and Cotterell, *Islam in Conflict: Past, Present and Future*, p. 192.

16 Ziauddin Sardar, *Desperately Seeking Paradise*, Granta, p. 12.

17 John Esposito, *Unholy War: Terror in the Name of Islam*, Oxford University Press, 2003, p. 160.

18 Aslan, *No God but God*, p. 266.

Chapter 16: Women in Islam

1 Eaton, *Islam and the Destiny of Man*, pp. 122–123.
2 Taheri, *The Cauldron: The Middle East Behind the Headlines*, Hutchinson, 1988, p. 254–255.
3 Fatna Sabah, quoted in Fatima Mernissi, 'Femininity as Subversion: Reflections on the Muslim Concept of Nushuz', in D. L. Eck and D. Jain, eds., *Speaking of Faith: Cross-Cultural Perspectives on Women, Religion and Social Change*, Women's Press, 1986, pp. 88–89.
4 Abdur Rahman I. Doi, *Women in Shari'ah (Islamic Law)*, Ta Ha Publishers, 1989, pp. 98–100, 175–176.
5 Grieve, *Islam: History, Faith and Politics: The Complete Introduction*, p. 256.
6 For example, Ayaan Hirsi Ali, *Infidel*, Free Press, 2007; Mona al-Munajjed, *Women in Saudi Arabia Today*, St Martins Press, 1997; Betty Mahmoody, *Not Without My Daughter*, St Martin's Press, 1987; Geraldine Brooks, *Nine Parts Desire*, Doubleday, 1995; Cherry Mosteshar, *Unveiled: One Woman's Nightmare in Iran*, St Martin Press, 1996; Phil and Julie Parshall, *Lifting the Veil: the World of Muslim Women*, Authentic Media, 2002; *Death of a Princess*, [[details]]; Jean Sasson, *Princess*, Wm Marrow & Co., 1992; Unni Wikan, *Behind the Veil in Arabia*, University of Chicago Press, 1982.
7 Benazir Bhutto, quoted in Ida Glaser and Napoleon John, *Partners or Prisoners? Christian Thinking about Women and Islam*, Paternoster, 1998, p. 75.

Chapter 17: 'Islamic terrorism'

1 This chapter is adapted from my *'Islamic Terrorism': Is There A Christian Response?*, Grove Books, 2005.
2 Esposito, *Unholy War: Terror in the Name of Islam*, p. 45.
3 Bernard Lewis, *The Crisis of Islam, Holy War and Unholy Terror*, Phoenix, 2004, pp. 109, 111.
4 Esposito, *Unholy War: Terror in the Name of Islam*, p. 56.
5 Ibid., p. 7.
6 Ibid., p. 157.
7 Turner, *Islam: the Basics*, p. 181.
8 Lewis, *The Crisis of Islam, Holy War and Unholy Terror*, p. 113.
9 Ibid., p. 137.
10 Ibid., p. 115.
11 *The Guardian Weekly*, 9–15 September 2005, p. 8.
12 Quoted in Riddell, *Christians and Muslims: Pressures and Potential in a Post 9/11 World*, p. 81.
13 Zaki Badawi, *Thought for the Day*, BBC Radio 4, 13 September 2001, quoted in Riddell and Cotterell, *Islam in Conflict*, p. 183.
14 Ziauddin Sardar, 'My Fatwa on the Fanatics', *Sunday Observer*, 23 September 2001, quoted in ibid., p. 184.

15 Esposito, *Unholy War: Terror in the Name of Islam*, p. ix.

16 Lewis, *The Crisis of Islam, Holy War and Unholy Terror*, p. 132.

17 Esposito, *Unholy War: Terror in the Name of Islam*, pp. 34–35.

18 Lewis, *The Crisis of Islam, Holy War and Unholy Terror*, p. 27.

19 Abul A'la Mawdudi, *The Islamic Way of Life*, Khurshid Ahmad and Khurram Murad, eds., UTIM Dawah Centre, 1998, p. 32.

20 See my *Islam and the West*, chapter 2, 'Islamic mission in the past', pp. 29–56.

21 Esposito, *Unholy War: Terror in the Name of Islam*, pp. 22, 24.

22 Ibid., p. 67.

23 Lewis, *The Crisis of Islam, Holy War and Unholy Terror*, p. 130.

24 Riddell and Cotterell, *Islam in Conflict*, p. 192.

Part Three title page

1 Hooker, *Uncharted Journey*, p. 23.

2 William Montgomery Watt, *Times Literary Supplement*, insert on Islam, 30 April 1976, p. 513.

3 *Journals and Letters of Henry Martyn*, ed. S. Wilberforce, Seeley and Burnside, 1937, vol. 2, p. 373.

Chapter 19: Social and political issues

1 See my *Whose Promised Land?*

Chapter 22: A deeper look at the main Muslim objections

1 David Brown, *The Cross of the Messiah*, SPCK, 1969, p. 31.

2 Ibid., pp. 29–30.

3 Kamel Hussein, *City of Wrong (Qaryatu Zalimah)*, Kenneth Cragg, trans., Djambatan, 1959, p. 222.

4 Moucarry, *Faith to Faith*, pp. 138–141.

5 Cragg, *The Call of the Minaret*, pp. 265–268.

6 Geoffrey Parrinder, *Jesus in the Qur'an*, Faber and Faber, 1965, p. 109.

7 Mahmoud Ayoub, 'Towards an Islamic Christology II: The Death of Jesus: Reality or Delusion?', *The Muslim World*, vol. LXX, April 1980, pp. 91–121.

Chapter 23: Learning from the controversies of the past

1 See Jean-Marie Gaudeul, *Encounters and Clashes: Islam and Christianity in History*, Pontifical Institute for Arab and Islamic Studies, 1984, pp. 28–33.

2 Ibid., pp. 39–44.

3 Ibid., pp. 49–54.

4 Ibid., pp. 89–90.

5 Ibid., pp. 158–161.

6 *Journals and Letters of Henry Martyn*, vol. 2, no. 26 (1811), p. 371; and see Gaudeul, *Encounters and Clashes*, p. 255.

7 Gaudeul, *Encounters and Clashes*, pp. 256–261.

8 Constance Padwick, *Temple Gairdner of Cairo*, SPCK, 1929, pp. 148–149.

Chapter 24: Exploring dialogue

1 This section is an adapted version of my chapter 'An Agenda for Dialogue', in David Thomas and Clare Amos, eds., *A Faithful Presence: Essays for Kenneth Cragg*, Melisende, pp. 384–403.
2 Isma'il al-Faruqi, in *Christian Mission and Islamic Da'wah: Proceedings of the Chambésy Consultations*, Islamic Foundation, 1982, pp. 47–48.
3 Ahmad, *State Politics and Islam*, pp. 11–12.

Part Four title page

1 Arne Rudvin, preface to Jens Christensen, *The Practical Approach to Muslims*, p. vii.
2 Muhammad Hamidullah, *Introduction to Islam*, Centre Culturel Islamique, Paris; Sh. Muhammad Ashraf, Lahore, 1968, p. 53.
3 Abul A'la Mawdudi, *Murtaddki Saza Islami Qawmi Mein*, Islamic Publications, Lahore, 8th ed., 1981.
4 Ahmad, *State Politics and Islam*, pp. 11–12.

Chapter 25: Theological questions

1 Michael Nazir-Ali, *Frontiers in Muslim-Christian Encounter*, Regnum, 1987, p. 20.
2 Sheikh, *I Dared to Call Him Father*.
3 Charles Kraft, *Christianity in Cross-Cultural Perspective. A Study in Dynamic Biblical Theologizing*, Orbis, 1981, p. 402.
4 Troll, *Muslims Ask, Christians Answer*, p. 43.
5 Gaudeul, *Encounters and Clashes*, p. 130.
6 Norman Daniels, *Islam and the West: the Making of an Image*, Edinburgh University Press, 1980.

Chapter 26: The Islamic view of Jesus

1 Kenneth Cragg, trans., *Readings in the Qur'an*, Collins, 1988.
2 Barbara F. Stowasser, *Women in the Qur'an, Traditions and Interpretation*, Oxford University Press, 1994, p. 72.
3 M. Ali Merad, 'Christ According to the Qur'an', *Encounter*, Pontifical Institute for Arabic and Islamic Studies, 69, November 1980, p. 7.
4 Ibid., p. 15.
5 Khalidi, *The Muslim Jesus*, pp. 74, 34.
6 Tha'alibi, *Stories of the Prophets*, in F. E. Peters, *A Reader on Classical Islam*, Princeton University Press, 1994, chapter 8, 'Islamic theology', pp. 389–390.
7 Rippin, *Muslims: Their Religious Beliefs and Practices*, p. 27.
8 Christensen, *The Practical Approach to Muslims*, pp. 379–380.
9 Cragg, *The Call of the Minaret*, pp. 219–220.
10 Khalidi, *The Muslim Jesus*, pp. 5–6, 44, 15.
11 Henri Michaud, quoted in Parrinder, *Jesus in the Qur'an*, p. 166.

Chapter 27: The qur'anic view of Christians

1 Jane Dammen McAuliffe, *Qur'anic Christians: An Analysis of Classical and Modern Exegesis*, Cambridge University Press, 1991, pp. 204–239.
2 Maqsood, *Teach Yourself Islam*, p. 177.
3 See further McAuliffe, *Qur'anic Christians*.

Chapter 28: Crucial differences: the parting of the ways

1 Al-Faruqi, in *Christian Mission and Islamic Da'wah: Proceedings of the Chambésy Consultations*, pp. 47–48.
2 Abdulaziz A. Sachedina, 'The Creation of a Just Social Order in Islam', in Ahmad, *State Politics and Islam*, p. 116.
3 Mawdudi, *The Islamic Way of Life*, p. 3.
4 Hamidullah, *Introduction to Islam*, p. 53.

Chapter 29: Thinking biblically about Islam

1 Alfred Guillaume, *Islam*, Penguin, p. 61.

Chapter 30: Counting the cost of conversion

1 Mawdudi, *Murtaddki Saza Islami Qawmi Mein*.
2 Kenneth Cragg, in *Christian Mission and Islamic Da'wah*, p. 92.
3 Maulvi Muhammad Ali, *The Holy Qur'an: Arabic Text with English Translation and Commentary*, Ahmadiyyah Anjuman-i-Ishaat-I-Islam, 1920, pp. 98–99.
4 Maqsood, *Teach Yourself Islam*, p. 259.
5 Al-Baidhawi, quoted in Samuel Zwemer, *The Law of Apostasy in Islam*, Marshall Brothers, 1924, pp. 33–34.
6 Abdullahi Ahmed An-Na'im, 'The Law of Apostasy and its Modern Applicability: A Case from the Sudan', *Religion* 16, 1986, p. 211.
7 'Murtadd', in H. A. R. Gibb and J. H. Kraemers, eds., *Shorter Encyclopedia of Islam*, Brill, 1961, p. 413.
8 Abul A'la Mawdudi, *The Punishment of the Apostate According to Islamic Law*, trans. Syed Silas Husain and Ernest Hahn, 1994, p. 17.
9 Al-Faruqi, in *Christian Mission and Islamic Da'wah*, pp. 92–93.
10 Hasan Abdallah al-Turabi, *The Diplomat*, Second Issue, Muharram 1417, June 1996, pp. 38–39.
11 Rafiq Zakaria, *Muhammmad and the Qur'an*, Penguin, 1991, pp. 86–87.
12 An-Na'im, 'The Law of Apostasy and its Modern Applicability: A Case from the Sudan', p. 213.
13 See my *Islam and the West*, chapter 5, 'Human rights', especially pp. 123–127.
14 Mohammed Talbi, in my *Islam and the West*, 'Human rights', pp. 139–145.
15 Ann Elizabeth Mayer, *Islam and Human Rights: Tradition and Politics*, Pinter, 1995, p. 183.
16 See my *Islam and the West*, chapter 5, 'Human rights', pp. 137–138.

17 Al-Razi, in Mahmoud Ayoub, *The Qur'an and Its Interpreters*, State University of New York Press, 1984, p. 254.
18 Sayyid Qutb, in ibid., p. 255.

Chapter 31: Facing the political challenge of Islam

1 Christensen, *The Practical Approach to Muslims*, p. 53.
2 *Suffering and Power in Christian-Muslim Relations, Transformation*, vol. 17, No. 1., January/March 2000, p. 3.
3 Cragg, *Islam and the Muslim*, p. 17.
4 Michael Nazir-Ali, *Martyrs and Magistrates: Toleration and Trial in Islam*, Grove Books, 1989, p. 12.
5 In Grieve, *Islam: History, Faith and Politics: The Complete Introduction*, pp. 72–75.
6 Nazir-Ali, *Conviction and Conflict: Islam, Christianity and World Order*, p. 61.
7 A. Yusuf Ali, *Holy Qur'an: Text, Translation and Commentary*, p. 447.
8 W. Montgomery Watt, *Muhammad at Medina*, Oxford University Press, 1977, pp. 359–360.
9 A. Guillaume, *Ibn Ishaq's The Life of the Apostle of God*, p. 525.
10 Quoted in Gaudeul, *Encounters and Clashes*, vol II. Texts, p. 65.
11 Nazir-Ali, *Martyrs and Magistrates: Toleration and Trial in Early Islam*, p. 12.
12 Ibn Khaldun, quoted in Bat Ye'or, *The Dhimmi: Jews and Christians Under Islam*, Associated University Presses, 1985, p. 162.
13 Mohammed Talbi, 'Christian-Muslim Encounter in the Middle East', in *Middle East Perspectives*, Middle East Council of Churches, 4–5, July–August 1985, p. 10.
14 Zakaria, *The Struggle Within Islam*, pp. 300–301.
15 For example, The Barnabas Fund, Christian Solidarity International, Open Doors and Middle East Concern.
16 *Suffering and Power in Christian-Muslim Relations*, pp. 19–20.
17 Ibid., pp. 20–23.
18 John Stott, *The Message of the Sermon on the Mount*, Inter-Varsity Press, 1978, pp. 107–113.
19 *Suffering and Power in Christian-Muslim Relations*, p. 2.
20 Nazir-Ali, *Frontiers in Muslim-Christian Encounter*, pp. 144–145.
21 *Suffering and Power in Christian-Muslim Relations*, pp. 2–3.

Part Five title page

1 Temple Gairdner, quoted in Padwick, *Temple Gairdner of Cairo*, p. 158.
2 Hooker, *Uncharted Journey*, p. 24.
3 Cragg, *The Call of the Minaret*, pp. 304–305.

Chapter 32: Natural openings in everyday life

1 Margaret Burness, *What Shall I Say to My Muslim Friends?*, Church Mission Society, 1989, pp. 11–12.

2 Bill Musk, 'Popular Islam: The Hunger of the Heart', in Don M. McCurry, ed., *The Gospel and Islam: A 1978 Compendium*, MARC, 1979, p. 219.

Chapter 33: Using the Bible

1 Kenneth Bailey has written about the parable of the two lost sons in three books: *The Cross and the Prodigal*, Concordia, 1973; *Poet and Peasant* and *Through Peasant Eyes*, Eerdmans, 1983, and *Finding the Lost: Cultural Keys to Luke 15*, Concordia, 1993.
2 Bailey, *Poet and Peasant*, p. 206.

Chapter 34: Starting from the Qur'an

1 B. D. Kateregga and D. W. Shenk, *Islam and Christianity: A Muslim and a Christian in Dialogue*, Paternoster, 1980, pp. 34–37.
2 Al-Baidhawi, quoted in Parrinder, *Jesus in the Qur'an*, p. 45.
3 Al-Razi, quoted in ibid., p. 46.
4 A. Yusuf Ali, *Holy Qur'an: Text, Translation and Commentary*, p. 133.
5 Parrinder, *Jesus in the Qur'an*, pp. 45–48.
6 'The Apology of John of Damascus', trans. John W. Voorhis, *Muslim World*, 1934, pp. 394–395.
7 Daoud Rahbar, *God of Justice: A Study in the Ethical Doctrine of God*, Brill, 1960.
8 Daoud Rahbar, 'A Letter to Muslim Friends', Hartford, 1 January 1960 (unpublished).

INDEX